Poetry and Contemporary Visual Culture
Lyrik und zeitgenössische Visuelle Kultur

Poetry in the Digital Age

Edited by Claudia Benthien

Advisory Board
Frieder von Ammon · Hannes Bajohr · Jörg Döring · Julia Lajta-Novak · María Mencía · Ralph Müller · Jesper Olsson · Paweł Piszczatowski · Jessica Pressman · Antonio Rodriguez · Hans Kristian Strandstuen Rustad · Holger Schulze · Eckhard Schumacher · Henrieke Stahl · Birgitte Stougaard Pedersen

Volume 3

Poetry and Contemporary Visual Culture
Lyrik und zeitgenössische Visuelle Kultur

———

Edited by / Herausgegeben von
Magdalena Elisabeth Korecka and Wiebke Vorrath

DE GRUYTER

This book series is part of the research project "Poetry in the Digital Age" that has received funding from the European Research Council (ERC) under the European Union's "Horizon 2020" research and innovation programme (grant agreement No 884177).

Views and opinions expressed here are those of the author(s) only and do not necessarily reflect those of the European Union (EU) or the European Research Council (ERC). Neither the EU nor the ERC can be held responsible for them.

European Research Council
Established by the European Commission

ISBN 978-3-11-221540-1
e-ISBN (PDF) 978-3-11-129933-4
e-ISBN (EPUB) 978-3-11-129940-2
DOI https://doi.org/10.1515/9783111299334

This work is licensed under the Creative Commons Attribution-NonCommercial-NoDerivatives 4.0 International License. For details go to https://creativecommons.org/licenses/by-nc-nd/4.0/.

Creative Commons license terms for re-use do not apply to any content (such as graphs, figures, photos, excerpts, etc.) not original to the Open Access publication and further permission may be required from the rights holder. The obligation to research and clear permission lies solely with the party re-using the material.

Library of Congress Control Number: 2023940196

Bibliographic information published by the Deutsche Nationalbibliothek
The Deutsche Nationalbibliothek lists this publication in the Deutsche Nationalbibliografie; detailed bibliographic data are available on the internet at http://dnb.dnb.de.

© 2025 the author(s), editing © 2025 Magdalena Elisabeth Korecka and Wiebke Vorrath, published by Walter de Gruyter GmbH, Berlin/Boston
This volume is text- and page-identical with the hardback published in 2023.
The book is published open access at www.degruyter.com.

Cover image: Rebecka Dürr
Typesetting: Integra Software Services Pvt. Ltd.
Printing and binding: CPI books GmbH, Leck

www.degruyter.com

Vorwort

Als Leiterin des mit einem ERC Advanced Grant geförderten Forschungsprojekts „Poetry in the Digital Age" freue ich mich, dass nun der erste interdisziplinäre Tagungsband und zugleich der dritte Band der gleichnamigen Buchreihe vorliegt. Er beruht wesentlich auf der ersten Tagung des Projekts, die im Mai 2022 federführend von Dr. Wiebke Vorrath und Magdalena Elisabeth Korecka, M.A., konzipiert und durchgeführt wurde; beide gemeinsam haben auch diesen Band als Herausgeberinnen verantwortet, wofür ich ihnen danken möchte.

Das Forschungsprojekt entwickelt Analyseparameter für die facettenreichen aktuellen Lyrik-Formate, die von populärkulturellen Werken bis zu elaborierter Sprachkunst reichen, indem es die Formen und Räume ihrer Präsentation und Performance untersucht: von der Theaterbühne bis zu Social Media, von der Schriftseite bis zum urbanen Raum, von Spoken Word bis zu experimenteller Lautpoesie – erschaffen von menschlichen oder posthumanen Agent:innen. Unsere Forschungen suchen, die folgenden Leitfragen zu beantworten:
- Welche Faktoren haben zur aktuellen Popularität von ‚Poetry' beigetragen?
- Wie können ihre Genres systematisiert werden und welche neuen Methoden und Theorien werden benötigt, um sie zu untersuchen?
- Wie unterscheiden, interagieren oder vermischen sich in ihnen Populärkultur und ‚Hochkultur'?
- Welche (ästhetischen, kulturellen, sozialen, politischen) Funktionen kommen den neuen Modi der Präsentation von Gedichten zu?

Als eine ‚Poetik neuer Formen' untersucht das Projekt die große Diversität, das mediale Spektrum und die Verbreitung zeitgenössischer Lyrik. Seine Forschungsergebnisse sollen in einer neuen, erweiterten Definition von Lyrik münden und die Art und Weise verändern, wie Wissenschaft, Dichter:innen und die Öffentlichkeit diese literarische Gattung betrachten. Dafür sind Expertisen unterschiedlicher Fächer gefragt, viele davon sind im Forschungsprojekt, aber auch in dem hier vorliegenden Band vertreten: Literaturwissenschaft, Performance Studies und Medienwissenschaft, Sound Studies, Musikwissenschaft, Sprechwissenschaft, Psychologie, Soziologie, Kunstgeschichte, Visual Culture Studies, Kunst- und Filmwissenschaft. Unsere inter- und transdisziplinäre Forschung gliedert sich in drei Teilprojekte, die sich schwerpunktmäßig den Interart-Verhältnissen von (1) Lyrik und Performance, (2) Lyrik und Musik und (3) Lyrik und Visueller Kultur widmen.[1]

---

1 Vgl. https://www.poetry-digital-age.uni-hamburg.de/.

Dieser Band nimmt die Untersuchungsfragen des Teilprojekts 3, „Poetry and Contemporary Visual Culture", auf und führt sie darüber hinaus hin zu anderen Gegenständen und weiteren disziplinären Ansätzen. Gedichte in digitalen Medien transformieren ästhetische Verfahren, die von der Avantgarde und Neo-Avantgarde konzipiert wurden. Ikonische und kinetische Schrift sind dabei innovative Elemente, die sich lyrischer Verfahren wie der Wiederholung und Variation bedienen oder ihr visuelles Erscheinungsbild einsetzen, um Verfremdungseffekte zu erzielen. Um die Ästhetik sich auf der Fläche oder im Raum bewegender Poesie zu untersuchen, wird auf Forschungen zu Medienkunst und anderen Formen kinetischer Schrift rekurriert. Einige digitale Lyriker:innen programmieren ihre Texte, indem sie beispielsweise Algorithmen zur Generierung von visueller Poesie verwenden. Forschungen, die Genreklassifikationen für digitale Lyrik vorschlagen, bilden den Ausgangspunkt für eine nähere Auseinandersetzung mit dem Gegenstandsbereich, indem u. a. Multilingualität hinzukommt. Im Zeitalter des ‚Scrollens von Literatur' sind Phänomene wie Instapoetry für das Teilprojekt ebenfalls relevant, weil diese zumeist kurzen und einfach zu verstehenden, für Smartphones entworfenen Gedichte oft mit visuellen Elementen (Handschrift, Ornamenten, Zeichnungen, Fotos) verknüpft sind. Ermöglicht durch plattformspezifische Affordanzen weist ihre visuelle Gestaltung aber auch relevante gesellschaftspolitische Funktionen auf. Ein weiterer Gegenstand des Teilprojekts sind Poesiefilme; sie setzen Gedichte auf konzeptueller Ebene ein, häufig mithilfe von elegischen Bild-Ton-Kombinationen, die lyrische Verfahren in audiovisuelle Kompositionen transformieren. Bezugspunkte sind hier bestehende Forschungen zu Poesiefilmen sowie der Einsatz von Gedichten in Avantgarde- und experimentellen Filmen. Lyrik erfreut sich nach wie vor einer Beliebtheit in der etablierten Buchform. Daher untersucht das Teilprojekt auch gedruckte Gedichte, ihre visuellen Qualitäten – grafische Elemente ebenso wie die sprachliche Evokation von Bildern betreffend – und die Transformationen der Buchkultur im digitalen Zeitalter. Wie im Teilprojekt werden auch im vorliegenden Band, der Beiträge von Wissenschaftler:innen und Lyriker:innen aus unterschiedlichen Ländern versammelt, interdisziplinäre Forschungsansätze und Theorien für die Erforschung von Lyrik und Visueller Kultur fruchtbar gemacht.

Claudia Benthien

Inhaltsverzeichnis

Vorwort —— V

Wiebke Vorrath and Magdalena Elisabeth Korecka
Poetry and Contemporary Visual Culture / Lyrik und zeitgenössische Visuelle Kultur: An Introduction —— 1

1 Sites and Sights: Modes of Contemporary Poetry

Karin Nykvist
Here, There, Everywhere: Situating Contemporary Multimodal Poetry —— 25

Vladimir Feshchenko and Olga Sokolova
Visualising Deixis in Avant-Garde and Contemporary Poetry "On and Off the Page" —— 49

Roberto Simanowski
Reading, Seeing, Clicking: Kinetic Concrete Poetry —— 73

Heinz Drügh
Von Überraschungseiern, Gummibärchen und anderem Eye Candy – Überlegungen zur gegenwärtigen Lyrik und den kommodifizierten Bildern —— 87

2 Visibly Visual: Sociopolitical Poetry on the Web and in Films

Astrid Böger
U.S. American Poetry in the Digital Age: Participation, Performance, Protest —— 105

Magdalena Elisabeth Korecka
Platformized Visual Intimacies: Visibility in Feminist Instapoetry —— 121

Sophie Ertel
Poetische Pluralität: Kollaborative und visuelle Strategien im Poesiefilm *LESBIAN* —— 145

3 Viewpoints: Artistic Practices in Digital Poetry and Poetry Films

Chris Kerr and Daniel Holden
Optimizing Code for Performance: Reading *./code --poetry* —— 167

María Mencía
Navigating the Poetic-Aesthetic Space of E-Poetry —— 185

Lucy English
Finding a New Approach: The Use of Visual Images in Spoken Word Poetry Film —— 207

4 Poetic Images: (Audio)Visuality in Contemporary Book Poetry

Esther Kilchmann
Vexierbild Gedicht: Schriftbildlichkeit, intermediale und interlinguale Translation in der Lyrik Heike Fiedlers und Jörg Piringers —— 225

Hiroshi Yamamoto
„Schneiden, Spleißen und punktgenaue Mutation!" Zu Text-Bild-Korrespondenzen im digitalen Zeitalter in Gerhard Falkners und Yves Netzhammers *Ignatien* —— 241

Tijana Koprivica
Film Techniques and Poetic Procedures in Vladan Krečković's Poetry Collection *Pariz, Teksas* —— 263

List of Figures —— 285

Authors —— 289

Wiebke Vorrath and Magdalena Elisabeth Korecka
Poetry and Contemporary Visual Culture / Lyrik und zeitgenössische Visuelle Kultur: An Introduction

Poetry and visuality have had an eventful history of medial correlations, ranging from poetic devices and genres such as ekphrasis and text-image combinations in emblematic poems to poetic forms like *carmina figurata* (*Figurengedichte*), visual and concrete poetry, right up to current poetic practices in audiovisual media. If we consider the further diversification of poetry in regard to inter- and transmediality, and the emergence of new poetic types across various media (cf. Mønster 2017, 235–236; Schaefer 2015, 169–170), it appears that the relationship between poetry and visual culture has intensified once more in the age of digitalization. The visual dimensions of contemporary poetry encompass, for instance, iconic and kinetic script in digital poetry, visual elements (e.g., drawings or pictures) in social media poems on networking platforms such as the photo and video sharing service Instagram, and spoken and written text in combination with moving pictures in poetry films. Going beyond poetry on screen and on the internet, poems can be found in public spaces in the form of light projections and murals (cf. Benthien and Gestring 2023), they adorn everyday items such as mugs or posters, and short poems or lyrics are sometimes even tattooed onto skin. Poetry employing visual layers in book publications has also endured and offers a different kind of aesthetic appeal in the digital age (cf. Borsuk 2018; Pressman 2020).

    We are deliberately giving this overview here because the ERC project "Poetry in the Digital Age" (overseen by Claudia Benthien at the Universität Hamburg, 2021–2025) investigates these phenomena of poetry and visual culture alongside the complexes of poetry and performance as well as poetry and music. As part of the research project, this publication focuses on the visual dimensions of contemporary poetry and opens up the field to further objects of research and perspectives from different disciplines. It presents contributions by scholars from various countries working in a range of research fields, such as literary, media, and film studies, cultural and visual culture studies, and linguistics, as well as in poetic practice. In doing so, this book aims to broaden the scope of visual culture studies, which mainly considers approaches from art history, popular culture studies, and media studies, by bringing in objectives and methods from poetry research as well as from lyricology. The term *lyricology* is currently being established among European scholars and describes the ongoing endeavor to unite the international study of poetry and advance its genre theory (see, for instance, Hillebrandt et al. 2019; Müller and Stahl 2021; Zymner 2009).[1]

Research on visual culture from the perspective of literary studies has so far generally focused on narrative texts and intermedial relations, e.g., between literature and photography or film (see, for example, Bathrick and Preußer 2012; Becker and Korte 2011; Beckman and Weissberg 2013; Brosch 2004; Cruz 2014; Lüdeke and Greber 2004; Voßkamp and Weingart 2005; Zima 1995). While visual culture studies has not adequately taken poetry into account, the visuality of poetry has played a major role in explorations that have been undertaken in poetry research: There is a significant number of contributions concerning emblematic, ekphrastic, and other visual poetic forms from various epochs (see, for instance, Bohn 2013; Dencker 2011; Ernst 1991; Krieger 1992; Robillard and Jongeneel 1998; Scholz 2002; Wandhoff 2003). Worth mentioning here is the special issue of *Humanities*, "Modernist Poetry and Visual Culture" (Kinnahan 2022), with articles focusing on poetry from the late nineteenth to mid-twentieth centuries. Regarding contemporary poetry, research on the visual and multimedia aspects of poetry has mainly been conducted in digital literary scholarship, which views visuality as something inextricably linked with media and their interfaces (see, e.g., Chasar 2020; Hayles 2008; Morris and Swiss 2006; Rettberg 2019; Stein 2010). While some contributions trace developments from print to digital poetry, only few of them integrate approaches from visual culture studies in particular.

Taking previous investigations into account while examining objects of research ranging from twenty-first century poetry in digital media and books to poetry films, this volume attempts to map the field of poetry and contemporary visual culture from European scholarly perspectives – thereby performing a cultural survey of knowledge production in order to enter the global discourse on contemporary poetics. The main goal of this undertaking is to assess the significance of visual culture for the production of poetry today and, in turn, to sound out the insights poetry might generate into contemporary visual culture. Considering the great variety of poetry, this volume will also discuss how the genre is changing by first and foremost asking how visual culture is applied, exposed, reflected on, and debated in poetic practices. The central hypothesis is that the medial correlations addressed here have crucial political implications and that poetry in the digital age therefore holds considerable potential for digital as well as post-digital language, image, and media criticism (cf. Cramer 2016, 31; Schmitt 2021, 7–8; Stiegler 2014, 161–162). Since the notions, topics, and objects of research in question are as diverse as the disciplines examining them, the following delib-

---

[1] See also https://lyricology.org/.

erations about key terms and concepts serve as a general basis and starting point for the subsequent discussions in this volume.

Across visual culture studies and poetry research

Visual culture studies, a research field that is interdisciplinary in itself, emerged in the 1990s with the objective of investigating contemporary visuality at large and flourished until the 2010s. It started with the observation that, due to the rapid development of media technology in the twentieth century, postmodern life is centered around visual media, that there is an image (and information) overload, and that pictures hold power over societies and individuals. In the light of this "hypervisuality" (Mirzoeff 2002, 4) or "new power of images" (Maar and Burda 2004), advocates of visual culture studies and *Bildwissenschaft* have proclaimed a pictorial, iconic, or visual turn. Referring back to the linguistic turn, they have criticized the enduring dominance of the text-image distinction in cultural and literary studies (cf. Benthien and Weingart 2014, 1–4), most frequently discussed in relation to the Laocoon debate.[2] The distinction between poetry as a time-based art form and the visual arts as spatial art forms has been challenged multiple times throughout this debate. At the latest since the advent of the personal computer – the epitome of the intermedium – it has become especially evident that it is no longer possible (and probably never has been) to maintain this dichotomy. Just as there are only mixed media, or in Mitchell's words, "the very notion of purely visual media is radically incoherent" (Mitchell 2008 [1992], 15; cf. also Rimmele and Stiegler 2019, 17), all cultural production now relies on digital technology, even when it is presented in analog form – which is what is meant here by the term *post-digital*, i.e., that differentiating between analog and digital today is near untenable (cf. Bajohr and Gilbert 2021, 14; Cramer 2016, 31).

Closely related to the suspension of dichotomies like spatial and time-based art, text and image, and analog and digital spheres is the dissolution of the dis-

---

[2] As the history and emergence of visual culture studies have already been broadly surveyed in previous research, we will refrain from providing an in-depth review here. For a discussion of the differences between Anglo-American visual culture studies and German *Bildwissenschaft*, and their relationship to media studies, see, for example, Stiegler 2014; cf. also Rimmele and Stiegler 2019, 158–164. For a disambiguation of the terms *pictorial*, *iconic*, and *visual turn*, and their interrelation with other cultural studies turns, see, for instance, Bachmann-Medick 2006; Benthien and Weingart 2014; Mitchell 2008 [1992]. References to and discussions of the Laocoon debate can be found in the aforementioned articles and many more on image-text relations (see also Mirzoeff 1999).

tinction between "popular" and "high" culture that was promoted in the field early on. Whereas art history has focused its study on products of so-called high culture and the fine arts, visual culture studies has aimed to develop a comprehensive theory of the visual that allows scholars to investigate visuality in every domain – from literature to the visual arts and mass media (cf. Benthien and Weingart 2014, 5; Mitchell 2008 [1992], 15; Rimmele and Stiegler 2019, 15–21). The term visual culture therefore encompasses a vast area of visuality that includes objects from the arts and products of popular culture as well as visual aspects of everyday life and therefore indicates a wide notion of culture (cf. Benthien and Weingart 2014, 7; Mirzoeff 1999, 12–13). As a theoretical discipline, the scope of visual culture studies ranges from investigations into the objects of traditional art history analysis such as paintings, to architecture and photography, right up to everyday items and manifestations of visuality on websites and social media, in commercials, and on the news. At present, its main focus lies on digital images, not only regarding their technological nature and circulation but also as a source of knowledge production in scientific and scholarly research and institutions.[3]

Hence, there are various approaches in visual culture studies: Whitney Davis (2018), for instance, tries to access visual culture in a way that mainly relies on art history. Scholar Irit Rogoff (2005), who is also classically trained, has moved beyond pure art criticism and conducted research on various visual cultures and their participatory ideals for a few decades now. For Nicholas Mirzoeff (2017; 2023), who has been greatly influenced by cultural studies, however, the boundaries between high and popular culture no longer exist – to be more precise, he actually renounces the addressing of any differences. Today, both visual culture studies and poetry research have resolved this distinction as it does not seem to serve any valid function and, moreover, does not account for a great variety of contemporary poetic forms. For instance, code poetry, i.e., poems written in source code that can sometimes even be executed by computer programs, have some characteristics that could be associated with a traditional understanding of high culture. These include the hermeticism and complexity of codework, its small, distinguished audience, and therefore the lack of a mass market value for the poems (even more so than for book poetry). On the other hand, they often use

---

[3] Of mention here is above all the research center Das Technische Bild ("The Technical Image"), founded in 2000 by art historian Horst Bredekamp, which is dedicated to exploring knowledge production through technical images in research, institutions, and networks with the aim of expanding visual history with the addition of perspectives and methods from technological, social, and media history. The research center's findings are published annually by De Gruyter in the book series *Bildwelten des Wissens: Jahrbuch für Bildkritik* (see https://www.kulturtechnik.hu-berlin.de/en/research/the-technical-image/).

popular culture content – such as intermedial references to various "nerd cultures" (see Kohout 2022), online discourses, and typographies with chat aesthetics – and they are mainly distributed on the internet (cf. Holden and Kerr in this volume).

Another example is book publications of social media poetry, which reflect the existence of a phenomenon that is often considered "pop-cultural" in various media, "non-traditional" and "traditional" alike. Such publications expose specific digital aesthetics, writing practices, and parallel, overlapping modes of reading in an analog form. A case in point is Sarah Berger's publication *Lesen und Schreien* (2020), in which visual chats in varying colors and multi-layered pictures are superimposed onto the "original" poetry published online, thereby demonstrating the highly visual conditions in which it was written as condensed images (cf. Pflock 2022, 230–238). Thus, various media variations of and in poetry intersect with, and deconstruct, assumptions about "high" and "low" culture. Current poetry research and lyricology are therefore striving to expand upon existing genre theory, in particular regarding the remarkable development of contemporary poetic genres, which are "increasingly exploring previously unfamiliar publication formats and breaking away from conventional modes of publication" (Müller and Stahl 2021, 5; cf. Mønster 2017, 235). In this manner, the research on poetry and visuality being conducted, for example, by organizations like the Electronic Literature Organization (ELO)[4] or in research projects such as Poetry Beyond Text: Vision, Text and Cognition[5] refrains from drawing lines between high and popular culture, instead paying attention to (born) digital practices (cf. Hayles 2008, 3), multimedia aesthetics – e.g., of images and pictures – and their effects on readers.

Visual culture studies differentiates between pictures and images, which W. J. T. Mitchell formulated in the oft-cited phrase: "you can hang a picture, but you can't hang an image" (Mitchell 2008 [1992], 16; see also Benthien and Weingart 2014, 10; Mirzoeff 1999, 7). Hence, the term *pictures* denotes, for instance, photographs or paintings but also virtual visualizations on screen and online (which one cannot hang physically but which do have a visible form). *Images*, by contrast, are understood in an immaterial sense as imaginations, *dispositifs*, motifs, or metaphors – which are equally important notions for poetic practice and poetry research – circulating in various media and pictures. Thus, pictures in poetry, *as* poems, or accompanying them do not stand alone but are embedded within discourses, i.e., images, their reproductions, and remediations. Since the pictorial turn postulated by Mitchell (cf. 2008 [1992]) and the interrelated iconic

---

4 https://eliterature.org/.
5 https://www.poetrybeyondtext.org/.

turn proposed by Gottfried Boehm (cf. 1994), the constant stream of pictures and images has increased once more as smartphones and social media platforms have become permanent fixtures of everyday life. The discussion has therefore moved into the digital sphere.

Olga Moskatova speaks of a "circulatory turn," thereby describing "image mobility" as a marker of our present visual culture (Moskatova 2021, 13). In addition, Mark B. Hansen states that contemporary culture is being shaped by a "regime of the digital image" (Hansen 2004, 11–12) and that digitalization has altered the meaning of images as such. Rather than proclaiming a "dissolution" of the image in the tradition of Lev Manovich – with whose theory he contrasts his own – Hansen explains that the digital image is the "embodied processing of information," thereby also portraying the human being as an integral component of the digital age (Hansen 2004, 9–10). In doing so, he refers to the digital image as an entity necessary for understanding big data experientially, as "it is in the form of the image [. . .] that digital information is rendered apprehensible" (Hansen 2004, 10–11). Thus, creating images – and furthermore new media art – from big data in an interactive, embodied manner can be and is a means of exploring the state of contemporary digital culture. Furthermore, the circulation of images is tied to networking and network effects: they mostly relate to scale and refer to how platforms are built around this structuring, meaning that "the more users who join a network, the more valuable that network becomes" (Poell et al. 2022, 37). As the growth of user numbers on platforms is linked with the distribution of images, pictures, and increasingly videos, and due to the logics of circulation as well as reproduction (cf. Moskatova 2021, 12), network effects can and do ascribe political as well as economic value to images and pictures.

Photographs of celebratory events such as representative gatherings (e.g., of politicians or celebrities at galas or weddings) but also horrifying pictures of wars as currently of the war in the Ukraine – at times even morbidly used as media spectacles – and of social media protests against oppressive regimes in Iran, for instance, are circulating daily through our media devices. These protest pictures are marked by their affectivity and are highly iconized, displaying and reproducing symbolic imagery, often in static pictures, e.g., photographs, which are frequently reenacted in varying political contexts (cf. Schankweiler 2019, 25–29; Sontag 2003, 29). Thus, it is not only possible to utilize aesthetics as a poetic means in themselves; rather, they can also become a political device, as Astrid Böger argues. Her contribution examines the participatory and activist functions of visual aspects of US poetry by looking at examples from Instapoetry, an online poetry magazine, and a virtual reality performance. For instance, the Poetry Foundation's collection *Poems of Protest, Resistance, and Empowerment* displays a highly colorful and retro-style illustration by CHema Skandal!, which is reminiscent of the poster art of Russian Constructivism. The poetic renderings Böger analyzes make use of visual playfulness to evoke seriousness, e.g., in the form of Blackout poetry that deconstructs the US national anthem or in Instapoetry created in the context of the Black Lives Matter movement that remediates photographs of street protests.

The omnipresence of visual representations may benefit media companies, voyeuristic readership or witnessing, practices of "astroturfing" (Schankweiler 2019, 45), or the visual and commercial appropriation of protest movements, but at the same time, these images are also intricately intertwined with the dissemination of crucial information (cf. Schankweiler 2019, 37), not only in poetic activism. Questions relating to the relationship between media, power, and perception that are shared by visual culture, media, and literary studies have therefore lost none of their relevance. The tasks of scrutinizing the power relations and dimensions of the visual, and developing a critique of both their hegemonial structures and the medial dominance of certain types of visibility, visuality, and also imagery (*Bildlichkeit*) are still at the heart of visual culture studies (cf. Stiegler 2014, 160–161) and are discussed in this volume. Karin Nykvist analyzes Caroline Bergvall's multilingual and multimodal poetry with a special focus on the poet's examination of representations of forced migrants[6] in the media and their societal (in)visibility. Regarding Bergvall's collaborative practice of creating poetry with other artists online, e.g., in livestreams during the Covid lockdown periods, Nykvist moreover suggests some innovative terminology for situating different kinds of contemporary poetry: she defines live performances of poetry as "here" poetry, printed poems in book publications as "there" poetry, and poetic formats on the internet as "everywhere" poetry.

Contemporary poetry is therefore situated within the media environment and the specific (post-)digital image culture described above, not only on platforms but also in contemporary visual culture in general. Poems range from conscious utilizations of pictures and/or images for socio-political purposes to aesthetic, formal, and critical examinations of images on a conceptual level in various print, online, multimedia, and performative formats. Additional layers of meaning emerge in all aesthetic aspects of poetry (i.e., visual, audio, tactile) that we need to consider when encountering contemporary poems. For example, digital multidimensional computer illustrations may stand alongside "pure" text in book poetry that has been remediated or influenced by weblogs or social media; three-dimensional poetry

---

6 See https://reliefweb.int/report/world/migrants-refugees-terminology-contested-powerful-and-evolving.

also exists as holograms or sculptures in exhibition spaces,[7] questioning the distinction between poetry and the visual arts once again. Not only is contemporary poetry taking on sculptural forms and expanding into new spaces, the concept of time-based art is also experiencing constant changes. For instance, Twitter poetry about real-time societal events with intermittently added user comments is ongoing and exists until it is taken down, although it does not exhibit physical materiality (cf. Pflock 2022, 223–227). Poetry film displays multilayered aesthetic elements simultaneously, e.g., written or spoken poetry and moving pictures (see Konyves 2012; Orphal 2014; Tremlett 2021). Here, reading processes break with linearity and the chronology of the solitary reader focusing on a book page and left-justified, black-and-white, text-only poems – an outdated image of poetry that remains prevalent, despite the genre's manifold forms. Considering the seriality and reproducibility of images and pictures on the internet, it can be said that poetry stands alongside "meme aesthetics" (Goriunova 2014, 62), i.e., humorous, subcultural, mediated, and repeatedly circulated motifs that dominate digital spaces.

Poetry attempts to sustain its position in the flow of innumerable online pictures by adapting or resisting specific visualities. The intricacy of the relationship between art and the economy becomes especially visible in online spaces and in light of the seeming commercialization of poetry, as Heinz Drügh argues. In his article, he presents his reflections on the relationship between contemporary poetry and commodified images and pictures – by looking at examples from Instapoetry and book poetry that incorporate or refer to the advertising aesthetics of commodities, from designer clothing to gummy bears. Poetic references to such media content stand in a longer tradition, e.g., of neo-avantgarde poetry that addresses visual culture, often in a critical manner. For example, Rolf Dieter Brinkmann utilized pictures of celebrities and pinups from advertisements or poems about photography itself to problematize text-image and interart relations as well as questions of gender and media conditions (cf. Weingart 2005, 228–232).

To summarize: of interest for the examination of poetry and contemporary visual culture are not only pictures as material, tactile objects but also many more facets of visuality (cf. Benthien and Weingart 2014, 7; Davis 2018, 279; Mirzoeff 1999, 12–13). In regard to the production and reception of poetry, this involves questions of text-image relations, of iconography and iconology, the visual

---

7 Most recently, sculptural and 3D poetry, as well as other poetry objects from the 1960s to the present, were displayed in two exhibitions in Germany, namely *Skulpturale Poesie* ("Sculptural Poetry," Weserburg in Bremen, March 26 to August 14, 2022; https://weserburg.de/ausstellung/skulpturale-poesie/) and *Dichtung in 3D* ("Poetry in 3D," Deutsches Buch- und Schriftmuseum in Leipzig, April 8, 2022, to January 8, 2023, https://www.dnb.de/DE/Ueber-uns/DBSM/DBSMAusstellungsarchiv/dichtung3D.html).

dimensions of writing, books, and film, and, furthermore, practices of watching, seeing, and reading, as well as dynamics of cultural visibility and invisibility (cf. Davis 2018, 197; Dencker 2011, 863–864; Stiegler 2014, 160; see also Bucher 2012; Cancik-Kirschbaum et al. 2012; Horstkotte and Leonhard 2006; Mergenthaler 2002; Mirzoeff 2017; 2023). This volume's contributions explore these aspects of visuality in the form of case studies of recent poetry books and films as well as digital and social media poetry in order to examine their aesthetic effects and political implications.

From visual and digital literacy to poetic criticism

At the beginning of this introduction, we claimed that contemporary poetry holds considerable potential for (post-)digital language, image, and media criticism. In this section, we will flesh out how this hypothesis relates to both visual culture studies and poetry research, and to our previous discussions of poetic reflections on visuality and their political potentials. Considering the global dissemination of pictures and images, and the changing qualities of visuality and visibility, one of the key concepts of visual culture studies is "visual literacy," meaning the development of strategies and skills to critically analyze, understand, and deconstruct visual artifacts and their (political, ideological, cultural) implications (cf. Benthien and Weingart 2014, 6; Mitchell 2008 [1992], 11–12; Mirzoeff 1999, 3; Stiegler 2014, 161–163).

Whitney Davis, for instance, also speaks of an "aspective view" (Davis 2018, 321) as a method for analyzing visual culture, which takes a diverse array of aspects into account (e.g., analogies and ruptures in "seeing as"/"seeing-like"), moving beyond solely visual, objective, material interpretations. This means that the "visible salient features" of analyzed works of art or other visual objects "are embedded in a network of forms of likeness including external aspective relations, or analogies" (Davis 2018, 321). Thus, a comparison of "visible" Instapoetic retro-style writing may evoke the "invisible" presence of the Blackout poetry movement of the 1960s and 1970s ("seeing-as"), which alters the final interpretation with consequences for the poetic field. Similarly, visually comparing code poems with the poetry of neo-avantgarde movements influences their reception, for example, in academia. In her contribution, María Mencía examines visuality in digital poetry as an aesthetic strategy that she uses in her own poetic practice. In doing so, she connects her digital art with avantgarde movements in visual poetry. She furthermore speaks of "in-between" spaces – between sound or text and images as the "poetic-aesthetic space" – in order to explore experimental strategies concerning materiality but also social issues in what she refers to as a "poetics of data."

The terminology from visual culture studies is to be seen in general correlation with the demand for "digital literacy" often made, especially in the past ten years, with regard to the constantly expanding impact of digitalization in every domain of contemporary life. With this term, scholars from different contexts formulate the need for a media competence that allows users to critically interact with and reflect upon digital technologies. Johanna Drucker, for example, investigates visual knowledge production in digital environments in her monograph *Visualization and Interpretation* (2020). In addition, calls for "source code criticism" (as in the workshop of the same name held by Hannes Bajohr in March 2022) proclaim that people should require skills to read, interpret, and understand source code and algorithms, which Mark. C. Marino also postulates in his publication *Critical Code Studies* (2020). Digital literacy is furthermore inextricably linked with the often-cited concept of *affordances*, i.e., the general properties of digital spaces, which are dependent on technology as well as the media competence of poets and users in general. Extending the approach taken by Jenny Davis – who updates the earlier concepts defined by James Gibson and Don Norman – and applying it to poetic production, affordances can thus be understood in a twofold manner: they can positively facilitate artistic creation or production, but they can also alter or diminish possibilities for action as well (cf. Davis 2020, 18–22; cf. also Gibson 1986 [1979]; Norman 2013).

But what do the terms *visual* and *digital literacy* have to do with poetry? Contemporary poetry and its encounter with visuality manifests and questions the medial correlations addressed here and their political potentials in various ways: In continuation of avant-garde and neo-avant-garde poetic practices, recent poetry oftentimes foregrounds layers of the visual (and the auditory) that generate meaning. In doing so, poems display automatisms in the use of images, pictures and language (relating to speech and writing), now in an updated manner regarding the further developments that have been made in media technologies (cf. Mønster 2017, 243; Müller and Stahl 2021, 12). Alongside image and media criticism, this is where the question of language criticism comes in – which, of course, is also interconnected with the literary dimensions of text, visuality, and picturality. It is worth mentioning here that the terms visual literacy and digital literacy themselves employ literature as a metaphor for a highly constructed system that we can only understand, interpret, and criticize if we acquire its language. As the term *literacy* furthermore possesses a pedagogical connotation, we propose speaking of poetic visual and digital criticism instead.

One example of current poetic practices that implement media and language criticism is digital poetry: generative poems and code poems employ digital language technology in order to explore the functions of algorithms and source code. They thereby lay bare the often hidden functional logics of digital media such as "the dissolution of the text/image difference in multimodal AI,"[8] which Hannes Bajohr addressed in connection with the readability and visuality of algorithmic works of poetry. Moreover, and returning to code poems, it can be argued that they reflect on the relationship between programming languages and "natural" languages. In doing so, they not only raise questions concerning human-machine relations and challenge concepts of authorship but also make visible the underlying programs in the form of scripts of (the predominantly visual) media interfaces (cf. Cayley 2002, 1–2; Funkhouser 2007, 320–321; Mirzoeff 1999, 3, 6; see also Vorrath 2022). Transformation, for example of bits and bytes into linguistic and visual signs, is therefore a crucial aspect that must be scrutinized.

The poet Chris Kerr and the programmer Daniel Holden specifically create and inspect these interwoven aspects of visuality, auditory meaning, and language as a material in their own code poetry. The question of how the visual qualities of different script systems in code poems can then be further transformed into oral performance is at the heart of their article. Moreover, the fusion of human and machine languages could be taken as a form of multilingualism, which – in the traditional understanding of the use of two or more "natural" languages – is still an integral component of some contemporary book poetry. In her article, Esther Kilchmann investigates visual aspects of translation in Heike Fiedler's multilingual book poetry and in Jörg Piringer's digital poetry. She thereby pays particular attention to minimal, formal interventions such as vowel shifts and line or break placements, and argues that visual strategies bring forth new meanings between the languages and language technologies used within the poems.

Reading and writing between media

In the digital age, poetry books are still favored by various authors as a publication format and they persist as relevant works alongside the manifold poetic genres in different media. With her concept of "bookishness," Jessica Pressman explains that book publications offer a different kind of aesthetic appeal, which demonstrates the validity of the book in the face of digital developments and as "a creative moment invested in exploring and demonstrating love for the book as

---

8 Hannes Bajohr. "Digital Ekphrasis: The Dissolution of the Text/Image Difference in Multimodal AI." Talk at the conference "Poetry and Contemporary Visual Culture / Lyrik und zeitgenössische Visuelle Kultur" held at Universität Hamburg from May 19 to 21, 2022.

a symbol, art form, and artifact" (Pressman 2020, 1). Nevertheless, printed books now rely on digital technology during the production process (cf. Bajohr and Gilbert 2021, 19). What is more, they sometimes even deliberately engage with digital themes and aesthetics, as the example analyzed by Hiroshi Yamamoto illustrates: he explores intersections between text and image in the collaborative poetry book *Ignatien* by poet Gerhard Falkner and visual computer artist Yves Netzhammer. While Falkner's poems reveal a negative view of a digitalized world, Netzhammer's images exhibit a clear-cut digital aesthetic, which develops a prolific tension between the verbal and visual layers. Concerning the interrelation of poetry and film, Tijana Koprivica investigates interart connections in book poetry by looking at the example of Vladan Krečković's poetry collection *Pariz, Teksas*. Of particular interest in her contribution are transfers of filmic elements from Wim Wender's movie *Paris, Texas* to Krečković's poetry. Koprivica argues that the poet transforms cinematic techniques into poetic ones, and that this relationship between poetry and film creates specific visualities and atmospheres within the written poems.

The cohesion of visuality and writtenness in general can be described as a dynamic but inextricable constellation. A good example of the fact that texts and images as well as reading and seeing should not be conceptualized as complete opposites is the German term *Schriftbild* (literally: script-picture; cf. Benthien and Weingart 2014, 6, 9–10; see also Cancik-Kirschbaum et al. 2012). It encompasses the specific appearance of something written, the way the typography and layout of a text look, but it can also mean a picture consisting of letters and words, for example. The concept's abstractness therefore reveals itself in a double-vision, in how written words are themselves visual constructs that can be read and seen in two ways: as visible and visual typographic elements embedded within a certain layout or as carriers of meaning (cf. Strätling and Witte 2006, 7–9). The display of the interrelations between the verbal and the visual becomes particularly evident in concrete and visual poetry (for an overview of their varieties, see Greber 2004). Two articles in this volume provide an insight into these poetic forms and their development, from the avant-gardes to their updated versions in digital media:

Roberto Simanowski discusses how the interrelation of reading, seeing, and clicking influences or brings forth diverse layers of meaning in kinetic concrete poetry. He thereby outlines the history of concrete and experimental poetry, from print to digital forms, which exhibit further levels of expression. This article can be referred to as a historical document in itself as it was first published in German in 2005 and therefore illustrates a particular moment in the development of digital poetry. Now, Simanowski's article is finally available in English and has been updated for this volume with examples from the 2020s. In their linguistic article, Vladimir Feshchenko and Olga Sokolova look at the historical context of deixis in visual poetry before turning to contemporary poems. They analyze examples that display deictic units, e.g., highlighted by colored font or combined with photographs, with a particular emphasis on the visual properties of language-based poetic practices in US, Russian, and Ukrainian literature. According to the authors, poets utilize deixis as an integral component of everyday language and deictic markers of spatial relations in their poetry to exhibit the materiality of language in the digital sphere. In doing so, the discussed poems also address current issues and societal conditions such as the Covid pandemic and the war against Ukraine.

Contemporary developments in the tradition of visual poetry that have brought about new forms such as interactive poems, multimedia adaptations of concrete poems, and poetry installations demonstrate that the interrelation between verbal and visual representation is even more profound than the dual nature of written letters – in fact, the alphabet itself possesses auditory dimensions, too. As Mitchell has pointed out numerous times, there are no purely visual media; rather, media can be described as mixed formations with complex correlations between diverse (e.g., semiotic, symbolic, perceptive) modes (cf. Mitchell 2008 [1992], 15; Gil 2014, 193–194) which also accounts for poetry, not only but especially in its multimodal and intermedial forms. Poetry's inherent multimodality can be most visibly detected in the increasingly popular genre of poetry film, as discussed by Lucy English. Her article focuses on this poetic form as a truly collaborative endeavor between poets and filmmakers, situated in between text, images, sound, and a seeming tactility. By scrutinizing terminology pertaining to poetry films and her own collectively created poetic work, the author proposes the term "lyrical spoken word poetry film" for the specific type she analyzes. She thereby focuses on the various influences and consequences this kind of artistic interart practice has on conceptualizations of poetic speech and writing in cinematic examples.

Furthermore, concepts of authorship and reception, of reading, seeing, and writing, are increasingly being challenged in new media and post-digital environments when, for instance, poetry on social media platforms or code poetry utilizes non-human, that is, algorithmic authors. As algorithms "read" or interpret data and then "write" or produce a textual output, Lori Emerson speaks of circular *reading writing* practices (cf. Emerson 2014, xiv). Poets sometimes creatively explore these developments and display the resulting visual materiality or hidden "invisible visual culture" (Rothöhler 2021, 82) of multiple authorships or of the internet's black box. We can even speak of "algorithmic 'platform seeing'" (Rothöhler 2021, 82) as a further visual influence on the aesthetics of poetry, with algorithms and the accompanying technology on platforms as additional relevant agents. Platforms "see," meaning they play a decisive and integral role in the uniformity of certain forms of social media poetry, for instance.

One related topic, to which correlations of poetic language and audiovisual media call attention, are changes in production as well as reception practices.

New poetry formats with their specific materiality and mediality not only result in a transformed writtenness and literality but also contribute to the reevaluation of reading and writing practices in digital spaces. While poets are becoming "poet-programmers" (Funkhouser 2007, 330), interaction can transform readers of poetry into "produsers" (Bruns 2008, 21). The boundaries between reading, seeing, and using, or interacting blur, resulting in altered modes of perception. "Readers" likewise engage with the poems as with each other, thereby establishing online communities revolving around sociopolitical agendas and participatory cultures (cf. Jenkins 2009). Sociopolitical agendas, moreover, were and are still marked by specific, immediately recognizable aesthetics, e.g., influenced visually by brightly colored, flat Russian Constructivist poster collages (cf. Brunner 2021) as indicated above. Contemporary poets continue these practices of unifying aesthetics, for instance, in socio-politically engaged forms of poetry on the internet, in protest poetry on weblogs, or on social media.

Collaborative and participatory artistic practices can also be found in online poetic collectives or anthologies and in the genre of poetry film, where they are often visibly exhibited, as Sophie Ertel's contribution demonstrates. With regard to its community-building potential, she argues that poetry film can become a space for discussions of queer and lesbian sexuality. By looking at the example of *LESBIAN* by Rosemary Baker, Ertel analyzes how the poetry film deconstructs the stereotypical images and pictures perpetuated by the news and in digital media, and thereby calls for a diversification of the gaze. The interrelation of visuality and visibility is relevant to mention in this context again as many poetry formats reflect upon these aspects of "visualities" which are, according to Donna Haraway, connected to social power. She argues that "politicality [exists] in the rift between representation and non-representation" (Haraway 1991, 188), referring to the visibility of bodies as a crucial aspect of belonging and being (cf. Leese 2016, 144). Seemingly democratic online spaces are highly ambivalent, enabling minoritized community-building but also diminishing and simultaneously suppressing it, i.e., consistently alternating between granting visibility and creating invisibility. For instance, minoritized bodies are seen but also "sensored" (Olszanowski 2014, 83), controlled, used and appropriated as "visual capital" (Mirzoeff 2019) in social media practices. This further influences poetry on networking platforms, which brings about an ambivalence that Magdalena Elisabeth Korecka discusses by investigating the example of feminist Instapoetry and its visual (in)visibilities. The described strategies result in varying stylistic communities, from a black-and-white aesthetic to colorful carousel posts on Instagram, which she examines in terms of platform features and affective community interventions, in particular by paying attention to the work of Hollie McNish.

In this introduction, we have laid out a theoretical foundation to explain the reciprocal relationship between poetry and visuality, building upon approaches from visual culture studies and poetry research. We have thereby outlined the diverse types of and publication formats for contemporary poetry, including the highly accessible and instantaneous genre of Instapoetry, collaborative efforts in multimodal online formats such as live streams and audiovisual poetry films, experimental renderings in digital poetry like kinetic poetry and code poems, protest poetry in magazines and on social media, multilingual poetry in book and online publications, and interart and ekphrastic strategies in poetry books and films. The following contributions from various research fields investigate this great diversity by asking how contemporary visual culture and the facets of visuality addressed here are applied, reflected on, exposed, or debated in poetry today in order to examine their potential for poetic (visual, linguistic, digital, and/or media) criticism.

Structure of this volume

This book is subdivided into four thematic sections which focus on different aspects of the complex of poetry and contemporary visual culture. The first section "Sites and Sights: Modes of Contemporary Poetry," comprises four contributions written from the perspectives of literary, media, and cultural studies, and linguistics. KARIN NYKVIST discusses current visual and spatial practices in contemporary multimodal poetry and the influence of poetry's spatiality on visual aesthetics in the multidimensional works of Norwegian artist Caroline Bergvall. VLADIMIR FESHCHENKO and OLGA SOKOLOVA examine spatial relationality by looking at the explicit linguistic as well as poetic strategy of deixis in examples of historical and contemporary poetry from the US, Russia, and Ukraine. The influence of space is also relevant in ROBERTO SIMANOWSKI's contribution, which not only traces the evolution from print-based to digital concrete poetry but also places emphasis on the dynamic situation of audiovisual, kinetic renderings in the digital sphere in a discussion of Jim Andrews's poetic work. Moreover, the placement of poetry within a culture dominated by advertising both on- and offline results in several types of poetry, as HEINZ DRÜGH asserts: on the one hand, serial, commodified pop artifacts in the form of Instapoetry appear on networking platforms like the photo- and video-sharing service Instagram, while, on the other, poets like Marion Poschmann and Dirk von Petersdorff critically engage with the sensory dimensions of consumerist pop culture in their poems.

"Visibly Visual: Sociopolitical Poetry on the Web and in Films," the volume's second section, deals with issues of sociopolitical as well as algorithmic visibility and invisibility and their relation to the visuality of online protest poetry, Instapoetry, and poetry films. ASTRID BÖGER analyzes the issues manifest in US protest poetry on Instagram and beyond, focusing on the Black Lives Matter movement and racial inequality. MAGDALENA ELISABETH KORECKA investigates the visual intimacies in Hollie McNish's multimodal feminist Instapoetry as an aesthetically appealing and platformized entity and as a part of various stylistic Instapoetic communities. In her contribution, SOPHIE ERTEL explores a collaboratively created poetry film by poet lisa luxx and filmmaker Rosemary Baker that addresses the lesbian gaze and the creatively implemented aesthetic dimensions of in-between spaces in the audiovisual rhythms of the production's film shots.

In the next section, "Viewpoints: Artistic Practices in Digital Poetry and Poetry Films," contributions from poetic practice reveal the valuable research positions taken by digital and spoken word poets themselves: the code poetry duo CHRIS KERR and DANIEL HOLDEN present their online and printed poetry collection *./code --poetry* and connect its specific audiovisual as well as performative aspects to the traditions of avant-gardist poetry performances. Digital and e-poet MARÍA MENCÍA gives insight into her poetic practices with examples such as her data visualization piece *Gateway to the World* by discussing its poetics of data as well as its historical connections to experimental visual and concrete poetry. Spoken word artist LUCY ENGLISH analyzes her collaborative poetry film projects *The Book of Hours* and *I Want to Breathe Sweet Air* with regard to poets' speaking practices and filmmakers' visualization techniques, proposing a new approach to spoken word poetry films.

Finally, the section "Poetic Images: (Audio)Visuality in Contemporary Book Poetry" concentrates on the enduring relevance of book publications by looking at the example of contemporary German, Serbian, and multilingual poetry. ESTHER KILCHMANN investigates visual strategies in poetry books, with a focus on translation practices in the multilingual works of Heike Fiedler and in digital poetry by Jörg Piringer. HIROSHI YAMAMOTO examines text-image correspondences in the collectively created book *Ignatien* by visual computer artist Yves Netzhammer and poet Gerhard Falkner. Furthermore, TIJANA KOPRIVICA analyzes the relationship between cinematic and poetic techniques in Vladan Krečković's anthology *Pariz, Teksas* as an artistic artifact of engagement with Wim Wender's film *Paris, Texas*.

This edited volume is written in German and English due to the disciplinary background of the editors in German and Anglophone literary and cultural studies, and as an endeavor to bring together decentralized European poetry research, and diverse practices of poetry and visual culture studies in the digital age. Furthermore, the contributions cover poetry in German, English, Polish, Ukrainian, Russian, Norwegian, and Serbian, as well as a number of multilingual works. The book thus aims to promote international exchange between poetry researchers and stimulate further investigation into current relations between poetry and visuality from additional research perspectives and languages.

Acknowledgments: This book is the result of the German-English conference "Poetry and Contemporary Visual Culture / Lyrik und zeitgenössische Visuelle Kultur," held within the scope of the ERC project "Poetry in the Digital Age." It would not have been possible without the hard work and patience of all authors and poets in this volume, as well as their critical engagement with the interrelations of poetry and visual culture. We would therefore like to sincerely thank them for their contributions and for their time and the trust they put in us to curate this book. We would also like to kindly thank the whole PoetryDA team, whose expertise, support, and critical feedback led us on this path, from the initial conception of the conference to this anthology. Special thanks to Claudia Benthien for making this volume possible as the Principal Investigator and for supporting the book with her expertise at various stages. Our thanks also go to Anna Hofman, who lent us her support with critical readings of various chapters. We would like to extend our thanks to the research fellows who provided invaluable advice on the conference and/or the volume during their time in Hamburg: Birgitte Stougaard Pedersen, Hans Strandstuen Kristian Rustad, and Daniela Silva de Freitas. Massive thanks also go to the student research assistants at the Universität Hamburg, Marisa Laugsch, Chiara Meyer, and Benedikt Stamm for their help and dedication in acquiring images and literature, and for all edits, especially during the final phases of this volume. Our gratefulness extends to our copy editor Lydia J. White, who, with her eye for detail and expert knowledge in academic English, contributed immensely to the quality of this book. Thank you to all the artists who provided the copyrights for the images and without whose work this book would not exist. We would also like to acknowledge the team at De Gruyter for helping with the cover and manuscript layout as well as the ERC for making this project possible with its financial support.

References

Bachmann-Medick, Doris. *Cultural Turns. Neuorentierungen in den Kulturwissenschaften*. Reinbek: Rowohlt, 2006.

Bajohr, Hannes. "Digital Ekphrasis: The Dissolution of the Text/Image Difference in Multimodal AI." Talk at the conference "Poetry and Contemporary Visual Culture / Lyrik und zeitgenössische Visuelle Kultur" at Universität Hamburg from May 19 to 21, 2022.

Bajohr, Hannes, and Annette Gilbert. "Platzhalter der Zukunft: Digitale Literatur II (2001–2021)." *Digitale Literatur II*. text + kritik: special issue. Ed. Hannes Bajohr and Annette Gilbert. Munich: Richard Boorberg, 2021. 7–21.

Bathrick, David, and Heinz-Peter Preußer (Ed.). *Literatur inter- und transmedial/Inter- and Transmedial Literature*. Amsterdam and New York: Rodopi, 2012.
Becker, Sabina, and Barbara Korte (Ed.). *Visuelle Evidenz. Fotografie im Reflex von Literatur und Film*. Berlin and New York: De Gruyter, 2011.
Beckman, Karen, and Liliane Weissberg (Ed.). *On Writing with Photography*. Minneapolis, MN: Univ. of Minnesota Press, 2013.
Benthien, Claudia, and Norbert Gestring. *Public Poetry. Lyrik im urbanen Raum*. Berlin and Boston, MA: De Gruyter, 2023 [forthcoming].
Benthien, Claudia, Jordis Lau, and Maraike M. Marxsen. *The Literariness of Media Art*. New York: Routledge, 2019.
Benthien, Claudia, and Brigitte Weingart. "Einleitung." *Handbuch Literatur & Visuelle Kultur*. Ed. Claudia Benthien and Brigitte Weingart. Berlin and Boston, MA: De Gruyter, 2014. 1–28.
Berger, Sarah. *Lesen und Schreien. Social-Media-Collagen*. Berlin: Frohmann, 2020.
Boehm, Gottfried. "Die Wiederkehr der Bilder." *Was ist ein Bild?* Ed. Gottfried Boehm. München: Fink, 1994. 11–38.
Bohn, Willard. *Reading Visual Poetry*. Vancouver: Fairleigh Dickinson Univ. Press, 2013.
Borsuk, Amaranth. *The Book*. Cambridge, MA: MIT Press, 2018.
Brosch, Renate (Ed.). *Ikono/Philo/Logie: Wechselspiele von Texten und Bildern*. Berlin: Trafo, 2004.
Brunner, Christoph. "Relaying Resistance – Translocal Media Aesthetics and Politics in the Feminist Intervention 'A Rapist in Your Path.'" Online talk in the lecture series "Performative Power and Failure of Dissent: Aesthetics of Intervention in Eastern Europe and Beyond" at TU Dresden. January 10, 2021, https://videocampus.sachsen.de/category/video/Relaying-Resistance-Translocal-Media-Aesthetics-and-Politics-in-the-Feminist-Intervention-Christoph-Brunner/812dd22025a5da0b99f95045b4759df0/14 (November 20, 2022).
Bruns, Axel. *Blogs, Wikipedia, Second Life, and Beyond. From Production to Produsage*. New York and Vienna: Lang, 2008.
Bucher, Taina. "Want to Be on the Top? Algorithmic Power and the Threat of Invisibility on Facebook." *New Media and Society* 14.7 (2012): 1164–1180.
Cancik-Kirschbaum, Eva, Sybille Krämer, and Rainer Totzke (Ed.). *Schriftbildlichkeit. Wahrnehmbarkeit, Materialität und Operativität von Notationen*. Berlin: Akademie, 2012.
Cayley, John. "The Code is not the Text (Unless It Is the Text)." *Electronic Book Review* (2002): 1–21. http://electronicbookreview.com/essay/the-code-is-not-the-text-unless-it-is-the-text/ (October 13, 2022).
Chasar, Mike. *Poetry Unbound. Poems and New Media from the Magic Lantern to Instagram*. New York: Columbia Univ. Press, 2020.
Cramer, Florian. "Postdigitales Schreiben." *Code und Konzept. Literatur und das Digitale*. Ed. Hannes Bajohr. Berlin: Frohmann, 2016. 27–43.
Cruz, Décio T. "Literature and Film: A Brief Overview of Theory and Criticism." *Postmodern Metanarratives*. London: Palgrave Macmillan, 2014. 38–49.
Davis, Jenny L. *How Artifacts Afford. The Power and Politics of Everyday Things*. Cambridge, MA: MIT Press, 2020.
Davis, Whitney. *A General Theory of Visual Culture*. Princeton, NJ: Princeton Univ. Press, 2018.
Dencker, Klaus-Peter. *Optische Poesie. Von prähistorischen Schriftzeichen bis zu den digitalen Experimenten der Gegenwart*. Berlin and New York: De Gruyter, 2011.
Drucker, Johanna. *Visualization and Interpretation. Humanistic Approaches to Display*. Cambridge, MA and London: MIT Press, 2020.

Emerson, Lori. *Reading Writing Interfaces. From the Digital to the Bookbound*. Minneapolis, MN: Univ. of Minnesota Press, 2014.

Ernst, Ulrich. *Carmen Figuratum. Geschichte des Figurengedichts von den antiken Ursprüngen bis zum Ausgang des Mittelalters*. Cologne, Weimar, and Vienna: Böhlau, 1991.

Funkhouser, Christopher. "Digital Poetry: A Look at Generative, Visual, and Interconnected Possibilities in its First Four Decades." *A Companion to Digital Literary Studies*. Ed. Ray Siemens and Susan Schreibman. Malden, MA: Blackwell, 2007. 318–335.

Gibson, James J. "The Theory of Affordances." *The Ecological Approach to Visual Perception*. Hillsdale, NJ: Lawrence Erlbaum Associates, 1986 [1979]. 127–137.

Gil, Isabel Capeloa. "Von der Semiologie zur 'visuellen Literalität.'" *Handbuch Literatur & Visuelle Kultur*. Ed. Claudia Benthien and Brigitte Weingart. Berlin and Boston, MA: De Gruyter, 2014. 193–211.

Goriunova, Olga. "The Force of Digital Aesthetics: On Memes, Hacking, and Individuation." *The Nordic Journal of Aesthetics* 24.47 (2014): 54–75.

Greber, Erika. "Das konkretistische Bildgedicht. Zur Transkription Bildender Kunst in Visuelle Poesie." *Intermedium Literatur. Beiträge zu einer Medientheorie der Literaturwissenschaft*. Ed. Roger Lüdeke and Erika Greber. Göttingen: Wallstein, 2004. 171–208.

Hansen, Mark B. N. *New Philosophy for New Media*. Cambridge, MA and London: MIT Press, 2004.

Haraway, Donna J. *Simians, Cyborgs, and Women. The Reinvention of Nature*. New York: Routledge, 1991.

Hayles, N. Katherine. *Electronic Literature. New Horizons for the Literary*. Notre Dame, IN: Univ. of Notre Dame Press, 2008.

Hillebrandt, Claudia, Sonja Klimek, Ralph Müller, and Rüdiger Zymner. "Einleitung. Wer spricht das Gedicht?" *Grundfragen der Lyrikologie. Bd. 1: Lyrisches Ich, Textsubjekt, Sprecher?* Ed. Claudia Hillebrandt, Sonja Klimek, Ralph Müller, and Rüdiger Zymner. Berlin and Boston, MA: De Gruyter, 2019. 1–22.

Horstkotte, Silke, and Karin Leonhard (Ed.). *Lesen ist wie Sehen. Intermediale Zitate in Bild und Text*. Cologne, Weimar, and Vienna: Böhlau, 2006.

Jenkins, Henry. *Confronting the Challenges of Participatory Culture. Media Education in the 21st Century*. Cambridge, MA: MIT Press, 2009.

Kinnahan, Linda (Ed.). *Humanities*. Special Issue: "Modernist Poetry and Visual Culture" (2022).

Kohout, Annekathrin. *Nerds. Eine Popkulturgeschichte*. Munich: C.H. Beck, 2022.

Konyves, Tom. "Videopoetry a Manifesto." *Critical Inquiry* (2012): 1–7. https://critinq.wordpress.com/2012/10/13/videopoetry-a-manifesto-by-tom-konyves/ (March 16, 2023).

Krieger, Murray. *Ekphrasis. The Illusion of the Natural Sign*. Baltimore, MD: Johns Hopkins Univ. Press, 1992.

Leese, Matthias. "'Seeing Futures.' Politics of Visuality and Affect." *Algorithmic Life. Calculative Devices in the Age of Big Data*. Ed. Louise Amoore and Volha Piotukh. London and New York: Routledge, 2016. 143–158.

Lüdeke, Roger, and Erika Greber (Ed.). *Intermedium Literatur. Beiträge zu einer Medientheorie der Literaturwissenschaft*. Göttingen: Wallstein, 2004.

Maar, Christa, and Hubert Burda (Ed.). *Iconic Turn. Die neue Macht der Bilder*. Cologne: DuMont, 2004.

Marino, Mark C. *Critical Code Studies*. Cambridge, MA and London: MIT Press, 2020.

Mergenthaler, Volker. *Sehen schreiben – Schreiben sehen. Literatur und visuelle Wahrnehmung im Zusammenspiel*. Tübingen: Niemeyer, 2002.

Mirzoeff, Nicholas. *White Sight. Visual Politics and Practices of Whiteness*. Cambridge, MA: MIT Press, 2023.

Mirzoeff, Nicholas. "Visual Thinking in Dangerous Times." FreshEye. 2019, http://fresh-eye.cz/video/spe cial-guest-lecture-nicholas-mirzoeff-visual-thinking-in-dangerous-times/ (November 20, 2022).
Mirzoeff, Nicholas. *The Appearance of Black Lives Matter*. Miami, FL: NAME Publ., 2017.
Mirzoeff, Nicholas. "The Subject of Visual Culture." *The Visual Culture Reader*. Ed. Nicholas Mirzoeff. New York: Routledge, 2002. 3–23.
Mirzoeff, Nicholas. *An Introduction to Visual Culture*. London and New York: Routledge, 1999.
Mitchell, W. J. T. "Pictorial Turn." *Bildtheorie*. Ed. Gustav Frank. Frankfurt a. M.: Suhrkamp, 2008 [1992]. 101–135.
Morris, Adelaide, and Thomas Swiss (Ed.). *New Media Poetics. Contexts, Technotexts, and Theories*. Cambridge, MA: MIT Press, 2006.
Moskatova, Olga. *Images on the Move. Materiality – Networks – Formats*. Bielefeld: Transcript, 2021.
Mønster, Luise. "Contemporary Poetry and the Question of Genre. With a Special View to a Danish Context." *Dialogues on Poetry. Mediatization and New Sensibilities*. Ed. Stefan Kjerkegaard and Dan Ringgaard. Aalborg: Aalborg Universitetsforlag, 2017. 235–257.
Müller, Ralph, and Henrieke Stahl. "Contemporary Lyric Poetry in Transitions between Genres and Media." *Internationale Zeitschrift für Kulturkomparatistik* 2 (2021): 5–24.
Norman, Don. *The Design of Everyday Things*. New York: Basic Books, 2013.
Olszanowski, Magdalena. "Feminist Self-Imaging and Instagram. Tactics of Circumventing Sensorship." *Visual Communication Quarterly* 2 (2014): 83–95.
Orphal, Stephanie. *Poesiefilm. Lyrik im audiovisuellen Medium*. Berlin and Boston, MA: De Gruyter, 2014.
Pflock, Magdalena. "nicht NUR Twitter & nicht NUR das Internet. Prozesshaftes Schreiben mit und auf Sozialen Medien am Beispiel von Sarah Berger." *Literatur nach der Digitalisierung. Zeitkonzepte und Gegenwartsdiagnosen*. Ed. Elias Kreuzmair and Eckhard Schumacher. Berlin and Boston, MA: De Gruyter, 2022. 215–243.
Poell, Thomas, David B. Nieborg, and Brooke Erin Duffy. *Platforms and Cultural Production*. Cambridge and Medford, MA: Polity Press, 2022.
Pressman, Jessica. *Bookishness. Loving Books in a Digital Age*. New York: Columbia Univ. Press, 2020.
Rettberg, Scott. *Electronic Literature*. Cambridge, MA: Polity, 2019.
Rimmele, Markus, and Bernd Stiegler. *Visuelle Kulturen / Visual Culture. Zur Einführung*. Hamburg: Junius, 2019.
Robillard, Valerie, and Els Jongeneel (Ed.). *Pictures into Words. Theoretical and Descriptive Approaches to Ekphrasis*. Amsterdam: VU Univ. Press, 1998.
Rogoff, Irit. "Looking Away: Participations in Visual Culture." *After Criticism. New Responses to Art and Performance*. Ed. Gavin Butt. Oxford and Medford, MA: Blackwell Publishing, 2005. 117–134.
Rothöhler, Simon. "Calm Images. The Invisible Visual Culture of Digital Image Distribution." *Images on the Move. Materiality – Networks – Formats*. Ed. Olga Moskatova. Bielefeld: Transcript, 2021. 73–86.
Schaefer, Heike. "Poetry in Transmedial Perspective: Rethinking Intermedial Literary Studies in the Digital Age." *Acta Universitatis Sapientiae / Film and Media Studies* 10 (2015): 169–182.
Schmitt, Peter. *Postdigital. Medienkritik im 21. Jahrhundert*. Hamburg: Felix Meiner, 2021.
Scholz, Bernhard F. *Emblem und Emblempoetik. Historische und systematische Studien*. Berlin: Schmidt, 2002.
Schankweiler, Kerstin. *Bildproteste. Widerstand im Netz*. Berlin: Klaus Wagenbach, 2019.
Sontag, Susan. *Regarding the Pain of Others*. New York: Picador, 2003.
Stein, Kevin. *Poetry's Afterlive. Verse in the Digital Age*. Ann Arbor, MI: The Univ. of Michigan Press, 2010.

Stiegler, Bernd. "Visual Culture." *Handbuch Literatur & Visuelle Kultur*. Ed. Claudia Benthien and Brigitte Weingart. Berlin and Boston, MA: De Gruyter, 2014. 159–172.

Strätling, Susanne, and Georg Witte (Ed.). *Die Sichtbarkeit der Schrift*. Munich: Fink, 2006.

Tremlett, Sarah. *The Poetics of Poetry Film. Film Poetry, Videopoetry, Lyric Voice, Reflection*. Chicago, IL: The Univ. of Chicago Press, 2021.

Vorrath, Wiebke. "Unter der Oberfläche? Programmierte Schriftlichkeit in digitaler Lyrik." *Schriftlichkeit. Aktivität, Agentialität und Aktanten der Schrift*. Ed. Martin Bartelmus and Alexander Nebrig. Bielefeld: Transcript, 2022. 55–68.

Voßkamp, Wilhelm, and Brigitte Weingart (Ed.). *Sichtbares und Sagbares. Text-Bild-Verhältnisse*. Cologne: DuMont, 2005.

Wandhoff, Haiko. *Ekphrasis. Kunstbeschreibungen und virtuelle Räume in der Literatur des Mittelalters*. Berlin and New York: De Gruyter, 2003.

Weingart, Brigitte. "In/Out. Text-Bild-Strategien in Pop-Texten der sechziger Jahre." *Sichtbares und Sagbares. Text-Bild-Verhältnisse*. Ed. Wilhelm Voßkamp and Brigitte Weingart. Cologne: DuMont, 2005. 216–253.

Zima, Peter V. (Ed.). *Literatur intermedial. Musik – Malerei – Photographie – Film*. Darmstadt: Wissenschaftliche Buchgesellschaft, 1995.

Zymner, Rüder. *Lyrik. Umriss und Begriff*. Paderborn: mentis, 2009.

1 Sites and Sights: Modes of Contemporary Poetry

Karin Nykvist
Here, There, Everywhere: Situating Contemporary Multimodal Poetry

Introduction

Here, there, and *everywhere*. Those are the words that linger when Paul McCartney sings, in the beautiful Beatles song about love invading every little space of the world: the specific here, the distant there, and the ungraspable everywhere.

As we all know, love and poetry have lots in common. One thing is that while they are both eternal, they never stay the same. Another is that poetry really can be found here, there, and everywhere. This observation may seem corny, and of course it oversimplifies things – but McCartney's simple and so very singable triad of settings can be useful in helping us to remember the importance of situatedness, of place, space, and time when it comes to how poetry is written, performed, perceived and experienced. And it could help us study it, too.

In this chapter I study these three basic ways of situating poetry, with a special regard to the visual properties of the genre as they come across in different media. I explore and reflect on how the lyric aesthetic as well as the interpretation potential of the poem changes with the way its situatedness is dominated by the *here*, the *there*, and the *everywhere*. While I am aware of the bluntness of this triad when regarded as a theory about the situatedness of the poetic genre, I aim to show its advantages when used pragmatically in a discussion on actual poetic practice. If I start with the notions of *here, there,* and *everywhere* when studying a poetic event, the way that poetry works differently in various settings becomes more visible.

In order to discuss this research question with any precision, I will therefore turn to the art of poetry itself. The transmedial and multimedial poetic and artistic practices of Caroline Bergvall provide excellent material to study this phenomenon in depth. As an artist, Bergvall is always mindful of the visual aspect of experiencing art: both in regard to the way her art works with visual media such as film, photography, and computer images, and in the way her art investigates the ontology and epistemology of seeing, observing, perceiving. This attention to seeing brings the question of embodied orientation and situatedness to the fore. Before delving into some of Bergvall's work I will, however, offer a brief discussion on my terminology.

∂ Open Access. © 2023 the author(s), published by De Gruyter. [CC BY-NC-ND] This work is licensed under the Creative Commons Attribution-NonCommercial-NoDerivatives 4.0 International License.
https://doi.org/10.1515/9783111299334-002

The *where* of the poem

The poetry taught at European universities in the twentieth century – where and when, incidentally, I started studying it – was almost exclusively presented in print. Sometimes it was to be found in books, sometimes in magazines and periodicals, but the main materiality of poetry as presented to the reader was the physical paper, the page. Poetry was found in artefacts that were to be handled, studied, stowed away, and taken back out. It was *there*, to be looked at, touched, weighed in my hand: in his study on how technology and its different materialities inform how we read, Andrew Piper talks about the "graspability" of the book (Piper 2012, 2). If it was not new, it was stored between dusty covers in the basement of libraries. Along with all this language in print came the theories to go with it: in the version of Roland Barthes (1977, 158–160), for example, the *there* poetry on the page was to be seen as a work that became a text when the mind of the reader took it in.

Bearing this in mind, I would suggest that while poetry has never had a moment when it has been exclusively constricted to print – consider Paul McCartney's song lyrics, for example! – in Western literary tradition, however, there has been a clearly discernible parenthesis of a *there* paradigm: a short era of a few hundred years, from Romanticism and onwards, when poetry in print was clearly its dominant form – to critics, historians, and readers. I borrow the notion of a dominant form of the art event from Philip Auslander, who in his study on the relationship between live and mediatised events of art writes that "at any given historical moment, there are dominant forms that enjoy much greater cultural presence, prestige, and power than other forms" (Auslander 1999, 162). Auslander goes on to say that nondominant forms "will tend to become more like the dominant ones but not the other way around" (Auslander 1999, 162). One result of the *there* paradigm of poetry is visible in the stage performances of poetry, which, in the twentieth century often were referred to as 'readings.' Poetry found in other art forms than literature was studied elsewhere – in art, theatre studies or perhaps in anthropology.

The dominance of the printed poetry collection works well with a culture that promotes monolingualism. It is therefore worth noting that the era of the *there* poetry coincides with what Germanist Yasmine Yildiz has named the monolingual paradigm. She uses the term to describe those few hundred years mentioned above when literature played an important part in the imaginary that knitted nation, language, and national literature closely together in a unit that was nearly impossible to unthink (cf. Yildiz 2012, 6–10). The printed poetry collection was produced in a print culture that, by the twentieth century, was part of a national literary system with clear boundaries made up by copyright laws as well as the boundaries of the imagined national community in Benedict Anderson's sense of the word. In his seminal work *Imagined Communities,* Anderson points out that "national print-languages" were of central ideological and political importance to the rise of what he calls Old-world nationalism from the early 1800s and onwards (cf. Anderson 2006, 67). Even though the literary arts are not his main focus, his argument holds for them as well. This imagined collective was experienced as natural and self-evident, and relied on as well as it was built through the existence of literature's national distribution and monolingual readership. It was not until the rights of literary texts were sold and properly translated that they officially crossed any international borders and entered another nation's literary system.

In this paradigm of the monolingual, printed volume, the visual aspects of poetry would become important in the early twentieth century, when poets such as Guillaume Apollinaire and e.e. cummings played with the iconographic possibilities of the printed page. The dominance of the printed poetry collection waned around the end of the twentieth century, much due to the rise of poetry slam and the newly re-awakened interest for spoken word. In their book on poetry in performance around the turn of the millennium, Mark Eleveld and Marc Smith – the latter being the Chicago-based inventor of the poetry slam – regarded this movement as no less than a revolution, as can be understood from the title, *The Spoken Word Revolution (Slam, Hip Hop & the Poetry of a New Generation)* (2003). The very alive body of the author made a comeback, confusing everyone who, after reading Michel Foucault, Roland Barthes and others, thought the author had been dead for decades (on the discussion on the death of the author see Burke 1998). The live event of poetry performance has been with poetry from its very start, although, as Philip Auslander (1999, 57) points out, the idea of "live" needs the mediatised variety as its binary and therefore did not exist as a concept before the age of reproduction. The reawakened interest in live poetry brought embodied performance and reception of poetry back into focus and made the fallacies that had been central to the teachings of new criticism outdated and obsolete. Today, poetry performances are not always called readings anymore. The book is no longer the obvious centre of poetry, which has made it possible for other aspects of the poetic genre and other media to come to the fore.

As I see it, *here* poetry does not always have to be a poem performed live on a stage. It does not always require the artist to be present while being performed; its quality of *hereness* may be evoked even if it is mediatised, for example when the poem is physically placed in the world and specifically situated in one place and time. A very illustrative example of how important setting can be is the piece "Heaven Is A Place Where Nothing Ever Happens" (2008) by the Scottish artist Nathan Coley. He chose it when he was commissioned to place a work of art next to the cathedral of Lund in southern Sweden for a few months in 2017. One could argue that it was placed *there*, by the cathedral, but in the experience of the work, its *here* quality gave it its potential: to experience the work one had to place one's body between the cathedral and the artwork, with the back to the former while still experiencing its shadow on the latter. As the cathedral in Lund is dense with symbolic value, the importance of the setting for the production of meaning of the artwork cannot be exaggerated. Dating from the eleventh century, it was once the seat of the archdiocese of all of Scandinavia (cf. Carelli 2012, 130–132), and has as such been important to the christening of the Nordic region. Today it is an active and powerful administrative and theological centre for the Swedish Church in southern Sweden. Coley's large work measures six times six metres and consists of an illuminated quote from the Talking Heads' song "Heaven" from 1979 on a piece of aluminium scaffolding. The placement of the work next to this iconic and important cathedral informed the meaning of the piece – as well as the meaning of the church placed next to it. Locals found that it talked back to the church and were surprised to find that it was commissioned by the church itself, whose leaders wanted to initiate a conversation about the role of the church in the city (cf. Lunds domkyrka 2017).

The acute setting of the *here* poetry places it not only in space but in time as well. It is poetry that often appears and then disappears: the performance of poetry has an evanescent quality and installations such as the Nathan Coley piece visiting Lund often occur within a timeframe. This ephemerality gives them a processual quality and underlines their being events rather than artefacts – even if they are, as in this case, built around artefacts which in different ways can be seen as undermining their liveness. In her influential study on the aesthetics of the performance, Erika Fischer-Lichte writes about art as a process and event:

> Be it in art music, literature, or theatre, the creative process tends to be realized in and as performance. Instead of creating works of art, artists increasingly produce events which involve not just themselves but also the observers, listeners, and spectators. Thus, the conditions for art production and reception [have] changed in a crucial aspect. The pivotal point of these processes is no longer the work of art, detached from and independent of its creator and recipient, which arises as an object from the activities of the creator-subject and is entrusted to the perception of the recipient-subject. Instead, we are dealing with an event, set in motion and terminated by the actions of all the subjects involved – artists and spectators. (Fischer-Lichte 2008, 22)

An important idea to Fischer-Lichte is how the performative event of art breaks down the imagined binary of art and reality, art/artist and spectator. Willmar Sauter expresses similar thoughts in his study *The Theatrical Event. Dynamics of Performance and Perception* (2000) when he discusses the importance of the where and when of the cultural artefact or event (Sauter 2000, 95–107). To him, communication in time and space is a key concept. To both Fischer-Lichte and Sauter, theatre is the example, but the theories are valid in many art forms.

As seen from the performative perspective proposed by Fischer-Lichte and Sauter, the Nathan Coley piece cannot be discussed outside of its setting, i.e., outside of its placement, its viewers, and how viewers and passers-by interacted with the piece while it was placed outside of the cathedral: by taking pictures, talking about Christian doctrines of the afterlife, personal beliefs, and by reflecting on the field of energy that was experienced in the space between the piece and the outer medieval walls of the cathedral. After it was gone, that space was somewhat changed – at least for a time (cf. Anjou 2017). Thus, while the scholar of printed poetry can choose to ignore the processual and temporal aspects of the collection at hand, that option is not possible when analysing and studying the poetry of the *here*. Perhaps it is no coincidence that the comeback of the *here* poetry coincided with a theoretical movement that turned to performance studies – even though the discussion on literature as performative often stayed within the book and explored the performative qualities of the printed text (cf. Culler 2000, 506–512). In literary studies, there was an obvious rise in both the interest of the performative and the visual aspects of literature at the turn of the millennium (cf. Bachman-Medick 2016, 86–88, 264). A vivid discussion on the advent of the performative and pictorial turns in the discipline was led and inspired by theorists such as Jonathan Culler (2000), Erika Fischer-Lichte (2000), and W. J. T. Mitchell (1994).

The ephemeral quality of the *here* poetry can be discussed and problematised: scholars such as Peggy Phelan have argued that the one quality that singles out the live performance is the fact that it cannot be saved (cf. Phelan 1993, 146) while others, such as Philip Auslander, point out that there are almost always aspects of the live performance that use remediation or mediatisation in one way or another (cf. Auslander 1999). Auslander also argues that the idea of the purely live performance is just an idea. It is nevertheless fruitful to consider *here* and *there* from the perspective of dominance. While both aspects can be at work at once, the receiver's attention and thus their experience can be radically different based on the situation and what is deemed to be more important. What happens when we experience the *there* – the printed matter – to be the basis of our study, and thus the event of reading our main source of information, or the multisensorial *here* of the performance, and thus the audiovisual, acutely embodied, and situated experience as our main object of interest? And perhaps more interesting – what happens when we experience that the two are combined and their borders are blurred – as they almost always turn out to be? The Coley piece can be taken down and erected somewhere else and a poem may also be performed in different venues, a fact that seems to underline the *there* of the works – but their apparitions are in a *here* that will always be new.

With the advent of the World Wide Web and the tsunami-like rise of social media, literary scholars have been challenged further to consider the situatedness of poetry – and the experience of poetry. The implicit possibility of poetry to be experienced more or less simultaneously in different places was of course always there with printed poetry and became even more acute with radio and television programming. The Internet, however, and its vast possibilities of text, image, and sound being stored, spread, and manipulated digitally at a very low cost and often without the necessary requirement of any special skills – as well as the humming of servers in places we might know of, if we have a special interest, but really do not think about in our every day – all enable poetry to exist in every pocket at once, in a paradoxical mashup of the *here, there*, and *everywhere*. "Digital texts are somewhere, but *where* they are has become increasingly complicated, abstract, even forbidden," Andrew Piper writes (2012, 15). Furthermore, the webpage allows for new possibilities for how poetry looks and sounds. Radically new ways for the poem to be "written," "read," and even to exist have opened up (cf. Morris 2006, 19–31).

In short, the ontology of poetry has changed, becoming more multimodal in the process, with audial and visual layers often at its centre. New forms of poetry range from the often quite easily digested poetry spread through platforms such as Instapoetry and TikTok and experienced on a planetary scale by millions of users (cf. Miller 2021, 161–171; Saxena 2022, 83–85), many of whom take on the role of *produsers* (as suggested by Axel Bruns, 2005), to the avantgarde digital poetry mapped by scholars such as Christopher Funkhouser (2007), Marjorie Perloff (2006), N. Katherine Hayles (2006) and others. Because of the Internet, poetry can be eerily experienced as detached from space and time (even though, of course, from a technical, material perspective, it is situated in very material servers in geographical places) – as being *nowhere* and *everywhere* at the same time, while it in its immediacy and intimacy – the AirPods in your ears placing the voice of the poet almost inside your body, the moving image of her body and face always there, in the phone in your pocket that is always exactly located through its GPS function – evoke an eerie notion of the *here*.

And paradoxically enough, this rise of the *everywhere* and *anytime* poetry has spurred an interest in its opposite: the poetry of the more commonly understood notion of *here*. Ephemeral live readings, poetry happenings, and poetry performances are becoming more common in the twenty-first century and as the example of German shows, they are beginning to gather quite large audiences (cf. Benthien 2021, 1). This tension between the contemporary dissolution of situatedness and the rise of the specific place has been discussed more generally by Doris Bachmann-Medick in her above-mentioned study on cultural turns. To her, what is new in the spatial turn of contemporary culture is that the two inform one another: "the rediscovery of the local, for instance, is not identical with the securing of safe havens from the demands of globalization" (Bachmann-Medick 2016, 214). To put it in the terms and scope of this chapter: the *here* of contemporary poetry is different, changed by the *everywhere*.

But what about the poetry of the *there*? Books of poetry are clearly still being written, manufactured, stored, and sold. But they are not the centre of the poetry world anymore. Today's landscape of poetry has a much more complex make up. To sum it all up, contemporary poetry exists in a landscape of here, there, *and* everywhere poetry. All is connected in different ways, and poetry travels between these three spheres, changing while doing so, borrowing the interface of one form while travelling into another. If a poet or book publisher works exclusively with published poetry collections, that is a conscious choice in a way it was not just a few decades ago. In short, today's poetry aesthetic is informed and altered through the changes in the situatedness of poetry. But how? How are the *here*, *there*, and *everywhere* poetries connected? How is the *there* poetry of the book connected to the *here* poetry of the performance? And how is the *here* quality of the performance transformed, when it is connected to or turned into files of sights and sounds on the Internet, thus connecting to the *everywhere* quality of the World Wide Web? It may be useful here to consider the suggestion that Heike Schaefer makes regarding contemporary literature:

> Rather than think of intermediality as a relation between distinct media and focus mainly on questions of media change, media borders and media specificity [. . .] intermedial literary studies should conceive of literature as a transmedial practice and make it a priority to study *the media of literature*. (Schaefer 2015, 178)

Or differently put: the aim of this exploration is to follow the literature to its different spatialities rather than to consider in depth the different media where the literary text appears. Seen this way, the processuality of the literary text becomes more evident; it moves through different media, bringing the aesthetics from one category to another as it goes, blending and enriching all of them along the way. How this processuality works and how it, in turn, changes and opens new possibilities to the genre of poetry, are questions that the contemporary poetry scholar must consider. In the remainder of this text, I will turn to the work of French–Norwegian multimodal and multimedial poet Caroline Bergvall, in order to address them.

The example of Caroline Bergvall

Caroline Bergvall was born in Hamburg in 1962 but grew up in different locations in Europe and North America. She made London her base in the early 1990s but continues to publish, collaborate, and perform internationally. Her very biography then, belies the fundamentals of national print poetry, a fact that becomes visible in the very aesthetics of her work. Early on, her poetry, performance work, installations, films, and drawings started to focus on the concept of plurilingualism and migration. Her interest in the practices of transit and movement across borders, across time and space, extends to that of human beings as well as to that of information and languages. Bergvall's keen interest in processual work, in movement and collaboration, and her presence on the Internet – she has a homepage that is continually up to date and curated, as well as Instagram, Twitter, Vimeo, and Facebook accounts that are continously being updated – makes her understand the challenges and the possibilities of the notion of the *everywhere* well. But she works across the whole spectrum: she makes performances that are centred on poetic text, and she regularly publishes collections of poetry. These very different practices inform one another in interesting ways and here I will just discuss a few different examples. During the Covid lockdown of 2020–2021, Bergvall initiated two co-writing sessions over the Internet that were in part performances, in part creative workshops, and in part visually powerful art installations. The sessions were streamed in real time and were open for everyone everywhere. Bergvall called the sessions "Night and Refuge."

The "Night and Refuge" sessions

The first "Night and Refuge" session was put together quickly during the very first lockdown and was intended to be a singular event. On the evening of 21 May 2020, Bergvall met up digitally with four other poets: Vahni Capildeo, Will Harris, Leo Boix and Nisha Ramayya for a creative session that was streamed live, openly, on the Internet. While UK-based, the session's poets were all multilingual and part of minoritised groups in different ways; thus, they all explore special relationships with the English language in their work in one way or another: Trinidadian-Scottish Capildeo writes across many languages – Spanish, French, Portuguese, and Old Norse – while Leo Boix is Argentinian-British and writes in Spanish and English. Poet and critic Will Harris as well as poet and scholar Nisha Ramayya both use dictionaries in their work that in different ways interrogate the English that they have grown up talking. Together, these five poets and their multitude of languages and different geographical heritages as well as positions made for a deterritorialising experience of English poetry writing.[1] Although frequent performers of their own poetry at *here* poetry events such as readings and festivals, the four invited poets are more known for their printed poetry collections, their *there* poetry. One might suggest that these forms were brought into play in the *everywhere* "Night and Refuge" poetry session and steered the visuality of the work in certain directions – a question I will return to shortly in my analysis.

The second session was put together after a commission from the Oslo International Poetry Festival. It followed the pattern of the first and was organised during the second lockdown later that year, on 28 November. For that event, Bergvall invited Norwegian multimedial poet Gunnar Waerness, British-Zimbabwean poet Mandla Rae, Greenlandic-Danish poet Jessie Kleemann, Canadian-Galician poet Erín Moure and the Nuyorican-British poet Edwin Torres. While still all multilingual in different ways, these poets are also all known for writing across media in more diverse ways than the poets of the first session. Bergvall's curation of the event also bore witness to a more apparent translingual, transmedial, and transcultural ambition and intention than the first, because of the more quickly curated initial session following the pandemic outbreak. For this second session, the process and its output were even more thoroughly deterritorialised: instead of writing a stanza each, all poets wrote simultaneously in the main document, editing and changing each other's lines as they went, adding words and phrases in several languages, thus underlining the processual quality and in turn changing how the created poetry was visually presented on the digital screen.

Both sessions were deeply collaborative, not only between the poets' writing but also in inviting people following the live stream to contribute via the hashtag #nightandrefuge on Twitter. Bergvall read from the feed intermittently during the session, and although the writings of the viewers were not written down in the shared document on the screen, their contributions were discussed. They thus became an important part of the event, influencing the poetic writing that took place. Later, the Twitter feeds were saved; the first one can be accessed through Caroline Bergvall's homepage.[2] Thus, the events combined the temporal ephemerality of the *here*, the live writing and performance event, with the situatedness of the *everywhere* that the Internet brings. But the poetry of the *there* was also present, through the writing that appeared to the left on the screen, a live process that was later finalized in a written poem that, albeit published on the Internet,

---

[1] Many scholars have found the terminology and theory of Deleuze and Guattari useful when discussing Bergvall's work – and I agree with them. See, for example, McMurtry 2018, 814–817.
[2] https://carolinebergvall.com/.

bears the visual resemblance of the finality and stability of poetry in print. The fact that all of the poets in the project have published poetry collections, furthers the *there* quality of the event and informs how it is received. And since the live stream is stored digitally in the *there* of a server and can be accessed again, this additional layer further adds to the poetry being out *there*.

At both events, Bergvall collaborated with Palestinian interdisciplinary artist Mays Albaik. Like Bergvall, Albaik works in different media and modes: film, text, performance, sculpture, and image. On her homepage her work is presented as an "interdisciplinary visual practice," which "investigates how a sense of placehood is formed, reflected and refracted by that which mediates it – the body, language, and their various intersections."[3] This investigative poetics is quite apparent in her work for "Night and Refuge," for which she designed the visual layout. The first time around, the interference with the interface of the Zoom application was kept to a minimum so that the event looked like most streamed events at the time of the pandemic – perhaps mirroring the shock of the world transitioning to Zoom and Microsoft Teams and to how the experience of zooming was still new to many people.

For this live stream session, a major part of the screen was taken up by a shared grey screen, on which seven open Google documents were posted, all in different colours. The largest one was white and thus resembled a white sheet of paper. It was on there that the collective poem was to be written during the session. The use of the Times New Roman font made the connection to printed poetry even stronger. On a smaller, bright blue document called "brief," the rules for the evening were written down: the poem should be written in five parts, each consisting of four stanzas, and the poets would take turns in writing tercets or couplets. Following the layout of the Zoom application's interface, the poets, along with Albaik, could be seen on the right-hand side of the screen throughout, as they were talking, reading, and reacting to what was written – much like a Zoom seminar of the time. Although simple, the effect was quite strong. The viewer of the event could see and hear the poets, as well as curiously study the rooms that they were sitting in – with book cases, art objects, and changing light, emanating from windows and or lamps – as well as the screen and the documents that they too were watching and interacting with – a double point of view that is rare in film and television, for example, and that underlined the *everywhere* quality of the session. At the same time, the live cams answered to the name of the event: from the refuge of where they were watching, the viewers followed the writers in their places of refuge, into the darkness of the night.

---

[3] https://maysalbaik.com/.

For the second session, more work had been put into the visual design from the beginning onwards: instead of on a white paper-like document that for the first session had been filled with Times New Roman text, the poem was written in white on a blue background in an internet-friendly sans serif font, a change that weakened the session's echo of the *there* poetry aesthetics of the printed page, and made the *everywhere* quality of the screen stronger. While all poets had their cameras on, only the poet that happened to be speaking would appear on screen: instead of the first sessions' small squares of streams from live cams, blocks of poetry, written by the participating poets, showed up and disappeared on the screen's right-hand side. They did so along with images from live cams placed in and operated from different locations, possibly reproducing the poets' points of view, showing different times of day, from bright daylight to the pitch black of night. These live images – which also came and went – made the writing collaboration paradoxically situated in a multitude of specific places, while still focused on the *everywhere* of the globally shared streamed live session. The viewer got the impression of watching what the poets saw when they were writing: cars passing by, the night falling.

All in all, the visual make up of this second session was much busier, with images and documents appearing and disappearing while the speaking poet was shown in the top right corner and the live document of the poem being written took up the left half of the screen. Sometimes lines from Bergvall's earlier writings appeared and disappeared on the dark blue screen as well. There was lots of visual information to take in, but as the session lasted three hours, the changes to the screen were happening at a slow pace – mirroring the pace of the reflections and interventions that were brought forth by the contributors on screen.

Afterwards, both three-hour events were uploaded to the Internet, where they can be re-experienced until taken down (cf. Bergvall 2020a; Bergvall 2020c). The first event also lives on in a nineteen-minute-long edited version that can be viewed on Vimeo (cf. Bergvall 2020b). Bergvall calls this shorter film a "documentary" on her own website, and on Vimeo the word "experience" is used. This latter version has been edited by the film-maker Andrew Delaney, with sound design by Jamie Hamilton.

In the nineteen-minute film version of the first session, the visual design was quite reworked and the three-hour session heavily edited, even new film material was added. In the film, the recorded sequences of the poets are enlarged, doubled, shown in the negative as well as in their original colour. The discussions are edited as well, with voices often overlapping, underlining the processual quality of the work. A new backdrop has also been added: the different film clips and text documents are shown against an image of an apartment building at night, with silhouettes of people visible in the apartments and on the balconies. The pic-

Fig. 1: Still from "Night and Refuge" [edited film version] by Caroline Bergvall. May 21, 2020.

ture aptly captures the Covid moment: people alone in their apartments because of the Covid lockdown but still in proximity of each other and belonging to the same structures and networks (Fig. 1).

The whole design of the screen underlines the sense of collaboration, of messy processual work, of co-presence but also the acute embodied experience of being apart. This excitingly busy film sequence, where lots of things are happening at once, is, however, tidily framed, starting (and ending) with sans serif white titles on a black background, which presents the title of the work as well as Bergvall's name, along with an additional paratext, an excerpt from the Brazilian thinker Paolo Freire:

> This shock between a yesterday which is losing relevance but still seeking to survive, and a tomorrow which is gaining substance, characterises the phase of transition as a time of announcement and a time of decision. Its potential force would depend upon our capacity to participate in the dynamism of the transitional epoch. (Bergvall 2020b)

The chosen motto underlines the implicit ambition of the project: to interact with the world during a time of change and transition. The film ends with the finished (though unedited) poem being read by the writers of each stanza while headings of the different stanzas appear in white against a background that goes from light grey to black. This gradual transition follows the five astronomical phases of twilight and night that make up the subheadings of the poem. In addition to these visual add-ons, new sound designs are added by sound artist Jamie Hamilton. Thus, this edited documentary leans heavily on both its visual and auditive aspects, even in the section that makes up the reading of the poem.

The two streaming events of "Night and Refuge" focused specifically on transition, movement, and process while underlining exactly where the poets were situated in the world: when the session started, each poet was asked to state the exact position from where they were streaming. Thus, the specific *here and now* of their performances was combined with the *everywhere* of the media they were using. Through this working method, the session managed to thoroughly blur not only borders between countries but those between artists and viewers as well. In the first session, a spontaneous discussion broke out between the poets about the fact that instead of working together around a table in a closed room, they were creating poetry on a global stage, along with social media users. Later, when the session was uploaded to YouTube, this *everywhere* event also became an *anytime* event, at least partly: the possibility of interacting was, of course, lost.

The "Night and Refuge" sessions are illustrative examples of poetry that combines the *now* of the *here* with the *always* of the *everywhere*. I would argue that the *there* quality of the printed book is also implicitly present in the sessions because of the finished work. This is especially apparent in the first session where the finished poem is read from the screen's Google doc that echoes the printed page with its bold headings and Times New Roman font.

Bergvall's practice abounds with examples that combine the *there* of the book with the *here* of the performance and the *everywhere* of the Internet. One project where this happens is her work "Drift" (cf. 2014–ongoing), which will be examined in the following section.

The multifaceted work of "Drift"

"Drift" itself is a multimodal, multimedial process-oriented work that is probably finished – as is often the case with Bergvall's work, there is no clear end to the process of it, no definite version, and on her homepage, she dates the work as "2014–ongoing."[4] So far, the work has consisted of art installations and exhibitions, as well as performances, a book, and theoretical writings. The exhibitions themselves have consisted of drawings, sound files or audiotexts, electronic text masses, photographs, and murals. This multi-layering is an important characteris-

---

4 https://carolinebergvall.com/work/drift-performance/.

tic of the *Drift* book as well as of its performance. In addition to the book, the performances and the exhibitions, there are also video clips from the performances published online, clips that Bergvall herself calls "performance edits." These can also be regarded as being part of the work.

The act of thinking in categories and with boundaries is examined and put into question in the work in many ways. On an aesthetic level, it questions and opens up the boundaries between art forms, and on a thematic and philosophical level, it interrogates the idea of boundaries between people and countries. Therefore, it is congenial with the aesthetic of the work that it is the fruit of many collaborations with other artists, thus also putting the romantic notion of the single and brilliant artist and author as the poetic work's originator and creator into question. Although this notion was contested by many, it has been of great influence since Romanticism (cf. Boym 1991, 5). In the performance, Bergvall cooperates with the Norwegian percussionist Ingar Zach and the Swiss digital artist Thomas Köppel, turning the performance into an event that combines song, music, sound art as well as visual art and lighting, and the book combines poetry with drawings and artwork by Bergvall as well as other artists.

All of these different expressions in different modes and media – some stable, some ephemeral – point in different directions and give "Drift" a centrifugal force. The many intertexts that are activated in the work – ranging from the medieval *Völuspa* and the old English poem "The Seafarer" to the songs of Iggy Pop and David Bowie – also give the work its deterritorialised quality. It does not belong in one place or one time. But the different parts also communicate with each other, making the porosity of its different sources, their times, and their places of origin visible. The fact that it originates in a translation project that has taken on a life of its own, where Bergvall has abandoned her dictionary and started to pseudo-translate through sound play and connotations (cf. Bergvall 2014a, 130–132) rhymes well with the very theme at the core of the work, which is about tearing down borders, drifting, losing control while making and finding something new: a constant movement between deterritorialising and reterritorialising forces. It is apparent that the work makes use of the many possibilities of the *there*, the *here*, and the *everywhere*. Its aesthetic shows that the boundaries between these categories should be regarded more like a helpful model in order to interrogate poetic works rather than stable empirical categories.

Already the name "Drift" points to the work's status as a constantly evolving, processual work that is changing as it moves through time and space. Considering that it is a multilingual work, the title can be read in different ways: in English it points toward the verb "to drift," to be carried aimlessly by wind or water, or to move with no goal in mind. In Norwegian, one of Bergvall's many languages, it would rather be read as a noun, meaning drive, as in sex drive, or death drive, or the drive to live, to survive, to reproduce. The act of drifting helplessly at sea is at the centre of "Drift" but the work also depicts and reflects temporal, linguistic and spatial drifting, as well as the experience of being adrift more existentially. An important and recurring word is the Old Norse word *hafville*, which means lost at sea: the book contains songs called "Hafville 1," "Hafville 2," et cetera, and the word is repeatedly used in the verses (cf. Bergvall 2014a, 36–45).

Thematically, *Drift* expresses deep sorrow as well as anger in regarding the failure of the international community to deal with some of the main problems of our time. Ultimately, one understands that the whole world is adrift, in its overexploitation of goods, materials, and people, which leads to climate change, pollution, involuntary migration as well as political and financial injustice. In the foreground, however, is the event that has come to be known as the "left-to-die-boat" case, where in March and April of 2011, seventy-two migrants from Sub-Saharan Africa, after being forced to leave Libya by the local military, drifted for two weeks on the Mediterranean without food or fuel in a rubber boat that was built to carry twenty-five people. Although the boat was observed and photographed by fishing boats, aircraft, and satellites, it did not receive any aid and drifted back to the Libyan shore. Only nine people survived (cf. Heller et al. 2014, 17–23). The incident is at the centre of the book, both thematically and literally: the poems all concern drifting in different ways, and the middle pages are taken up by a chapter called "Report," which stands out as it is printed in white letters on black pages, as if draped in sorrow.

The fact that the forced migrants were observed but not really seen, in any ethical sense, turns visuality and visual representation into one of the book's most important themes. In the opening poems, which are reworkings of the anonymous "Seafarer" poem, the loss of visuality at sea is the main theme. Later in the "Hafville"-suite, the loss of visuality at sea is expressed in the very form of the poem, where sounds and letters are dropped until only one letter remains: the letter "t," which stutteringly takes up more than two pages. For the person lost at sea, to lose one's sight is akin to losing one's mind – after that, death awaits. In the performance of the work, the iteration of the letter "t" is performed with a quiet calm, while a sea of "t"s are shown behind the performing Bergvall (Fig. 2) – reminding the viewer both of an armada of ships without sails, and of the many crosses of a Christian graveyard (cf. Bergvall 2018).

The fact that visuality as well as visual representation is at the heart of the "Drift" project, is underlined by the opening of its *there* project, the book. Instead of lines of poetry, the reader is presented with sixteen drawings on as many pages. In a study of these sketches, Catherine Humble has suggested that they invite the reader to consider the act of seeing, witnessing, and that they bring the role played by the image in the current crisis on the Mediterranean into question: as Humble points out, the people on the "left-to-die-boat" were both "dreadfully hyper-seen

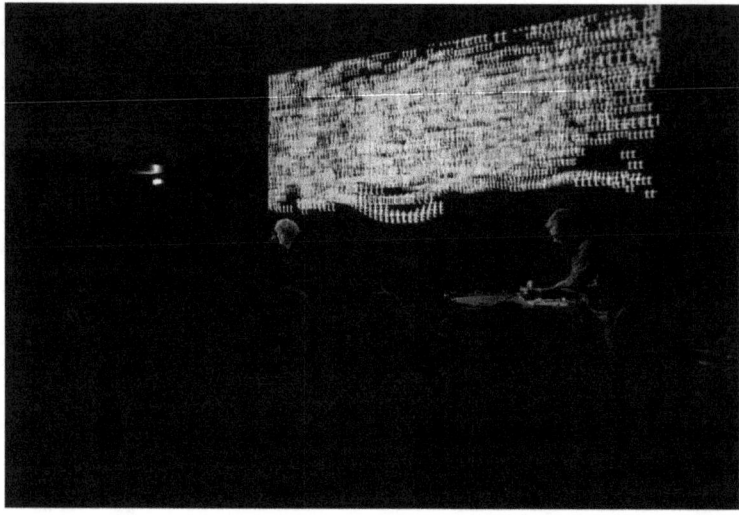

Fig. 2: Photo from "Drift" [performance] by Caroline Bergvall. 2014.

and unseen" (Humble 2021, 109) while they themselves were watching those who were watching them. Humble also brings up the role of the visual in the (impossible) representing of trauma, and the ethically difficult act of bearing witness and representing the trauma of the other (cf. Humble 2021, 119).

The act of watching interrogated

Central to *Drift* is a photograph taken by a French reconnaissance plane on March 27, 2011, believed to be of the "left-to-die-boat." To a contemporary Western consumer of news media, the image of a boat of refugees on the Mediterranean is not a rare occurrence (cf. Heller and Pezzani 2017) but what Bergvall seems to ask us, is if we really *see* these images. Such an interrogation is much in the vein of visual studies theorist Nicholas Mirzoeff, who with the term "persistent looking" asks that people take on a "strategy of engagement: going back, and going back, and staying with it" (Mirzoeff and Szcześniak 2015, 6). Working on the photograph, Bergvall collaborated with artist and photographer Tom Martin, who explored it through macro enlargements of details, and made enlargements that are so blown up that all that the viewer really sees are pixels (Fig. 3).

The image is reprinted in the *Drift* book in black and white and was included in colour in the "Drift" exhibition at Callicoon Gallery in New York in 2015. The uncannily beautiful blue colour of the original artwork makes a clearer connection to

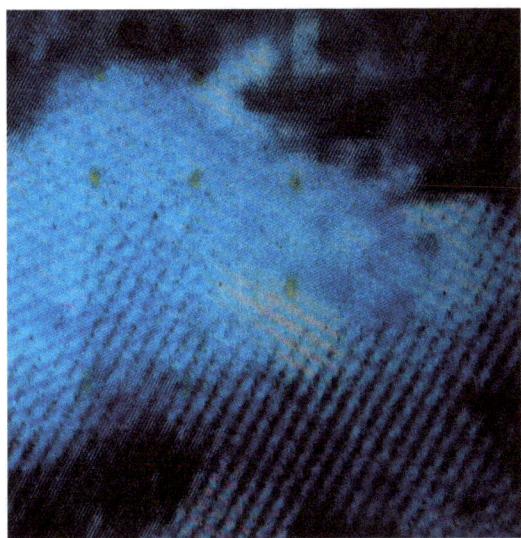

Fig. 3: Tom Martin. *Passenger*. 2014.

the Mediterranean, while the black and white of the *Drift* publication further remove the image from its motif. In neither case it is, however, possible to decode the image and see the human beings that are visible in the original photograph. On his homepage, Martin writes about the underlying idea of these images: "In this way, the macro processing of the image does not de-sensitise the content by making it abstract, but activates it beyond its original purpose – beyond the dossiers and official reports, beyond the consumed and discarded newspapers and on-line articles." (Martin 2014) It is obvious that the hyperbolic enlargements of this image have many layers, ethical, aesthetical, and political. The fact that the viewer cannot discern what the image portrays, adds a meta-reflection to it and seems to call out the blindness of the world community. The leaders of the world observe but do not seem to fully understand or act upon what they see. The failure to do so is a catastrophe and deeply unethical, perhaps even criminal: the research group "Forensic Architecture," based at Goldsmith College, has used the photograph in order to call out how international law was broken when the boat was being observed but not given assistance (cf. Heller et al. 2014, 52).

In a theoretical article, Bergvall has commented on her discussion about the photograph with Tom Martin and what she wanted to achieve:

> How one might imagine and hold visually the memory and the reality of these passengers beyond morbid voyeurism. How one might activate both inquisitiveness and empathetic connection not only in a forensic but also in an experiential way. So that seeing can be radi-

cally slowed down and the viewing of the news item can be experienced as a material, opaque, inescapable trace of observed and shared life. (Bergvall 2017, 17)

The call for a slowing down of seeing that Bergvall discusses, can be compared to the interventions into contemporary visual culture made in the work by the above-mentioned Nicholas Mirzoeff. He talks about how the "banality of images" (Mirzoeff 2005, 67), due to the huge flow of images circulating in different media takes away the effect of the image – among his examples are the pictures taken in the Abu Ghraib prison in 2004 that had no impact on the US election that year.

Shake that megavoice

The way that "Drift" uses visual representation changes with its different settings: the book, the performance, and the art show all echo one another but are not at all identical in their use of visuality. But it is obvious that the blurring of borders is an important part of its foundation. Bergvall activates the *there* of the book in her performance, for example, with the artwork of Thomas Köppel filling the wall behind her, where words from the printed book are moving on a large black screen.

How this blurring of borders between the *here*, *there*, and *everywhere* is achieved, becomes apparent when we follow the poem "Shake" from the book to the webpage. In the book, the poem follows directly after the chapter "Report." There, it consists of fourteen stanzas spread out over fourteen pages. Each stanza consists of five to six lines of about the same length, and the layout of the poem – which expresses an intense but controlled rage – follows the aesthetic of the traditional poetry collection. The stanzas are centred, tidily arranged on the pages, and stand in stark contrast to the affect that the lines express. In the performance, the poem was preceded not only by the "Report," but also by a low-key performance of the Tim Buckley song "Song to the Siren." The performance of "Shake" that follows, unleashes the affect that is being held in in the book version: the performance is quite dramatic, and the words spoken by Bergvall are underlined by the intense work of the percussionist Ingar Zach and the text masses that Thomas Köppel projects on the black screen behind the performers. They move faster and faster – shake, one could say – all the while reiterating words from the book.

In the version uploaded to the virtual *everywhere* or *nowhere* of the Internet, the "Shake" poem is quite changed. Bergvall calls the five-minute-long video clip a *Performance edit* (see Bergvall 2014b). The voice in the clip is Bergvall's, and the sound is a recording from the live performance. But the sound fades out after half of the fourteen stanzas: the viewer will not experience the climax, which was an important part of the performance. The most critical change, however, is that the screen is made up by the moving electronic text masses only. That stands in stark contrast to the performance of "Drift," where Bergvall took centre stage, anchoring the poem, and the percussionist Zach was visible to the right, on the stage as well. But in the film clip, only her disembodied voice is present, along with Ingar's sound effects. Her body could be anywhere. Percussionist Ingar Zach cannot be seen either. Instead of watching them perform, the viewer is drawn to watch the digital art of Thomas Köppel: words in white and blue, moving across a dark background on the screen, suggesting an archipelago of words.

This archipelago of words turns the theme of drifting into a powerful image while the words are drifting too: between English and Old Norse, between the sensical and the non-sensical. This suggests a theory behind the work – or at least that a theory can be drawn from it. In his article "Thinking with the archipelago," Jonathan Pugh suggests a productive way of thinking about art as archipelago, as "fluid tropes of assemblages, mobilities, and multiplicities" (Pugh 2013, 10). I would suggest that this aesthetic can be found at the heart of Bergvall's work, but that Pugh's line of thought also aptly describes the world view that is expressed through her practice: in its form as well as in its major themes. The fact that Bergvall writes about reading Édouard Glissant while working on "Drift," makes the archipelago as a productive image even more plausible (cf. Bergvall 2014a, 154–155).

The viewer of the "Shake" video listens to the voice and sound performances while taking in this archipelago of moving words on the screen. The words keep growing larger and larger, as if they are shouting the viewer in the face – all up until the end when the screen and the sound of Bergvall's voice and Zach's sound effects suddenly go mute. This moment is just about when they were starting to really pick up volume and tempo in the performance. Instead, the words from the poem can be read, silently, on the screen:

> Bang that pan rig that sail
> Shake that megavoice
> Wake the intergang
> Dont go back in hold the game
> With our softness with our give

The words are taken from the eighth stanza of the book's poem, but the stanza is shorter. This variation is in line with the processual character of Bergvall's work; the book version is not to be regarded as the original in any way. The lines are performative, addressing the viewer wherever they may be, urging them to act. The words reach beyond the screen out into the here and now of the world: do something, make some noise of your own, do not go back in. And this is where the border between the *everywhere* of the Internet and the *here* of the performance is overcome.

Conclusion

"What is a poem's mode of existence?" Derek Attridge (2019, 1) opens his study on experience with this question. Already in their ground-breaking *Theory of Literature*, published in 1949, René Wellek and Austin Warren asked pretty much the same: "Where is the 'real' poem, where should we look for it; how does it exist?" (Wellek and Warren 1956, 129). I would suggest that the question needs to be asked again and again: poetry is never still; its ontology can never be pinpointed once and for all.

This fact becomes even more obvious when one considers contemporary work like that of Caroline Bergvall. Her processual oeuvre shows that poetic practice can never be securely placed in the *there* of the book, the *here* of the performance, or the *everywhere* of the World Wide Web. The different evocations of a poetic work may stand alone – but, when placed together, one can see that they are all informed by one another. The book is changed by the Internet, and the poetry video borrows its aesthetic from the printed book. In the "Night and Refuge" sessions, the poets were carefully and outspokenly situated in exact places on the planet. But at the same time, they were part of something that happened everywhere. In the work of Nathan Coley, a Talking Heads' piece of music, which can be experienced *here* or *everywhere*, is turned into material text, a *there* artefact. But then it is placed *here* – next to a church in the medieval centre of a town in the northern periphery of Europe. And all those places, spaces, modes, and media make it into the work.

In her study on cultural turns, Doris Bachmann-Medick points out that space "is now no longer seen as a physical territorial concept but as a relational one" (Bachmann-Medick 2016, 216). My point and main suggestion, then, is that we should be careful not to study the *there* poetry without considering the *here* or the *everywhere*. The three categories are all present in one another. In this chapter I have shown how these different qualities inform the practice and experience of poetry while exploring how the visual aesthetic changes when the work moves across different media and settings – as for example in the "Shake" poem of "Drift," where different strategies are used in the performance, the printed poem, and the short digital video. In the "Night and Refuge" sessions, it is obvious that the visual set up informs the (sometimes interactive) viewers' as well as the performers' experience of the poem in becoming: through streams from live cams, poetry is connected to specific humans and geographic places while at the same time becoming global: with the *everywhere* of the Google Document format it becomes part of the poem's production of meaning. The "Night and Refuge" sessions also show that the visual aesthetic of the book can become part of the visual set up of a digital screen – but that the digital image of the white, printed page is something other than the white page itself. Through the "Drift" project and its use of Tom Martin's *Passenger* image, the ethical problems of seeing and watching, of the arbitrary lines between the visible and invisible are brought to the fore. When a digital surveillance image makes the transition into the *here* of the art show, and the *there* of the poetry collection, something happens to it. Through the artist's and audience's acts of what Mirzoeff calls "persistent watching," the visual object of surveillance remains what it is but also turns into a political object of counter visibility.

It has become apparent that although simple, the notions of the *here*, the *there*, and the *everywhere* offer a fruitful way to think about contemporary poetic practice, even though – or rather, since – these practices in many ways always override the imagined borders of the triad. As all users of models know, reality and poetry are always more complex and multi-layered than any model would suggest. But in this case, the triad becomes a tool that makes it possible to study how different aesthetics, theories, and poetic strategies bleed into one another as the situatedness of the poem changes. This way it becomes apparent how the aesthetic of one situation informs the other. I suggest that contemporary poetry should always be considered as situated, in the *here*, the *there* as well as in the *everywhere*. To concentrate on just the one would be to miss out on all the ways that poetic meaning is produced. As always, it turns out that the Beatles were worth a listen.

References

Albaik, Mays. *MAYS ALBAIK*. Homepage. https://maysalbaik.com/ (October 29, 2022).
Anderson, Benedict. *Imagined Communities. Reflections on the Origin and Spread of Nationalism*. London: Verso, 2006.
Anjou, Marika. "Himmelskt budskap lyser i Lund." *Sydsvenskan*. November 17, 2017, https://www.sydsvenskan.se/2017-11-17/himmelskt-budskap-lyser-i-lund (April 3, 2023).
Attridge, Derek. *The Experience of Poetry. From Homer's Listeners to Shakespeare's Readers*. Oxford: Oxford Univ. Press, 2019.
Auslander, Philip. *Liveness. Performance in a Mediated Culture*. London and New York: Routledge, 1999.
Bachman-Medick, Doris. *Cultural Turns. New Orientations in the Study of Culture*. Transl. Adam Blauhut. Berlin and Boston, MA: De Gruyter, 2016.
Barthes, Roland. "From Work to Text." *Image, Music, Text*. Transl. Stephen Heath. London: Fontana, 1977. 155–164.
Benthien, Claudia. "Poetry in the Digital Age." *Theories of Lyric. An Anthology of World Poetry Criticism*. 2021, https://lyricology.org/poetry-in-the-digital-age/ (October 15, 2022).
Bergvall, Caroline. *Caroline Bergvall*. Homepage. https://carolinebergvall.com/ (October 31, 2022).
Bergvall, Caroline. *Drift*. Callicoon, NY: Nightboat Books, 2014a.
Bergvall, Caroline. *Performance edit. Shake / DRIFT*. [Film] 2014b, https://vimeo.com/133971915 (October 31, 2022).

Bergvall, Caroline. "Infra-materiality and Opaque Drifting." *Minding Borders. Resilient Divisions in Literature, the Body and the Academy.* Ed. Nicola Gardini, Adriana X. Jacobs, Ben Morgan, Mohamed-Salah Omri, and Matthew Reynolds. Cambridge: Legenda, 2017. 67–75.

Bergvall, Caroline. "Drift." [Performance] Festival Operaestate, Bassano del Grappa, Italy. September 4, 2018.

Bergvall, Caroline. "Night and Refuge." [Public Collaborative Writing Event] Recorded May 21, 2020a, https://carolinebergvall.com/work/night-refuge/ (October 11, 2022).

Bergvall, Caroline. "Night and Refuge." June 24, 2020b, https://vimeo.com/432290058 (August 8, 2022).

Bergvall, Caroline. "Caroline Bergvall & Sonic Atlas present: Night & Refuge. Live Writing." Recorded November 27, 2020c, https://www.youtube.com/watch?v=IGjDld-PEcQ (October 30, 2022).

Bruns, Axel. "Some Exploratory Notes on Produsers and Produsage." 2005, https://distributedcreativity.typepad.com/idc_texts/2005/11/some_explorator.html (January 16, 2023).

Boym, Svetlana. *Death in Quotation Marks. Cultural Myths of the Modern Poet.* Cambridge, MA: Harvard Univ. Press, 1991.

Burke, Seán. *The Death and Return of the Author. Criticism and Subjectivity in Barthes, Foucault and Derrida.* Edinburgh: Edinburgh Univ. Press, 1998.

Callicoon Fine Arts. "Caroline Bergvall: Drift." [Exhibition] January 9–February 15, 2015, https://www.callicoonfinearts.com/exhibitions/caroline-bergvall/installation-views?view=slider (October 31, 2022).

Carelli, Peter. *Lunds historia – staden och omlandet. 1. Medeltiden. En metropol växer fram.* Värnamo: Elanders Fälth & Hässler, 2012.

Culler, Jonathan. "Philosophy and Literature: The Fortunes of the Performative." *Poetics Today* 21.3 (2000): 503–519.

Eleveld, Mark, and Marc Smith. *The Spoken Word Revolution (Slam, Hip Hop & the Poetry of a New Generation).* Naperville, IL: Sourcebooks Mediafusion, 2003.

Fischer-Lichte, Erika. "Vom 'Text' zur 'Performance.' Der 'performative Turn' in den Kulturwissenschaften." *Kunstforum International* 152 (2000): 61–63.

Fischer-Lichte, Erika. *The Transformative Power of Performance. A New Aesthetics.* Transl. Sakskya Iris Jain. London and New York: Routledge, 2008.

Funkhouser, Christopher. "Digital Poetry: A Look at Generative, Visual, and Interconnected Possibilites in its Firs Four Decades." *A Companion to Digital Literary Studies.* Ed. Ray Siemens and Susan Schreibman. Malden, MA: Blackwell, 2007. 318–335.

Hayles, N. Katherine. "The Time of Digital Poetry: From Object to Event." *New Media Poetics. Contexts, Technotexts, and Theories.* Ed. Adalaide Morris and Thomas Swiss. Cambridge, MA and London: MIT Press, 2006. 181–209.

Heller, Charles, Lorenzo Pezzani, and SITU Studio. "Forensic Oceanography. Report on the 'Left-To-Die-Boat'." Part of the European Research Council project "Forensic Architecture." Center for Research Architecture, Goldsmiths, Univ. of London, 2014.

Heller, Charles, and Lorenzo Pezzani. "Drifting Images, Liquid Traces: Disrupting the Aesthetic Regime of the EU's Maritime Frontier." *antiAtlas journal* 2 (2017): https://www.antiatlas-journal.net/02-drifting-images-liquid-traces/ (April 3, 2023).

Humble, Catherine. "Exposed to the Other. Responding to the Refugee in Caroline Bergvall's *Drift*." *Wild Analysis. From the Couch to Cultural and Political Life.* Ed. Shaul Bar-Haim, Elizabeth Sarah Coles, and Helen Tyson. London and New York: Routledge, 2021. 105–124.

Lunds domkyrka. *Nathan Coleys verk tar plats på Krafts torg vid Domkyrkan.* 2017, https://lundsdomkyrka.se/2017/11/14/nathan-coleys-verk-tar-plats-pa-krafts-torg-vid-domkyrkan/ (August 8, 2022).

Martin, Tom. *DRIFT + Aircraft Sighting: 33°40′ N, 13°05′ E.* 2014, http://martinandmartin.eu/#/drift/ (August 17, 2022).

McMurtry, Áine. "Sea Journeys to Fortress Europe: Lyric Deterritorializations in Texts by Caroline Bergvall and José F. A. Oliver." *The Modern Language Review* 113.4 (2018): 811–845.

Miller, Alyson. "A Digital Revolution? Insiders, Outsiders, and the 'Disruptive Potential' of Instapoetry." *arcadia* 56.2 (2021): 161–182.

Mirzoeff, Nicholas. *Watching Babylon. The War in Iraq and Global Visual Culture*. London: Routledge 2005.

Mirzoeff, Nicholas, and Magda Szcześniak. "Persistent Looking in Times of Crisis." *View. Theories and Practices of Visual Culture* 11 (2015): https://www.pismowidok.org/assets/files/article-pdf/issue-11/mirzoeff-szczesniaczi.pdf (April 3, 2023).

Mitchell, W. J. T. *Picture Theory. Essays on Verbal and Visual Representation*. Chicago, IL: Univ. of Chicago Press, 1994.

Morris, Adalaide. "New Media Poetics. As We May Think /How To Write." *New Media Poetics. Contexts, Technotexts, and Theories*. Ed. Adalaide Morris and Thomas Swiss. Cambridge, MA and London: MIT Press, 2006. 1–46.

Perloff, Marjorie. "Screening the Page/Paging the Screen. Digital Poetics and the Differential Text." *New Media Poetics. Contexts, Technotexts, and Theories*. Ed. Adalaide Morris and Thomas Swiss. Cambridge, MA and London: MIT Press, 2006. 143–162.

Phelan, Peggy. *Unmarked. The Politics of Performance*. London and New York: Routledge, 1993.

Piper, Andrew. *Book Was There. Reading in Electronic Times*. Chicago, IL: Univ. of Chicago Press, 2012.

Pugh, Jonathan. "Thinking with the Archipelago." *Island Studies Journal* 8.1 (2013): 9–24.

Sauter, Willmar. *The Theatrical Event. Dynamics of Performance and Perception*. Iowa City, IA: Univ. of Iowa Press, 2000.

Saxena, Akshya. "Spoken Wor(l)ds: Anglophony, Poetry, Translation." *Wasafiri* 37.3 (2022): 82–92.

Schaefer, Heike. "Poetry in Transmedial Perspecitve: Rethinking Intermedial Literary Studies in the Digital Age." *Acta Universitatis Sapientiae. Film and Media Studies* 10 (2015): 169–182.

Torres, Lourdes. "In the Contact Zone: Code Swiching Strategies by Latino/a Writers." *MELUS* 32.1 (2007): 75–96.

Wellek, René, and Austin Warren. *Theory of Literature*. New York: Harcourt, Brace & Co., 1956 [1949].

Yildiz, Yasemin. *Beyond the Mother Tongue. The Postmonolingual Condition*. New York: Fordham Univ. Press, 2012.

Vladimir Feshchenko and Olga Sokolova
Visualising Deixis in Avant-Garde and Contemporary Poetry "On and Off the Page"

This article deals with the linguistic poetics of deixis as one of the key mechanisms for expressing subjectivity in poetic communication.[1] The aim of the study is to discuss the specifics of deictic words and constructions in visually innovative poetic discourse. The particular focus of analysis is on the functions of personal, spatial and discourse (textual) deixis in the visual layout of a poetic text (spatial design of verse). The material for analysis extends from early avant-garde practices of visualising deixis (in e.e. cummings' experimental verse) through neo-avant-garde conceptual poetry (in Moscow Conceptualism and American Language Writing) to contemporary poetry that foregrounds the deictic units as carriers of new subjectivities in the age of digital media (namely in poems of the Covid pandemic as well as Ukrainian anti-war poems). We will argue that the deictic means of language, interacting with the visual space of the poetic text, actualise the dynamic subjectivity of the aesthetic utterance "on & off the page" (Perloff 1998).

In poetic discourse, the spatiality, length, and duration of the utterance (message) as such is a particularly active field of indexicality. Thus, the visual properties of poetic texts become tightly intertwined with poetic deixis that locates the reader's attention in the space of the poem. Before we turn to contemporary poetic examples of visualised deixis, we will, firstly, give insight into the theoretical linguistic premises and, secondly, into the historical context from poetic practice. The first section, then, presents an overview of theories of deixis in relation to poetry. More precisely, the role of spatial deixis is highlighted with respect to the texts' visuality. In the second section, our linguo-poetic analysis focuses on how experimental deixis interacts with the visual layout of the poem in cases from avant-garde (e.e. cummings) and neo-avant-garde (Luis Camnitzer, Lev Rubinstein, Vsevolod Nekrasov, John Cage, Robert Grenier, etc.) language-centred writing. Further on, in section three we consider new deictic functions in the poetry of the Covid pandemic analysing the poem "Notzeit (After Hannah Höch)" by one of the leading American Language poets Barrett Watten. This discussion focuses on transcoding between paper and digital forms of the texts (and vice versa) that

---

[1] The research is funded by grant № 22-28-00522 of the Russian Science Foundation and is carried out at the Institute of Linguistics, Russian Academy of Sciences.

Open Access. © 2023 the author(s), published by De Gruyter. [CC BY-NC-ND] This work is licensed under the Creative Commons Attribution-NonCommercial-NoDerivatives 4.0 International License.
https://doi.org/10.1515/9783111299334-003

underlies several deictic shifts that the poet himself highlights with colour and italic font. Finally, the fourth section dwells upon the spatial deixis in cases of contemporary Ukrainian anti-war poets, such as Olga Bragina, Lyudmila Khersonskaya, Julia Kolchinsky Dasbach and Danyil Zadorozhnyi who publish their texts online. In Ukrainian poetry dealing with the ongoing war's consequences, the deictic "here" acquires complex meanings, functioning as a spatial, discourse and personal marker of displacement and catastrophe.

Deixis in poetic discourse: theoretical premises

Being a basic linguistic mechanism, deixis serves as one of the tools for shaping up the subjectivity of a statement or text. It assembles and reassembles the subject from disparate words and phrases in the process of speech production. It binds language units and expressions to specific spatio-temporal coordinates and living subjects of speech, making each communicative event unique and personalised. Deixis is furthermore commonly studied within the framework of the theory of performativity as a manifestation of a subject's utterance in his/her speech act. Modern linguistics defines deixis as "the name given to those aspects of language whose interpretation is relative to the occasion of utterance: to the time of utterance, and to times before and after the time of utterance; to the location of the speaker at the time of utterance; and to the identity of the speaker and the intended audience" (Fillmore 1966, 220). Deixis therefore becomes an operating mechanism only in a specific language use, in particular kinds of discourse.

Our focus in this paper is on visual properties of deixis in poetic discourse. In linguistics, the German scholar Karl Brugmann was the first to study deictic words, in the early twentieth century, paying attention to how personal pronouns function in Indo-Germanic languages (see Brugmann 1904). Another prominent German linguist, Karl Bühler, further developed this approach in his studies of the "indexical field of language." He identified the basic scheme of deixis in language, consisting of three components: "I – here – now." The convergence of these components in the act of utterance marks the "starting point" of subjectivity, which Bühler calls "origo" (Bühler 2011, 102). Bühler's theory of indexicality is based on the analysis of everyday language and does not contain any literary references. He does not move beyond a discussion of everyday language, only once appealing to poetry to equalise the powers of deixis in ordinary and poetic speech.

Roman Jakobson, however, who named deictic words "shifters" (Jakobson 1957), and some other scholars in linguistic poetics made further observations on the functioning of deictic units in poetry. The Russian linguist Vyacheslav Ivanov, for example, noted the increasingly active role deixis played in twentieth century lyric poetry, which focuses on "the expression of the poet's personality in the moment of the very act of poetic speech" (Ivanov 1979, 106; own translation). Worthy of note in this regard is the study by British literary scholar Keith Green (1992), devoted to the problem of deixis in lyric poetry. This work is an attempt at a systematic and consistent linguistic approach to the functioning of various deictic categories in a poetic text. He posits that the instance of the self in poetry is the starting point for the spatio-temporal coordinates of the deictic context. In this case, the deictic context is not the external context of the utterance, but the very space of the poetic text, the world that is created anew each time in each specific poem. In lyric poetry this origo may be unknown, hence the deixis is not determined in advance by the knowledge of the reader but is constituted in the organisation of the text. Stephen Levinson distinguishes five types of deixis in language: person deixis, place deixis, time deixis, social deixis, and discourse deixis (cf. Levinson 1983, 68–94). In poetic language, with its peculiar subjectivity, materiality and spatiality, personal deixis (the poetic persona) is intricately intertwined with discourse deixis (the focus on the message as such) and spatial deixis (the visual layout of the poem on the page or on screen).

The visual culture of the twentieth and early twenty-first centuries has been highly dependent on the transformation of media. Poetry of the avant-garde and the neo-avant-garde was intensely experimenting with the space of the poem within the book, the picture, the environment. Towards the late twentieth century, the digitalisation of print media foregrounded the importance of the *interface* between the author, the text, and the reader/user. The new interfaces of poetic practices reconfigured the relations between the person, the text, and the space in the process of aesthetic communication. The personal deixis sets the coordinates of the subjects participating in poetic communication, whereas discourse deixis organises the situational frame of the act of utterance, and spatial deixis positions this act of utterance in the real or imaginary space of the text. Focusing on spatial deixis in early modern English lyric, Heather Dubrow claims that "since 'here'/'there,' 'this'/'that,' and 'come'/'go' often involve subjectivity, they interact with pronominal deixis" (Dubrow 2015, 5). Dubrow also emphasises that it could be productive to look how "recent media inflect the issues about spatiality and temporality that deixis introduces" (Dubrow 2015, 63), which we will examine further in this paper. In addressing the issue of space in the poetic text, we will make use of Marjorie Perloff's notion of "spatial design" (Perloff 2010, 69), which includes, among other things, the composition of language units within the visual layout of the text. We will argue that deictic units constitute a considerable part of the text's linguistic design contributing to the overall spatial design. First, we will address several cases from the history of avant-garde and neo-avant-garde poetry, which actualise the experimental effects of deixis in the visual configuration of the poetic text.

Deictic markers as elements of spatial design: experimental poetry

We have elsewhere discussed such concepts as bodily deixis and vocal deixis (cf. Proskurin and Feshchenko 2019), in cases where markers of corporality or physical voice are involved in the indexical field of a work of art or literature. One of the first modern poets to exploit bodily and vocal deixis together with the text's enforced iconicity was e.e. cummings, who was not only a poet but also a talented painter. Visually eccentric verse was for him an experiment with the typescript and the typeset, a modern technical medium reinforcing the graphical potentialities of the poetic text (Fig. 4).

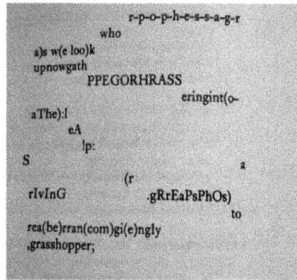

Fig. 4: e.e. cummings. "r-p-o-p-h-e-s-s-a-g-r." *Complete Poems, 1904–1962*, 2013. 396.

In cummings' famous 1932 "grasshopper" visual poem, deictic markers make up a significant part, including the personal deictics ("who," "we"), the temporal ("now"), the spatial ("up," "to"), and the articles as shifters of (in)definiteness ("the," "a"). cummings tries to capture the moment of transition from the symbolic and iconic way of signification to the indexical-deictic one. The poem models the very process of reading and conveying the meaning of the verse, with the help of experimental deixis located within the space of the poem. In poems like "ecco a letter" (1940), discourse markers are foregrounded both linguistically and graphically:

> ecco a letter starting"dearest we"
> unsigned:remarkably brief but covering
> one complete miracle of nearest far
>
> "i cordially invite me to become
> noone except yourselves r s v p"
> (cummings 2013, 504)

Subjectivity is transferred from the author to the message itself, which, in turn, opens many possible subjective relations: "dearest we," "i cordially invite me," "noone except yourselves." The Italian word *ecco* ("here") used in the first line is a deictic particle that not only refers to the entire origo (this – here – now), but also includes the subject in the emphatic act of pronouncing the word itself (as in the Latin phrase *ecce homo* – "behold the man"). The "r s v p" (French abbreviation of "please answer") in the final phrase is addressed simultaneously to the recipient of the "letter" and its sender (as the anomalous personal deixis testifies: "i invite me"). The use of speech marks ("") visually highlights the shifting subjectivity of who writes this poem/letter to who reads it. Miscapitalisation of the pronoun "I," characteristic of most of cummings' work, serves as a graphic tool of foregrounding the personal deictic. Particularly interesting is cummings' treatment of the pronoun "I," miscapitalised and recapitalised as the noun "eye" in this 1963 poem:

i
never
guessed any
thing(even a
universe)might be
so not quite believab
ly smallest as perfect this
(almost invisible where of a there of a)here of a
rubythroat's home with its still
ness which really's herself
(and to think that she's
warming three worlds)
who's ama
zingly
Eye
                        (cummings 2013, 827)

Here, the indexical field of the poem, comprising numerous deictics ("I," "never," "any," "a," "so," "this," "where," "there," "here," "herself," "she," "who's"), coalesces with the iconic field – the poem is laid out as a visual representation of the eye-ball. The longest central line in it is a cluster of spatial deictics pointing to the message itself, which turns out to be a language game between "where," "here," and "there": "(almost invisible where of a there of a)here of a." This iconicity reflects cummings' orientation towards visual perception by the author and reader, which seems to be peculiar to him as a "poet-and-painter." Abstract painting, as the cutting-edge technique in arts of his time, served as a visual model for the poem's linguistic and spatial design.

Deixis, as a powerful linguistic mechanism, becomes even more involved in the poetics of the neo-avant-garde after the Second World War, on the wave of the "performative turn" that went hand in hand with the spatial and pictorial/visual turns (cf. Bachmann-Medick 2016). Simultaneously with scientific interest in linguistic performativity (e.g., by John Austin, John Searle and by Emile Benveniste), artistic discourse begins to experiment with locutionary, illocutionary and perlocutionary meanings of statements in the space of a text, art object or performance. New forms of interaction between verbal and visual matter play an important role beyond the borders between a poem and a picture as stable traditional formats of expression. The most striking manifestation of this turn was John Cage's famous maxim "I have nothing to say, and I'm saying it" – a classic performative statement from the point of view of the theory of speech acts, and a "liar paradox" from the point of view of logical analysis.[2] In fact, this statement is part of Cage's visual and poetic composition published under the title "Lecture on Nothing" in his book *Silence* (1961). The text begins with the deictic phrase "I am here" and unfolds as a series of fragmented sentences, many of which deliberately emphasise their deictic constituents ("and there is nothing to say," "If among you are," "somewhere," "any moment," "now," "and that is," "for I'm making it," "an i-dea may occur in this . . . talk," etc.; see Cage 1961, 109–127). The spatial configuration of the "Lecture" is reminiscent of cummings' "grasshopper" poem, with the breakdown of the text into columns and clusters. This lecture-poem speaks about itself and about the process of performative creativity. With its spatiality, combined with rich deictic markup, it marks a new type of verbal art – performance writing.

Similar visual-verse experiments were undertaken, since the 1950s, all over the world. For example, in textual objects by the Uruguayan conceptual artist Luis Camnitzer, an ordinary statement placed in a frame and divided into lines, reads like a poem with an indefinite deictic reference (Fig. 5):

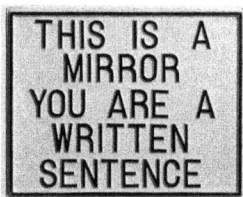

Fig. 5: Luis Camnitzer. *This Is a Mirror. You Are a Written Sentence*. 1966–1968.

On another plate containing the phrase "THIS IS A MAP YOU ARE HERE," there is only one proper content word ("map") surrounded by mere deictics, which makes viewer-reader participation the only valid way to actualise this statement. The plates, being exhibited in a gallery hall, serve as 'mirrors' that reflect the reader/viewer's thoughts about these art objects. Particular locations within the space of

---

2 A liar paradox in philosophy is a statement of a liar that they are lying, in declarations such as "I am lying," "this statement is not true," "a majority of what Jones says about me is false," etc.

an exhibition will shift the viewer's deictic focus, or origo, in relation to these artistic statements. Conceptual art and poetry sought to reconsider the deictic frameworks of an artistic text, opening up new ways of interaction between word and image, verbality and visuality.

Within the same period of the 1950–80s, in the former Soviet Union, performative art and poetry was developing within a highly censored underground environment and manifested itself to a greater extent in the deconstruction of the official language of power. Poetry was increasingly inhabited by everyday expressions that opposed the poeticisms of official Soviet literature. Already in the first conceptualist paintings and objects by Ilya Kabakov, deictic expressions play a major role. The replicas of the characters (Soviet citizens) organise the composition of the canvases, which, in turn, resemble book pages or bureaucratic Soviet documents with poetic-like verbal structures. The new pragmatics of poetry in Moscow Conceptualism consisted in the critique of ordinary and political discourses. Some of the texts, like the ones by Vsevolod Nekrasov, are overwhelmed by deictic words such as "we," "itself," "here," etc., turning poetry into a machine for dismantling the official language of Soviet society. Some of the poems are entirely made of deictic and performative words:

верю
верю что верю
верю

In this minimalist poem (Nekrasov 2012, 290), the recursive use of the epistemic verb in "я верю что я верю" ("I believe that I believe") is placed in the visual composition of a Suprematist cross, actualising both the semantics of religious belief and the pragmatics of certainty. On the opposite page of this edition, the expression containing the same verb "believe" is rendered differently: The poetic line "верю верю в" ("I believe I believe in") is located right against the margin of the page, on the upper right side, actualising the dual reference of the deictic preposition "в" ("in"): the conceptual *believe in something* and the visual-performative *I believe inside this*, an anomalous use of the word *believe* as a spatial, rather than mental, verb. In much of Moscow Conceptualist poetry, the reader is faced with fragments of inner or outer speech performed on the page, as if it was performed on the (theatrical) stage. This principle of staging the ordinary discourse is probably most vividly realised in the poetry of Lev Rubinstein. The poetic text here is transformed into verbal performance, with utterances sporadically interspersing each other:

1
Well, what on earth is there to say?
2
He knows something, but won't tell.

> 3
> Who knows, maybe you're right.
> 4
> It's good for you, and tasty too.
> 5
> At seven, by the first train car.
> 6
> It goes on about the student.
> 7
> Let's go. I'm also heading there.
> 8
> Have you decided something now?
> 9
> I rode the bus to the last stop.
> 10
> Hey, listen to what I just wrote.
>   (Rubinstein 2014, 139)

The lines in this poem are visually arranged as a numbered list, parodying the official Soviet bureaucratic documents that contained often senseless and endless enumerations of actions to be performed by a Soviet citizen. The typical Soviet concept of 'standing in line, or queue' is embodied into a poetic sequence. Each line reads here as an everyday phrase heard from people standing in a queue for something. There are no logical connections on the surface between these utterances, yet, if interpreted poetically, they acquire metaphorical or even metaphysical meanings: What is saying? What is writing? Knowing? Deciding? Going where? Etc. They sound as replicas by anonymous characters, mystical as much as ordinary, who play a language game in a ruled grid of the page's layout.

In the USA, a close analogue to this kind of performativisation of the word and verbalisation of the visual image was the Language Writing movement. One of the principles of its poetics was the emphasis on writing, that is, not so much the sound form of verse, but rather the graphical and spatial. To a large degree, this spatial turn was inspired by Charles Olson's "Projective Verse" theory and practice of spatial arrangement of language on the page (cf. Olson 1950). But in language writing, the metalinguistic function of the utterance came to the fore in order to challenge the boundaries of poetry and non-poetry, yet staying within the poetic function. Robert Creeley's visually condensed verse was another forerunner of the 'turn to language' in the American tradition. Discourse markers and deictic units as carriers of metalinguistic reflection were a characteristic feature of his poetics, which can be seen already from the titles of his poetic works: *The Kind of Act Of; If You; Listen; His Idea; Away; Thanks; Was That a Real Poem and Other Essays; Later; It; So There; If I Were Writing This*. Quite often, Creeley's poetic line consists of only one deictic word or short expression, which creates a minimalistic space of the verse's subjectivity and materiality.

It is characteristic of Language Poetry that the name of one of the first journals was *This*, which is both a spatial and discourse deictic marker, indicating both the actualisation of the utterance itself ("this message") and the space that surrounds it ("the journal itself"). The first issue of the journal was logically called *This 1*. Minimalism became one of the basic features of Language Writing. For example, Robert Grenier's cycles of the 1970s and 1980s are made out of a special typographic placement in the space of the book. In this special format, his series *Sentences* (1978) was created, consisting of five hundred large-format index cards, each of which contains a short poem of just a few lines. Freed from the constraints of a bound book, this work can be read in any order, either as separate texts or as one long poem with dynamic relationships between its parts. The deictic shifts both within and between the separate pages are actualised by particular deictic units, such as in: "why you say you see later" (Grenier 1978, n. pag.). These short performative poems appear to be prototypes for instant messaging in Internet communication.

Discourse, or textual deixis, serves in Language Writing as a tool of self-reflection, as in Clark Coolidge's "Larry Eigner Notes" (1984) and many writings of this kind, blending the genres of poem and essay. The self-reflexivity and the spatiality of language poetry can probably be best illustrated by Rachel Du Plessis's poem called, as it is, "DEIXIS" (*Drafts* series, 2001), exposing an interest to this phenomenon both on conceptual and on practical poetic planes. In addition, one of the major language poets, Ron Silliman, draws a lot from Internet genres in writing and publishing text such as in the blogging format of writing, for example, in his large poem deictically called "YOU" (Silliman 2008). He published parts of this poem daily throughout the year 1995 as prose poetry miniatures on his personal blog. In the following sections, we will investigate new functions of the above-mentioned types of deixis in contemporary poetry, in particular, in poetic texts published on the Internet. Digital media have changed the communication model influencing both ordinary language and poetic discourse by focusing on the interface as the new communication tool between the author, the text, and the reader/user.

Digital interfaces of poetry: cases from the Covid pandemic

Building upon Perloff's concept of "spatial design" (Perloff 2010), we will project the 'on' and 'off' distinction onto a specific interface that is being formed in recent poetry in the space of new media. It is the digital interface that conveys new communication forms and displays the transformation of all communication parameters, according to Roman Jakobson's communication model, beginning with the dominance of information channels and including the modification of codes and roles of communication participants. Contemporary poetry is characterised by increased attention to the structural and pragmatic organisation of the utterance, which allows us to consider it in terms of media theory based upon Vilém Flusser's model of a "significant surface" (Flusser 1984, 6) and as a "two-dimensional plane" both, from a material and metaphorical perspective (Galloway 2012, 30). According to Lev Manovich, the interface "far from being a transparent window into the data inside a computer, [. . .] brings with it strong messages of its own" (Manovich 2001, 65). The interface is not just a tool for accessing data, but the medium that "shapes how the computer user conceives of the computer itself" and "determines how users think of any media object accessed via computer" (Manovich 2001, 65). Shifting attention from material interface objects to virtual processes, Alexander R. Galloway argues that "interfaces are not things, but rather processes that effect a result of whatever kind" and points out the idea of "interface effect" (Galloway 2012, vii). Poetry of our times uses the digital interface as an interactive structure in which relations are distributed between different layers of information, message and meaning formation codes, in the creation of which both the addresser and the addressee take an active part. It is a consistent theme of the recent humanities that a great social shift brings about a great discursive shift in the era of the pandemic. The discursive shift is common for various discourses, including media, political, medical, etc. Unlike other discourses, in poetry the shift manifests itself in emphasising the pragmatic coordinates of the utterance.

The problem of textualising new deictic and pragmatic coordinates in the period of self-isolation and lockdown was actualised by several American and Russian contemporary poets. For example, many American poets posted their texts written during the pandemic in the "poets corner" of the *gchschautauqua* webpage.[3] Publishing their texts during the pandemic, some contemporary poets mark the reference to the lockdown in the titles of poetic books like Italian poet Valerio Grutt in *L'amuleto. Appunti sul potere di guarigione della poesia* (Grutt 2021; "The Amulet. Notes on the Healing Power of Poetry") and Charles Bernstein in "Covidity" (Bernstein 2021, 144). The authors also comment on poetic texts to emphasise the period of writing like Barrett Watten in his "Note for online publication" to his *Notzeit (After Hannah Höch)* (2020): "'Notzeit (After Hannah Höch)' was written over a five-week period, from 23 March to 26 April 2020 [. . .]. I de-

---

3 https://www.gchschautauqua.com/bl-poets-corner.html.

cided I would continue writing on a daily basis through the duration of our period of isolation, not knowing how long that would be" (Watten 2020c, 26). Similar statements can be found in the content of various "pandemic" art platforms.[4]

Considering the manuscript *Notzeit (After Hannah Höch)* by Watten as a representative example of the above-mentioned issue,[5] we can argue that the author gravitates here toward the conceptualist method, deliberately refraining from such traditional means as metaphors in favour of pragmatic means: The most active elements of his poetic language are deictic markers. The poet describes his text as "the poem of the COVID duration" (Watten 2020b) as it is a hybrid text of the diary-testimony of the lockdown period. Limited communication of the lockdown period expands to include components of self-communication and numerous digital discourses. The poem consists of headlines and banners, fragments of conversations and news feeds, political and social events. We can trace how the scale of cognitive perspective created in the text has changed during and after the lockdown. Watten posted fragments of his poem daily on his blog: The text was originally called "Isolate flecks" (Watten 2020a) and referred to William Carlos Williams' text "To Elsie," including an epigraph from Williams: "It is only in isolate flecks that / something / is given off / No one / to witness / and adjust, no one to drive the car" (Watten 2020a; Watten 2020c, 1). Watten emphasised the idea of self-isolation as a new form of communication that breaks the standard connections between people with the help of the visual text. Above the epigraph, the poet placed an abstract digital image of spots that centrifugally diverge and multiply with the help of mirroring.

Watten finally changed the poem's name using the title of a watercolour by the Dada artist Hannah Höch from her period of "inner emigration" in 1940s Berlin. The picture is filled with images of people with sketchy bodies and faces. The artist uses a broken, non-linear, perspective, which blurs the line between static and dynamic human bodies. Their faces are like spots, at the same time scattered over the sheet and compressed by the page boundaries. Compared to the digital image of the spots, which the poet used for the first version of the poem, this abstract watercolour expresses the sense of suffering and sadness. It conveys the relationship between tragic loneliness in the crowd and the impossibility of harmonious unity with oneself even in isolation. Höch's title *Notzeit* (1943) translates

---

4 See, for instance, https://www.pandemia-art.com/250/#unghigno0.
5 A great resonance of this book can be confirmed by a recent issue of the Russian literary magazine *Nosorog*, which was published with the subtitle "Travel Around the Room (Following Barrett Watten's *Notzeit*': Six Poets on the Experience of Isolation)" (2020), focusing on the experience of self-isolation through the extensive use of pragmatic markers of transcoded subjectivity and addressing such subjectivity-related strategies.

to "Time of Suffering," but Watten explained that he prefers "the sense of duration," namely "not time": "Höch's title means 'Time of Suffering,' but I like better the sense of duration: 'not time.'" (Watten 2020c, 27) This interpretation can express the idea of metalinguistic translation of words in poetic language, which converge on the ground of paronymic attraction, namely a similar sound. Bridging the boundaries between languages extends to other boundaries including time and space: suffering exists beyond any limits, as a part of human existence.

The concept of inner immigration, 'going in,' is obviously a central concern of the poem (cf. Watten 2020c, 27). The last meaning refers to the pragmatic and deictic coordinates. In the poem, not only has the title changed, but also the communication perspective. The first version of the poem, as it was published on the poet's blog, included diary dates, and did not have any graphic coloured emphasis:

> 21 MARCH 2020
> What I am to think about, in a room with others, is the nature of Zero Hour—our new life.
>   Our colloquy is an opening to that question.
> 22 MARCH 2020
> The poet often sees oneself as an *isolato*, "a person who is physically or spiritually isolated from others." We are collectively isolated, as well.
> This is the common condition we have sequestered ourselves within. These are the occasions for what I am now writing: *here begin*
>
> (Watten 2020a)

If we compare the text posted on the blog with the final version published after the end of the lockdown with the new title, we can see the accents that were placed by the poet himself in the final version. He highlighted egocentric words in red to emphasise them:[6]

> I
> What *I* am to think about, in *this* room without others, is the nature of
> Zero Hour—the new life. *Our* inquiry is an opening to *that* question.
> II
> The poet sees *himself* as an isolato, "a person . . . physically or spiritually
> isolated from *others*." *You* are collectively isolated, *each* in *their* turn.
> *That* is the common condition *we* have sequestered *ourselves* within. *This* is the occasion
>   for what *I* now undertake to write: *here* begin
>
> (Watten 2020c, 1)

---

[6] For the printed version of this volume we have marked emphasised words in terms of colour in the following excerpts (which are both red and formatted with italics in the original) with bold and italic formatting, instead.

As Watten commented in the afterword to this last version, "I have italicised and highlighted in red all pronouns, relative pronouns, and deictics of time and space. I have done this in order to foreground their varying patterns and to point out the possibility of their mutual substitution" (Watten 2020c, 28). We would like to underline that the poet not only highlights egocentric words but also changes the interpretation mode.

According to the theory of linguistic pragmatics, there are two main modes of interpretation: primary deixis, which underlies the dialogue mode, or the classical situation of communication, and deictic projection (cf. Lyons 1977, 579), or secondary deixis (cf. Lyons 1995, 310). The deixis of literary discourse also belongs to the second type. Whereas "I – here – now" has a literal meaning in the dialogue mode, the deictic center in the narrative mode can refer not to the speaker's position, but to the object of the story's position. For example, in the phrase "He only now realised how much he loves her," the "now" can mean both the time of the utterance and the moment in the past preceding it, when the hero of the story realised something important (cf. Apresjan 1995, 276). Watten reflects on different deictic shifts: between dialogic and narrative types of deixis, as well as the shift between narrative and discourse types of deixis. So, a lack of communication during a period of isolation has become a trigger to experience new perceptions and to broaden traditional communication frames using deictics markers. The poet experiments with online communication, rethinking each deictic sign in a new way: "here," "now," "this," "that," etc. All of them become ambiguous when there is a shift between an everyday speech situation to an online communication mode and – vice versa.

We can trace the pragmatic shifts that occur between two versions of the text. The following types of shifts can be distinguished as an intermediate zone between different interfaces and communication modes: "a room – *this* room"; "our new life – *the* new life"; "The poet often sees oneself as an *isolato* – The poet sees *himself* as an isolato"; "We are collectively isolated, as well – *You* are collectively isolated, *each* in *their* turn"; "This is the common condition – *That* is the common condition"; "These are the occasions – *This* is the occasion." Such shifts express an overlap of the cognitive "zoom-in and zoom-out" mechanisms when the object is simultaneously approaching and moving away from the addressee. The deictic shift "near speaker – away from speaker" is rendered with the help of various language markers. The poet changes the degree of determinativeness. This function expresses meaning on a scale from definiteness to indefiniteness of the object. Its indicators are articles, possessive pronouns, and demonstratives which refer to the place where the speaker finds him/herself such as "here" and "there." The shift of determiners leads to the change of the degree of object proximity. At the same time, there is a shift along the line of distance – from the personal pronoun to the definite article or from the first person pronoun to the second person, as well as between the demonstrative pronouns, from a proximal deictic expression to a distal one. These shifts express by verbal means the change in visual perspective reminiscent of Hannah Höch's watercolour.

The verbal description of a visual work of art, in this case, a depiction of the crucial elements, namely in the form of a non-linear perspective, operates as ekphrasis by combining different types of artistic media to express a common idea. Another function of these shifts is to convey a communication strategy of transcoded subjectivity along the referential line of zooming in and zooming out. Building upon cognitive linguistics research (Foulsham and Cohn 2020; Hill and MacLaury 1995), we use the "zooming in" and "zooming out" conceptions in the meaning of a semantic shift aimed at switching between full and close-up scenes and bringing the object to the spotlight of attention. These conceptions are significant for our study since they function as visual metaphors conveying the idea of visual perception of verbal text. This perception is similar to the impression from Hannah Höch's watercolour also using the shift from zooming in to zooming out because of the broken, non-linear, perspective.

In the case of personal deixis, the poem activates a shift from possessive pronouns of the first and second person in the function of determinativeness as more definite and direct participants in communication (such as "the displacement of *my* body onto *yours*") to the quantifier "both" and, further, to the third person indicator "it," which goes beyond boundaries of the communicative act. According to Émile Benveniste, the "third person" "represents the unmarked member of the correlation of person" as a "non-person" (Benveniste 1971, 221). Such a shift signals the distancing of the subject – both grammatical and pragmatic – in relation to one's own "I," which, paradoxically, moves away in a communicative situation of self-isolation: "The displacement of *my* body onto *yours* signifies the destruction of *both*. / *It* is the universal figure, projected onto a macabre display" (Watten 2020c, 24). This deictic shift denotes a change in distance, the imposition of zoom-in and zoom-out mechanisms within one utterance. The poet here complements the direct nomination with deictic markers indicating the distance and degree of objects' remoteness: "*his* Great Isolation"; "*each* must find *their* place."

The shift from the distal to the proximal deixis goes along with nominalisation of the deictics with the help of quotation marks and violation of the ordinary collocation due to the use of 'out *there*' and 'in *here*' in an isolated position: "The only mitigation between 'out *there*' and 'in *here*' is doubt about / social hierarchies and the boundaries of the property system" (Watten 2020c, 5). Actualisation of polysemy leads to the increase of expressiveness of the deictic "out *there*," which at the same time means 'over there,' 'outside,' and 'someone or something that is out-there is very extreme or unusual,' whereas "in **here**" signifies 'the inner part of a building or room.' The indefinite article ("a person") is an indicator of the determinative change, shifting between abstraction and concretisation, as well as within the boundaries of visual perspective. This indefinite nomination forms a rhetorical question in combination with an interrogative construction ("What is . . .?"): "***What*** is a person and ***what*** do ***you*** care? ***I*** care about ***himself*** and ***those*** dear / to ***us***, ***who*** have been statistically modeled to an optimal number" (Watten 2020c, 12). The third person reflexive pronoun "***I*** care about ***himself***" marks an increase in the degree of determination and concretisation. The same effect is achieved by the use of a definitive subordinate clause related to the pronoun "those" ("***those*** dear to ***us***, ***who*** . . ."). At the same time, as we can see from the context, the lexical meaning turns out to be the opposite, expressing indefiniteness, and denotes abstract "dear" ones, who have become a part of the digital reality: "***those*** dear / to ***us***, ***who*** have been statistically modeled to an optimal number."

In addition, let us point out the shift between animateness and inanimateness as a characteristic for the distancing strategy, which marks the loss of human contact and the mechanisation of communication. Grammatically, this phenomenon manifests itself through a shift from the third person pronoun "he" to the pronoun "it," denoting inanimate objects: "***He*** would be a bar graph, a projection curve, a downward spiral of case / acceleration, a bubble on a map ***that when we*** clicked on ***it*** got larger" (Watten 2020c, 10). Thus, the deictic shift leads to the automation of the communication participants themselves. This shift transfers the idea of digital procedures and can be compared with pseudo-communication with Internet bots, namely software application imitating human activity such as messaging on the Internet.

Numerous shifts in the field of personal deixis mark the physical coordinates of the subject's position and indicate the current communicative situation. The variation of deictics as well as the designation of corporality ("embodiment") in a situation of distancing and loss of connections between the subject and the object allow us to apply the concept of "deixis in carnal form" by Norman Bryson (1983, 88). The more the physical coordinates of communication dissolve in the new conditions of media technologies, the more the poetic subject seeks to grasp the elusive coordinates. Lexical ("The displacement of ***my*** body onto ***yours*** signifies the destruction of ***both***"; Watten 2020c, 24) and pragmatic markers such as reflexive pronouns ("When ***you*** see ***yourself*** in a clear light, ***you*** will know the body as ***it*** opens / up"; Watten 2020c, 24) come to the fore, signifying, on the one hand, corporality through the frequent use of deictics and their graphic highlighting with colour and italic type. On the other hand, the loss of corporality is implied here, which is performed through the deictic shift. It also refers to the non-linear visual perspective in Hannah Höch's watercolour, which is also manifested through verbal means. In Watten's own view, his text marks a temporal and technological "zero point" (Watten 2020c, 26). Thus, at the centre of Watten's metapoetic reflection is the transcoding of the text between digital and everyday reality and vice versa. In the text, there is an emphasis of the shift between the virtual and the real, performed through linguistic markers of subjectivity – deictic words and deictic shifts. Following Galloway, we can claim that the poet's focus is on the dynamic interface processes, or the "interface effect," which manifests itself not in stable objects, but in their dynamics.

The last case we would like to discuss is spatial deixis in poetry in digital media. It acquires new functions in contemporary anti-war Ukrainian poetry, where space comes into focus. The Ukrainian poets express – with the help of deictic markers – a new and changed sense of the habitual space, which has three dimensions: the surrounding as well as remote and virtual aspects.

Contemporary anti-war poetry: shifts of spatial deixis

The last section of the paper investigates texts of very recent social and political poetry, which were written by Ukrainian and Russian poets as reaction to the war of Russia against Ukraine and published from the end of February 2022 onwards. There is still no definite term to designate Ukrainian and Russian poetry against the war. Some authors use the terms "war poetry" (Ivashkiv 2022), "poems of war" (Kelly 2022), or "anti-war" literature and poetry (Kobylko et al. 2022, 94). In our paper, we will use the last term – "anti-war poetry" as it allows to express the poets' attitude towards the atrocities of the war. We have collected a corpus of texts that were published in various sources: poems with hashtags on Internet portals such as #nowar on Sigma, #StandWithUkraine and #TranslationMonth on the pages of Ukrainian and Russian poets on Facebook; in poetic magazines and collections such as in *Ukrainian Poetry in Translation Part I* and *Part II* published by the National Translation Month (NTM 2022); in the volume *Invasion. Ukrainian Poems about the War* (Kitt 2022); and in anti-war poetry online projects, such as "Dear Ukraine" by Julia Kolchinsky Dasbach (2022). All these projects use virtual space of the page to combine verbal texts with visual images, such as representations of sunflowers, known as the symbol of Ukraine, on the one hand, and shelters, and bombed-out buildings, on the other hand. Visual representations serve to draw the reader's attention to a huge contrast between a peaceful past and a terrible present as two remote times and spaces.

Much of this poetry is designed not so much by means of specific text graphics, but with the help of interactions of poetic discourse with everyday speech. Anti-war poetry employs fragmented diary narratives close to those specific in "docu-poetry." Quite often, such hybrid media texts are made up of Facebook posts that poets begin to write during the war, and which look like reformatted fragments of everyday speech in off- and online communication. Such is the cycle *Kyiv Diary* by Ukrainian poet Olga Bragina (February–March 2022), which comprises a selection of Facebook posts written during the siege of Kyiv. In the analysed anti-war poetry, poetic subjectivity emerges as a process of transition between non-historical, historical and individual experience, as a result of the forced relocation from the besieged Ukrainian cities to the European Union. The trauma of the war presence translates into fragmented poetic testimonies about the war. We have detected several new functions of deictic markers that come into focus in anti-war poetry. The most representative of them is the shift of spatial deixis with the function of determinativeness.

In a fragment from *Kyiv Diary* by Olga Bragina, the marker "here" is combined with the locative predicate "to stay," denoting 'in this situation' and expressing the common meaning of location in a definite place:

> I tell Dad: "The best people in the city are here. If it weren't for the war, you'd think it was New Year's Eve."
>
> I tell Mom: "We are here, like in Akhmatova's poem Requiem."
>
> Mom says: "We are standing our ground now—here—so that things don't get worse, as they did in the poem."
>
> (Bragina 2022)

The marker "here" acquires a narrower and more specific meaning 'at the point where the speech act takes place,' namely, in besieged Kyiv. The temporal marker "now," which is graphically marked "now—here," as well as the verbal indicator of a present continuous tense emphasise the synchronism of what is happening in relation to the poetic speech act and the desire to involve the addressee in the interaction. The publication of *Kyiv Diary* on the Internet combines text and visual presentation of a shelter, one from the thousands, where Ukrainian people have to seek asylum, which allows a reader to achieve deeper immersion in the actual communicative situation of the text. The picture of the basement shelter presented on the site resonates with the visual image of the fragmented text of the diary (Fig. 6).

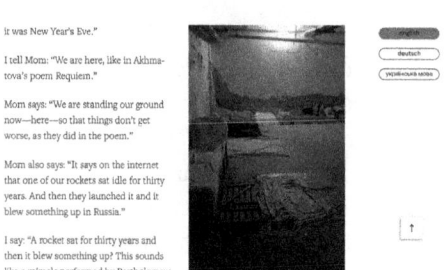

Fig. 6: Olga Bragina. "Excerpts from 'Kyiv Diary'." 2022.

In this text, we can also detect the intertextual dialogue with the poem "Requiem" (1934–1963) by Anna Akhmatova, notorious as the narrative about human suffering under Stalin's genocidal policy, known as the Great Terror or Great Purge that targeted political oppositionists, academics and artists, ethnic and national minorities as well as rivals in the Communist party in the Soviet Union among many others. The reference to Akhmatova's "Requiem" signifies the eternity of the terror machine, which continues to grind people's lives even in the post-Soviet space. Another Ukrainian author, Lyudmila Khersonskaya, includes in her text the word "here" in the adversative construction, the first part of which is specified by the nominative group "a carnival in venice." The second part to this construction, which is opposed to the first, is marked by the adversative conjunction "while here":

> she says it's a carnival in venice, it's spring,
> while here a leader is peeling open his eyelids swollen with sleep,
> while here, a louse is readying itself to drink some blood,
> she says it's carnival time, your partner is masked,
> and here we have masked fighters, slits instead of their eyes,
> she says, over there the masks are different, fancy masks,
> and here a new death is added to the anniversary of a death,
> to call a war a provocation – this takes some smarts [. . .].
> (Khersonskaya 2022)[7]

The indefinite article "a" in the context "a carnival in venice" expresses the abstract nomination of the 'holiday, peaceful life.' This abstract idea of a 'peaceful life' is opposed to the war, which is not named directly, but denoted with the deictic "here" and descriptions in the present tense: "while here a leader is peeling," "while here, a louse is readying itself." The deictic marker "here" denotes not only a specific communicative situation, but also a specific country – Ukraine, and a specific historical time – the ongoing war. Moreover, the comparison of two opposite

---

7 The original text is written in Russian and was translated by Nina Kossman.

events ("carnival" vs. "war") marks a highly grotesque dimension of the text, emphasising destruction not only at the material, but also at the cultural and communication levels. The text presents and is written in the form of an indirect dialogue between two persons who cannot understand each other. They discuss the same things, like "masks," but employ different meanings. The terms "carnival mask" and "military mask," or "balaclava helmet" evoke different visual images of two masks and different sentiments in the reader: the joy of the holiday and the horror of the war. Using this grotesque dimension, the poet draws the reader's attention to the misunderstanding between communicants, presented in the form of a dialogue where interlocutors cannot come to a mutual understanding.

Another issue that became the focus of Ukrainian poets' self-reflection is the lack of understanding between people speaking in different languages, who can have common pro-Ukrainian interests, but cannot engage in a dialogue. The interactive poem "Dear Ukraine" with the subtitle "A global community poem" by Julia Kolchinsky Dasbach offers the opportunity for people to communicate with each other as part of a "poetic community." Kolchinsky Dasbach comments on the idea of the project as a platform, where one can submit a text to express involvement in the anti-war movement: "We believe poetry and the arts can be an essential way to respond to trauma, make meaning, and connect communities across languages and borders." (Kolchinsky Dasbach 2022) The poem is recorded in three languages (English, Ukrainian, and Russian), so readers with the knowledge of these languages can enter a poetic dialogue by clicking on the link with their native language. This digital project is open to further poetic comments and allows for every poet supporting Ukraine to share their voices in a feedback mode. In Kolchinsky Dasbach's poem "Dear Ukraine" the discursive marker "even" emphasises an indication of a specific location of the subject, denoting a referent known to the addressee, namely Ukraine: "Even here, they soak the earth." In addition, the "here" expresses a metatextual meaning, that is, "in this song": "Take shelter, if only in this / song and soil, if only / for a moment, take shelter here." (Kolchinsky Dasbach 2022).

The metatextual use of "here" in the poem "Russian Warship, Go Fuck Yourself" (2022) by Danyil Zadorozhny signals several deictic shifts: from the poetic communicative situation in which the subject finds him/herself, to another alternative communicative situation presented in the form of a video recording of Russian prisoners of war: "Watch the video of Russian prisoners of war / saying on camera that they didn't know where and why they were sent. That they are not welcome here and have no need for this war / to happen." (Zadorozhnyi 2022) Importantly, the poem indexes the markers of Russian invasion through visual modes and technological media ("photographs," "camera") describing them as visual pictures rather than real people, such as "photographs of the bodies of their dead soldiers." The first deictic shift is from the indefinite pronoun "where" to the demonstrative "here." However, several grammatical functions and pragmatic perspectives are hidden within the "here" itself. The "here" corresponds to two deictic centres at a time. Firstly, to the point at which the soldiers found themselves against their own will: "They are asking their / mothers to please bring them back." (Zadorozhnyi 2022) Secondly, to a distant point of presence of the poetic subject – his homeland, Ukraine, in which he would like to be, but which he had to leave. In this case, the spatial deictic "here," which implicitly includes both proximal and distal deictic positions, "introduces issues about spatial, temporal and affective distance and proximity" and renders the idea of "othering," to use a term by Heather Dubrow (2015, 63). "Othering" here has different meanings depending on the subject (persona) of perception: it marks the poet's 'homeland' which is far away, but the text allows to zoom it in with the help of homonymy of spatial and discursive meanings. The "here" also has an opposite meaning: Russian soldiers are physically located at the "here" point, but this space is zoomed-out by them as they feel themselves as "others," who got here against their will.

The use of the deictic marker "here" in contemporary anti-war poetic texts reflects an attitude towards increasing definite reference in the poetic statement. "Here" acquires a communicative meaning, indicating a position in space or time relative to the deictic centre, including both subjective and historical parameters. The specific functioning of deictic "here" in anti-war poetry indicates, firstly, a dichotomy of a movement between a "close" home and forced removal from it. Secondly, "here" takes on a metatextual function, when the meaning of war shifts from the remote category to the point 'here-and-now' of the subject, becoming a part of his/her personal communicative space and an element of discourse deixis – the "here" of the poetic text. Thirdly, the deictic "here" acquires a new meaning according to new media as a (non-)site position of the subject on the Internet (off the page): It can signify 'everywhere' and 'nowhere' at the same time. The idea of the subject's remote presence in digital media can be compared with the technological affordance of 'telepresence,' allowing a person to go beyond any space limitations and overcome the basic oppositions of 'local – distant,' 'material – virtual,' and 'human – digital.' Performing this function, discursive and spatial deixis also serve as a trigger to involve the addressee in the interaction, which is carried out due to shifts between the categories of verbal and visual, personal and technological, local and distant, abstract and concrete, empirical and metatextual.

Conclusion

Deixis in experimental poetry, thus, is a powerful mechanism for the subjectivation of the author, the lyrical persona, and the reader through poetic discourse and through specific texts. Numerous shifts in the field of personal deixis mark the physical coordinates of the subject's position and – through spatial design "on or off the page" – provoke the reader's active reconsideration of themselves in this world. The interfaces of the Internet era have suggested new modes of operating with subjectivity both in ordinary and poetic discourses. Poetry has been making productive use of the recent communicative transformations, which is especially the case with language-centred poetry, experimenting with the very materiality of the text's creation.

We have analysed the key types of deixis in experimental poetry over the twentieth and early twenty-first centuries: personal, spatial and discourse deixis. The tendency towards the visualisation of deictic markers signifies an increased attention of poets to the spatial design of a poetic text and their interest in experimenting with multimedia, especially in avant-garde and neo-avant-garde poetry of the twentieth century. The poetic discourse of the twenty-first century increasingly interacts with everyday language and digital user interfaces, which contributes to a more active involvement of the addressee in the communicative interaction. Both in avant-garde and contemporary poetry, visualised deixis becomes a specific tool of metareflection and is a participant in the formation of new strategies of artistic subjectivation. Among these strategies we distinguish the transition from interiorisation to exteriorisation within the poetic reference, the use of zooming in and zooming out mechanisms, and the combination of different positions in one deictic centre ('here,' 'everywhere,' and 'nowhere' at the same time). Deictics as linguistic subjectivisers significantly contribute to the enhanced role of the poem's visuality in avant-garde and contemporary poetry writing, typesetting and publishing practices.

References

Apresjan, Yury. "Дейксис в лексике и грамматике и наивная модель мира (Deixis in Vocabulary and Grammar and a Naive Model of the World)." *Избранные работы*. Т. 2 *(Selected Works.* Vol. 2). Moscow: Languages of Russian Culture, 1995. 629–650.

Bachmann-Medick, Doris. *Cultural Turns: New Orientations in the Study of Culture*. Berlin and Boston, MA: De Gruyter, 2016.

Benveniste, Émile. *Problems in General Linguistics*. Miami, FL: Univ. of Miami Press, 1971.

Bernstein, Charles. *Topsy-Turvy*. Chicago, IL and London: Univ. of Chicago Press, 2021.

Bragina, Olga. "Excerpts from 'Kyiv Diary'." Transl. Olga Livshin. 2022, https://lcb.de/diplomatique/excerpts-from-kyiv-diary/ (October 15, 2022).

Brugmann, Karl. *Die Demonstrativpronomina der indogermanischen Sprachen. Eine bedeutungsgeschichtliche Untersuchung*. Leipzig: Teubner, 1904.

Bryson, Norman. *Vision and Painting. The Logic of the Gaze*. New Haven, CT and London: Yale Univ. Press, 1983.

Bühler, Karl. *Theory of Language. The Representational Function of Language*. Amsterdam and Philadelphia, PA: John Benjamins Publishing, 2011.

Cage, John. "Lecture on Nothing." *Silence. Lectures and Writings*. Middletown, CT: Wesleyan Univ. Press, 1961. 109–127.

Coolidge, Clark. "Larry Eigner Notes." *The L=A=N=G=U=A=G=E Book: Poetics of the New*. Carbondale and Edwardsville, IL: South Illinois Univ. Press, 1984. 224–226.

cummings, e.e. *Complete Poems, 1904– 1962*. New York: Liveright, 2013.

Dagognet, François. *Faces, Surfaces, Interfaces*. Paris: Vrin, 1982.

Dubrow, Heather. *Deixis in the Early Modern English Lyric. Unsettling Spatial Anchors Like "Here," "This," "Come."* Basingstoke: Palgrave Macmillan, 2015.

Du Plessis, Rachel. *Drafts 1–38, Toll*. Middletown, CT: Wesleyan Univ. Press, 2001.

Ehlich, Konrad. "Anaphora and Deixis: Same, Similar or Different?" *Speech, Place, and Action. Studies in Deixis and Related Topics*. Ed. Robert J. Jarvella and Wolfgang Klein. New York: John Willey & Sons, 1982. 313–338.

Fillmore, Charles J. "Deictic Categories in Semantics of 'Come'." *Foundations of Language* 66 (1966): 219–227.

Flusser, Vilém. *Towards a Philosophy of Photography*. London: Reaktion Books, 1984.

Foulsham, Tom, and Neil Cohn. "Zooming In on Visual Narrative Comprehension." *Memory & Cognition* 49 (2021): 451–466.

Galloway, Alexander R. *The Interface Effect*. Cambridge: Polity Press, 2012.

Green, Keith. *A Study of Deixis in Relation to Lyric Poetry* [PhD thesis]. Univ. of Sheffield, 1992.

Grenier, Robert. *Sentences towards Birds*. Kensington, CA: L Publications, 1978.

Grutt, Valerio. *L'amuleto. Appunti sul potere di guarigione della poesia (The Amulet. Notes on the Healing Power of Poetry)*. Otranto: AnimaMundi, 2021.

Hill, Jane H., and Robert E. MacLaury. "The Terror of Montezuma: Aztec History, Vantage Theory and the Category of 'Person'." *Language and the Cognitive Construal of the World*. Ed. John R. Taylor and Robert E. MacLaury. Berlin and New York: De Gruyter, 1995. 277–330.

Kitt, Tony (Ed.). *Invasion. Ukrainian Poems about the War*. Transl. Anatoly Kudryavitsky. Dublin: SurVision Books, 2022.

Ivanov, Vyacheslav. "Категория определенности-неопределенности и шифтеры (The Category of Definitive-Indefinitive and Shifters)." *Категория определенности-неопределенности в славянских и балтийских языках (The Category of Definitive-Indefinitive in the Slavic and Baltic Languages)*. Moscow: Nauka, 1979. 90–117.

Ivashkiv, Roman. "Translating Ukrainian War Poetry into English: Why It Is Relevant." *East/West* 9.1 (2022): 37–65.

Jakobson, Roman. *Shifters, Verb Categories and the Russian Verb*. Cambridge, MA: Harvard Univ. Press, 1957.

Kelly, Martha M. F. "'Bleed – My Heart – Bleed.' Ukrainian Poems of War by Boris Khersonsky, Iya Kiva, and Vasyl Makhno." February 2022, https://lareviewofbooks.org/short-takes/ukrainian-poems-of-war-khersonsky-kiva-makhno/ (October 19, 2022).

Khersonskaya, Lyudmila. "Two Poems about the War." Transl. Nina Kossman. 2022, https://eastwestliteraryforum.com/rus/translations/ludmila-khersonskaya-two-poems-on-war/ (October 15, 2022).

Kobylko, Nataliia, Oleh Honcharuk, Larysa Horbolis, and Svitlana Antonovych. "Features of Modern Ukrainian Military Prose (on the Example of Bohdan Zholdak's Film Story 'Ukry' and Yevhen Polozhii's Novel 'Ilovaisk')." *Amazonia Investiga* 11.53 (2022): 92–100.

Kolchinsky Dasbach, Julia. "Dear Ukraine." 2022, https://dearukrainepoem.com/ (October 15, 2022).

Levinson, Stephen C. *Pragmatics*. Cambridge: Cambridge Univ. Press, 1983.

Lyons, John. *Semantics*. Vol. 2. Cambridge: Cambridge Univ. Press, 1977.

Lyons, John. *Linguistic Semantics. An Introduction*. Cambridge: Cambridge Univ. Press, 1995.

Manovich, Lev. *The Language of New Media*. Cambridge, MA: MIT Press, 2001.

National Translation Month. Special Feature: "Ukrainian Poetry in Translation Part I." 2022, https://nationaltranslationmonth.org/wp-content/uploads/2022/03/Ukrainian-Poetry-in-Translation_Part-I.pdf (January 19, 2023).

National Translation Month. Special Feature: "Ukrainian Poetry in Translation Part II." 2022, https://nationaltranslationmonth.org/wp-content/uploads/2022/03/Ukrainian-Poetry-in-Translation_Part-II.pdf (January 19, 2023).

Nekrasov, Vsevolod. *Стихи 1956–1983 (Verses 1956–1983)*. Vologda: Biblioteka Moskovskogo kontseptualizma Germana Titova, 2012.

Olson, Charles. "Projective Verse." *Poetry New York* 3 (1950): 13–22.

Perloff, Marjorie. *Poetry On & Off the Page. Essays for Emergent Occasions*. Evanston, IL: Northwestern Univ. Press, 1998.

Perloff, Marjorie. *Unoriginal Genius: Poetry by Other Means in the New Century*. Chicago, IL: Univ. of Chicago Press, 2010.

Proskurin, Sergey, and Vladimir Feshchenko. "Voice and Bodily Deixis as Manifestation of Performativity in Written Texts." *Semiotica* 227 (2019): 317–374.

Rubinstein, Lev. *Complete Catalogue of Comedic Novelties*. New York: Ugly Duckling Press, 2014.

Silliman, Ron. *The Alphabet*. Tuscaloosa, AL: The Univ. of Alabama Press, 2008.

Watten, Barrett. "Entry 40: Isolate flecks." March 23, 2020a, https://barrettwatten.net/2020/03/ (October 15, 2022).

Watten, Barrett. "Entry 42: Hello, Indiana!" December 25, 2020b, http://barrettwatten.net/tag/readings/ (October 15, 2022).

Watten, Barrett. *Notzeit (After Hannah Höch)*. Unpublished manuscript, 2020c.

Zadorozhnyi, Danyil, and Yuliya Charnyshova. "'One Heart Left for Us All': Poems from Ukraine." Transl. Yuliya Charnyshova and Elina Alter. 2022, https://lareviewofbooks.org/short-takes/poems-from-ukraine-charnyshova-zadorozhnyi/ (October 15, 2022).

Флаги (Flagi project). "Вслед за 'Notzeit' Барретта Уоттена: шесть поэтов об опыте изоляции (Following Barrett Watten's 'Notzeit': Six Poets on the Experience of Isolation)." *Носорог (Nosorog)* (2020): https://flagi.media/piece/203 (January 20, 2023).

Roberto Simanowski
Reading, Seeing, Clicking: Kinetic Concrete Poetry

Concrete poetry in print media

In literary history the connection between reading and seeing has always been present, though not always very well known.[1] Such a connection already existed in antiquity, in text that possessed a semantic surplus through the arrangement of its letters. In *Labyrinthgedichten* (labyrinth poems), the line of text wiggles across the paper as if walking a labyrinth, thus keeping this metaphor visually present alongside the message of the text. In *Figurengedichten* (figure poems), the arrangement of the text forms a specific figure, at first often a cross, in the Baroque period also secular figures such as a goblet as on the occasion of the wedding of a Bremen burgher couple in 1637 (cf. Simanowski 2005, 165). This poem reveals an early form of interactive literature that prompts the reader to turn either the page or the head to read. The deeper meaning, i.e., joke of this formal gimmick is that after turning the paper, one feels as dizzy as if one had already emptied a goblet full of wine. The philosophy behind this play with form, behind this shift of attention to typography, is to liberate the word from its merely representational, signifying function. In literature the physicality of language, its graphic aspect, for instance, usually plays no role and is even rejected as undermining the authority of the text. In this case, however, the visual side of the word is used as an additional layer of meaning. The word not only represents an object but it *presents* it on the visual level. The goblet is visible even before one starts reading.

After 1910 attention to the visual materiality of language received a new impetus, when Futurists like Filippo Tommaso Marinetti or Dadaists like Tristan Tzara or Kurt Schwitters carried out their typographic experiments. These experiments on the physical level of language came to an end with Surrealism, which used language only on the linguistic level. The typographic experiment was renewed in the 50s and 60s of the twentieth century, now under the title of concrete poetry. The unifying element of this worldwide literary movement, the only worldwide literary movement after the Second World War, was that the texts could not be read aloud for their design would have been lost in orality. The texts

---

[1] This article is a slightly modified and updated English version of "Lesen, Sehen, Klicken: Die Kinetisierung konkreter Poesie" (Simanowski 2005, 161–177).

∂ Open Access. © 2023 the author(s), published by De Gruyter. [CC BY-NC-ND] This work is licensed under the Creative Commons Attribution-NonCommercial-NoDerivatives 4.0 International License.
https://doi.org/10.1515/9783111299334-004

are visual texts or, as Franz Mon, one of the main representatives of concrete poetry, called them in an essay, "poetry of the surface" (cf. Mon 1994).[2]

A very famous example is Reinhard Döhl's "Apfel" ("Apple") from 1965 – here the repetition of the word "apple" forms an apple, with the punchline that the word "worm" is hidden in-between. An equally famous example is Eugen Gomringer's text "Schweigen" ("Silence") from 1954 – here several instances of the word "schweigen" are placed horizontally and vertically next to each other, with the word saliently missing in the centre of the text block. This blank space is the message of the arrangement for which all the words around it are only a preparation. It is the missing word "silence" that conveys that silence is not expressed in its naming but only in the absence of language. The statement lies not in the semantic sense between the lines but in the graphic sense between the words. However, the representative function of the word is by no means abandoned here in favour of a purely visual presentation. The irony of Gomringer's "Schweigen" lies in the fact that it utters the real value of silence rather through redundancy, for the gap around the missed word does not require the first and the last line to be understood or even read.

```
silence silence silence
silence silence silence
silence         silence
silence silence silence
silence silence silence
```
(Gomringer 1954; see Bann 1967)

The message is seen rather than read, but this presupposes a preceding reading of the surrounding words. This is precisely the meaning of the term concrete poetry: concrete is the descriptive or the graphic, in contrast to the abstraction of a word. Concrete poetry is about the relationship between the visible form and the signifying substance of the word; it is visual not because it uses images, but because it adds the visual gestures of the words to their phonetic and semantic ones as a complement, by extension or negation. Intermediality does not consist in the change of media but in the change of the media-typical act of reception, in this case from the semiotic system of reading, typical of literature, to the system of viewing, typical of the visual arts.

---

[2] For important collections of concrete poetry see Spoerri 1957; Bann 1967; Williams 1967; Solt and Barnstone 1968; Gomringer 1972. For a historical overview of experimental literature as a whole see Dencker 2002. Johanna Drucker refers to Ilia Zdanevichs *Poetry of Unknown Words* of 1949 as a "first exhaustive anthology of concrete and experimental typology" (Drucker 1994, 227).

Concrete poetry in digital media

In the realm of digital media, concrete poetry gains two further levels of expression. While in classical concrete poetry the graphic quality of the words becomes the constitutive element of the text alongside the linguistic one, in digital media time as well as interaction also generate additional meaning. The text can appear, move, disappear, and it can do so because of an action by the reader. In such a context, the worm can finally eat the apple as in Johannes Auer's digitised adaptation "worm applepie for doehl": The worm eats its way through the fruit, eradicating the linguistic signifier along with the visual one – and since digital technology has no concept of end or death, the worm can eat the apple over and over again.[3]

The works of the Brazilian poet Augusto de Campos and the Argentinean artist Ana María Uribe are examples of the personal continuity of experiments in concrete poetry in analogue and digital media. Campos' *poema bomba* (1983–1997) realises the explosion, which was first concretised by scattered letters on paper and in the digital medium finally by means of sound and movement;[4] Uribe, after her print works, which she calls "Typoem," developed digital works, which she calls "Anipoem" – animated poem – and which combine an elegant objectivity with refreshing humour such as the *Gimnasia* pieces of 1998. In them the circular substitution of the letters P and R, or of the letters I, T, Y, V, X with the respective following letter creates an association with gymnastic exercises.[5] An equally elegant – though more complicated – programmed example of the behaviour of text in time is "A Fine View" from David Knoebel's *Click Poetry*.[6] It is a short text about a roofer's fall, which gradually unwinds from a tangle of words – like the cigarette's smoke the roofer lights at the height of their workplace – and which comes towards the reader with increasing speed and size – like the abyss towards the falling.

While this form of kinetic concrete poetry is reminiscent of the text films or video and TV poetry of the late 1960s and early 1970s, the further development of concrete poetry to an interactive relationship with the reader exits the cinema situation again. An example of this is Urs Schreiber's "Das Epos der Maschine" ("The Epic of the Machine"),[7] winner of the Arte Liter@turwettbewerb in 2000, a competition of digital literature. In this elaborately programmed, technology-

---

[3] http://auer.netzliteratur.net/worm/applepie.htm.
[4] https://artsandculture.google.com/asset/poema-bomba/vgHdr0QTZQrFbg?hl=de and https://www.youtube.com/watch?v=h3gzuQ-3R94.
[5] https://amuribe.tripod.com/gimnasia3.html and https://amuribe.tripod.com/gimnasia.html.
[6] http://home.ptd.net/~clkpoet/fineview/fineview.html.
[7] http://kunst.im.internett.de/epos-der-maschine.

critical work, the question of the meaning and function of technology builds up word by word in the form of a question mark, the dot of which is the word "truth." While the other words move slightly back and forth, "truth" stands as rigidly as described in the text. Clicking on it causes all the words to disappear behind it, as if they were seeking refuge there or as if truth was devouring that by which it is questioned. No matter how one reads this disappearance, it does not last long. If one now moves the mouse, "truth" follows the cursor, followed by those other words that emerge again in the pull of gravity and remain on the heels of "truth," wherever it escapes. If the mouse stops, all words disappear again behind "truth." Once questions have been raised – a possible interpretation – they can no longer simply be erased, provided there is movement in the discourse. That this lies in the hands of the users, is the realisation that literally results from the direct interaction of the users with the work.

The audiovisual rollover love poem "YATOO" (2001) by the Viennese net artists Ursula Hentschläger and Zelko Wiener also relies entirely on the action of the user. This piece initially appears as a pentagonal star, which, when the user moves the mouse over its parts, sounds the words of a love poem spoken by a woman and a man. As the parts of the star are activated by mouse contact, they simultaneously change their shape (Fig. 7). One soon notices that the exact following of the programmed sequence not only leads to a correct sentence – the first sentence of the man clarifies the initials of the title: *You are the only one* – but also always to a new geometrical harmony. The verses seem simplistic and schematic and certainly do not belong to the finest moments of English-language poetry. This results in part from the poetics of constraint, to which each verse is subjected insofar as it must convey its message in exactly five words. However, the poetics of constraint – this is new and is what actually makes the work interesting – not only affects the process of creation but also the process of perception: If the recipients lack a certain dexterity in clicking on the corresponding parts, while at the same time avoiding touching the other parts, all one gets is a chaos of acoustic and visual signs.

The superimposition of the graphics and the sound files, which are activated by touch, results in an incalculable sequence on different verse levels instead of a dialogue between woman and man. It is precisely this confusion that is the point here. The superimposition of the sound files, the incalculability that has occurred, seems like a commentary on the title's declaration of unconditionality. It seems to signify scepticism or is at least an indication that in the long run, mutual understanding only works under certain conditions – though it is open to the recipient to perceive the very chaos as a refreshment and possibly also as a liberation from old communicative tracks. The condition to be observed and complied with in the present case is precise navigation; the constraint aspect thus itself becomes part of the message.

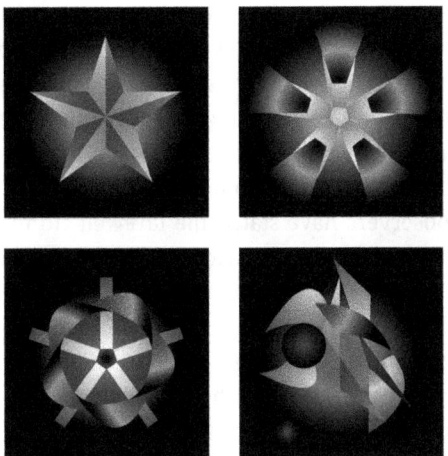

Fig. 7: Snapshots from "YATOO" by Zeitgenossen (Ursula Hentschläger and Zelko Wiener). 2001.

These examples may suffice to give a first impression of kinetic concrete poetry in the digital medium. This inventory is now replenished by some reflections on the poetology of concrete poetry in the print medium and in digital media.

Decoration and message

Experimental poetry – to which concrete poetry is assigned – has sometimes been reproached for its opaque language, which makes it a private matter and thus seems unsuitable to have an effect on the consciousness of the reader, and therefore unsuitable for political intervention. The counter-argument is that the focus on the material of the text also entails a critical reflection on language and its use, which leads to a sensitisation that works against any instrumentalisation of language (cf. Einhorn 1978, 1–4). "Through the isolation of words from the usual 'flow' of language," says Gisela Dischner, "the self-evident of the language habit suddenly appears new, questionable, incomprehensible; the intended language habits are broken. The aesthetic not taking for granted of the self-evident could be a model for the social not taking for granted of the usual, 'normal'." (Dischner 1978, 38; own translation) Johanna Drucker notes a similar intention for the typographic experiments of Dadaism: "[it] was concerned with opposing the established social order through subverting the dominant conventions of the rules of representation." (Drucker 1994, 65) In this respect, concrete poetry is enlightenment and some see its revolutionary content precisely in this dismantling play with the hierarchically alienated language system (cf. Bezzel 1978, 35). Can a similar pathos be found in kinetic concrete poetry?

One should first note that concrete poetry and its digital continuation are not only separated by media, but also by decades of social development. Since the thematisation of the postmodern condition, disillusionment set in with regard to such liberation projects. In addition, with the passing of the *grand narratives*, the emphatic message in literature was basically replaced by reflection on the preconditions of writing, i.e., the creation of messages, or by noncommittal everyday depiction. Regarding visual arts, too, observers have stated the farewell "to the holy seriousness of utopian designs, to ideologies of world improvement and claims of effect on society as a whole" (Wick 1999, 11; own translation) and declared a trend towards the sensual and playful. The aesthetic consequence of this cultural disposition is obvious: where no emphatic message seems to be possible anymore, the external comes to the fore. This was already the case with Mannerism, which is a crisis phenomenon in a similar manner to postmodernism. For this reason, Umberto Eco, in his *Postscript to the Name of the Rose*, wonders "if postmodernism is not the modern name for mannerism as a metahistorical category" (Eco 1984, 66).

As far as current cultural trends are concerned, Andrew Darley, in his study *Visual Digital Culture*, notes a "shift away from prior modes of spectator experience based on symbolic concerns (and 'interpretative models') towards recipients who are seeking intensities of direct sensual stimulation" (Darley 2000, 3). He also sees audiences "in pursuit of the ornamental and the decorative, modes of embellishment, the amazing and the breathtaking, the nuances of the staged effect and the virtuoso moment, the thrill of vertigo or the *agôn* of competition." (Darley 2000, 169) According to Darley, the domination of technology and image over content and meaning – also manifested in computer-generated films such as *Star Wars* (1977), *Total Recall* (1990), and *Terminator 2: Judgment Day* (1991) – leads to a "culture of the depthless image" (Darley 2000, 192). Darley speaks of films, MTV and computer games but the tendency towards the visual and sensual can also be observed in print media. One thinks of the designer David Carson, who uses letters only as ornaments which are difficult to decipher – they basically appear as images – and remodels information as an aesthetic event in design that has been called "post-alphabetic text" (Kirschenbaum 2000). As far as written texts in multimedia contexts are concerned, some speak of a replacement of the classical security of the strict word. It is substituted by a restless dynamic, the endless abundance of images, and described as the replacement of "Protestant enlightenment" by "Catholic emotion" (cf. Schmitz 1997, 144; own translation).

Thrown into this context of shifting attention to surface effects, it is hardly surprising that the digital version of concrete poetry rarely shows its Enlightenment heritage with regard to the meaningful reflection of its materiality. Very often it remains at the level of an interesting effect or witty conceit, very often it does not even presume to catch up semantically with the effect, but simply flexes its 'technical muscles.' In this case – as with Mannerism – language celebrates itself. In the digital realm language is, of course, no longer just the word or the image, but it is the digital code beneath the screen surface that is responsible for the appearance of word and image in space and time and in the interaction with the audience. And if code is the language, it is no wonder that the new type of artist is the "software artist," as Lev Manovich notes in his essay "Generation Flash." This software artist, according to Manovich, turns to the language of abstraction and modernist design, "to get away from figuration in general, and cinematographic language of commercial media in particular. Instead of photographs and clips of films and TV, we get lines and abstract compositions." (Manovich 2002a, 6) The announced retreat from the language of commercial media seems to take back the transformation of artists into designers that, in the 1920s, helped "[to change] the formal radicality of early modernism into the seamless instrument of corporate capitalist enterprise." (Drucker 1994, 238) However, that Generation Flash does not waste its energy on media critique, as Manovich further notes, weakens such an assumption:

> This is the new generation that emerged in the 1990s. In contrast to visual and media artists of the 1960s–1980s, whose main target was media – ads, cinema, television – the new generation does not waste its energy on media critique. Instead of bashing commercial media environment, it creates its own: Web sites, mixes, software tools, furniture, cloves, digital video, Flash / Shockwave animations and interactives. (Manovich 2002a, 7)

Another argument against such an assumption is the fact that the non-cinematic Flash aesthetic (which was ground-breaking in the 1990s and 2000s) was basically very well suited to serve as the language of a new, rapidly commercialised medium. It should be considered that most software artists also work as designers and create commercial products anyway, such as online games, web toys and multiuser environments.

One example is the group of designers, artists, and musicians Squid S o u p, whose piece "Untitled" – a navigable 3-D space made of transparent text walls – represents software art under the banner of the non-figurative and at the same time of "post-alphabetic texts" (see my review with screenshots in Simanowski 2001). Both, the visualised letters and the mumbled, barely comprehensible words randomly sampled from a book, represent the transformation of text into design and sound. A visitor of this project is visually and acoustically drawn into the project and feels the "feeling of being somewhere," that Squid S o u p states as the intention of their project. It is not about a deeper meaning, hidden between the lines, only recognisable after a long study and repeated reading, it is about fascination in itself (Fig. 8).

Fig. 8: Snapshot from "Untitled" by Squid S o u p. 2001.

An example, which almost paradigmatically embodies the development of concrete poetry, is "Enigma n" by the Canadian programmer and net artist Jim Andrews. "Enigma n" was first developed in 1998 as an anagrammatic play with the word "meaning," of which an updated version from 2022 is available (Fig. 9). In the print form of concrete poetry, the transformation of meaning through letter rotation could perhaps have been made clear in the form of horizontal and vertical rows, which would, of course, soon have revealed the anagrammatic excess of the letter n. In Andrews' digital form, the message is conveyed through the constant shifting of letters, with the title – "Enigma n" – and the source and target word – *meaning* – forming the lexemic bracket. The ongoing rearrangement of the letters simultaneously reintegrates the surplus letter n, for in this way meaning is not only enigma, but indeed n-enigmas. Andrews calls this work "a philosophical music & poetry toy for poets, musicians & philosophers from the age of 7 up." (Andrews 2022 [1998]) This self-description emphasises the play character of the piece, which, due to the necessary clicking actions of the audience, goes far beyond the play character of concrete poetry in the print medium.

In 2002, Andrews presented an audiovisual development of the piece, which perhaps does not necessarily increase the play character of the piece, but certainly its sensual effect. In "Enigma n^2," the initial word "meaning" is no longer shown in rearranged form but spoken, with the programme randomly selecting the starting point of the underlying sound line and determining the duration and number of repetitions of the activated section (cf. Andrews 2002). As Andrews explained in an email to me on November 12, 2002:

> The sound itself starts out with the word 'meaning' backwards and then there are two normal repetitions of the word 'meaning.' The program randomly selects a starting point in the sound and a random end point (after the start point). And it selects a random number of times between 1 and 6 to repeat the playing of that segment.

In another email from November 9, 2002 Andrews stated that he considers "Enigma n^2" "as a kind of continuation of "Enigma n" in that it is concerned with the enigma of meaning." However, whereas "Enigma n" required contemplating the deconstruction one sees on the screen, "Enigma n^2" is a work whose suggestive singsong, similar to "Untitled" by Squid S o u p, puts the listener in a hypnotic mood and pushes the original philosophical intent of the anagrammatic game into the background. Andrews described this further as "[a] kind of strange generative/interactive sound poetry/music. I have my stereo hooked up to my computer, so my computer speakers are my stereo's speakers. I play it sometimes (fairly loudly) for a few minutes to hear if I can figure out more about that sort of music." (Email from November 9, 2002) Concrete poetry has passed over into music, the purposeful play with form ends in sensation rather than beginning an intellectual process of material reflection.

Fig. 9: Screenshots from "Enigma n" and "Enigma n^{2022}" by Jim Andrews. 2022 [1998].

Erotics of art

Concrete poetry is apparently undergoing the same shift from "symbolic concerns" towards "intensities of direct sensual stimulation" (Darley 2000, 3) that Darley states for visual digital aesthetics. Behind this, on the side of production as well as reception, lies a condition of the technical that could be critically described as an expression of digital kitsch. It is based on Ludwig Giesz's definition of kitsch as the end of any distance between I and the object in favour of a feeling of fusion and surrender to the object (cf. Giesz 1954, 407). Such a take of course results from an academic perspective that is obsessed with meaning and dismisses phenomena such as ornament and spectacle as inferior. Darley rightly questions such an attitude: "Is ornamentation, style, spectacle, giddiness really aesthetically inferior or, rather, just different (other) from established motions of literary, classical modern art? Is an aesthetic without depth necessarily an impoverished aesthetic, or is it rather, another kind of aesthetic – misunderstood and undervalued as such?" (Darley 2000, 6) Darley can draw on Susan Sontag, who noted as early as 1964 in her famous essay "Against Interpretation":

> In a culture whose already classical dilemma is the hypertrophy of the intellect at the expense of energy and sensual capability, interpretation is the revenge of the intellect upon art. Even more. It is the revenge of the intellect upon the world. To interpret is to impoverish, to deplete the world – in order to set up a shadow world of 'meanings' (Sontag 1966, 7).

Sontag recommends an increased interest for the form in art and ends her essay with the famous line: "In place of a hermeneutics we need an erotics of art." (Sontag 1966, 14) Similarly, Darley also recommends approaching the "'poetics' of surface play and sensation" (Darley 2000, 193) openly and without any reservations based in cultural pessimism. With this call Darley can also draw on art history, for in a way the aesthetics of the sensual, the culture of the depthless image is reminiscent of the debate in formal aesthetics at the beginning of the twentieth century. At the time the visual sign was thought of in terms of its self-valence and called for to be freed from its meaning-bearing role to a pure visibility (for an international context of this debate see Drucker 1994; Wiesing 1997).

Does "Enigma n^2" – and especially those examples of software art that are consciously oriented towards "surface play and sensation" – signify a return to formal aesthetics? Is the autonomous technical effect that only refers to itself the contemporary equivalent of the principle of pure visibility? Does the aesthetic of "surface play" and "sensation" correspond exactly to the "event society" as the end of the twentieth century has been described (cf. Schulze 1993) and to its technological achievements? In this context, one may also ask whether one should not rather demand works that still invest and practice interpretative energy, against the sell-out of meaning. Reception theory and constructivism have taught us that the meaning of an artwork does not lie in the hand of the artist (alone) but (also) depends on the approach of the audience to the work. The production of meaning takes place in the specific media constellation of the present, which, not only with regard to digital media, is characterised by impatience and a lack of willingness to a deeper intellectual engagement with the work.

One example of the fact that even authors with more serious intentions have to reckon with this kind of reception is Urs Schreiber's "The Epic of the Machine." Schreiber quite aptly compares the reading of his hypertext in the introduction to diving, swimming, and rummaging. He also promises in an interview that those who "use the mouse pointer with interested patience [. . .] will not only encounter a spectacle of the surface but also one in the head" (Simanowski and Schreiber

2000, 4; own translation). However, as a reader attests, the encounter with kinetic concrete poetry can very well omit any closer reading: "ideal to plunge web designers into admiration and depression" stated an enthusiastic comment, and: "the handling of typeface and typography alone! I don't need to read any more! how words slide into each other and circle and appear and disappear and and and!"[8] It seems that the media constellation itself induces this attitude of surface. Digital media, characterised by the gesture of click activity and the ideal of instant access, favour curiosity about what is promised behind the link at the expense of curiosity about what is hidden between the signs.

This notion from almost twenty years ago has been confirmed by later digital artworks that employ text. One example is *bit.fall* by Julius Popp from 2006. In this roughly two-meter high and five-meter wide installation, hundreds of valves release drops of water so that they form letters which horizontally form words.[9] The words are taken from Internet announcements of world events and have a visual life of only two or three seconds. As Popp himself said, this "waterfall of letters" was supposed to express the fleeting nature of what we think is important (cf. Popp in Bit.Fall 2006). Of course, the irony is that the words disappear before they even have truly appeared. From the very beginning, they are not read as meaningful series of letters but are rather viewed as a fascinating phenomenon. We do not read words made of water. We touch them, we stick our arms into them, we wet our brows with them and we jump through them. Words of water can also be enjoyed from the rear. *bit.fall* invites people to encounter text on a visual actionist level. Meaning plays no role in this encounter. The text does not want to be decoded, just seen (for an extensive discussion of *bit.fall* see Simanowski 2012, 194–198).

Another, more recent example, is Refik Anadol's data sculpture *Archive Dreaming* (2017) that translates hundreds of thousands of cultural documents from an open source library in Istanbul into an immersive architectural space.[10] Thus, texts and images that usually require attention and understanding are turned into an immersive experience, if not into ambient art equipped to embellish airports, malls, or the entrance hall of an office building. When Anadol states: „Research in artificial intelligence is growing every day, leaving us with the feeling of being plugged into a system that is bigger and more knowledgeable than ourselves," (Anadol 2023) one suspects that the deeper meaning of this shift from "symbolic concerns" towards "intensities of direct sensual stimulation," to apply Darley's words

---

8 This comment on the Internet Literatur *Webring* "bla" is no longer online.
9 https://www.youtube.com/watch?v=ygQHj1W0PPM.
10 https://refikanadol.com/works/archive-dreaming.

again, is the beautification and sublimation of data. It is the transfer of "invisible and 'messy' phenomena [. . .] into ordered and harmonious geometric figures" (Manovich 2002b), as Lev Manovich described the visualisation of data as early as in 2002. It is beauty beyond meaning (for a discussion of digital art as sublimation with reference to Jean-François Lyotard and Immanuel Kant see Simanowski 2011, Ch. 5).

Examples such as "A Fine View," "YATOO" or "Der Epos der Maschine" have shown that kinetic concrete poetry can contain effects that are heavy with meaning. These effects are based on the semantic levels of time and interaction that concrete poetry gains through the underlying technology in the digital medium. In terms of both generating and perceiving the artwork, however, there is a clearly discernible tendency that technology as such will be placed at the centre of the action, as works like *bit.fall* and *Archive Dreaming* illustrate. The possible historical points of contact of this tendency towards "pure visibility" and sensation within formal aesthetics have been addressed, as have the obvious cultural-critical objections. The aesthetic and social consequences of this tendency are to be discussed elsewhere and beyond the digital media. One question of this discussion will be which side the producers of kinetic concrete poetry will take – and which side the audience will expect them to take. I discuss the aesthetic and social consequences as well as the background of this tendency with special regard to the "Farewell of Interpretation" and the shift from a culture of meaning towards a culture of presence proposed by Hans Ulrich Gumbrecht in the "Introduction" and "Epilogue" of my study *Digital Art and Meaning* (Simanowski 2011, 1–26; 208–230).

References

Anadol, Refik. *Archive Dreaming*. 2017, https://refikanadol.com/works/archive-dreaming (March 8, 2023).
Anadol, Refik. "Art in the Age of Machine Intelligence," https://www.ted.com/talks/refik (March 8, 2023).
Andrews, Jim. "Enigma n^{2022}." 2022 [1998], https://enigman.vispo.com/ (March 8, 2023).
Andrews, Jim. "Enigma n^2." 2002, http://www.vispo.com//animisms/enigman2/index.htm (March 8, 2023).
Auer, Johannes. "worm applepie for doehl." 1997, http://auer.netzliteratur.net/worm/applepie.htm (March 8, 2023).
Bann, Stephen (Ed.). *Concrete Poetry. An International Anthology*. London: London Magazin Editions, 1967.
Bezzel, Chris. "dichtung und revolution." *Konkrete Poesie I. Experimentelle und konkrete Poesie*. text + kritik 25. Ed. Heinz Ludwig Arnold and Nicolaus Einhorn. Munich: Boorberg, 1978. 35–36.
Bit.Fall – Discovery Channel Short Film. 2006, https://www.youtube.com/watch?v=AICq53U3dl8 (March 8, 2023).
Campos, Auguste de. *poema bomba*. 1983, https://artsandculture.google.com/asset/poema-bomba/vgHdr0QTZQrFbg?hl=de (March 8, 2023).

Campos, Auguste de, and Cid Campos. "Poema-bomba." *Poesia É Risco*. 1987, https://www.youtube.com/watch?v=h3gzuQ-3R94 (March 8, 2023).

Darley, Andrew. *Visual Digital Culture. Surface Play and Spectacle in New Media Genres*. London and New York: Routledge, 2000.

Dencker, Klaus Peter (Ed.). *Poetische Sprachspiele. Vom Mittelalter bis zur Gegenwart*. Stuttgart: Reclam, 2002.

Dischner, Gisela. "Konkrete Kunst und Gesellschaft." *Konkrete Poesie I. Experimentelle und konkrete Poesie*. text + kritik 25. Ed. Heinz Ludwig Arnold and Nicolaus Einhorn. Munich: Boorberg, 1978. 37–41.

Drucker, Johanna. *The Visible Word. Experimental Typography and Modern Art, 1909–1923*. Chicago, IL and London: Univ. of Chicago Press, 1994.

Eco, Umberto. *Postscript to the Name of the Rose*. San Diego, CA: Harcourt, 1984.

Einhorn, Nicolaus. "Zeigen was gezeigt wird." *Konkrete Poesie I. Experimentelle und konkrete Poesie*. text + kritik 25. Ed. Heinz Ludwig Arnold and Nicolaus Einhorn. Munich: Boorberg, 1978. 1–4.

Giesz, Ludwig. "Was ist Kitsch." *Deutsche Literatur im Zwanzigsten Jahrhundert. Gestalten und Strukturen*. Ed. Hermann Friedmann and Otto Mann. Heidelberg: Rothe, 1954. 405–418.

Gomringer, Eugen (Ed.). *konkrete poesie. deutschsprachige autoren*. Stuttgart: Reclam, 1972.

Hentschläger, Ursula, and Zelko Wiener. "YATOO." 2001, [the poem's website is no longer active].

Kirschenbaum, Matthew G. "The Other End of Print: David Carson, Graphic Design, and the Aesthetics of Media." 2000, http://web.mit.edu/comm-forum/legacy/papers/kirsch.html (March 8, 2023).

Knoebel, David. "A Fine View." 2000–, http://home.ptd.net/~clkpoet/fineview/fineview.html (March 8, 2023).

Manovich, Lev. "Generation Flash." 2002a, http://manovich.net/content/04-projects/038-generation-flash/35_article_2002.pdf (March 8, 2023).

Manovich, Lev. "The Anti-Sublime Ideal in Data Art." 2002b, https://silo.tips/download/lev-manovich-the-anti-sublime-ideal-in-data-art (March 8, 2023).

Mon, Franz. "Zur Poesie der Fläche." *Gesammelte Texte 1. Essays*. Berlin: Janus Press 1994. 77–80.

Popp, Julius. *bit.fall*. [video documentation of the installation at MOMA NY] 2008, https://www.youtube.com/watch?v=ygQHj1W0PPM (March 8, 2023).

Schmitz, Ulrich. "Schriftliche Texte in multimedialen Kontexten." *Sprachwandel durch Computer*. Ed. Rüdiger Weingarten. Opladen: Westdeutscher Verlag, 1997. 131–158.

Schreiber, Urs. "Das Epos der Maschine." 2000, http://kunst.im.internett.de/epos-der-maschine (March 8, 2023).

Schulze, Gerhard. *Die Erlebnisgesellschaft. Kultursoziologie der Gegenwart*. Frankfurt a. M. and New York: Campus, 1993.

Simanowski, Roberto. "Text as Event: Calm Technology and Invisible Information as Subject of Digital Arts." *Throughout. Art and Culture Emerging with Ubiquitous Computing*. Ed. Ulrik Ekman. Cambridge, MA: MIT Press, 2012. 191–204.

Simanowski, Roberto. *Digital Art and Meaning. Reading Kinetic Poetry, Text Machines, Mapping Art, and Interactive Installations*. Minneapolis, MN and London: Univ. of Minnesota Press, 2011.

Simanowski, Roberto. "Lesen, Sehen, Klicken: Die Kinetisierung konkreter Poesie." *Literarität und Digitalität. Zur Zukunft der Literatur*. Ed. Simone Winko and Harro Segeberg. Munich: Fink, 2005. 161–177.

Simanowski, Roberto. "Squid S o u p: 'Untitled': Wände aus Text und Sound." *Dichtung Digital. Journal für Kunst und Kultur digitaler Medien* 3.19 (2001): 1–4. https://doi.org/10.25969/mediarep/17475 (March 8, 2023).

Simanowski, Roberto, and Urs Schreiber. "Das Epos der Maschine: Interview mit Urs Schreiber." *Dichtung Digital. Journal für Kunst und Kultur digitaler Medien* 2.13 (2000): 1–9. https://doi.org/10.25969/mediarep/17386 (March 8, 2023).

Solt, Mary Ellen, and Willis Barnstone (Ed.). *Concrete Poetry. A World View*. Bloomington, IN: Indiana Univ. Press, 1968.

Sontag, Susan. *Against Interpretation and Other Essays*. New York: Noonday Press, 1966.

Spoerri, Daniel (Ed.). *Kleine Anthologie konkreter Dichtung*. Darmstadt: Self-publishing, 1957.

Uribe, Ana María. "Gimnasia." 1998, https://amuribe.tripod.com/gimnasia.html (March 8, 2023).

Uribe, Ana María. "Gimnasia 3." 1998, https://amuribe.tripod.com/gimnasia3.html (March 8, 2023).

Wick, Rainer K. "Im Rückspiegel. Vorbemerkungen zum historischen Verhältnis von Kunst und Design." *Global Fun. Kunst und Design von Mondrian, Gehry, Versace and Friends*. Exhibition catalogue. Ed. Susanne Anne. Ostfildern: Cantz, 1999. 11–47.

Wiesing, Lambert. *Die Sichtbarkeit des Bildes. Geschichte und Perspektiven der formalen Ästhetik*. Reinbek: Rowohlt, 1997.

Williams, Emmet (Ed.). *Anthology of Concrete Poetry*. New York: Something Else Press, 1967.

Heinz Drügh

Von Überraschungseiern, Gummibärchen und anderem Eye Candy – Überlegungen zur gegenwärtigen Lyrik und den kommodifizierten Bildern

> auch in unsern so unpoetischen Tagen
> (Friedrich Schiller: „Über Bürgers Gedichte")

Nach einer zentralen Bestimmung aus Kants *Kritik der Urteilskraft* funktioniert das Ästhetische als ein *subjektiv Allgemeines*. Mit dieser paradox klingenden Formulierung begreift Kant die Spezifik des Ästhetischen: die Vermittlung höchsteigener und möglicherweise idiosynkratischer Subjektivität mit einer Gemeinschaft von Anderen, und dies in einer Gesellschaft, die sich am Ende des 18. Jahrhunderts erst auf den Schritten hin zu einer demokratischen Öffentlichkeit befindet. Es geht Kant darum, in seinem Modell des Ästhetischen die drei sehr unterschiedlichen Vermögen, Sinnlichkeit, Gefühl und Intellekt, in ein Spiel zu versetzen, eine spezifische Mixtur aus genauem Hinhören und -sehen und dem, was wir dabei empfinden, sowie dem, was wir dabei denken. Und das alles auch noch so, dass dabei das Bedürfnis entsteht, sich mit anderen darüber auszutauschen, also höchst individuelle Erlebnisse mit anderen in einer Gemeinschaft zu kommunizieren, sie ihnen *anzusinnen* oder *zuzumuten*, so Kants sprechende Begriffe (vgl. Kant 1974 [1790], 124–131).

Wenn man sich diese anspruchsvolle Struktur noch einmal genauer vor Augen führt – ein einzelnes Selbst vermittelt seine Sinnlichkeit und seine Emotionen mit dem Intellekt und beansprucht, sich darüber mit einer Allgemeinheit auszutauschen – dann könnte man auf die Idee kommen, dass wir in goldenen Zeiten des Ästhetischen lebten. Denn was wäre Social Media mit ihrer Kultur der Memes anderes – wenn doch jede Userin ihre höchst idiosynkratischen Bilder, versehen mit *catchy* Textchen, mit bis vor wenigen Jahren unvorstellbar hoher, um nicht zu sagen *allgemeiner* Reichweite verbreiten kann, zum Liken wie zur Diskussion. Ist das nicht Ästhetik in Kant'scher Reinform? Dass wir über eine solche Engführung vielleicht lächeln, ja die visuelle Kultur der Social Media intuitiv als eher *anästhetisch* beargwöhnen, zeigt, wie sehr wir Adornos kulturkritische Haltung verinnerlicht haben, die uns trotz aller interaktiven und kollaborativen Aspekte eines Web 2.0 oder 3.0 nach wie vor oder vielleicht mehr denn je vermuten lässt, dass die „anthropologischen Veränderungen unter den spätindustriellen, von totalitären Regimes und Riesenkonzernen gesteuerten Massenkultur, [...] die Menschen zu bloßen Empfangsapparaten, Bezugspunkten von conditioned reflexes reduziert" haben – und dass nur „das Kunstwerk, welches das äußerste von der eigenen Logik und der eigenen Stimmigkeit wie von der Konzentration des Aufnehmenden verlangt" jene Instanz ist, die vor diesem Medienkomplex nicht „kapituliert" (Adorno 1991a [1981], 124f.).

Kunst wäre demnach die ideale Exit-Kandidatin in einer massenmedial und kapitalistisch zugerichteten Sinnlichkeits- und Gefühlslandschaft. Ein recht erfolgreiches Narrativ, da es nicht zuletzt ein gehöriges Quantum Legitimation vermittelt. Doch stimmt das auch? Schauen wir einmal genauer auf die Exit-Leistungen der Literatur, und setzen wir einmal voraus, dass wir über Gegenstände reden, die wenn vielleicht nicht ein Äußerstes, so aber doch ein erfreuliches Maß an formaler Stimmigkeit aufweisen. Wie hoch schätzen wir nun ihre Leistung bei der Markierung und Prozessierung von subjektiver Allgemeinheit tatsächlich ein? Beim Roman, jenem viel beschworenen demokratischen Genre, sind wir da einigermaßen *safe*. Wenn Literatur allgemeine Aufmerksamkeit erlangt, dann in aller Regel Prosa. Nicht zuletzt der jüngste Trend der Autofiktion scheint eine in vieler Hinsicht interessante zeitgenössische Ausprägung jener schon von Friedrich von Blanckenburg aufgeworfenen Frage zu sein, wie der Roman im Unterschied zum vormodernen Epos das fühlende und handelnde Individuum als öffentliches, politisches Wesen artikuliert. Auch die visuelle Kunst des Theaters gilt – wie das Kino – als prototypischer Ort von Öffentlichkeit, auch wenn YouTube und Streamingdienste das Bild verändert haben. Als kollaborativen Künsten gilt beiden, dem Kino wie dem Theater, aber vielleicht nicht das Hauptaugenmerk, wenn es um die Frage der Artikulation emphatischer Subjektivität geht. Anders bei der Lyrik, der vermeintlichen Königsdisziplin dafür, „Subjektivität als solche" auszuloten, die „ganze Stufenleiter der Empfindung" (Hegel 1984 [1832–1845], 205) zu bespielen, wie Hegel schreibt. Die ziselierende Stimmungs-Nuancierung gehe allerdings, meint Hegel, durchaus auf Kosten gesellschaftlicher Kompatibilität des „zu einem Weltreichtum sich ausbreitenden Zusammenhange". Hegel markiert das Problem der Lyrik damit ziemlich genau: als Spalt zwischen dem „einzelne[n] Subjekt", dem „Vereinzelte[n] der Situation und der Gegenstände" (Hegel 1984 [1832–1845], 203) und der von Kant beschworenen Allgemeinheit im Ästhetischen.

Fassen wir das noch einmal mit der dreistufigen Kürzestgeschichte der Lyrik, die Jonathan Culler anbietet: Lyrik ist demnach zunächst einmal ein „Medium gehobenen Sprachgebrauchs" und befördert dadurch die „elegante sprachliche Umsetzung kultureller Werte" (Culler 2002 [1997], 108). An deren Stelle tritt mit dem Erlebnisgedicht und der allgemeinen Subjektivierung der Kultur im 18. Jahrhundert, in deren Schema auch die Erfindung der Ästhetik gehört, Lyrik als „Ausdruck überwältigender Gefühle" (Culler 2002 [1997], 108) – dies jedoch, wie Hegel meint, mit der Folge ihrer Marginalisierung. In der Moderne wird Lyrik dann, so weiter mit Culler, zu einer „Arbeit an der Sprache", zum literarischen Experimentierfeld *par excellence*, zu einer Stätte der „Irritation von Kultur" (Culler 2002 [1997], 108). Das führt einerseits dazu, dass gegenwärtige Lyrik Adornos Forderung nach einem Äußersten an Durchgeformtheit auf Objekt- und entsprechender Konzentration auf Rezipient:innenseite zwar ausgezeichnet entspricht. Der Effekt davon aber ist andererseits, dass Lyrik, wie etwa Christian Metz in seinem immerhin eine „Blütezeit der deutschsprachigen Lyrik" (Metz 2018, 9) ausrufenden Buch *Poetisch Denken* einräumt, „sicherlich nicht mehr der Gefühlsbeweger Nummer 1 ist" (Metz 2018, 47). Oder, um es etwas schroffer mit dem amerikanischen Dichter und Literaturprofessor Ben Lerner zu sagen: Lyrik nervt, und zwar aufgrund ihrer nach wie vor suggerierten „ungeheuren sozialen Bedeutung" (Lerner 2021, 15) – und eine solche hat sie auch nach Adorno als das „Zarteste, Zerbrechlichste", das sein „Wesen geradezu daran hat, die Macht der Vergesellschaftung [...] nicht anzuerkennen" oder sogar „zu überwinden" (Adorno 1991b [1981], 50) – „verbunden", so Lerner, „mit dem Gefühl ihrer ungeheuren sozialen Marginalisierung." (Lerner 2021, 15)

Das mit Hölderlins *Stimme des Volks* muss jedenfalls zeitgenössisch noch einmal überdacht werden. Denn was es heißt, wenn Lyrik es doch einmal schafft, zu so etwas zu werden wie einer Stimme des Volks, sehen wir zum Beispiel an der indisch-kanadischen Autorin Rupi Kaur und ihrem in 40 Sprachen übersetzten Band *Milk and Honey* mit Gedichten, die aus Instapoetry hervorgegangen sind (siehe Penke 2022). Mit mehr als 3,5 Millionen verkauften Exemplaren war es diesem Gedichtband vorbehalten, Homers *Odyssee* als erfolgreichste Versdichtung aller Zeiten abzulösen. Die ihrerseits versifizierte Selbstetikettierung am Ende des Buchs – „milk and honey takes readers through / a journey of the most bitter moments in life / and finds sweetness in them / because there is sweetness everywhere / if you are just willing to look" (Kaur 2015, 208) – lässt freilich eher an Poesiealben denken denn an das, was Adorno sich unter dem Äußersten an formaler Stimmigkeit und Konzentration vorgestellt hat. Oder nehmen wir den Auftritt der jungen afroamerikanischen Poetin Amanda Gorman bei Joe Bidens Amtseinführung. „Where can we find light in this never-ending shade?" (Gorman 2021, 11), fragt ihr dort vorgetragenes Gedicht, um die Vision einer Zeit zu zeichnen, „where a skinny Black girl / descended from slaves and raised by a single mother / can dream of becoming president" (Gorman 2021, 14), eine Zeit, die nicht fern sein muss, „if only we're brave enough to see it. / If only we're brave enough to be it" (Gorman 2021, 32). Nicht zuletzt vor dem Hintergrund des Kapitolsturms ist das mit der pushenden Wiederholung „If only we're brave enough" und dem nicht gerade kunstvollen, aber in diese Stimmung passenden Reim „see it" – „be it" (Gorman 2021, 32) durchaus bewegend. Aber ist das insgesamt gelungene Lyrik? Oder ist das eine ganz falsche Frage?

Amanda Gorman und ihre Botschaft jedenfalls wurden in Windeseile zu einem Meme – in ihrem sonnengelben Mantel mit knallrotem Haarband, beides von Prada; und in unterschiedlichsten Montagen: am Assoziationsfaden der Farbkombination gemeinsam mit Ronald McDonald,[1] mit einem verzwergten Donald Trump,[2] auf dem eisernen Thron aus der Serie *Game of Thrones*[3] oder mit dem ob seiner ostentativen *Grumpiness* während Joe Bidens Inauguration seinerseits memefizierten Bernie Sanders.[4] „Alle reden über das Gedicht der 23-Jährigen", klagt merkwürdigerweise dennoch Alice Schwarzer in der *Emma*, „niemand redet über die Werbe-Ikone", nichts anderes sei Gorman schließlich mit ihrem „Prada-Stirnband für 360 € (ausverkauft)", wie Schwarzer eifert, und dem „Prada-Mantel zu 2.800 €" (Schwarzer 2021). Und dann sei sie auch noch auf dem Cover der amerikanischen *Vogue* gelandet.[5] Aber ist das ein zündendes Argument? Ob Alice Schwarzer schon einmal davon gehört hat, dass Tyler Mitchells Foto von Beyoncé für das Cover der amerikanischen *Vogue* im Mai 2019 das erste *Vogue*-Titelfoto eines afroamerikanischen Fotografen gewesen ist,[6] und damit ein Politikum ersten Ranges, weil ein solches Cover eines der großen Magazine, wie Niklas Maak dazu anmerkte, „eine Form der Bildproduktion" ist, die wirklich gesellschaftliche Realitäten herstellt und viel mehr prägt als beispielsweise: „Kunst" (Maak 2019, 33). Bei Amanda Gorman machte übrigens niemand Geringeres die Aufnahme als die Fotografinnenlegende Annie Leibovitz.

Was ich damit sagen will: Amanda Gorman und ihr Gedicht sind besser *sub specie* Pop zu begreifen als durch herkömmliche literarische Kritik und Wertung; als Pop, wie ihn Diedrich Diederichsen begreift: An die Stelle von Klagen über ein „Zuviel an Reizen, Formen, Zeichen" und die „Suche nach dem Sinn (The big Sinn)" (Diederichsen 1983, 176), wie Diederichsen das nennt, rückt eine offensive Ausrichtung auf Stil und Oberflächenästhetik – und nicht mehr nur die musikalische Verfasstheit eines Songs oder seine *lyrics* sind ausschlaggebend, sondern ebenso und gleichberechtigt das Artwork und Format eines Albums, Clips oder Auftritte im TV oder auf Youtube oder in sozialen Medien, das Live-Konzert, die textile Kleidermode der Band, Körperhaltung, Posen, Make-up etc. und nicht zu-

---

[1] Die hier genannten Bilder können unter den nachfolgend angegeben Links angesehen werden: https://i.redd.it/nctmhpke0qc61.jpg.
[2] https://i.imgur.com/ggyKMCGl.jpg.
[3] https://imgur.com/4DawnuG.
[4] https://twitter.com/emmaspacelynn/status/1352674737579679748.
[5] https://assets.vogue.com/photos/6064ac1bb475e844532aab98/master/w_1600,c_limit/VO0521_Cover_A.jpg.
[6] https://assets.vogue.com/photos/5b63464a56dfa111db8629e2/ master /w_2700,h_3263,c_limit/09-beyonce-vogue-september- cover-2018.jpg.

letzt: ihre „Haltung und Bezug zum gesellschaftlichen Kontext" (Diederichsen 2014, 232f.; siehe auch Huber 2019, 229–246). Amanda Gormans Memefizierung und Covergirl-Karriere sind also vielleicht nicht nur interessanter als ihr Gedicht; ihr Gedicht ist losgelöst davon gar nicht adäquat zu verstehen.

Dies kollidiert allerdings in so mancher Hinsicht mit unserem herkömmlichen Verständnis von Lyrik. Denken wir noch einmal systematischer über diesen Punkt nach. Lyrik scheint nach wie vor das Objekt der Wahl zu sein, wenn die Bedeutsamkeit einer Situation – etwa bei runden Geburtstagen, Hochzeiten oder eben bei einer Amtsinauguration – nach irgendwie hochkultureller Auszeichnung oder Singularisierung verlangt. So viel ist durchaus noch aktuell von Cullers Lyrik der Stufe 1 als eleganter Markierung kultureller Werte. Subjektive Empfindsamkeit ist dabei vorzugsweise von Autorinnen gefragt, „die sich", wie Dirk von Gehlen schreibt, „im 20. Jahrhundert nie (und in den Jahrhunderten zuvor erst recht nicht) auf diese Weise äußern konnten" (von Gehlen 2020, 18) – „a skinny Black girl / descended from slaves and raised by a single mother" (Gorman 2021, 14). Nur dass von Gehlen diese Formulierung gar nicht auf Lyrik bezieht, sondern auf die Produktion von Memes als eine Art digitaler „Volkskultur" (von Gehlen 2020, 18). In Bezug auf Memes wird freilich niemand bestreiten, dass diese Form der Vermittlung von Individualität, die Möglichkeit, „eine Stimme" (von Gehlen 2020, 22) zu bekommen, immer auch eine ökonomische Signatur hat. Denn „Aufmerksamkeit" ist im Informationszeitalter nicht mehr eine besonders konzentrierte Rezeptionshaltung, sondern schlicht die „wertvollste Ressource" (von Gehlen 2020, 22), die sich in Klickzahlen bemisst. Was zirkuliert, ist wertvoll, und umgekehrt.

Lyrik, Warenwelt und (post-)autonome Ästhetik

Lyrik, als „das Zarteste, Zerbrechliste" (Adorno 1991b [1981], 49), tut sich schwer mit der nicht unbedingt für Subtilität bekannten Warenwelt: „Ich erinnere mich", schreibt Ben Lerner in *The Hatred of Poetry*, „als in Topeka der Hypermarket eröffnete, ein 25000 Quadratmeter großer Kasten von einem Supermarkt mit riesigen, hoch aufragenden Gängen voller grell beleuchteter, grell verpackter Waren, erinnere mich besonders an den Gang mit Frühstückszerealien, wo sich Cap'n Crunch-Schachteln in ‚Familiengröße' wiederholten, so weit das Auge reichte" (Lerner 2021, 92). Hier hat man zunächst einmal die angestammten Topoi des Supermarkts als eines ikonischen Orts des Konsumkapitalismus (siehe Drügh 2015): Grellheit, Gleichheit, Überfülle, eine merkwürdige Infantilisierung (Cap'n Crunch), eine leichte Peinlichkeit gegenüber der gespreizten Produkt- oder Werbesprache in Lemmata wie „Frühstückszerealien" (Lerner 2021, 92), die hier allerdings eher durch die Übersetzung akzentuiert wird, sowie eine irgendwie unangenehme Überdrehtheit, die Lerner – etwas lahm, wie er zugibt – zunächst einmal allegorisch zu lesen versucht:

> Und zwischen diesen zuckrigen Unendlichkeiten fuhren auf Rollerskates – ich mache keine Witze – junge uniformierte Arbeiterinnen umher, uniformiert sowohl in dem Sinne, dass sie die Kluft der Kette trugen, als auch in dem Sinne, dass sie uniform die Konventionen der Teenage-‚Schönheit' befolgten – die nicht Schönheit war, sondern ein Höchstmaß an vollkommener Austauschbarkeit, wobei die Rollerskates ein wenn auch angejahrter Verweis auf die Wendigkeit des Kapitals waren. (Lerner 2021, 92 f.)

Und wenn man schon dabei ist, sich beim Verbreiten angejahrter Gemeinplätze zu ertappen, dann ist es vielleicht einmal angesagt die Gegenrichtung auszuprobieren und über ästhetische Anknüpfungspunkte des Hypermarkts nachzudenken: „Die Energie, die mich im Hypermarket – einem Laden, der für mich kleine Rotznase das Gleiche war wie der Mont Blanc für Shelley – durchströmte, machte mich zunichte – ich halte diese Energie für einen wesentlichen Bestandteil der Dichtung" (Lerner 2021, 93). Was Lerner hier zeichnet, ist die postmoderne Supermarkt-Version des Erhabenen, das den Einzelnen zunichte zu machen droht, ähnlich wie es Percy Bysshe Shelley einst am Mont Blanc empfunden hatte. Ringt der englische Romantiker seine Poesie der schroffen, abweisenden, menschenfeindlichen Natur ab, so tut sich für Lerner im neuen Hypermarket von Topeka, wo sich anstelle der alpinen Steinmassen riesengroße Packungen von Frühstückszerealien zu zuckrigen Unendlichkeiten stapeln, die nicht weniger anspruchsvolle Aufgabe auf, sich dichterisch zu behaupten: „Thou art there" (Shelley 2012 [1817], 82), wie es bei Shelley heißt – aber wie weiter?

Die entscheidende Wende in Lerners Text ist also, dass er diesem Szenario nicht einfach den Rücken dreht, sondern hinschaut und dies als Dienst an der Poesie, als Arbeit an ihrer Gelenkigkeit in der Welt und somit als Versuch begreift die subjektive Allgemeinheit der Dichtung auf aktuelles Niveau zu heben. Eine Möglichkeit, die in diesem Zusammenhang immer von Nutzen ist, wäre Susan Sontags Camp-Strategie: „how to be a dandy in the times of mass-culture" (Sontag 1966 [1964], 280) bzw. „[c]amp sees everything in quotation marks" (Sontag 1966 [1964], 288), eben auch die Schönheit bzw. Hässlichkeit des Hypermarkets: „it's good, because it's awful" (Sontag 1966 [1964], 291). Lerner geht darüber aber einen Schritt hinaus, wenn er die Austauschbarkeit der Ware in strukturelle Homologie zur Dichtung oder im Wortsinn zur subjektiven Allgemeinheit des Ästhetischen setzt: „Eine Cola ist eine Cola, und egal für wie viel Geld, man kriegt keine bessere Cola als die, die der Penner um die Ecke trinkt. Alle Colas sind gleich, und alle Colas sind gut" (Warhol 2006 [1975], Kapitel 6, zit. nach Lerner 2021, 64), zitiert er Warhols berühmten Spruch und nennt Warhol den „Whitman des Konkreten" (Lerner 2021, 64), einen ästhetischen Demokraten – eben weil Whitman beabsichtigt hatte, als Lyriker „zu allen und für alle" (Lerner 2021, 93) zu sprechen. Lerner behauptet also, dass Whitmans Maxime der „gleiche[n] Gutheit" und „gute[n] Gleichheit" (Lerner 2021, 93), sich im Hypermarkt in nichts anderem zeigt als in der Ware.

Vergleichbares gilt, wie gesehen, auch für Amanda Gorman oder Rupi Kaur, mindestens mit Blick auf die Distribution ihrer Texte und Bilder. „Als Kunst gilt, was zugleich nicht Kunst ist" (Ullrich 2022, 38), benennt Wolfgang Ullrich die Faustformel einer zeitgenössisch postautonomen Kunst. Diese vertraut nicht mehr auf die gängigen Mechanismen ihrer Geltungskraft, wie sie für autonome Kunst gut eingespielt waren, insbesondere nicht mehr auf die programmatische Distanz zu allem anderen – Heidegger hat diese mit allem Pathos formuliert: „Je einsamer das Werk, festgestellt in die Gestalt, in sich steht, je reiner es alle Bezüge zu den Menschen zu lösen scheint, um so einfacher tritt der Stoß, daß solches Werk ist, ins Offene, um so wesentlicher ist das Ungeheure aufgestoßen und das bislang geheuer Scheinende umgestoßen" (Heidegger 1977 [1935/1936], 55, hier zit. nach Ullrich 2022, 38). Bei Lerner läuft die Sache anders: Verbundenheit statt Stoß könnte die Formel dafür sein. Mit Wallace Stevens stellt er fest: „Dichtung ist eine Art Geld [...]"; und „wie Geld vermittelt sie zwischen dem Individuum und dem Kollektiv, löst Ersteres in Letzterem auf oder lässt Ersteres aus Letzterem neu entstehen, worauf es sich wieder auflöst" (Lerner 2021, 93). Das bedeutet natürlich nicht, dass Dichtung sich radikal in Kommerz auflöste. Der Punkt ist vielmehr, dass postautonome Kunst nicht mehr unumwunden auf ihre Autonomie vertraut, sondern über ihre Verflochtenheit mit einer Reihe von Fremdbestimmungen nachdenkt – um aus dieser Bewegung neue „Energie" (Lerner 2021, 93) zu gewinnen (hier ist auch an Stephen Greenblatt zu denken; vgl. Greenblatt 1993, S. 9–24), eine Autonomie auf höherer Stufe. Das Gefühl, „ein vorläufiger Knotenpunkt in einem grenzenlosen Netzwerk von Waren und Flüssen zu sein" – „auch das ist Dichtung" (Lerner 2021, 93). Und so fragt Lerner: „Der Affekt des abstrakten Austauschs, das Gefühl, dass alles austauschbar ist – was ist sein Lied?" (Lerner 2021, 93)

Ich möchte diese Frage, den Wunsch künstlerisch „eine Struktur hinter dem Alltäglichen" zu entdecken, „Flecken der nicht grundierten Leinwand, die durch das Wirkliche hindurchscheinen" (Lerner 2021, 95 f.), noch einmal gegenwartsästhetisch aufgreifen und pointieren. Wer Ästhetik sagt, spricht natürlich weiterhin von einer *vollzugsorientierten Wahrnehmung*, wie der Frankfurter Philosoph Martin Seel sie nennt, von einer Sinnlichkeit also, die nicht als Transportmittel bloßer Sinnesdaten gilt, sondern die um ihrer selbst willen vollzogen wird, das heißt von Selbstreferenz gekennzeichnet ist (vgl. Seel 2003, 48). Und dies geschieht mit dem Effekt, dass mit ihr die Welt nicht nur schärfer wahrgenommen, sondern auch präziser zu erfühlen ist – aka „das Zarteste, Zerbrechlichste" (Adorno 1991b [1981], 49). Dass wir dadurch auch kognitiv stimuliert werden, betont Kant mit der schönen Formulierung, das Ästhetische gebe immer auch „viel zu denken" (Kant 1974 [1790], 249). Auf der Basis dieses Zusammenspiels von Wahrnehmung, Gefühl und Intellekt entsteht das Bedürfnis, sich mit anderen darüber auszutauschen, also höchst private Erlebnisse in einer Gesellschaft zu kommunizieren, sie anderen *anzusinnen* oder *zuzumuten*, so Kants bereits erwähnte Termini. Nur dass dies, so die These, heute mit anderen Parametern anzureichern bzw. zu aktualisieren wäre; etwa mit Blick auf die Sphäre des Populären, wie sie der Medienwissenschaftler Jochen Venus diskutiert:

> Die Selbstreferenz populärer Kulturen konstituiert (und stimuliert!) – und zwar gemäß ihres ästhetischen Prinzips – ein selbstähnliches Formenrepertoire. Wann immer populäre Kulturen einen Aufmerksamkeitserfolg erzielen, kristallisiert an diesem Erfolg sofort ein Konvolut ähnlicher Produkte. Jedes Faszinosum geht unmittelbar in Serie, strahlt aus, metastasiert und bezieht immer mehr Rezipienten in die spezifische Form spektakulärer Selbstreferenz ein. Auf diese Weise emergieren *Stilgemeinschaften normalisierten Spektakels*. (Venus 2013, 67)

Ich möchte behaupten, dass sich die Arbeit einer Lyrikerin wie Rupi Kaur ziemlich präzise mit dieser Struktur beschreiben lässt. Der Aufmerksamkeitserfolg setzt auf Instagram (und davor schon auf Tumblr) ein. Die wachsende Follower:innenschaft stimuliert die Weiterproduktion des Nachgefragten als „selbstähnliches Formenrepertoire" (Venus 2013, 67) auch im Printformat – und beschäftigt damit dann auch die Literaturkritik, etwa insofern, als ebenso gefragt wird, ob diese Art Dichtung, ob ihre Einfachheit, Popularität und emotionale Intensität überhaupt noch Lyrik im herkömmlichen Sinn ist, wie und ob sie vielleicht *die Lyrik überhaupt* retten könne (vgl. Hill und Yuen 2018) – was zusammengenommen nichts anderes heißt, als zu fragen, ob und wie sich an diesem Erfolgsfall eine Reihe ähnlicher Produkte anlagern kann. Auch der Punkt der Stil- oder Fangemeinschaften liegt auf der Hand, wenn man bedenkt, dass Rupi Kaur bei Instagram 4,5 Millionen Follower:innen hat; normalisiertes, d. h. auf Dauer gestelltes und nicht unbedingt transgressives Spektakel. Oder doch transgressiv? Die vielen Rupi Kaur-Fans würden sich jedenfalls beschweren, würde man behaupten, dass die Texte qua formaler Naivität schlicht affirmativ bleiben und somit nicht dem von Venus gekennzeichneten Popularitäts-Ideal entsprechen, nämlich innerhalb des Systems kommodifiziert sinnlichen Erlebens „reflexive Distanznahmen" und „Spielräume persönlicher Souveränität" (Venus 2013, 71) zu ermöglichen, qua künstlerischer Produktion „eine Struktur hinter dem Alltäglichen" aufzudecken, wie Lerner das nennt. Kurz gefragt: warum ist der Post vom 10. Mai auf Rupi Kaurs Insta-Account: „i get so lost / in where i want to go / i forget that the place i'm in / is already quite magical" (@rupikaur_, 10. Mai 2022) nicht eine zeitgenössische Formulierung des Shelley'schen *thou art there*? Und da landen wir dann eben doch wieder bei dem Punkt, dass der Text *als Text* das halt nicht hergibt in seiner Instapoetik, wie sie Faith Hill und Karen Yuan prägnant in *The Atlantic* beschreiben: als „bite-size lyric, the tidy aphorism, the briefly deliverable quote. Most Instagram poems advise how to live a better life – how to move on from a broken heart, how to believe in one's self, how to pursue one's dreams. On a platform full of idealized lifestyles in food, travel, and fashion, poetry presents yet more aspirational philosophies", also nichts als „quick consumption" (Hill und Yuen 2018). Aber wie könnte das aussehen, die Markierung eines lyrisch überzeugenden *thou art there* in dieser konsumistischen Welt mit ihren *bite-size, tidy, cuten* Sprüchen und Bildern, ihrem Eye-Candy und ihrem verbalen Soulfood?

Vielleicht wäre der Hip-Hop, selbst durch und durch kulturindustrielles Produkt und nah dran an den schnellen Szenen der Gegenwart, die geeignete Adresse, um der Frage nach der Lyrik in der gegenwärtigen *Visual Culture* nachzugehen (vgl. Lerner 2021, 87; siehe auch Bradley 2017; Greif 2012; Levin-Becker 2022; Wolbring 2015). Hier aber möchte ich nun in zwei knappen Skizzen vorführen, wie zwei deutschsprachige Lyriker:innen der Gegenwart, Dirk von Petersdorff und Marion Poschmann, ihre Fühler in Richtung industriell gefertigtem Candy ausstrecken: nach Gummibärchen und Überraschungseiern, dem Terrain des Pop.

Pop verdankt seinen Namen (u. a.) einem künstlichen Süßgetränk, dem Sodapop (also der Limonade), und diesem Umstand huldigen Lyrics auf unterschiedlichste Weise, von Beyoncés *Lemonade* zu Bilderbuchs *Softdrink* (*Coca-Cola, Fanta, Sprite, 7Up, Pepsi alright*) bis zu *Lola* von den Kinks, „where you drink champagne and it tastes just like coca cola". Solche Getränke und sonstiger Industrie-Candy hat in der gegenwärtigen Lyrik eher keinen Ort. Die Anmutung von, sagen wir, Haribo, ist denkbar non-*arty*, wie sich auch einem bekannten Werbeclip mit Thomas Gottschalk entnehmen lässt. „Ich versteh ja kaum was von moderner Kunst" kommt Gottschalk darin naiv strahlend in einem Museum für moderne Kunst um die Ecke, „aber ich liebe diese Skulptur". Damit meint er ein überdimensioniertes goldgelbes Gummibärchen unter einer Glaspyramide. „Lockruf des Goldbären" heiße diese Skulptur; „und hört ihr, wie sie lockt?", fragt Gottschalk. Und mit den souffierten Worten „iss mich, Thomas, iss mich" legt er seine Hand auf das Schutzglas, worauf ein Alarm losgeht. „O.k., o.k., wenn du gleich losheulst", holt Gottschalk nun eine Tüte wirklicher Gummibärchen aus der Innentasche seines Jacketts, „ess ich halt Deine kleinen Freunde." Wie befand schon Arthur Schopenhauer – dass es der höchste Ausdruck ästhetischen Banausentums sei, wenn jemand vor einem Stilleben das Wasser im Mund zusammenläuft, eine „Aufregung des Willens [...], die jeder ästhetischen Kontemplation des Gegenstandes ein Ende macht" (Schopenhauer 1911 [1859], 245). Aber Thommy setzt das ebenso fröhlich in Szene, wie sich die Kunst üblicherweise kein bisschen um Gummibärchen schert. Aber schauen wir einmal auf eine Ausnahme, ein Haribo-Gedicht von Dirk von Petersdorff, in dem es doch tatsächlich zentral um die sinnliche Erfahrung, die geschmackliche Textur dieser Süßigkeiten geht.

> Fruchtgummi
> Wir nach der Schule auf dem Weg zum Bus
> und angeln aus der Tüte Gummitiere:
> Die Fledermäuse geben Zungenkuss,
> die saure Gurke, die ich neu probiere.
> Wie das im Gaumen zieht, die Zunge schwirrt,
> die Teufel, Schnuller, voll verklebte Zähne –
> wir stehen, kauen, schmecken ganz verwirrt
> und haben nur die Frühlingsluft als Lehne.
> Da ist der Wind in Haaren als Gekräusel,
> ein Pinsel, der durch nasse Tusche wischt,
> an süßen Schlangen kleben saure Streusel,
> das rote und das schwarze Zeug gemischt,
> dass einer an der Kreuzung träumend warte,
> und unterm Sweatshirt hängt die Monatskarte.
> (von Petersdorff 2021, 42)

Es geht um die sinnliche Erfahrung der Fruchtgummi-Warenpalette, das genaue Hinschmecken, neu probieren, schwirren, im Gaumen ziehen – orale Aisthesis in Reinform, und natürlich ist der Mund auch ein sehr poetologischer Ort. Das macht sich denn auch in der Lautlichkeit des Gedichts bemerkbar, seinem Gezischel, wenn ein Pinsel „durch nasse Tusche wischt", oder in einem Paradigma weiterer s- oder z-Laute: „süße[] Schlangen", „saure Streusel", „schwarze[s] Zeug, gemischt", „Sweatshirt". Ein anderes berühmtes Schmeck-Gedicht eines Lautvirtuosen, Rilkes 13. der *Sonette an Orpheus*, lässt im spätsommerlichen Geschmack der Früchte Auflösung, Tod und Leben zusammenfließen: „Voller Apfel, Birne und Banane, / Stachelbeere ... Alles dieses spricht / Tod und Leben in den Mund" (Rilke 1986 [1922], 683). Eine Sprache der Natur im Schmecken des Süßen. „Wo sonst Worte waren, fließen Funde, / aus dem Fruchtfleisch überrascht befreit", eine Feier des Hiesigen und der Aisthesis im Angesicht der Vergänglichkeit:

> Wagt zu sagen, was ihr Apfel nennt.
> Diese Süße, die sich erst verdichtet,
> um, im Schmecken leise aufgerichtet,
>
> klar zu werden, wach und transparent,
> doppeldeutig, sonnig, erdig, hiesig -:
> O Erfahrung, Fühlung, Freude -, riesig!
> (Rilke 1986 [1922], 683)

Petersdorffs Frühlingsgedicht übersetzt die natürliche Fruchtsüße in die radikale Künstlichkeit von Fruchtgummi; und als Frühlingsgedicht genregemäß in das Erwachen des Eros, was hier auch noch kindliche Tapsigkeit und pubertäre Verwirrung heißt wie auch bürgerliches Wohlbehütet-Sein: so das schöne Bild am Schluss, mit dem Sehnsucht und Aufbruchswunsch formulierenden, auch drucktypisch ein bisschen in der Luft hängenden Konzessivsatz, „dass einer an der Kreuzung träumend warte" (von Petersdorff 2021, 42), und der eher ernüchternden Ersetzung des Herzschlags durch eine unterm Sweatshirt hängende Monatskarte – ohnehin die Leine, an der man, ob man will oder nicht, zurück zu den behütenden Eltern geführt wird. Über dem Ganzen schwebt natürlich Romantik. Dem Gemeinen, ganz Gewöhnlichen – Bushaltestelle, Gummibärchen – wird, mit Novalis gesagt, „ein geheimnisvolles Ansehen" verliehen, was aber für das „Höhere", als das sich die Poesie begreift, stets auch eine „Erniedrigung" (Novalis 1978 [1798], 334) bedeutet.

Consuming the Romantic Utopia (Illouz 1997), könnte man daher mit dem Titel eines Buchs der Soziologin Eva Illouz über dieses Gummibärchengedicht schreiben, nur dass es bei Petersdorff nicht diese düstere Note gibt, die romantische Utopie hier also gar nicht verzehrt, aufgezehrt oder vernichtet wird in ihrer Verknüpfung mit der Warenwelt, sondern eher dorthin übersetzt wird, ein eigenes Gepräge bekommt. Das wäre also Petersdorffs konsumästhetische Antwort auf Ben Lerners Frage: „Der Affekt des abstrakten Austauschs, das Gefühl, dass alles austauschbar ist – was ist sein Lied" (Lerner 2021, 93)? Dass man einfach einmal nachschauen und -fühlen sollte, was genau die Erfahrung von Gummibärchen ist. Wenn man so will, eine konsequente Antwort auf jene peinigende Situation bei einem Zahnarzt, von der Ben Lerner berichtet, und bei der der Zahnarzt ihn in der ohnehin schon peinlichen und untersuchungsbedingt einseitigen Kommunikation der Art *Sie sind also Dichter* – „beinahe mit einem Spiegel erstickte, als wäre er auf der Suche nach meinen innersten Gefühlen" und im Grunde nach Lerners Vermutung dabei denkt, „kannst du dir denn keinen richtigen Job suchen und diesen Kinderkram hinter Dir lassen" (Lerner 2021, 15f.). Haben sie doch, Ben Lerner, als Professor für Englische – und Dirk von Petersdorff als Professor für Deutsche Literatur.

Eine andere Nuance fügt Marion Poschmann der Bedichtung der Warenwelt hinzu – mit einem programmatischen, „Kunststoff" betitelten Gedicht:

Kunststoff
Votivkerzen, Schluckbildchen, Wettersegen –
Meine Tanten schritten den ersten eigenen Teppich ab,
Länge mal Breite, ihr goldenes, ihr Verlies,
In das sie zurückgekehrt waren nach Jahren
In Schwesterwohnheimen, Abendschulen,
nach Jahren, in denen sie niemals verneinten frei zu sein

Das Kunststoffwunder veränderte alles,
Ließ neue Geräusche ins Zimmer,
Die sich zu Gebilden formten,

> Zum quietschenden Drehverschluß eines Cremetiegels,
> Zum schmatzend entspannenden Bauch einer Shampooflasche
> Zum knackenden Deckel auf einem Schälchen Heringssalat.
> Durch das gekippte Küchenfenster drängte noch immer
> Geruch von Dung, aber wenn sie jetzt abwuschen, standen
> die Tanten ganz anders da, standen anders im Raum,
> Standen locker wie Schäume, Vliese und Flocken,
> Weichmacher lagen auf ihren Gesichtern, Füllstoffe
> Um ihre Hüften, die waren viel näher dran,
>
> wenn von glänzenden Tellern das Wasser leicht abfloß
> wie Seide, sie fühlten sich selbst seidig, waren
> jetzt enger verbunden mit ihrer Umgebung, als hätte
> Verseifung stattgefunden, Vulkanisierung, Bestrahlung.
> Meine Tanten bevorzugten lebenslang Kleider
> von Delmod: Nylon, Polyester, Polyamid.
>
> Ich habe mich sofort daran gewöhnt.
> Seltsam, daß Dinge wie Haarspray mit mir zusammen
> Zur Welt kamen. Meine Kindheit jene der Tetrapaks,
> Plastiktüten und Kühltruhen. Letztens erst trieben
> Im Müllstrudel Tausende Überraschungseikapseln
> Mit Spielzeug gefüllt an den Strand von Langeoog.
> (Poschmann 2020, 44f.)

Die Kunst des im epischen Präteritum gehaltenen Gedichts ist es, unsere Affäre mit dem Kunststoff zu erzählen, mit Plastik und anderen synthetischen Stoffen. Marion Poschmann, die laut der Jury des Bremer Literaturpreises „mit großem Formbewusstsein die Tradition der Naturlyrik in das Zeitalter von Klimawandel und Artensterben" (Rudolf-Alexander-Schröder-Stiftung 2020) überführt, entwirft in diesem Gedicht ein Narrativ, in dem die Kunststoffwelt der 1970er Jahre zunächst als stimulierend und befreiend, geradezu als alles veränderndes „Kunststoffwunder" an die Stelle einer religiösen („Votivkerzen, Schluckbildchen, Wettersegen") oder von muffigeren Konsumwünschen geprägten Lebenswelt tritt – versinnbildlicht im „ersten eigenen Teppich", der nicht etwa ein Vlies ist, sondern dessen „Länge mal Breite" ein „Verlies" bildet. Nun aber dringen neue Geräusche ins Zimmer, die von neuartigen Gebilden ausgehen, dem quietschenden Drehverschluss eines Cremetiegels, dem schmatzend entspannenden Bauch einer Shampooflasche, dem knackenden Deckel eines Schälchens Heringssalat.

Quietschen, Schmatzen, Knacken, so die Kunststoff-Variante von Clemens Brentanos romantischem Natursound: „Summen, murmeln, flüstern, rieseln". Vorgetragen natürlich mit jener Ambivalenz, wie sie schmatzend sich entspannenden Bäuchen nicht so sehr lange nach Auschwitz gegenüber angemessen ist. „Ans Schmatzen" dürfe sich Lyrik nie „verraten", meinte Adorno (1991b [1981],

63). Ein wenig mithören lässt sich beim Lemma Bauch freilich auch der Slogan *Mein Bauch gehört mir*, mit dem die Frauenbewegung in der Bundesrepublik seit 1968 für das Recht auf Abtreibung kämpfte. Eine Art Emanzipation spürt man auch, wenn man betrachtet, wie die Tanten der lyrischen Sprecherin, die Heldinnen des Gedichts, inmitten der Kunststoff-Aisthetik „ganz anders da" stehen, „anders im Raum", „locker wie Schäume, Vliese und Flocken". Jetzt also doch *Vliese*, im Konsumkontext fällt dieser Begriff meist im Zusammenhang mit Einwegwindeln, auch dies umweltschädliche Wegwerfware, auch dies eine massive Erleichterung der Haushaltsführung mit Kindern. Im Detail erinnert sich der Text auch an ein anderes berühmtes Versprechen der Werbeindustrie, das beim Spülen Glanz ganz ohne Abtrocknen verhieß. Pril hieß die Marke, die mit den bunten Blumen, Flower-Power.

Die lyrische Sprecherin begrüßt denn auch in den entsprechenden Objekten ihre Weggefährten und Geschwister – in einer eigentümlichen Mischung aus Gewohnheit, Selbstverständlichkeit und Erstaunen: „Ich habe mich sofort daran gewöhnt. / Seltsam, da Dinge wie Haarspray mit mir zusammen / Zur Welt kamen. Meine Kindheit jene der Tetrapaks, Plastiktüten und Kühltruhen".

Und das Schlussbild? „Letztens erst trieben / im Müllstrudel Tausende Überraschungseikapseln / mit Spielzeug gefüllt an den Strand von Langeoog" (Poschmann 2020, 45). Die Überraschungseiflut auf Langeoog hat es tatsächlich gegeben. Im Januar 2017 wurden dort Hunderttausende solcher mit Spielzeug gefüllter Kapseln angespült. Sie stammten aus einem havarierten Schiffscontainer. Eine gemischte Empfindung, ob man will oder nicht, ein Müllstrudel ebenso wie eine nicht nur Kindergemüter entzückende Gabe.[7] Ökokatastrophe und quietschbunter Spaß teilen sich auf durchaus herausfordernde Weise ein Bild. Denken lässt sich dabei auch an den *Social Surrealism* einer Künstlerin wie Mika Rottenberg, die die künstlerische Erkundung unserer aisthetischen Verstrickung in die nicht selten aus wabbligem, brutzelndem, knisterndem und klackerndem Kunststoff bestehende Physis der Welt etwa in einer Videoarbeit wie *Spaghetti Blockchain* (2019) anhand von wabbligem Silikon, geschmolzenen Marshmallows, brutzelndem Schaum – und eben: klackernden bunten Plastikkugeln vornimmt.[8]

Die Herausforderung von Poschmanns Lied auf die Aisthesis der Konsumwelt, ihre haptischen, visuellen Oberflächen ebenso wie den emotionalen Response darauf, liegt darin, die Sache gegenwartsästhetisch scharf zu stellen und das heißt: (1) kulturpoetisch die unterschiedlichsten materialgebundenen Erzäh-

---

7 https://lokal26.de/nordsee/langeoog-tokio-langeooger-ue-eier-gehen-um-die-welt_a_50,6,2015043534-blocked.html.
8 https://mcachicago.org/Exhibitions/2019/Mika-Rottenberg-Easypieces/Described-Media/Spaghetti-Blockchain.

lungen zu rekonstruieren, die Formbarkeit von Körpern und Existenzen durch Stoffe, wie auch die Hoffnungen und Ängste, die sich in der Geschichte bestimmter Materialien manifestieren. Darin findet sich (2) immer schon der Übergang zur Sensitivität der wahrnehmenden Instanz wie zur Nuanciertheit des gedanklichen Urteils über das Wahrgenommene und zur Frage seiner angemessenen formalen und sprachlichen Prozessierung, womit (3) auch die Frage einer im Urteil entworfenen Allgemeinheit einer Stilgemeinschaft bzw. einer generationellen Erfahrung auftaucht.

Fruchtgummi und *Kunststoff* formulieren also zwei interessante lyrische Antworten auf die von Ben Lerner gestellte Frage nach dem Lied, das auch in der Warenwelt schläft, der wie auch immer „gute[n] Gleichheit" oder „gleiche[n] Gutheit" (Lerner 2021, 93) – Antworten einer Dichterin und eines Dichters, die den Sprung auf die Seite jener verweigern, die die Warenform offensiver annehmen und dadurch selbst Teil der gegenwärtigen visuellen Kultur werden.

Quellenverzeichnis

Adorno, Theodor W. „Der Artist als Statthalter". *Noten zur Literatur*. Hg. Rolf Tiedmann. Frankfurt a. M.: Suhrkamp, 1991a [1981]. 114–128.
Adorno, Theodor W. „Rede über Lyrik und Gesellschaft". *Noten zur Literatur*. Hg. Rolf Tiedmann. Frankfurt a. M.: Suhrkamp, 1991b [1981]. 48–68.
„Amanda Gorman auf dem eisernen Thron". [Abb.] Januar 2021, https://imgur.com/4DawnuG (23. Januar 2023).
„Amanda Gormans und Bernie Sanders". [Abb.] Januar 2021, https://twitter.com/emmaspacelynn/status/1352674737579679748 (23. Januar 2023).
„Amanda Gorman und Donald Trump". [Abb.] Januar 2021, https://i.imgur.com/ggyKMCGl.jpg (23. Januar 2023).
„Amanda Gorman und Ronald McDonald". [Abb.] Januar 2021, https://i.redd.it/nctmhpke0qc61.jpg (23. Januar 2023).
Bradley, Adam. *Book of Rhymes. The Poetry of Hip-Hop*. New York: Civitas Books, 2017.
Culler, Jonathan. *Literaturtheorie. Eine kurze Einführung*. Stuttgart: Reclam, 2002 [1997].
Diederichsen, Diedrich. „Die Auflösung der Welt. Vom Ende und Anfang". *Schocker. Stile und Moden der Subkultur*. Hg. Diedrich Diederichsen, Dick Hebdige und Olaph-Dante Marx. Reinbek bei Hamburg: Rowohlt, 1983. 165–188.
Diederichsen, Diedrich. *Über Pop-Musik*. Köln: Kiepenheuer & Witsch, 2014.
Drügh, Heinz. *Ästhetik des Supermarkts*. Konstanz: Konstanz Univ. Press, 2015.
Gehlen, Dirk von. *Meme*. Berlin: Wagenbach, 2020.
Gorman, Amanda. *The Hill We Climb*. New York: Viking Books, 2021.
Greenblatt, Stephen. „Einleitung: Die Zirkulation sozialer Energie". *Verhandlungen mit Shakespeare*. Frankfurt a. M.: Fischer, 1993. 9–24.
Greif, Marke. *Rappen lernen*. Berlin: Suhrkamp, 2012.

Hegel, Georg Wilhelm Friedrich. *Vorlesungen über die Ästhetik. Dritter Teil – Die Poesie*. Hg. Rüdiger Bubner. Stuttgart: Reclam, 1984 [1832–1845].

Heidegger, Martin. „Der Ursprung des Kunstwerkes". *Holzwege. Martin Heidegger: Gesamtausgabe*. Bd. 5, 1. Abteilung: *Veröffentlichte Schriften 1914–1970*. Hg. Friedrich-Wilhelm von Herrmann. Frankfurt a. M.: Vittorio Klostermann, 1977 [1935/1936]. 1–70.

Hill, Faith und Karen Yuan. „How Instagram Saved Poetry. Social Media is Turning an Art into an Industry". *The Atlantic*. 15. Oktober 2018, https://www.theatlantic.com/technology/archive/2018/10/rupi-kaur-instagram-poet-entrepreneur/572746/ (3. Januar 2023).

Huber, Till. „Lyrics als Literatur". *Handbuch Literatur & Pop*. Hg. Moritz Baßler und Eckhard Schumacher. Berlin und Boston, MA: De Gruyter, 2019. 229–246.

Illouz, Eva. *Consuming the Romantic Utopia. Love and the Cultural Contradictions of Capitalism*. Berkeley: Univ. of California Press, 1997.

Kant, Immanuel. *Kritik der Urteilskraft*. Hg. Wilhelm Weischedel. Frankfurt a. M.: Suhrkamp, 1974 [1790].

Kaur, Rupi. *Milk and Honey*. Kansas City, MO: Andrews McMeel, 2015.

Kaur, Rupi/@rupikaur_. Unbenanntes Gedicht. *Instagram*. 10. Mai 2022, https://www.instagram.com/p/CdWuziusTtV/ (6. Januar 2023).

Kremer, Klaus. „Strand von Langeoog". [Foto] 2017, https://lokal26.de/nordsee/langeoog-tokio-langeooger-ue-eier-gehen-um-die-welt_a_50,6,2015043534-blocked.html.2017 (23. Januar 2023).

Lerner, Ben. *Warum hassen wir die Lyrik?* Übers. Nikolaus Stingl. Berlin: Suhrkamp, 2021.

Leibovitz, Annie. „Cover der amerikanischen Vogue". [Abb.] Mai 2021, https://assets.vogue.com/photos/6064ac1bb475e844532aab98/master/w_1600,c_limit/VO0521_Cover_A.jpg (23. Januar 2023).

Levin-Becker, Daniel. *What's Good. Notes on Rap and Language*. San Francisco, CA: City Lights Books, 2022.

Lynn, Emma/@emmaspacelynn. „Amanda Gorman hopped on the Bernie train." 22. Januar 2021, https://twitter.com/emmaspacelynn/status/1352674737579679748 (23. Januar 2023).

Maak, Niklas. „Nie wieder Opfer! Warum das Cover der ‚Vogue' politischer sein kann als alle kritische Biennalenkunst: Der Fotograf Tyler Mitchell und sein ‚Black Utopia'". *FAZ*. 28. April 2019.

Metz, Christian. *Poetisch denken*. Frankfurt a. M.: Fischer, 2018.

Mitchell, Tyler. „Cover der amerikanischen Vogue". [Abb.] September 2018, https://assets.vogue.com/photos/5b63464a56dfa111db8629e2/master/w_2700,h_3263,c_limit/09-beyonce-vogue-september-cover-2018.jpg (23. Januar 2023).

Novalis. „Fragment Nr. 105". *Vorarbeiten zu verschiedenen Fragmentensammlungen 1798. Novalis: Werke, Tagebücher und Briefe Friedrich von Hardenbergs*. Bd. 2: *Das philosophisch-theoretische Werk*. Hg. Hans-Joachim Mähl und Richard Samuel. München: Carl Hanser, 1978 [1798].

Penke, Niels. *Instapoetry. Digitale Bild-Texte*. Berlin: Metzler, 2022.

Petersdorff, Dirk von. „Fruchtgummi". *Unsere Spiele enden nicht. Gedichte*. München: C.H. Beck, 2021.

Poschmann, Marion. „Kunststoff". *Nimbus. Gedichte*. Berlin: Suhrkamp, 2020.

Rilke, Rainer Maria. „Sonette an Orpheus". *Die Gedichte*. Frankfurt a. M.: Insel, 1986.

Rottenberg, Mika. *Spaghetti Blockchain*. Museum of Contemporary Art Chicago. 2019, https://mcachicago.org/Exhibitions/2019/Mika-Rottenberg-Easypieces/Described-Media/Spaghetti-Blockchain (9. Januar 2023).

Rudolf-Alexander-Schröder-Stiftung – Stiftung des Senats der Freien Hansestadt Bremen. „Der 67. Bremer Literaturpreis 2021 geht an Marion Poschmann – Der Förderpreis geht an Jana Volkmann". [Pressemitteilung] 14. November 2020, https://www.senatspressestelle.bremen.de/pressemitteilungen/der-67-bremer-literaturpreis-2021-geht-an-marion-poschmann-der-foerderpreis-geht-an-jana-volkmann-347223 (3. Januar 2023).

Schopenhauer, Arthur. „Die Welt als Wille und Vorstellung". *Arthur Schopenhauers Sämtliche Werke*. Bd. 1. Hg. Paul Deussen. München: Piper, 1911 [1859].

Schwarzer, Alice. „Werbe-Ikone Amanda Gorman". *EMMA*. 28. April 2021, https://www.emma.de/artikel/werbeikone-gorman-338597 (16. November 2022).

Seel, Martin. *Ästhetik des Erscheinens*. Frankfurt a. M.: Suhrkamp, 2003.

Shelley, Percy Bysshe. „Mont Blanc – Lines Written in the Vale Of Chamouni". *The Complete Poetry of Percy Bysshe Shelley*. Bd. 3. Hg. Nora Crook, Neil Fraistat und Donald H. Reiman. Baltimore, MD: The John Hopkins Univ. Press, 2012 [1817].

Sontag, Susan. „Notes on ‚Camp'." *Against Interpretation and Other Essays*. New York: Farrar, Straus & Giroux, 1966 [1964]. 275–292.

Ullrich, Wolfgang. *Die Kunst nach dem Ende ihrer Autonomie*. Berlin: Klaus Wagenbach, 2022.

Venus, Jochen. „Die Erfahrung des Populären. Perspektiven einer kritischen Phänomenologie". *Performativität und Medialität Populärer Kulturen*. Hg. Marcus S. Kleiner und Thomas Wilke. Wiesbaden: Springer VS, 2013. 49–73.

Warhol, Andy. *Die Philosophie des Andy Warhol – von A nach B und zurück*. Frankfurt a. M.: Fischer, 2006 [1975].

Wolbring, Fabian. *Die Poetik des deutschsprachigen Rap*. Göttingen: Vandenhoeck & Ruprecht, 2015.

2 **Visibly Visual: Sociopolitical Poetry on the Web and in Films**

Astrid Böger
U.S. American Poetry in the Digital Age: Participation, Performance, Protest

Introduction

Although its beginnings go back to the mid-twentieth century (see Funkhouser 2007), digital poetry has fully emerged roughly since the turn of the twenty-first century as an innovative literary form bringing together a diverse group of creative actors including not only poets of the traditional kind – by whom I mean writers who share their poems with the public across a variety of existing media channels – but also visual and performance artists. The one thing their wide-ranging poetic creations have in common is the reliance on internet-based media first to make and then disseminate individual artworks and, what is more, to enable readers to interact with them in ways not readily afforded by traditional, print-based poetry. In fact, it might be more appropriate to speak of users or even producers of digital poetry here, to invoke a cultural studies concept introduced by Australian media scholar Axel Bruns to describe the vital role of readers as active co-creators in the meaning-making process (cf. Bruns 2008, 9–33). Sharing common roots with text-based concrete poetry as well as its more recent manifestation, multimodal visual poetry (cf. Funkhouser 2007, 9; Sokar 2021, 3), digital poetry often makes use not only of visual elements such as illustrations, photographs, and videos, but also of hypertext elements, virtual, enhanced, and augmented reality environments as well as computer-generated animations and holograms, among others. Increasingly, then, poets in the digital age are using similar strategies aimed at attracting readers' attention as do authors working in other genres vying for visibility in an ever-expanding and seemingly amorphous, fast-digitizing literary marketplace. In fact, the increasing blurring of (genre) boundaries between traditional, print-based poetry and such digital forms that have emerged in the new millennium have led scholars like Louise Mønster to argue that "it makes no sense to maintain an unequivocal definition of poetry. It is much more appropriate to understand poetry as a dynamic and ever-expanding field that interacts with other genres and art forms and which has proved to be extremely flexible and adaptable." (Mønster 2017, 250)

As a consequence of such generic openness bordering on fuzziness, contemporary poetry has lost the precarious position or, depending on one's own position vis-à-vis the increasingly differentiated field of cultural production, the privileged cachet of an art form which, over the course of the twentieth century, had become increasingly secluded from the bigger literary business catering to more mainstream tastes and reading habits. Instead, poetry is now on its way to becoming a truly popular phenomenon again, arguably for the first time since the nineteenth century, not least thanks to widely-used social media platforms such as Instagram or TikTok, to name but two of the most prominent ones. Predictably, this development is not to everyone's liking. Mahmoud Moawad Sokar, for one, while acknowledging the (assumed) present-day reader's need for "a new, easy, simple, and flexible form of poetry that fits the massive technological development," has recently posed the controversial question whether "this new digitalized form of poetry [can] keep the genre's aesthetics and creativity?" (Sokar 2021, 1). Sokar clearly has his doubts, as he concludes his contribution with a rather critical assessment of what he considers its "de-aestheticization as the digital poem presents flashy direct ideas rather than aesthetic and figurative meanings" (Sokar 2021, 10).

In this article, my intention is not to support or refute such efforts at re-evaluating poetry's doubtlessly changing cultural status in the age of digital (re)production,[1] which invariably mirror the aesthetic standards of those critics comparing its contemporary emanations with older poetic forms typically imbued with considerably greater cultural esteem. Rather, my aim here is simply to highlight a range of different examples of digital or, as the case may be, digital*ized* poetry written and disseminated with the explicit intention to reposition poetry as a kind of public forum opening up spaces of resistance against certain ideologies deemed untenable by a majority of people today, with racism and misogyny clearly at the top of the list. In more concrete terms, I begin by looking at presentations of otherwise traditional, that is text-based poetry disseminated via internet platforms but then go on to discuss poetry posted on Instagram following a somewhat different aesthetic as well as activist regime. In the final part of my article, I briefly revisit *Chalkroom*, the acclaimed media art environment created by Laurie Anderson and Hsin-Chien Huang in 2017, which I consider to be a particularly interesting specimen of contemporary digital poetry conceived and rendered as a virtual reality performance aimed at opening up an interactive room of experiential possibility.

Throughout, my specific aim is to focus on U.S. American poetry in and of the digital age that affords new forms of participation, broadly defined, ranging from the formation of interactive literary communities on social media platforms but also encompassing public performances of protest, in the form of digital poetry,

---

[1] Other authors have invoked Walter Benjamin's well-known essay on "The Work of Art in the Age of Mechanical Reproduction" (1969 [1935]) to discuss the question whether digital reproduction further diminishes any aura poetry might still possess. See, for example, Kevin Stein, "Poems and Pixels: The Work of Art in an Age of Digital Reproduction" (2010).

against concrete policies or ideologies that demand public attention and, even more importantly, change. The dynamic interplay between literary and visual media elements within digital poetry will be explored, in line with the present volume's overall focus on poetry and contemporary visual culture. I will therefore ask in each case how language and visual content are juxtaposed, combined, or even merged, and what kinds of engagement on the part of readers/viewers this affords. Finally, I am wondering if digital poetry is a new artistic phenomenon or rather a continuation of older poetic forms with digital means – a question that has been broached by other scholars, as well (for example, see Baetens 2021), and that I will attempt to answer, albeit provisionally, in the concluding section below.

Poems of protest, resistance, and empowerment

The first example I would like to discuss is taken from a digital collection titled *Poems of Protest, Resistance, and Empowerment* and made available via the Poetry Foundation, an independent U.S. based literary organization established in 2003 whose stated aims are, first, "to discover and celebrate the best poetry and to place it before the largest possible audience" and, secondly, to "raise poetry to a more visible and influential position in our culture."[2] Without doubt, in today's world both aims are best achieved via digital publication, and in this context it bears mentioning that the Poetry Foundation is also publishing the renowned *Poetry* magazine, which has appeared since 1912 and is available both in print and digital form. Additionally, The Poetry Foundation is present on social media, namely on Twitter and Facebook, as well as Instagram. On their website, the following rationale is given for the Foundation's digital programs:

> The Poetry Foundation uses emerging technology to reach and engage a broad audience for poetry. Through its award-winning website, mobile applications, and social media, the Foundation seeks to create new readers of poetry, serve existing poetry fans, and support Foundation initiatives and programs.

From this mission statement, the purpose of using digital programs becomes quite clear: to reach out to or even "create" new audiences who would otherwise simply not exist or in any case connect to poetry – which can nowadays apparently be achieved best via "emerging technology" such as social media and mobile

---

2 https://www.poetryfoundation.org/foundation/about.

apps – while also catering to those readers already well-versed in accessing and reading poetry regardless of how it is presented.

As a visual introduction of sorts, the collection of *Poems of Protest, Resistance, and Empowerment* uses an eye-catching, colorful title image – at the same time the only image appearing along with the seventy-two poems selected – featuring a human hand clenched into a fist and holding up a pencil, revolutionary-style. This iconic presentation emphasizes the traditional craft of writing by hand, whereas the frame of the image suggests a television or computer screen through which the central message is transmitted, presumably to an imagined audience of like-minded comrades-in-arms. The style of the illustration itself, by Chicago-based artist CHema Skandal!, likewise transcends any perceived barriers between so-called old and new media, by using a traditional woodcut aesthetic often seen in older politically-engaged poster art, but which is here produced entirely through digital means.[3] The image's old-fashioned aesthetic creates a notable contrast with today's digitally-produced visual culture often relying on photoshopping or even fully digital production of visual content. On a meta-level, one might thus understand the title image as a visual commentary on the ways in which new media remediate older media, to invoke an influential concept originally proposed by Bolter and Grusin (2000). A related point has recently been made by Baetens, who has argued that "digitization of poetry takes on the shape [. . .] of a *ricochet*, that is, a profound transformation of old practices, rather than expressing itself directly, that is, by the appearance of an exclusively screen-based poetry" (Baetens 2021, 241). In a similar move, the title image heading the collection of *Poems of Protest, Resistance, and Empowerment* ricochets back and forth between old-style writing by hand and digital forms of transmitting texts, albeit presenting both as one harmonious and powerful unity.

The poems selected are for the most part by well-known or even famous poets from the United States and several other countries, most of whom are still alive. But the collection also includes some classic poems from the U.S. American lyrical canon by the likes of Walt Whitman, Langston Hughes, and Denise Levertov. As the editors explain in their introduction, the poems selected "call out and talk back to the inhumane forces that threaten from above. They expose grim truths, raise consciousness, and build united fronts." What is more, they "rail against complacency and demonstrate why poetry is necessary and sought after in moments of political

---

[3] Readers are kindly referred to the Poetry Foundation's website displaying the image as part of the collection, https://www.poetryfoundation.org/collections/101581/poems-of-protest-resistance-and-empowerment.

crisis."[4] Among the collected poems is a recent contribution by Sonia Sanchez, a well-known U.S. based poet, playwright, literature professor, and activist as well as one of the foremost leaders of the Black Arts Movement now in her late eighties. Her long poem "Haiku and Tanka for Harriet Tubman" (Sanchez 2018) originally appeared in *Poetry* magazine in 2018 and is, on the one hand, a straightforward homage to Tubman, the formerly enslaved person of color turned abolitionist and activist instrumental in operating the Underground Railroad, a secret network that helped escaped enslaved people toward freedom in antebellum North America. On the other hand, the poem is firmly rooted in the historical moment in which it appeared, more than a century and a half later, when many African Americans are still subjected to racist oppression and are thus clearly not enjoying the full rights granted by U.S. citizenship; instead, they face an ongoing struggle to convince fellow Americans that Black lives do, indeed, matter. Another presumable origin story of the poem is the Trump administration's (2016–2020) refusal to put Tubman's portrait on the twenty dollar bill, thereby reversing the previous administration's decision to replace Andrew Jackson's likeness with hers – a hugely political issue in the U.S. American context, considering that Jackson was not only an enslaver himself but more broadly stands for the pernicious ideology of white supremacy in mid-nineteenth century America and beyond.

Sanchez's poem, while consisting of words only, uses highly visual rhetoric and imagery throughout, starting each stanza as it does with the invitation to readers to "picture" or "imagine" Tubman in iconic scenarios where she bravely fights the institution of slavery for the greater good of saving her country from moral ruin. One might thus argue that this is an ekphrastic poem invoking Tubman even as it turns her into a work of art. Importantly, however, the poem emphasizes movement, not stasis, in line with its larger political message. What is more, as the title indicates, the poem takes the form of haiku and tanka, two short forms in classical Japanese poetry known for their precise language and imagery. This aesthetic ideal is palpable in Sanchez's poem, as well, with its focus on painting verbal images of its heroic subject in action, as seen in the central metaphor of the opening stanza: "Picture a woman / riding thunder on / the legs of slavery. . ." (Sanchez 2018). In consequence, "Haiku and Tanka for Harriet Tubman" presents a verbal account of an individual transformed into a heroic figure through vivid images painting Tubman as a powerful agent of history. It is, moreover, a verbal-visual testament to her historic achievement turned into a poetic call for the empowerment of people resisting and fighting racism today, as evidenced by the ninth stanza (out of twenty-four), which transgresses time and

---

4 https://www.poetryfoundation.org/collections/101581/poems-of-protest-resistance-and-empowerment.

space in order to invoke Tubman directly addressing contemporary audiences with the following powerful message:

> Picture her saying:
> *You have within you the strength,*
> *the patience, and the passion*
> *to reach for the stars,*
> *to change the world . . .*
> (Sanchez 2018).

Without any doubt, empowering passages such as the one above convey the poem's strong anti-racist message regardless of the way in which readers access the poem. And yet, due to the specific set-up of social media platforms and mobile apps affording not only personalized access but also easy shareability with others, the digitized version of Sanchez' poem arguably has much greater potential for community-building than individual acts of reading it in *Poetry* magazine's printed version, even when considering the latter's rather impressive circulation, reaching around 15.000 subscribers today.[5]

Protest through poetry

Compared to the strictly poetic efforts at empowerment and community building such as afforded by the Poetry Foundation's collection discussed above, *Protest Through Poetry* is a much more straightforwardly activist grassroots project. The platform was established in mid-2020 in the context of the Black Lives Matter (BLM) movement in the aftermath of the murder of George Floyd chiefly at the hands of a white police officer in Minneapolis. Notably, BLM had already been formed in 2013 by three female Black organizers, named Alicia Garza, Patrisse Cullors, and Opal Tometi, as a response to a whole series of racist hate crimes in the United States more often than not followed by the acquittal of their (mostly white) perpetrators. Remarkably, it is one of the earliest protest movements that originated on social media ("born digital"), with the hashtag #BlackLivesMatter. These online protests soon prompted massive protests in the physical world, as well, but without losing the internet as a common basis and amplifier of the movements' collective voice demanding change more desperately with each racist atrocity committed. The anthology *Protest Through Poetry* has directly spawned

---

5 See https://www.timothy-green.org/blog/poetry-journal-rankings/.

from the BLM movement, as the following excerpt from the all-female editors' introduction makes quite plain:

> *Protest Through Poetry* is an international collective of BIPOC [Black, Indigenous, People of Color] activist poets. We work together through writing seminars, poetry workshops, and demonstrate our protest publicly through multimedia and physical demonstrations. As BIPOC poets, our very gathering is inherently political and an act of resistance. We gather to correct injustice. Through poetry, we write to disrupt. We use our words to empower, our poetry for healing and visibility. Together, we share our stories and learn from one another's expertise. We want to provide a safe outlet for poets of color to gather in solidarity and process, protest, and refuel through poetry and activism. [. . .] Our community began through a 2-night seminar last summer in which BIPOC writers gathered digitally to affirm *Black Lives Matter*, establish solidarity and unity among BIPOC writers, and reflect on our role in protest poetry.[6]

While poetry has always been used by some activists and public intellectuals as a vehicle for voicing protest and appealing to like-minded audiences, *Protest Through Poetry* owes its entire existence to activism, and as a matter of fact directly grew out of it. The anthology is published both online and in print, with donations and proceeds being used to support the project as a whole as well as currently about thirty individual poets contributing their work to it. Especially in its online version, a sense of movement is rendered palpable to the extent that it can be slightly disorienting to navigate the webpage, with individual words and entire phrases moving in several directions at the same time. This purposefully-evoked confusion is no doubt an intended effect considering that *Protest Through Poetry*'s stated mission is to shake things up and to get these voices of protest out, *loud*, and to simultaneously make its anti-racist message more visible. Toward the latter end, a striking black-and-white color scheme is used throughout, which reinforces BIPOC's unambiguously political message focusing on racial violence while also invoking other black-and-white media formats such as older documentary photography, newspapers or traditional book printing, which further underscores the anthology's claim to historicity, authenticity, and overall truthfulness. Importantly, BIPOC poets are also present on social media platforms. In fact, visitors to the website are practically lured to Instagram. Thus, when scrolling down to the final section of the webpage, they are prompted to "FOLLOW US ON INSTAGRAM FOR MORE," with an arrow directly pointing to "@PROTESTHRUPOETRY" – which is likely where *Protest Through Poetry* finds its largest audience, with roughly 1200 followers.[7]

One poem from the collection achieves a particularly powerful effect through its use of visual elements in combination with text. Anna Li Bryant, an award-winning writer and high school writing teacher based in Chicago, has submitted a

---

6 https://protestthroughpoetry.com.
7 https://www.instagram.com/protesthrupoetry/.

poem titled "▬Anthem (a blackout poem of the National Anthem)." As indicated by the poem's subtitle, "▬Anthem" literally blackens out a large portion of the text of the national anthem more popularly known as the "Star-Spangled Banner." The original lyrics were written by Francis Scott Key in 1814 to celebrate the final victory over the British oppressors following the war of independence, inaugurating what became known as the "Era of good Feelings" in the happily United States of America. To put it mildly, any such positive feelings are thoroughly absent from "▬Anthem"'s text as represented by Bryant, blackout-style (Fig. 10). With only twenty-two words left and devoid of the patriotic praise of victory that the "Star-Spangled Banner" is known and admired for by most U.S. Americans, the foremost icon of national pride is here turned into its negative and deeply disharmonious, even fractured but nonetheless quite powerful mirror image:

▬Anthem"
(a blackout poem of the National Anthem)

we   gleaming

red glare,

star-spangled
and

towering

That
a country should leave us
blood   washed
No refuge
or
home of

our   s

Fig. 10: Anna Li Bryant. "▬Anthem (a blackout poem of the National Anthem)." *Protest Through Poetry*. 2020. 36–37.

Through its ingenious play on visibility versus invisibility, and by specifically blacking out the profusely heroic imagery of the national anthem, the poem gets rid of the pathos of patriotism and highlights instead the bare life (cf. Agamben 1998, 12–13) of those who have *not* found refuge in the United States, even today, and who are therefore continually at risk and unprotected, or left in the dark, in a manner of speaking, like people stuck in an extended power blackout without any resources. Remarkably, by rigorously striking out all the positive notes of one of America's most cherished national symbols, Bryant's disjointed blackout poem exposes a power failure affecting contemporary U.S. American society at large chiefly through its brilliant visual artifice.

Protest poetry on Instagram

I will now turn to poetry posted on Instagram with the explicit aim of connecting with protest movements in order to make their agenda more visible through the effective use of visual elements including photographs and hashtags. I should be careful to add that my interest here lies less with so-called Instapoetry, that immensely popular platform for publishing digital poetry today which has its own hashtag on Instagram as well as over five million posts and counting. With some noteworthy exceptions, Instapoetry tends to abstain from all-too specific, let alone activist, political causes or entire agendas in favor of (more or less) professional Instapoets' efforts at self-promotion through attracting followers and likes, often with the intention of making money off of it.[8] In order to monetize one's Instapoetry, it appears advisable to focus on personal experiences cast as more general human-interest concerns. Also, pleasing if not too distracting visual elements such as drawings added for illustration or emotional embellishment are clearly a plus judging from the most successful Instapoets' work. Strikingly often displaying what Tanja Grubnic has described as "nosthetics," or a return to a predigital, nostalgia-inducing aesthetics, the overall aim of such vintage illustrations is to accommodate viewers' longing for tangibility in social media's all-digital environment (Grubnic 2020, 146).

By contrast, the political protest poems I have selected likewise make use of visual elements, though less with the intention of pleasing viewers but rather to raise their awareness and, ideally, enlist their support. Admittedly, these poems are somewhat of a niche phenomenon – so much so, in fact, that some discerning

---

[8] For an illuminating study including a definition of what distinguishes Instapoets from other poets posting their work on Instagram, see Camilla Holm Soelseth's "When is a Poet an Instapoet?" (2022).

colleagues familiar with poetry on social media have doubted the relevance of individual posts if they have garnered only relatively few likes and followers such as the ones I am discussing below. I should therefore clarify that I have made my selection not on the grounds of certain postings' popular or commercial success but because I recognize in them a new quality of articulating protest digitally: in the form of poetry disseminated via social media platforms affording new means of connecting to others, sharing views and information and, more broadly, community building. And indeed, even though the numbers are modest by many people's standards, there is a whole world of protest poetry out there. Thus, when I last checked in March 2023, there were almost 5.100 entries under the hashtag #protestpoetry alone, as well as a plethora of others appearing under related hashtags such as #RiotPoems and #poetryofprotest, to name but a few. As with the other digital poetry collections above, I therefore had to be extremely selective and decided on just a few specimens that I found particularly evocative, not least for their innovative use of visual elements to convey their political messages.

The first example, posted by someone under the pseudonym mutteringbum in May 2022, is reminiscent of Bryant's blackout poem discussed above. After all, it uses a similar approach where only a few words remain visible against an otherwise black background displaying thick black lines, which appear as though they have been painted on by hand. The six words that do remain visible form the somewhat enigmatic, metaphorical phrase, "The / sky was filled with / resistance" (mutteringbum May 3, 2022). Fortunately for visitors to the post, mutteringbum has provided a bit of context, by letting them know in the captions that they had already "shared this poem 3 years ago [. . .]." What is more, according to its tagging the poem is dedicated to the American Civil Liberties Union and to Planned Parenthood, which suggests that the repost happened in reaction to the then-recent leak of the Supreme Court's likely revoking of Roe vs. Wade (which actually did come to pass shortly thereafter), the court's 1973 ruling that the U.S. Constitution protects the liberty of women to choose to terminate a pregnancy without undue government restrictions within a certain time-frame. Arguably, without such contextualization – reinforced by pertinent hashtags added further below – the poem would instill in viewers a rather vague notion of resistance, somehow looming above, as it were, but without referencing any specific cause or political agenda. No doubt in order to increase its circulation and, hence, visibility, mutteringbum has added a number of different hashtags indicating the various audiences and communities targeted, some of which are overlapping. They include #poetry, #poetrycommunity, #poetryisnotdead, #protestpoetry, #blackoutpoetry, #blackoutpoetrycommunity, #foundpoetry, #roevswade, and #seeyouincourt and, considered together, suggest that the post is relevant both to poetry and political communities, interestingly cast as related or even connected, via hashtag neighborship if nothing else.

Another interesting example, accessed on May 11, 2022 but deleted in the meantime, was posted by someone named westtrestle. Their posting likewise appeared under a number of poetry hashtags and raised intriguing questions about the poetic function or poeticity of language. Poeticity, following Russian-American linguist and semiotician Roman Jakobson, is achieved when language is perceived for its own sake and not merely as a conduit or verbal representation of objects or emotions, or when there exists "an 'aesthetic surplus' that exceeds the communicative function" (Benthien et al. 2019, 25). As Jakobson expounds in "What is Poetry,"

> Poeticity is present when the word is felt as a word and not a mere representation of the object being named or an outburst of emotion, when words and their composition, their meaning, their external and inner form, acquire a weight and value of their own instead of referring indifferently to reality (Jakobson 1987, 378).

Thus, if the text on the poster in the stark black-and-white photograph, "Black Lives Matter" (Fig. 11), is indeed perceived as poetic, this would indicate that it has acquired an aesthetic quality in its own right, thereby transcending any strictly referential characteristics or specific political meanings it has accrued by virtue of its prevalence in anti-racist protests around the globe in recent years. The fact that the poster is placed in the foreground and appears somewhat detached from the crowd gathered behind it supports this notion, as do the hands of the young Black woman holding the sign and seemingly pointing toward its unmistakable message. As Claudia Benthien, Jordis Lau and Maraike M. Marxsen argue, "[t]he foregrounding of speech or script creates a heightened awareness of sound, syllables, letters, or the process of production itself" (Benthien et al. 2019, 26), further testifying to the post's self-referential poeticity.

Fig. 11: westtrestle. "Black Lives Matter." Instagram. April 20, 2022.

At the same time, the fact that the image partakes of a traditional documentary aesthetics and was taken and posted in the context of BLM protests does make it likely that most viewers will associate it primarily with those concrete events and the underlying racist structures rather than the image's purely poetic function.

Similar to mutteringbum's blackout poem above, this is therefore another case of blurred boundaries between poetic and non-poetic language, where the dynamic verbal-visual rendition is open to multiple viewpoints and aesthetic responses. Arguably, however, the combination of image and text achieves a higher degree of poeticity than words or images by themselves would, by drawing attention to the central message represented in two media, writing and photography, which merge into one image and amplify each other as a result even as they push the core slogan to the fore.

jo.backhouse.96 (2020) uses a similar approach, by focusing on a makeshift, hand-held sign stating that "It is NOT enough to be non-racist – We MUST be Anti-racist" (Fig. 12). That the poem – if indeed we consider it as such – appeared under the hashtags #poetryofprotest and #blacklivesmatter provides further contextualization. This seems hardly necessary in this case, however, as the posting was made just about two weeks after the killing of George Floyd, or in early June of 2020. Even though only six people publicly expressed their liking it as of March 2023, the image/poem is visually quite effective in my opinion, as it puts viewers in the position of fellow demonstrators, who are implicitly getting on board not only with the anti-racist message but also with the physical Black Lives Matter movement itself.

Fig. 12: jo.backhouse.96. "It is NOT enough to be non-racist." Instagram. June 9, 2020.

Notably the last two examples of protest poetry on Instagram invite questions about the poeticity of digital poetry, while expanding Jakobson's original concept to include multimodal approaches, as well. My overall impression is that digital poetry has a way of broadening our understanding of what, indeed, constitutes poetry today, not least through the elevating of language many would not have considered poetic outside of the world of hashtags and hyperlinks to art. "As an expressive form," writes Funkhouser, "[digital poetry] matters not only as a free-ranging serious practice, but because it invites vibrant, transformative multimodal engagement for its practitioners and audience alike" (Funkhouser 2012, 4). Especially the co-presence of verbal and visual elements is further contributing to a new appreciation of poetry as an art of engagement – with others, with one's community, with the world at large – as visuals tend to add considerable weight to the evidentiary value of a given post and thereby increase its affective power. Unlike more typical

Instapoetry, which tends to focus on subjective feelings supposedly shared by many and is targeted at garnering clicks and likes usually with the aim of monetizing them, the poems of protest considered here de-emphasize individual experience in favor of larger, political causes potentially affecting multitudes. Even though this almost certainly means that they cannot easily be monetized given prevailing marketing rules in the digital age, the actual currency they deal in is social relevance, agency, and collective empowerment, not personal self-promotion.

Performing virtual realities

As announced at the beginning of this article, I would like to conclude my discussion of digital poetry by briefly revisiting a virtual reality environment designed by the U.S. American performance artist Laurie Anderson and Taiwanese new media creator Hsin-Chien Huang in 2017. Their collaborative work *Chalkroom* appeared in the U.S., in the U.K., in Denmark, and Taiwan; it was furthermore declared the winner of the Venice International Film Festival in the category of Best Virtual Reality Experience in that year. Visitors to *Chalkroom*, equipped with VR headsets where the piece was exhibited in the real world (and without, in the case of its digitally-preserved online version; see Anderson and Huang 2017), move through a long series of interconnected, fluidly-expanding spaces whose walls look like old-school blackboards displaying words as well as some simple graffiti-style drawings, all done in chalk, hence the title of the piece. In addition to the writing on the walls, more letters and half-formed phrases reminiscent of fractured e-mail messages or blog entries appear to sail through the air, seemingly floating toward the viewer. By thus integrating old and new media into one audiovisual performance, the piece can be placed in alignment with the other examples of digital poetry discussed here, which likewise bridge that gap through an innovative mix of verbal and image content, the latter strikingly often relying on older media practices such as photography and writing or drawing by hand.

Anderson's disembodied voice-over narration is frequently referred to as storytelling in reviews included in the "Press Highlights" section of the *Chalkroom* website. However, it seems rather more poetic than prosaic, as the phrases uttered form repetitive and dream-like, loose chains of associations in lieu of an actual story one could follow from beginning to end. The repetitive structure is also reflected by the writing on the walls itself, where a few phrases occur again and again, including, "(Some Say our) Empire is Passing, as all Empires do" and "Angels of Artifice" (Anderson and Huang 2017). Throughout the entire performance, the tone is meditative bordering on elegiac, adding to the overall poetic effect further underscored by the spherical music track accompanying the piece. In contradistinction to the kind of protest poetry I have highlighted in this article, this artwork appears to vaporize language, through both vision and sound, rather than use it to invoke any concrete objects or recognizable real-world scenarios. In consequence, referentiality is itself in question where words "fall into dust. They form and reform," as Anderson notes on her website. In other words, a virtual reality environment such as *Chalkroom* makes use of digital poetry in order to afford a remarkably immersive experience, where visitors are invited to enter the digital performance of a work of art approximating something akin to pure poeticity. As such, Anderson and Huang's virtual reality environment presents a different, and by comparison a rather more experimental take on digital poetry: one that aims to free language of its referential bind altogether, via multimedia art, thereby opening up an experiential dimension, where visitors are likewise "free to roam and fly" (Anderson and Huang 2017).

Conclusion

In this article, I have argued and tried to show that digital poetry has initiated a return to the genre's former relevance and cultural weight, which poetry had enjoyed since ancient times but which has been greatly diminished over the course of roughly the past 150 years for a number of reasons. While some blame the immense popularity of another genre, narrative fiction, for this loss of cultural value (cf. Stein 2010, 105), it is equally important, I believe, to take into account the different media channels in which poetry has appeared and which have hugely affected its cultural position over decades and, indeed, centuries. The twentieth century, in particular, saw a gradual migration of poetry to mostly small presses and prestigious academic journals, granting it considerable cultural esteem but reaching relatively few, highly educated readers as a consequence. Poetry's diminished presence in Western cultures becomes especially apparent when keeping in mind that it used to be much more of an everyday phenomenon, read by the literate and memorized by most others, both on special occasions and in daily settings, the latter being preserved in children's rhymes, for instance, even today. In other words, poetry used to be on (almost) everyone's lips. The larger point that I have attempted to make here is that there is a real possibility that today's digital forms of producing and disseminating poetry might restore what Stein terms "the resiliency and relevance of poetry's public appeal" (Stein 2010, 106). The fact that several renowned poetry platforms in the U.S., including the Poetry Foundation and the Academy of American Poets, offer an app service through which they send subscribers a 'poem of the day' seems to testify to the rekindled desire or even need for poetry in people's everyday lives – a need that can easily be satisfied via such new, web-based media channels.

These new venues do not only make poetry accessible to readers formerly not as cognizant of or in any case connected to it; what is more, they have also summoned a rising number of poets who use social media platforms in order to get their work out to a potentially global public, perhaps most visibly exemplified by today's legions of Instapoets vying for readers' attention. Toward this end, much digital poetry including Instapoetry makes use of visual elements, thereby adding another sensory dimension to an otherwise all digital and verbal presentation. The fact that these visual elements often refer back to older media practices supports Baetens's observation that the latter have a way of re-emerging in digital poetry in what he describes as a gradual, transformative process from print to screen culture (cf. Baetens 2021, 240–241). In the examples discussed above, moreover, culled from a branch of recent U.S. American poetry mainly intended as a vehicle for articulating voices of protest and empowerment, the visual elements serve another, namely a specifically activist function. As Alyson Miller writes, "by representing that which unsettles and confronts, protest poetry establishes a collective responsibility for readers to reckon with past and present injustices" (Miller 2021, 5). Harking back to the notion of the 'citizen poet' of the nineteenth century, authors of this ilk consider poetry a public forum for addressing social and political causes and, ultimately, for the exposure of, and resistance against, various kinds of oppression. To conclude, while one would be hard-pressed to argue that today's poetry is essentially different from pre-digital times, it is quite apparent that the new social media affordances including visualizations and meaningful interactions with readers and entire communities are changing the position of poetry in today's world considerably, thereby increasing not only its public appeal but also, importantly, its social relevance. Consequently, while it is difficult to anticipate poetry's further development in any concrete terms, it is fairly safe to assume that its importance in the digital age is only going to increase in the foreseeable future.

References

Agamben, Giorgio. *Homo Sacer. Sovereign Power and Bare Life*. Redwood City, CA: Stanford Univ. Press, 1998.

Anderson, Laurie, and Hsin-Chien Huang. "Chalkroom." 2017, https://laurieanderson.com/?portfolio=chalkroom (February 13, 2023).

Baetens, Jan. "No, Poetry is Not out of Date: Notes on Poetic Writing and Digital Culture." Transl. Marie-Claire Merrigan. *Mediating Vulnerability. Comparative Approaches and Questions of Genre*. Ed. Anneleen Masschelein, Florian Mussgnug, and Jennifer Rushworth. London: UCL Press, 2021. 238–251.
Benjamin, Walter. "The Work of Art in the Age of Digital Reproduction." *Illuminations*. Ed. Hannah Arendt. Transl. Harry Zohn. New York: Schocken Books, 1969 [1935]. 1–26. https://web.mit.edu/allanmc/www/benjamin.pdf (September 5, 2022).
Benthien, Claudia, Jordis Lau, and Maraike M. Marxsen. *The Literariness of Media Art*. New York: Routledge, 2019.
Bolter, Jay David, and Richard Grusin. *Remediation. Understanding New Media*. Cambridge, MA: The MIT Press, 2000.
Bruns, Axel. *Blogs, Wikipedia, Second Life, and Beyond. From Production to Produsage*. New York: Peter Lang, 2008.
Bryant, Anna Li. "▪Anthem (a blackout poem of the National Anthem)." *Protest Through Poetry*, 2020. 36–37.
Funkhouser, Christopher. T. *Prehistoric Digital Poetry*. Tuscaloosa, AL: The Univ. of Alabama Press, 2007.
Funkhouser, Christopher. T. *New Directions in Digital Poetry*. New York: Continuum Books, 2012.
Grubnic, Tanja. "Nosthetics: Instagram Poetry and the Convergence of Digital Media and Literature." *The Australasian Journal of Popular Culture* 9.2 (2020): 145–163.
Holm Soelseth, Camilla. "When is a Poet an Instapoet?" *Sciendo* 10.1 (2022): 96–120. https://www.sciendo.com/de/article/10.2478/bsmr-2022-0008 (September 8, 2022).
Jakobson, Roman. "What is Poetry." *Language in Literature*. Cambridge, MA: Harvard Univ. Press, 1987. 368–378.
jo.backhouse.96. "It is Not Enough to be Non-Racist." June 9, 2020, https://www.instagram.com/jo.backhouse.96/ (February 13, 2023).
Miller, Alyson. "Ideas, Language, Action: The Protest Poetry of #MeToo and Black Lives Matter." *Poetry Now*. TEXT Special Issue 64 (2021): 1–18.
Mønster, Louise. "Contemporary Poetry and the Question of Genre. With a Special View to a Danish Context." *Dialogues on Poetry. Mediatization and New Sensibilities*. Ed. Dan Ringgard and Stefan Kjerkegaard. Aalborg: Aalborg Universitetsforlag, 2017. 235–255.
mutteringbum. "The sky was filled with resistance." May 3, 2022, https://www.instagram.com/mutteringbum/ (February 13, 2023).
Sanchez, Sonia. "Haiku and Tanka for Harriet Tubman." *Poems of Protest, Resistance, and Empowerment*. The Poetry Foundation. 2018, https://www.poetryfoundation.org/poetrymagazine/poems/146231/haiku-and-tanka-for-harriet-tubman (February 11, 2023).
Sokar, Mahmoud Moawad. "Digital Poetry: Innovation and De-aestheticization." *Aswan University Journal for Human Sciences* 1.1 (2021): 1–12.
Stein, Kevin. "Poems and Pixels: The Work of Art in an Age of Digital Reproduction." *Poetry's Afterlife: Verse in the Digital Age*. Ann Arbor, MI: Univ. of Michigan Press, 2010. 78–113.
The Poetry Foundation. https://www.poetryfoundation.org/ (September 5, 2022).
westtrestle. "Black Lives Matter." Instagram. April 20, 2022 (accessed on May 11, 2022; in the meantime, the post has been deleted).

Magdalena Elisabeth Korecka
Platformized Visual Intimacies: Visibility in Feminist Instapoetry

Introduction

What started as a photographic series about menstruation on Tumblr with Rupi Kaur continues today as aesthetically specific multimodal Instapoetry.[1] To be exact, the hereby analyzed poetry on Instagram belongs to visually engaging feminist renderings from the Anglophone, German-, and Polish-speaking Instapoetics, showcasing an extract of a multifaceted range: from "bookish" (Pressman 2020, 31), print-alluring typewriter poetics to colorful, platform-mediating examples. Furthermore, the body as a central topic and as a poetic device stands out in the chosen media-specific, feminist writing. When one looks at the long history of feminist literature and visual art (see, e.g., Wentrack 2014, 148–167; Janz 1995, 30), it is clear how the female body has been utilized as a canvas on which to portray societal norms, as an object on which patriarchal norms have been visibly displayed and negotiated in discourses *about* the body. These experiential renderings have then been performatively – thus, repeatedly – enacted *with* the artist's body or a figurative illustration of the body, a drawing, or with the help of an evoked ekphrasis, with which the body is deconstructively broken, thereby creating disillusionment and anti-hegemonial moments of resistance through repetitive patterns (cf. Butler 1988, 519–531). As such, specific variants of Instapoetry can be precisely situated within feminist literary practices that center the body as a key marker covering topics such as reproductive rights, online harassment of embodied marginalization, the queer love of "othered" bodies, and sexual violence against bodies that are perceived as female. As Mike Chasar argues with regard to the all-pervasive media, Instapoetry focuses on a "tripartite liberation – media, body, and poetry." Moreover, the scholar states that Instapoetic feminist writing displays a "synergy of bodily, visual, poetic, and medial creative control" (Chasar 2020, 186; cf. also 187), benefit-

---

[1] This article forms part of my dissertation project, in which I elaborate further on feminist Instapoetic writing. For instance, the networked dimension of Instapoetry will become even clearer in my netnographic/media ethnographic analysis of the comment section of "pre-baby body" with its 68 comments. To do so, I will combine various media ethnographic approaches such as netnography (cf. Kozinets 2020, 129–160) with affect analysis (cf. Zappavigna's "ambient affiliation," 2011, 800). Furthermore, in my multimodal analysis I will extend and adapt previous approaches by Gunther Kress and Theo van Leeuwen, Carey Jewitt, David Machin, and Sigrid Norris among other scholars in this field.

Open Access. © 2023 the author(s), published by De Gruyter. This work is licensed under the Creative Commons Attribution-NonCommercial-NoDerivatives 4.0 International License.
https://doi.org/10.1515/9783111299334-007

ting the agency of the feminist writer. Here, he refers to the bypassing of influential editors, journalists, marketing specialists, and publishers as instapoets such as Rupi Kaur now embody these multiple roles themselves. Thus, "liberation" is meant as a positive outcome of this new movement, whereas the body in poetry is also regarded as a canvas, "as a medium" (Chasar 2020, 188). Nevertheless, this entrepreneurial undertaking by poets puts them under intense labor-intensive pressures that center around the sale of one's own work and one's 'brand' (Holm Soelseth 2022, 43–44). This fact thus complicates the 'freedom' poetry and poets are seemingly granted on Instagram. So, I argue that the poetic feminist space on social media is a space of ambivalence that grants agency but simultaneously diminishes it. The double logic of this poetic form – its embeddedness in a capitalist, profit-based platform and its simultaneous activist premises – stand at the forefront of this article's feminist Instapoetic examination. This article will first present theory pertaining to the visibility and affective paradigm of Instagram, initially conceptualized in 2010 as a visual photo-sharing application (cf. Leaver et al. 2020, 44–52), before continuing with a brief overview of stylistic communities in feminist Instapoetry. Finally, it will conclude with an analysis of the multimodality in Hollie McNish's Instapoem "pre-baby body" (2021a).

(In)visibilities: Feminist Instapoetry and ambivalence

The internet and social media platforms have made it possible for feminists to express themselves through and with "body territories" (Brunner 2021) such as via platform-specific poetry and self-publishing efforts. They thereby bypass some of the powerful gatekeepers of the literary industry like mainstream publishers, critics, and literary committees. As an alternative practice of writing, reading, and publishing, social media poetry revolves around creating "greater visibility for demographics that are usually underrepresented or misrepresented" (Manning 2021, 269) in the largely white, patriarchal public literary sphere, including the perspectives of Black[2] female poets and collectives, and those of post-migrant authors (cf. bruce 2022, 246–263; Leetsch 2022, 301; Matthews 2019, 400). One pressing issue here, however, is that this seeming openness can be easily contradicted by the platform policies themselves, which continuously censor female

---

2 I choose to capitalize "Black" in order to signal the political implications of race in accordance with scholars such as Jenn M. Jackson (2020, 107).

bodies, e.g., by not allowing female breasts to be displayed, with the exceptions of mastectomies and breastfeeding, resulting in hashtag campaigns such as #freethenipple (cf. Are 2021, 1).[3] Underlying these censorial practices is the white, racist, patriarchal, and specifically US-influenced gaze directed at gender and sexuality, which is fostered by multi-billion-dollar networks such as on Elon Musk's Twitter and Mark Zuckerberg's Meta (cf. Little and Winch 2021, 9; Noble 2018, 14, 64). These conventions are exemplified by the Meta community guidelines, which were drafted in alignment with a hypersexualized Victoria's Secret advertising campaign (cf. Are 2021, 2). Magdalena Olszanowski appropriately names this control of the female body "sensorship," a "censoring of the senses" (Olszanowski 2014, 83), which users actively and creatively circumvent and negotiate with regard to queer and female corporeality. She connects her observation with the visual dimension of visibility, the "networked image" (Olszanowski 2015, 237) of the artistic and visual Instagram post and its comments. With this terminology, Olszanowski describes a space where networking allows users to generate power by creating visibility, that is, by commenting, liking, and tagging, which also applies to Instapoetry.

Regarding public spaces in general, Zofia Burr rightfully looks at Maya Angelou's engaged poetry to rightfully argue that the public space is not a neutral ground for discussion, as gendered and racialized bodies are consistently marginalized and accordingly discussed in marginalizing terms (cf. Burr 2009, 428–436). Even though the public space of Instagram offers them opportunities to "write back" internationally as it partially bypasses the racialized, class-based, and gendered power of the literary industry,[4] it does not circumvent the hegemony of social media platforms or their cultural embedding *per se*. Practices of writing back therefore take place in an ambivalent space, as the logic of marginalization con-

---

3 Currently (as of January 2023), Meta's advisory board (for Facebook and Instagram) has suggested to overhaul the ban on the free exposure of breasts by women, non-binary and trans people. Meta has sixty days to decide how to act upon this decision, which was made official on January 17, 2023 (cf. Demopoulos 2023).
4 As US-based research by Claire Grossman, Stephanie Young, and Juliana Spahr ("The Index of Major Literary Prizes in the US") revealed, the current situation of the prize-based literary system is particularly painful "for writers who are not white, a troubling contradiction in what otherwise appears to be a moment of watershed inclusion." (2021) While the diversification of prize-winning authors may seem positive at the surface, institutional legacies paint a more complex picture that proves how the entering of these systems is necessary for a successful career. Especially Black and otherwise marginalized writers are, statistically speaking, required to prove themselves professionally to a higher degree, and are put under immense pressures to write about their own identity in a certain manner (for a European context see also: Łomnicka 2018; for the observation of gender see the VIDA/Women in Liberal Arts count 2019). In regards to gender, the inadequate representation of non-binary writers is another concern, as VIDA reported in 2019.

tinues to apply on Instagram in the form of "shadowbanning": the suppression of content by platform algorithms and/or moderators, making it less visible or completely invisible, i.e., removing it from explore, hashtag, and search pages. This means that content is partly or completely hidden for interested users without the content creators' knowledge. Algorithms are thereby "engaged in the filtering of what can be seen," resulting in "new visibilities and invisibilities" (Amoore and Piotukh 2016, 6). Furthermore, the practice of shadowbanning is carried out on a variety of marginalized groups and identities – affecting multiple possible points of contention, e.g., LGBTQIA+ populations or Black female content creators. When it comes to female bodies, shadowbanning is a "form of light and secret censorship targeting what Instagram defined as borderline content, particularly affecting posts depicting women's bodies, nudity and sexuality" (Are 2021, 1–3). Olszanowski also confirms this assertion, writing that posts and stories that are "nude, nonconforming to ideals of beauty, [or] dealing with violent subject matter" are examples of content that is potentially "flagged," "and/or removed via Instagram," shadowbanned, or even deleted (Olszanowski 2015, 233). The problematic implications for instapoets are that poems and posts are not visible on explore pages when users search by certain hashtags and/or content, thereby reducing existential income that specifically depends on content visibility. This exclusionary practice, highlighted by the negative and visual connotation of the shadow, leads to disillusionment about the so-called "safe space" rhetoric propagated by the platforms (cf. Olszanowski 2015, 240, with reference to bell hooks's critique of white feminist safe spaces).

Feminist Instapoetry is embedded precisely within this two-faced logic of the new media sphere, which has to be dissected and analyzed in terms of its visual style – a highly political endeavor – which can be achieved through "persistent looking," a "refusal to look away from what is kept out of sight" (Mirzoeff 2017, 85). Feminist Instapoetry is a space of continuous negotiation and resistance against platform policies and reflects a desire to carve out a space for diverse voices on social media. Instapoets and their followers thus operate within a neoliberal ambivalence, situated in "economies of visibility" (Banet-Weiser 2018, 21; cf. Glatt and Banet-Weiser 2021, 43) and embedded within the social media entertainment industry marked by "visibility labor" and "self-branding" (cf. Holm Soelseth 2022, 43–44; Pâquet 2019, 300–301). "Economies of visibility" describes "the ways in which the visibility of particular identities and politics, such as gender, race, and sexuality, circulates on multiple media platforms" (Glatt and Banet-Weiser 2021, 43), affecting female and/or Black and/or LGBTQIA+ populations in particular. Given these circumstances, it is revealing to see how the phenomenon of civically engaged Instapoetry manages to incorporate feminist creation, mirroring a certain discursive body politics circulating on social media in general.

In line with the ambivalence described above, "visual capital" (Mirzoeff 2019) on Instagram in the form of feminist Instapoetry can create a starting point for an aesthetics of resistance that incorporates certain female visibilities. This type of poetry can, however, also be commodified into visual capital once more, potentially with the same visible bodies it attempted to previously empower, which are then repurposed for a "postfeminist sensibility" (Gill 2017, 610; cf. Orgad and Gill 2021, 54–55). For instance, feminist Instapoems as such can be easily commodified through product-endorsements, e.g., when creators post period product advertisements. One example of this is Hollie McNish's (unnamed) poem on menstruation that was posted as part of the #EndPeriodPoverty campaign, where the brand Always donated one pad per like to the Red Box Project in the UK. This was problematic considering the brand's years-long body shaming practices and indicates a postfeminist "wokewashing" (Orgad and Gill 2021, 31) accompanying the in itself feminist content of the poem.

Moreover, the visuality of Instapoems is created by the "affordances" of social media that are central to the human-technology relationship, as argued by, e.g., Jenny Davis (cf. 2020, 22–30) and Taina Bucher and Anne Helmond (cf. 2018, 233–253). This concept describes "*how* objects shape action for socially situated subjects" and "how objects enable and constrain" action (Davis 2020, 18; 22). This means that affordances allow for all kinds of creative exploration in poetic writing but can also constrict certain artistic possibilities. Davis' theory is an extension of James Gibson's "affordances of the environment" (Gibson 1986 [1979], 127) and Dan Norman's design theory (2013) that is here applied to postdigital poetry. In other words, the affordances of networking and visibility are made possible by connecting the in itself valuable poetic work to hashtags, location tags, and captions as well as through the multimodal coloring, compositions, and the use of typography. But they are afforded in dependence on the media literacy of the poet and reader on Instagram as well as the technical conditions of the platform (cf. Davis 2020, 18; 22). While keeping the concept of affordances open and flexible, it can be argued that it plays a major role in the scrutinization of the possibilities and limitations associated with poetic creation in the digital age.

One result of this is the different visual elements and aesthetics, and ultimately various "stylistic communities" ("Stilgemeinschaften," Gross and Hamel 2022, 9–10) that emerge in visually non-monolithic Instapoetry. While Gross and Hamel mainly discuss elements such as punctuation, brevity, and irony, here, visual elements such as color are also poeticity creators. These will be explored in the following in discussions of poetry written in English, German, and Polish by Nikita Gill (@nikita_gill), Carina Eckl (@kursives_ich), and Rudka Zydel (@rudkazydel) respectively.

The visuality of feminist Instapoetry: Stylistic communities

In Nikita Gill's poem "Death Threat (Trigger Warning)" (2021) about the harassment of and violence against women in online spaces, she uses an affective mode of shock and anger. As this paper will later argue, this affect is a pre-emotional state that subsequently influences any action and is inextricably linked to the consequent emotions (cf. Paparachissi 2014, 5). In Gill's poem, affect and emotionality are exemplified by the use of swear words like "bitch" and connected to the trigger warning in the caption describing "violence against women," where the female author positions herself at the receiving end of misogynistic hate.[5] The visuals of the feminist poem are plain and simple, reminiscent of pen and paper, with a longer text in the caption that ends with the hashtag #poetry, thereby marking it as a poem and its author a member of the poetic community on Instagram. The use of black font against a white background stands out on the highly stylized platform, although this would not seem unusual in the material form of the book. Gill's feed – i.e., her profile (see Gill 2022), which comprises all the poems she has posted, sometimes in remediated audiovisual versions that circulate from the book page to the platform and back – is highly structured. It is consistent, alternating between black-and-white, "bookish" poems and colorful, promotional content, which creates the unique aesthetic that is associated with Instapoetry. In the poem itself, a serious topic is juxtaposed with a simple visual form, further emphasizing the poem's content through this stark contrast. Here, it makes an allusion to book culture and a certain type of nostalgia reminiscent of Instagram's early lo-fi, vignette-centered, "vintage" aesthetics – a "nosthetics" (Grubnic 2020, 145; cf. Leaver et al. 2020, 44–55).

Similarly, Carina Eckl's typewriter aesthetic, also often seen in Instapoetry, focuses on the corporeal dimension, the body, which is already manifest in her user name @kursives_ich, meaning "@cursive_me." To be specific, *kursiv* in German refers to italics and also sounds like the word "curvy" in English. The relation between these words, and therefore the inherent word play, is further enhanced by the fact that italics are a typographic form of writing that consist of malleable text, which here also points to the malleable body. When considering the phrase "soft body soft heart" in the author's bio, this relationship becomes even clearer. The account name is therefore a creative exploration of languages that ultimately and

---

5 As studies show, women and girls, and especially further minoritized women, experience disproportionate hate online, which is still fairly unregulated by EU and international law with regard to the digital sphere (cf. Bayer and Bárd 2020, 17).

formally centers poetic content on body image, a *topos* that permeates Eckl's poetry. In general, her whole profile is black and white, and short poems on e.g., queer love alternate with framed photographs of visual art and museum snapshots. One case in point is an unnamed poem that forms part of a postmodern aesthetic that utilizes "analog" materials, which are relocated into the post-digital sphere of a square Instapost by means of remediation, i.e., the poem was written on a typewriter and then photographed and uploaded to Instagram. Hence, Eckl layers visual materialities, which results in a truly "hybrid aesthetic" (Bassett 2015, 136), a marker of post-digitality, with the remediated typewriter font also showcasing a critique of "old-fashioned," patriarchal systemic ideas that need to be revised. The poem's scope and its meaning are also expanded through the political caption "your body, your choice" and with seven lines of hashtags, including repetitions of #yourbodyyourchoice and #feminismus, clear positions and visible feminist slogans (Fig. 13). These hashtags are part of a wider international feminist discourse centered on bodily autonomy. By changing the politically significant feminist slogan "my body, my choice" and its first-person pronoun to the second-person level with #yourbodyyourchoice, Eckl addresses the reader directly, in a poetic and activist manner.

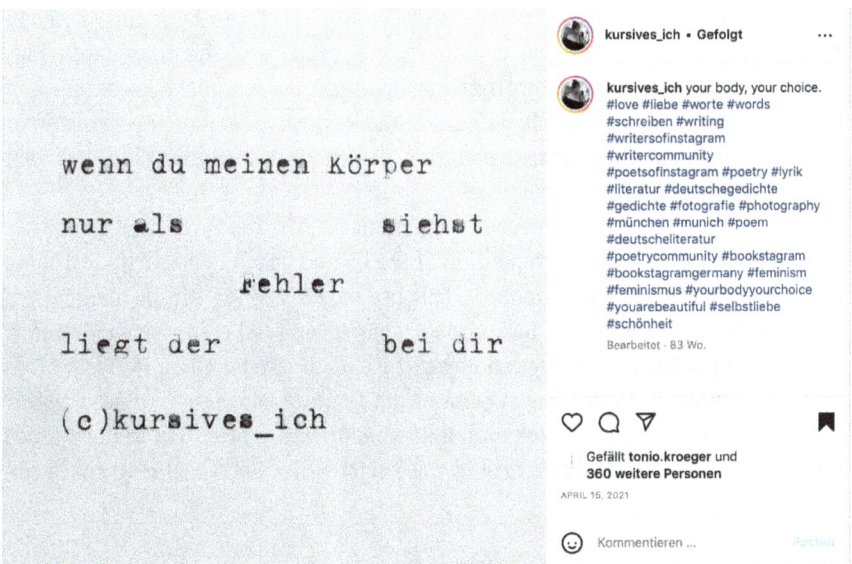

Fig. 13: @kursives_ich. Unnamed poem. Instagram. April 15, 2021.

Engaged or "activist" poetry has a more radical, materialist feminist aesthetic and its own stylistic community (cf. Baumgardner and Richards 2000, 95; Lorde 2009, 356). Audre Lorde formulates it in this way when discussing the existential necessity of poetry: "For women, then, poetry is not a luxury. It is a vital necessity of our existence. [. . .] Poetry is the way we help give name to the nameless so it can be thought." (Lorde 2009, 356) Thus, poetry is in itself actualizing this pivotal need – as in all discussed examples in this article –, as for instance, in poems that play a crucial role in activist strategizing. A specific case in point are poems that specifically draw upon current political movements and "tangible action," as in the feminist online anthology *Wiersz nie jest cudem* (*A Poem is Not a Miracle*; 2022). Here, poetry is functional and manifests a visual surplus, utilized by Polish feminists in the context of the Black Protests,[6] the #czarnyprotest, the #strajkkobiet ("womensstrike"). Particularly in the wake of the 2020 protests that took place on social media and the streets, the political movement initially founded in 2016 made visual art to propagate its opposition to the curtailing of reproductive rights in Poland and to show solidarity with the affected women (cf. Graff 2020, 230–235). Poetry on Instagram continues this protest by visually utilizing these specific symbols and content from the women's rights movement and therefore directly positions itself as a part of this political endeavor. For example, the title of Rudka Zydel's poem "Babskie wiersze" (Fig. 14), which can be found on her Instagram profile and in a longer version on the webpage of the online anthology, plays ironically with the minoritization of literature written by women, as it seemingly reduces this highly affective and critical poem to the category of "Women's poems," the direct translation of the original Polish title, but even more so reclaims the category.

The caption contains numerous movement-specific hashtags such as #piekłokobiet ("womenshell") and a repetition of the last poem's line #jebaćlukierróbmydym ("fuckfrostingletscreatesmoke"). This use of the hashtag can be aligned with Elizabeth Losh's statement of hashtags as "condensed [. . .] expressive cultural artifacts" (Losh 2020, 4), thereby rendering the symbol a poetic one in itself. Moreover, the famous red lightning symbol of the feminist movement, placed against the beige background and black font, immediately draws attention to the political endeavor and connects the excerpt of the longer poem with it. Due to space con-

---

[6] The "Black Protests" ("Czarny Protest") were the women's rights protests against the restrictions to abortion rights in Poland from 2016, to which everyone attending wears black clothes "as a sign of mourning for women's reproductive rights" (Graff 2020, 231). A not so obvious or well-known allusion is to the "spectacle of women wearing black during Anti-Russian demonstrations in 1861" (Graff 2020, 231). For a detailed discussion of the hashtag in the context of the feminist Black Protest movement see Nacher 2021.

Fig. 14: @rudkazydel. "Babskie wiersze." Instagram. October 26, 2020.

straints, Zydel has posted a rather short version of the whole poem on Instagram in the form of six lines, which is also visually indicated through three dots in brackets in the first line of the poem. Here, the poem's meta self-reflection clearly identifies the writing as feminist poetry ("feministyczne wiersze") and basically contradicts the figure of the sweet, obedient girl, replacing it with a loud, subversive, angry woman (cf. Graff 2020 232, 242). Such affects are used throughout this particular movement, the Czarny Protest and the Strajk Kobiet, and can be regarded as helping to embody a collectively visualized and subversive "feminist killjoy" character within the poem's lyrical persona and in the author persona as well as within the poetic reader-writer collective (cf. Ahmed 2010, 582).

Social media logics: Affectivity in platformized poetry

Feminist stylistic communities range from black-and-white "bookish" aesthetics to materialist collage styles and specific symbols rooted in material feminist movements outside of social media. In addition, they utilize platform features such as hashtags to visually and visibly create a specific feminist multimodal aesthetics. Its multimodality lies in the actual poetic units of text-image or text-moving image-sound accompanied by paratextual or epitextual elements such as the caption (the text beneath the poem), a location tag (the location indicated above an Instagram image connected to the platform's cartography), hashtags (words marked by a # sign or "a finding aid"[7] (Losh 2020, 3) linking the post to a theme, political movement, the Instapoetry writing scene, or providing additional self-definition), and the comment section (comments beneath the *poeimage* – a term I use to describe the inherent imagery of Instagram poems). These textualities are additionally entangled with the visual multimodal elements of Instapoems, such as typography, color, and composition (cf. Ledin and Machin 2020, 88–186). As such, Instapoetry inherently forms part of the platform and is marked by a tension between its given platform options and shared poetic feminist efforts. Therefore, Instapoetry is "platformized poetry." With this concept I am picking up on media and cultural studies scholars Thomas Poell, David Nieborg, and Brooke Erin Duffy and their theory of platformization as the "penetration of digital platforms' economic, infrastructural, and governmental aspects into the cultural industries, as well as the organization of cultural practices of labor, creativity, and democracy around the platforms" (Poell et al. 2022, 5). Feminist Instapoetry can be accordingly located in the sphere of cultural production and is highly entangled with the economic realm, precarious gig labor, and the diminished visibility of certain groups, meaning that it is a form of platformized creation and production (cf. Holm Soelseth 2022, 98).

The platformization of poetry is accompanied by the importance of visibility in a network marked by information and pictorial overload and scarce possibilities for action. If we relate it to the previously described control over female bodies and "sensorship" (Olszanowski 2014, 83), as well as Taina Bucher's theory of algorithms (2012), the concept of visibility is challenged by its opposite. Visibility as a notion has been discussed in visual culture and cultural studies most famously with regard to Michel Foucault's theory of the panopticon and its power-infused "regimes" of visibility. The panopticon, an architectural prison model designed by Jeremy Bentham, has an invisible observer at its center overseeing everyone from every possible angle, which compels people to discipline themselves accordingly, as Foucault claims (cf. 1995, 201). While this theory is useful for thinking about the invisible control exerted over female bodies by the internet's black box of largely hidden APIs, the post-digital sphere employs another oppositional concern: the possibility of disappearing, of not being considered important enough. In order to appear, to become visible, one needs to follow a certain logic embedded within the architecture of the platform (cf. Bucher 2012, 1171). In her study on algorithms on social media, Bucher speaks in this context of a "threat of invisibility on the part of the participatory subject" (Bucher 2012, 1164). Additionally, from an ontological

---

[7] As Elizabeth Losh researched, the hashtag was initially conceptualized for an additive phone button and its function was "sorting digital content into similar clusters" (Losh 2020, 2), which continues to exist as such on social media platforms.

standpoint, the more the poetic work is entangled with the platform's "visual capital" logic (Mirzoeff 2019) – i.e., the more one's livelihood depends on these (in)visibility structures – the more crucial it becomes to consider censorship practices on social media. Monetization efforts are thus a direct result of differing levels of platform dependency, further fueled by the gendered dimensions of gig work on platforms, such as unpaid brand labor by female creators (cf. Duffy 2015, 1). These implications cannot be ignored for feminist Instapoetry as it is grounded in the visibility of the female body – illustrated or drawn, ekphrastically evoked, photographed, in pictures made by the authors themselves and *of* themselves, and/or by other artists in collaborative efforts. Consequently, the threat of invisibility is productively and poetically challenged by the visualized body that circumvents all attempts to visually extinguish it.

Simultaneously, the capitalist, neoliberal environment of the platforms means that visibility at times fluctuates between "wokewashed" postfeminist poetry in the manner of representation politics (visibility for the sake of visibility) and feminist poetic content of resistance that cannot completely escape its neoliberal embeddedness but tries to resist it. As Zoë Glatt and Sarah Banet-Weiser rightfully argue in reference to the ambivalent status of social media creators, which can be applied to the Instapoetry described here, the

> emergence of exciting queer, intersectional, and progressive political content [. . .] working to transform hegemonic power relations [. . .] is fundamentally built on a platform designed with the capitalist logics of competition, hierarchy, and inequality. So, while some content creators aspire to be "transformational" – to change social norms, to challenge discrimination, to disrupt systems of power – as long as this kind of transformation is also transactional, there is a limit to its progressive potential. (Glatt and Banet-Weiser 2021, 54)

The following analysis will examine the extent to which the poetry by Hollie McNish aspires to resist and yet cannot escape the capitalist, transactional logic of Instagram. But before that, I would like to make a few remarks about Instapoetry's affective dimension.

Generally, a kind of "transformational" resistance in visible, online community feminist efforts is a commitment to *affectivity*, meaning to the affects evoked through Instapoetry and its paratextual elements, i.e., visually displayed in the audience's commentary. Theories of the affect on social media and its politics reflect the interconnection between the social media system, political movements, and feminist art. Affects and affectivity are understood here as the ability to invoke emotions, so deeply personal and intimate states of being such as love, hate, joy, anger, and hope (cf. Paparachissi 2014, 15; Ahmed 2014, 43–61; 82–100; 122–143). Affect is thus "a form of pre-emotive intensity subjectively experienced and connected to [. . .] processes of premediation or anticipation of events prior to their occurrence" (Paparachissi 2014, 5). To clarify the terminological use in this paper, when one speaks of affects, it is difficult to separate them from the resulting emotions that are therefore always considered together with affects. In addition, affects work through their close proximity to embodied subjects and objects, i.e., they create feelings of closeness across varying situations, such as across geographical distances. The affected subjects and their emotive responses are therefore further characterized by a directional "stickiness" (Ahmed 2014, 89–90). This logic is used on social media in order to politically mobilize readers through the use of hashtags, e.g., on Twitter (cf. Paparachissi 2014, 30–63, in particular her analysis of the Arab Spring as a hashtag movement; cf. Illouz 2010, 5, and her concept of "emotional capitalism"). Media scholar Zizi Paparachissi calls these practices of closeness and affect "affective affiliation," which manifest themselves in "affective publics" (Paparachissi 2014, 115–136). Hinting at a culture of feeling created by hashtags, linguist Michelle Zappavigna refers to them as "ambient affiliation" (Zappavigna 2011, 800).

In intersectional feminist theory, emotions are regarded as productive vehicles for radical change. Accordingly, "love," "anger," and "hope," among an array of emotional expressions, can further the equality of lived feminist realities presented in feminist Instapoems. Epistemologically, this view underpins an understanding of emotionality that is entangled with rationality and not erased from it (cf. Ahmed 2014, 43–61; 82–100; 122–143). This is important to mention here as there is a complicated and problematic history of the literary establishment rejecting young adult fiction and Instapoetry as objects of analysis for being genres that are "too emotional" – a highly debatable sentiment considering that a myriad of writers and readers that occupy these genres are young Black and Brown women (cf. Bronwen 2020, 90; see also Watts 2018). Do young female writers and readers then constitute targeted reading and writing communities? Paparachissi and Zappavigna, are wary of speaking of "communities," instead opting for terms like "publics" and "affiliations" in order to stress the "connective" (Poell and Van Dijck 2015, 534) character of social media that does not necessarily encompass enduring initiatives, i.e., communities. Here, the term community is used very consciously as something that indicates self-definition and emphasizes a seriality of feminist visuals – e.g., symbols, logos, or colors – that are not only indicative of a commodity culture but are also aspects of a visualized unity, feelings of belonging, and both aesthetic and affective sharing practices. While Instapoetry cannot escape its neoliberal placement, its focus on the "shared rituals" and "relational linkages" central to "virtual communities" (Parks 2010, 111) renders it fruitful for discussions of lived, feminist realities. Olszanowski fittingly names this visualized feminism on Instagram a "community *in* an image" and an "affective exchange" in the form of the post, the comments, the caption (Olszanowski 2014, 233). With reference to Hollie McNish's YouTube work, George Cox also speaks of the "affective ability to constitute a community" within the "poetics of platforms" (Cox 2020, 2).

Similarly, in Instapoetry, relationships of closeness characterize the relationship between the author and the audience, where captions and comments exhibit cultures of feeling on an intimate level in networks and in scale-dependent "network effects." Direct network effects explain why "the more users who join a network, the more valuable that network becomes" (Poell et al. 2022, 37; cf. also Franzen 2022, 116). This means that the economic value of a platform and its poems rises if a specific author puts out more poems or "content." The network also signalizes that only a few nodes in the network will ever achieve such a popular status. Thus, a few instapoets may relate to a huge number of followers or fans in an intimate way. Furthermore, Olszanowski speaks of affect as an inherent element of aesthetics when considering aspects that lead to interactions with others, creating layered meaning and potentials of action (Olszanowski 2014, 17). It could even be said that affect can be seen as an implicit element of aesthetic affordances in Instapoetic writing. Affective feminist visualities, moreover, can be traced back to DIY cultures, blogs in the alt-lit or alternative literary scenes of the 2000s, where playfulness toward gender and existing stereotypes resulted in the creation of "public selves" as part of a collective understanding called "community" (Harris 2012, 221–222). What is referred to as "feminist Instagram aesthetics" (Crepax 2020, 71) constitutes these subversive feminist practices inherent in the feminist Instapoetry discussed here. The unifying aspect is visualized through a "networked" quality, the aforementioned "relational linkage" (Parks 2010, 111) in the sharing of women's highly personalized lived realities and therefore in the shared "intimacies" of poetry and its dynamic media environments (cf. bruce 2022, 246).

Specifically, the angry figure of the "feminist killjoy," which refers to the expression of powerful feelings, furthers the advancement of women when everyday conversations become uncomfortable but productive (cf. Ahmed 2010, 582). This means that this figure's expression of anger – an often negatively connoted emotion for women – sheds a light on crucial issues. It can be said that, e.g., anger in networks about sexual violence, hopes for equal payment, and the love felt in sisterhoods are emotions that can be productively used. This is the case, for example, when shared emotions are acknowledged as valid expressions by individuals and institutions and they further the organization of public street protests. If these emotional states are expressed and shared in connection with highly personal topics in a public sphere, they are marked as "intimate publics" (cf. Olszanowski 2014, 232). Intimacy is thereby understood as something that reveals our "innermost" selves and can be traced back etymologically to the Latin root *intimus*. This intimacy is publicly shared through individual poems and collective practices of commenting, liking, and sharing, and is situated in cultural and contextual spaces (e.g., concerning the association of colors with femininity, for instance). These practices of intimacy are then visually expressed in feminist visual artistic renderings using multimodal elements such as colorful emojis or unifying hashtags that signify solidarity or belonging or, in general, through the "networked image" of the Instapoem. To summarize these considerations about the entanglement between multimodal visuality, visibility, and affect, feminist Instapoetry is a phenomenon of what I propose calling *platformized and networked post-digital visual intimacies*. I will now further explore these intimacies by analyzing an emblematic example, Hollie McNish's poem "pre-baby body."

Hollie McNish's "pre-baby body": Platformized visual intimacies

Hollie McNish (@holliepoetry) is a British poet and writer, whose Instagram bio states: "I love writing poems / Sunday Times Bestseller / Books: Slug, Plum, Nobody Told Me, Antigone / Agent @lewinsohnliterary / Bookings: oli@pagetoperformance. org" and contains a "linktr.ee," a categorized collection of links. These include a link to her books, tour dates, and a donation link to "Planned Parenthood" (cf. McNish 2022).[8] Thus, an initial glance at her Instagram page shows how McNish and/or her agent are positioning her as a successful poet: her bio mentions the *Sunday Times* bestseller status granted to her last collection of poetry, prose, and short stories *Slug: and Other Things I've Been Told to Hate* (2021d) as well as her poetry books *Plum* (2017) and *Nobody Told Me: Poetry and Parenthood* (2020), for which she received the Ted Hughes Award for New Work in Poetry. In addition, her official representation by an agent makes the account, which McNish curates herself, seem highly professional (email correspondence McNish, December 2022). Her follower count of 80,700 underlines her position as an avid social media poster who regularly uploads content. Her work is versatile and multimodal, and crosses genres; it ranges from poetry performances and album recordings at Abbey Road Studios to poetry readings and spoken word pieces on YouTube, the project "Poems in Pyjamas," and Instapoetry on Instagram. Thematically, McNish's poetry is centered around motherhood, sexuality, female empowerment, body image, and politics, and can therefore be considered feminist writing. For example, her poem "Embarrassed" (2013) about breastfeeding in public and the hyper-sexualization of mothers' bodies went viral on YouTube with

---

8 As of November 20, 2022, there were 2,677 posts on Hollie McNish's social media feed followed by 80,700 followers.

1,4 million views. It was then turned into a poetry film in collaboration with filmmaker Jake Dypka (2016). The artistic versatility of the poet, dramatist, spoken word artist, and host is also evident in her feed visuals.

Her Instagram profile displays visually static, colorful, highly saturated poems together with recorded poetry readings, audiovisual snippets and photographs of poetry performances and other artistic events, screenshots of Twitter posts, photographs of herself and with other poetic collaborators, a few advertisements for period products, and political calls for action. Her visual poetry is immediately recognizable due to the use of neon colors such as pink in the formally identifiable series "sketches," of which the poem "pre-baby body" (Fig. 15) is a part. This poem about motherhood was posted on July 21, 2021, was liked 1,470 times, and received 68 comments, with the paratextual caption description: "Today's sketching after reading a lot of Summer body / baby body back bollocks (for the last eleven years of motherhood) and imagining someone delivering my pre-baby body to me x." (McNish 2021a). A direct reference to the body, besides the obvious content of body politics, is the alliteration of "baby body back bollocks," pointing to the title "pre-baby body." Accordingly, semantics and sound ("baby," "body," "breasts," and "bones,") unite the poem and the caption, rendering it "authentic" (Lajta-Novak 2020, 324) and also approaching a seeming amalgamation of the implicit persona in the caption and the lyrical persona in the poem.

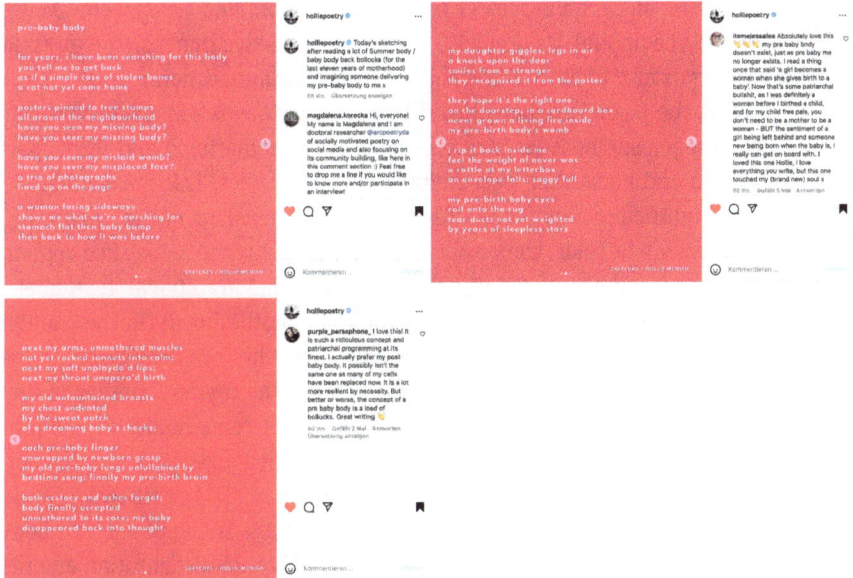

Fig. 15: @holliepoetry. "pre-baby body." Instagram. July 21, 2021.

However, the unity of the ironic take and simultaneous criticism of the societal expectations on a mother's body is visible not only in the caption and in the poem's semantic and poetic interconnections but also on the visual level. The connection between the poem's twelve stanzas of four lines on the one hand and the series "sketches" on the other is visibly marked by capital letters in the lower right-hand corner of the "poeimage." It consists of a so-called "carousel post," i.e., multiple slides or pages – in this case three – instead of one square image post, and cleverly circumvents the platform's space constraints. The visible contrast between the highly saturated pink in the flat background or foreground and the white font also strikes the reader immediately. The poeimage shares this aesthetic with other poems on the poet's profile and in the series, such as the poems "newborn" (McNish 2021b) and "no stones in her stomach" (McNish 2021c). Thus, "sketches" is a visual format, particularly with regard to its use of color. Making reference to multimodal theory and the interpersonal functions of language (cf. Ledin and Machin 2020, 8), "coherence," "ideas," and "attitude," we could say that the tripartite poem series with its ready-made aesthetic seriality is characterized by visual "coherence" (Ledin and Machin 2020, 91–96), and therefore unity in its format. In addition, there are two relevant dimensions of the interpersonal function and thus of an intermedial transfer of meaning-making. Visually addressed to the audience, "ideas" (Ledin and Machin 2020, 89–90) in the form of feminist discourse are also communicated through the modes of color, composition, and typography. Moreover, "attitude" (Ledin and Machin 2020, 90–91), an affective dimension expressed in various ways, is also implicit in the poem's visual communication.

In general, the poem "pre-baby body" by Hollie McNish is a visual deconstruction of the misogynistic body politics associated with motherhood and forms part of platformized and networked post-digital visual intimacies. This means that the poem displays and circulates the platform-specific dimensions of the poetry, i.e., the visual utilization of color, composition, and typography, the networked content in the caption and comments, the visual modes including 'traditional' textual elements, and the highly intimate content of embodied motherhood. On the content level, a lyrical persona is "searching for this body," i.e., the "pre-baby body" in the title – a seemingly non-essential object or an animal as the rhyming similes "a simple case of stolen bones" in line three and a "cat not yet come home" in line four suggest. The twice repeated "missing body" is a personified object in a missing person's report as the evocation of a photographed woman "facing sideways" on a "poster" indicates. This aesthetically postmodern montage is composed of a body semantics combined with negatively connotated adjectives of disfiguration and the affective dimension of disgust. Body parts such as "my mislaid womb" and "my misplaced face" are replaced with a separation between the female connoted body and motherhood, by e.g., "unmothered muscles," "pre-birth baby eyes," "soft, unplaydo'd lips," "throat unopera'd birth," "old unfountained breasts," "pre-baby finger," "pre-baby brain," and, finally, "body [. . .] unmothered to its core." The body is gradually dissected into its individual elements, from head to toe, only to refer back to the "brain," that is, the beginning and the "acceptance" of the body in an "unmothered" state. By distorting the visual image of the body through the peculiar-looking words – before the reader's inner eye as well – McNish poetically creates and exhibits a focus on the materiality of the body. Only the glitch in the flow of reading creates a "hésitation" (Valéry 1960, 637), a forced moment of reflection. Thus, the absurd image of a body being delivered disrupts the rules of convention by making a chronological break, by returning to a previously embodied state of personhood, devoid of motherhood. By utilizing text, color, typography, and composition as its core visual modes, without any photographic elements, and by evoking a female body by poetic means, the poem circumvents the "sensorship" regulations imposed on the female body (cf. Olszanowski 2014, 83). The ekphrastically evoked body, visible to the inner eye, cannot be registered by platform algorithms or censored.

By separating the body from motherhood on a semantic level through disgust, the "stickiness" of certain emotions toward maternal bodies, a gendered norm, is performatively revealed and simultaneously deconstructed. As feminist scholar Sara Ahmed argues, embodied disgust relies on "economies of disgust" that "also involve the shaping of bodies. When the body of another becomes an object of disgust, then this body *becomes* sticky" (Ahmed 2014, 92). The poem portrays a disembodied motherhood ekphrastically and visually as strange by negating body parts ("*un*mothered muscles," emphasis added) when they are removed from the embodied mother. The violation of such a separation also becomes manifest through the absurdness of returning to a "pre-baby body" that only aggressive force may achieve as the lyrical persona "rip[s] it back inside." This awareness of disgust sticking to the mother's body makes apparent the absurdity of such societal discourses, i.e., of returning to a "pre-baby body." That is when dissent about a visual, affective, and highly intimate level of the self becomes possible. When embodied collective feelings, "intimacies," connect the bodies of motherhood to other emotions such as love, they separate the body from disgust (cf. Ahmed 2014, 100).

In addition, the performed repetitiveness in relation to the body in the poem reenacts a further deconstruction of this societal discourse and the pressure on mothers to lose weight after birth. Lines seven to ten, the last two lines of stanza two, and the first two lines of stanza three read: "have you seen my missing body? / have you seen my missing body? / have you seen my mislaid womb? / have you seen my misplaced face?" These lines not only create a certain rhythmicality and musicality in the poem but are also subversive and deconstruct the "disgusting body." A "*stylized repetition of acts*" (Butler 1988, 519) enforces gender norms and constitutions. These repetitions visualize how a body may be affectively associated with certain characteristics through frequent use over time. This "subversive repetition" has a "transformational" potential, which is also how Glatt and Banet-Weiser (2021, 49–51) describe effective feminism. Accordingly, such a disclosure leaves room for the visibility of an affective and alternative possibility of (performed) gender expression. Thus, seriality and repetition are not only important in social media poetry as far as a commodified aesthetics are concerned; another act of feminist subversion and another attempt at visibility lies in the modal dimensions of color, typography, and composition.

Concerning color, the use of bright pink as a background color, highly energetic, i.e., creating a strong contrast with the white, lower-case font, catches the eye of the potential reader in the flow of pictures and information in Instagram's economy of attention. The color used here is saturated, conveying an "emotional temperature," and is also decidedly bright, rather flat, and u-modulated, signaling "truthfulness," i.e., conveying ideas within a clear worldview (cf. Levin and Machin 2020, 100; 107). The pink is a hybrid between white and red, the latter a color known to elicit attention and highlight importance, and thus affectively plays with a potential reader-writer (cf. Elliot 2015, 3). This means that it not only signals the importance of the poem's feminist message; rather, the use of the color pink in the poem also contradicts the expectations of the audience, which are created at first sight. While in Western culture pink is mostly associated with a conservative notion of womanhood, it is subversively and explicitly utilized here to deconstruct the gendered gaze. This means that the distinct use of stereotypical and gendered aesthetic notions forms part of a produced and celebrated "hyper-femininity," created with the help of visual elements such as color or even "glitter, [. . .] soft lighting, candy and pastel colors, pretty flowers." (Crepax 2020, 79) Such renderings are a case in point for post-digital feminism or a certain "feminist Instagram aesthetics," as Rosa Crepax claims (2020, 76).

These visualities are productively utilized in order to shed light on urgent feminist issues such as motherhood, sexuality, and reproductive rights. This creates visibility for feminist content, as in McNish's poem, and mocks misogynistic content on Instagram through visual playfulness. Nevertheless, "girly" feminism cannot entirely escape its "postfeminist sensibility," so, the placement of the poem in the capitalist, data-driven platform logic (cf. Crepax 2020, 76). In a highly restricted environment such as Instagram, such efforts mirror platform logics while simultaneously subverting them. For this reason, it can be argued that the criticism in the poem of the unrealistic body standards placed on women is reflective of Instagram culture itself, which is known to proliferate photoshopped body types. However, it is not only the mode of color that functions as a crucial meaning-maker in "pre-baby-body" – typography and composition fulfill additional functions.

With regard to the typography and the composition of "pre-baby body," the following visual characteristics situate the poem within nostalgic book culture. Clicking the three slides and looking at the open space on the right side of the square frame is like turning a page, visually signified by an arrow. The material and tactile dimension evoked here can be said to exist within the compositional mode. When specifically dissecting and persistently looking at the objects and subjects of analysis (cf. Mirzoeff 2019), the "modal configurations" (Norris 2011, 78) of typography and composition, and the following revelations become clear: the consistently left-justified text, which is written in lower-case letters, is characterized by a regular, horizontal, bold, and rounded font that signals openness, seriousness, and artistic playfulness (cf. Levin and Machin 2020, 135). Such aesthetics, leaning on the previously mentioned "nosthetics" (Grubnic 2020, 145), are a means of generating legitimacy and visualizing the literary establishment. Therefore, the modes of typography and composition lend it a rather 'traditional' literary visibility due to the manner in which the poem is placed visually within the Instagram environment and allude to the literary field (cf. Pressman 2020, 25–30; Bourdieu 2000 [1974]). Consequently, such an allusion not only seemingly grants prestige but also evokes products that are actually sold, such as McNish's books, which form one component of Instapoets' existential income as Instapoems are uploaded free of charge.

Conclusion

While feminist Instapoetry is actually a highly versatile poetic form in terms of its stylistic communities, which range from colorful, neon carousel posts to seemingly traditional "bookishness" and experimental collage cut-ups, feminist messages prevail on a continuum from micro-politics to activism. Moreover, the affective dimension together with the relational affordances of platformized poetry can give individual poems visibility as well as a certain aesthetic. This visibility is, in turn, highly important with regard to feminist embodiment practices as well as discriminatory and commodifying practices that (may) diminish the power of feminist poetry on Instagram. The circumstances shared intimately in poems, captions, and (potentially) in the comments sections, however, function as antidotes to the truly ambivalent, neoliberal media environment and lead to the formation of feminist post-digital platformized, networked visual intimacies. With regard to the affectivity analyzed here, the poem "pre-baby body" takes up the topic of "love" as a form of resistance by visually invoking the so-called "feminist killjoy" figure by utilizing productive anger as well as the visual, poetic dissection of the female body (cf. Ahmed 2014, 141).

While feminist Instapoems inherently move between platform conventions and authorial creativity, these platformized works of art continuously alter their visuality in accordance with the rapidly changing digital and visual culture of the internet. This is resulting in the numerous stylistic communities constantly being created and a variety of feminisms in poetry, representing current discourses, as well as moves toward more video and audio productions and developments toward a TikTok-like visual culture, as several discussions have lamented (cf. McCallum 2022). It is all the more surprising that poets like Hollie McNish are keeping up with the growing demands, changing platform practices, and continuing to create feminist poetry, e.g., on concepts of the body in motherhood, that stands in stark contrast to Instagram's censorship practices regarding the queer and female body. In this manner, Hollie McNish's "pre-baby body" deconstructs the constant work of the embodied, female self that platforms such as Instagram demand but also creates space for both readers and poets to carry out potential and continuing system critique.

In the various feminist Instapoetic stylistics, exemplified here in the work of Nikita Gill, Carina Eckl, and Rudka Zydel, it becomes clear that visuality is highly entangled with efforts to generate visibility that permeate existentially relevant modes of perseverance in platformized poetry. These stylistic communities also show that Instapoetry is not a visual monolith but encompasses various styles, techniques, and utilized materialities. In addition, Instapoetry serves individual poets and their fans, often writers themselves, and at times entire feminist movements, by enabling them to reflect and to express solidarity visually. Furthermore, the choice of colors, typography, layout, and the use of platform affordances in the form of hashtags, comments, and captions are means of mounting resistance against platform practices such as shadowbanning and literary exclusionary systems outside of social media. In this space of negotiation on Instagram, the examples shown here reveal how multimodal, aesthetically specific Instapoetry embraces a range of feminisms, e.g., material, queer, and post-feminist renderings, within culturally-specific contexts and beyond.

References

Ahmed, Sara. *The Cultural Politics of Emotion*. Edinburgh: Edinburgh Univ. Press, 2014.
Ahmed, Sara. "Killing Joy: Feminism and the History of Happiness." *Signs. Journal of Women and Culture in Society* 35.3 (2010): 571–594.
Amoore, Louise, and Volha Piotukh. *Algorithmic Life. Calculative Devices in the Age of Big Data*. Abingdon and New York: Routledge, 2016.

Are, Caroline. "The Shadowban Cycle: An Autoethnography of Pole Dancing, Nudity and Censorship on Instagram." *Feminist Media Studies* 21.1 (2021): 1–18.

Banet-Weiser, Sarah. *Empowered. Popular Feminism and Popular Misogyny*. Durham, NC: Duke Univ. Press, 2018.

Bassett, Caroline. "Not Now? Feminism, Technology, Postdigital." *Postdigital Aesthetics. Art, Computation and Design*. Ed. David M. Berry and Michael Dieter. Basingstoke: Palgrave McMillan, 2015. 136–150.

Baumgardner, Jennifer, and Amy Richards. *Manifesta. Young Women, Feminism, and the Future*. New York: Farrar, Straus, and Giroux, 2000.

Bayer, Judit, and Petra Bárd. "Hate Speech and Hate Crime in the EU and the Evaluation of Online Content Regulation Approaches." EU Policy Department for Citizens' Rights and Constitutional Affairs 2020, https://www.europarl.europa.eu/RegData/etudes/STUD/2020/655135/IPOL_STU(2020)655135_EN.pdf (November 20, 2022).

Bourdieu, Pierre. *Zur Soziologie der symbolischen Formen*. Frankfurt a. M.: Suhrkamp, 2000 [1974].

Bronwen, Thomas. "Literary Movements in the Network Era." *Literature and Social Media*. Ed. Bronwen Thomas. Abingdon, Oxon, and New York: Routledge, 2020. 83–97.

bruce, keisha. "'Everyone Has a Pic Like This in the Album!' Digital Diasporic Intimacy and the Instagram Archive." *Women's Studies Quarterly* 50.1–2 (2022): 246–263.

Brunner, Christoph. "Relaying Resistance – Translocal Media Aesthetics and Politics in the Feminist Intervention 'A Rapist in Your Path.'" Online talk in the lecture series "Performative Power and Failure of Dissent: Aesthetics of Intervention in Eastern Europe and Beyond" at TU Dresden, January 10, 2021, https://videocampus.sachsen.de/category/video/Relaying-Resistance-Translocal-Media-Aesthetics-and-Politics-in-the-Feminist-Intervention-Christoph-Brunner/812dd22025a5da0b99f95045b4759df0/14 (November 20, 2022).

Bucher, Taina, and Anne Helmond. "The Affordances of Social Media Platforms." *The SAGE Handbook of Social Media*. Ed. Jean Burgess, Alice Marwick, and Thomas Poell. Los Angeles, CA, London, and New Delhi: SAGE Publications, 2018. 233–253.

Bucher, Taina. "Want to be on the top? Algorithmic Power and the Threat of Invisibility on Facebook." *New Media & Society* 14.7 (2012): 1164–1180.

Burr, Zofia. "Of Poetry and Power: Maya Angelou on the Inaugural Stage." *Poetry and Cultural Studies: A Reader*. Ed. Maria Damon and Ira Livingston. Chicago, IL: Univ. of Illinois Press, 2009. 428–436.

Butler, Judith. "Performative Acts and Gender Constitution: An Essay in Phenomenology and Feminist Theory." *Theatre Journal* 40.4 (1988): 519–531.

Chasar, Mike. *Poetry Unbound. Poems and New Media from the Magic Lantern to Instagram*. New York: Columbia Univ. Press, 2020.

Cox, George. "Archived Bards: Platformalism, Hollie McNish & YouTube." *C21 Literature. Journal of 21st-century Writings* 8.1 (2020): 1–21.

Crepax, Rosa. "The Aestheticisation of Feminism: A Case Study of Feminist Instagram Aesthetics." *ZoneModa Journal* 10.1S (2020): 71–81.

Davis, Jenny. *How Artifacts Afford. The Power and Politics of Everyday Things*. Cambridge, MA: MIT Press, 2020.

Demopoulos, Alaina. "Free the Nipple: Facebook and Instagram Told to Overhaul Ban on Bare Breasts." *The Guardian*. January 17, 2023, https://www.theguardian.com/technology/2023/jan/17/free-the-nipple-meta-facebook-instagram (January 23, 2023).

Douglas, Marcia. "The 2019 Vida Count." VIDA, http://www.vidaweb.org/the-count/2019-vida-count/ (March 31, 2023).

Duffy, Brooke Erin. "The Romance of Work: Gender and Aspirational Labour in the Digital Culture Industries." *International Journal of Cultural Studies* 19.4 (2015): 1–17.

Dybka, Jake. "The Battle to Breast Feed | Embarrassed feat. Hollie McNish by Jake Dypka | Short Film | Random Acts." 2016, https://www.youtube.com/watch?v=S6nHrqIFTj8 (December 18, 2022).

Eckl, Carina/@kursives_ich. Unnamed poem. April 15, 2021, https://www.instagram.com/p/CNsa-QuhZJl/ (November 20, 2022).

Elliot, Andrew J. "Color and Psychological Functioning: A Review of Theoretical and Empirical Work." *Frontiers in Psychology* 6.368 (2015): 1–8.

Foucault, Michel. *Discipline and Punish: The Birth of the Prison*. New York: Vintage Books, 1995.

Franzen, Johannes. "Die Trennung von Publikum und Autor: Neue Näheverhältnisse in der literarischen Öffentlichkeit nach der Digitalisierung." *Sprache und Literatur* 51.125 (2022): 116–133.

Gibson, James J. "The Theory of Affordances." *The Ecological Approach to Visual Perception*. Hillsdale, NJ: Lawrence Erlbaum Associates, 1986 [1979].

Gill, Nikita/@nikita_gill. "Death Threat (Trigger Warning)." May 12, 2021, https://www.instagram.com/p/COxxaaYL-Yf/(November 20, 2022).

Gill, Nikita/@nikita_gill. "Feed." 2022, https://www.instagram.com/nikita_gill/ (December 18, 2022).

Gill, Rosalind. "The Affective, Cultural, and Psychic Life of Postfeminism: A Postfeminist Sensibility 10 Years On." *European Journal of Cultural Studies* 20.6 (2017): 606–626.

Glatt, Zoë, and Sarah Banet-Weiser. "Productive Ambivalence, Economies of Visibility, and the Political Potential of Feminist YouTubers." *Creator Culture. An Introduction to Global Social Media Entertainment*. Ed. Stuart Cunningham and David Craig. New York: New York Univ. Press, 2021. 39–56.

Graff, Agnieszka. "Angry Women: Poland's *Black Protests* as 'Populist Feminism.'" *Right-Wing Populism and Gender. European Perspectives and Beyond*. Ed. Gabriele Dietze and Julia Roth. Bielefeld: Transcript, 2020. 231–250.

Gross, Pola, and Hanna Hamel. "Neue Nachbarschaften: Stil und Social Media in der Gegenwartsliteratur." *Sprache und Literatur* 51.125 (2022): 1–17.

Grossman, Claire, Stephanie Young, and Juliana Spahr. "Who Gets to Be a Writer?" Public Books. April 15, 2021, https://www.publicbooks.org/who-gets-to-be-a-writer/ (March 31, 2023).

Grubnic, Tanja. "Nosthetics: Instagram Poetry and the Convergence of Digital Media and Literature." *The Australasian Journal of Popular Culture* 9.2 (2020): 145–163.

Harris, Anita. "Online Cultures and Future Girl Citizens." *Feminist Media. Participatory Spaces, Networks and Cultural Citizenship*. Ed. Elke Zobl and Ricarda Drüeke. Bieleld: Transcript, 2012. 213–225.

Holm Soelseth, Camilla. "When is a Poet an Instapoet?" *Baltic Screen Media Review* 10.1 (2022): 97–120.

Illouz, Eva. *Cold Intimacies. The Making of Emotional Capitalism*. Cambridge and Malden, MA: Polity Press, 2010.

Jackson, Jenn M. "Private Selves as Public Property: Black Women's Self-Making in the Contemporary Moment." *Public Culture* 32.1 (2020): 107–131.

Janz, Marlies. *Elfriede Jelinek*. Stuttgart: J.B. Metzler, 1995.

Kozinets, Robert V. *Netnography. The Essential Guide to Qualitative Social Media Research*. Los Angeles, CA and London: SAGE Publications, 2020.

Lajta-Novak, Julia. "Performing Black British Memory: Kat François's Spoken-Word Show *Raising Lazarus* as Embodied Auto/Biography." *Journal of Postcolonial Writing* 56.3 (2020): 324–341.

Leaver, Tama, Tim Highfield, and Crystal Abidin. *Instagram. Visual Social Media Cultures*. Cambridge and Medford, MA: Polity Press, 2020.

Ledin, Per, and David Machin. *Introduction to Multimodal Analysis*. London and New York: Bloomsbury Academic, 2020.

Leetsch, Jennifer. "From Instagram Poetry to Autofictional Memoir and Back Again: Experimental Black Life Writing in Yrsa Daley-Ward's Work." *Tulsa Studies in Women's Literature* 41.2 (2022): 301–326.

Little, Ben, and Alison Winch. *The New Patriarchs of Digital Capitalism. Celebrity Tech Founders and Networks of Power*. London and New York: Routledge, 2021.

Losh, Elizabeth. *hashtag*. New York and London: Bloomsbury Academic, 2020.

Lorde, Audre. "Poetry is not a luxury." *Poetry and Cultural Studies. A Reader*. Ed. Maria Damon and Ira Livingston. Chicago, IL: Univ. of Illinois Press, 2009, 355–358.

Łomnicka, Mirosława. "Nagrody literackie: znak jakości, popularności czy medal z ziemniaka?" *Rynek-Ksiazki*. September 27, 2018, https://rynek-ksiazki.pl/czasopisma/nagrody-literackie-znak-jakosci-popularnosci-czy-medal-z-ziemniaka-cz-1/ (March 31, 2023).

Manning, Maria. "Crafting Authenticity: Reality, Storytelling, and Female Self-Representation Through Instapoetry." *Storytelling, Self, Society* 16. 2 (2021): 263–279.

Matthews, Kristin L. "'Woke' and Reading: Social Media, Reception, and Contemporary Black Feminism." *Journal of Audience and Reception Studies* 16.1 (2019): 390–411.

McCallum, Shiona. "Instagram U-Turns on TikTok-Style Revamp." *BBC News*. July 29, 2022, https://www.bbc.com/news/technology-62345306 (November 20, 2022).

McNish, Hollie/@holliepoetry. "Feed." 2022, https://www.instagram.com/holliepoetry/ (December 18, 2022).

McNish, Hollie/@holliepoetry. "pre-baby body." July 21, 2021a, https://www.instagram.com/p/CRmIC8dhpr0/ (November 20, 2022).

McNish, Hollie/@holliepoetry. "newborn." 2021b, https://www.instagram.com/p/CTXl1QnsLKv/ (November 20, 2022).

McNish, Hollie/@holliepoetry. "no stones in her stomach." 2021c, https://www.instagram.com/p/CTxdeyFsX7y/ (November 20, 2022).

McNish, Hollie. *Slug. And Other Things I've Been Told to Hate*. London: Little, Brown Book Group, 2021d.

McNish, Hollie. *Nobody Told Me. Poetry and Parenthood*. London: Little, Brown Book Group, 2020.

McNish, Hollie. *Plum*. London: Pan Macmillan, 2017.

McNish, Hollie. "Embarrassed || Spoken Word by @holliepoetry." 2013, https://www.youtube.com/watch?v=KiS8q_fifa0 (December 18, 2022).

Mirzoeff, Nicholas. "Visual Thinking in Dangerous Times." FreshEye. 2019, http://fresh-eye.cz/video/special-guest-lecture-nicholas-mirzoeff-visual-thinking-in-dangerous-times/ (November 20, 2022).

Mirzoeff, Nicholas. *The Appearance of Black Lives Matter*. Miami, FL: NAME Publications, 2017.

Nacher, Anna. "#BlackProtest from the Web to the Streets and Back: Feminist Digital Activism in Poland and Narrative Potential of the Hashtag." *European Journal of Women's Studies* 28.2 (2021): 260–273.

Noble, Safiya Umoja. *Algorithms of Oppression. How Search Engines Reinforce Racism*. New York: New York Univ. Press, 2018.

Norman, Don. *The Design of Everyday Things*. New York: Basic Books, 2013.

Norris, Sigrid. "Modal Density and Modal Configurations: Multimodal Actions." *The Routledge Handbook of Multimodal Analysis*. Ed. Carey Jewitt. London and New York: Routledge, 2011. 78–90.

Olszanowski, Magdalena. "The 1x1 Common: The Role of Instagram's Hashtag in the Development and Maintenance of Feminist Exchange." *Hashtag Publics. The Power and Politics of Discursive Networks*. Ed. Nathan Rambukkana. New York: Peter Lang, 2015. 229–242.

Olszanowski, Magdalena. "Feminist Self-Imaging and Instagram: Tactics of Circumventing Sensorship." *Visual Communication Quarterly* 2 (2014): 83–95.

Orgad, Shani, and Rosalind Gill. *Confidence Culture*. Durham, NC and London: Duke Univ. Press, 2022.

Paparachissi, Zizi. *Affective Publics. Sentiment, Technology, and Politics*. New York and Oxford: Oxford Univ. Press, 2014.

Pâquet, Lili. "Selfie-Help: The Multimodal Appeal of Instagram Poetry." *Journal of Popular Culture* 52.2 (2019): 296–314.

Parks, Malcolm R. "Social Network Sites as Virtual Communities." *A Networked Self. Identity, Community, and Culture on Social Network Sites*. Ed. Zizi Paparachissi. New York: Routledge, 2010. 105–123.

Poell, Thomas, David B. Nieborg, and Brooke Erin Duffy. *Platforms and Cultural Production*. Cambridge and Medford, MA: Polity Press, 2022.

Poell, Thomas, and José Van Dijck. "Social Media and Activist Communication." *The Routledge Companion to Alternative and Community Media*. Ed. Chris Atton. New York: Routledge, 2015. 527–537.

Pressman, Jessica. *Bookishness. Loving Books in a Digital Age*. New York: Columbia Univ. Press, 2020.

Staśko, Maja (Ed.). *Wiersz nie jest cudem*. http://haart.e-kei.pl/prezentacje/projekty/5020-wiersz-nie-jest-cudem.html (November 20, 2022).

Valéry, Paul. *Œuvres II*. Paris: Gallimard, 1960.

Watts, Rebecca. "The Cult of the Noble Amateur." *PN Review* 44.3 (2018): https://www.pnreview.co.uk/cgi-bin/scribe?item_id=10090 (November 20, 2022).

Wentrack, Kathleen. "Female Sexuality in Performance and Film: Erotic, Political, Controllable? The Contested Female Body in the Work of Carolee Schneemann and VALIE EXPORT." *Kunsthistorisk tidskrift/Journal of Art History* 83.2 (2014): 148–167.

Zappavigna, Michelle. "Ambient Affiliation: A Linguistic Perspective on Twitter." *New Media & Society* 13.5 (2011): 788–806.

Zydel, Rudka/@rudkazydel. "Babskie wiersze." October 26, 2020, https://www.instagram.com/p/CG0cQtjnYUT/ (November 20, 2022).

Sophie Ertel
Poetische Pluralität: Kollaborative und visuelle Strategien im Poesiefilm *LESBIAN*

Kollaboration, Kooperation und die Entstehung des Poesiefilms *LESBIAN*

„Wir werden miteinander oder wir werden gar nicht", schreibt Donna Haraway in *Unruhig bleiben* und betont sowohl die Notwendigkeit als auch das Potenzial, zumindest temporär, Kollektivität anzustreben (Haraway 2018, 13). Sie hegt damit genauso wie das Schweizer Architekt:innenkollektiv RELAX mit ihrem provokanten und nicht minder radikal klingenden Ausspruch „Allein denken ist kriminell" (RELAX 2017) Kritik am vorherrschenden Denken des Singularen. Denn auch, wenn es gegenwärtig so wirkt, als ob man im Kunst- und Kulturbereich am Begriff des Kollektivs und dem Themenkomplex des kollaborativen Arbeitens nicht mehr vorbeikommt, bezeugt diese Kritik die immer noch vorherrschende Omnipräsenz singulärer Autor:innenschaft (vgl. Mader 2022, 182). Dieser Beitrag stellt daher die im Kunstdiskurs immer wichtiger werdenden Begriffe des Kollektiven, der Kooperation sowie der Kollaboration vor und beleuchtet das Genre des Poesiefilms, das vor allem im letzten Jahrzehnt immer mehr Beachtung erfährt. Exemplarisch werden am Film *LESBIAN* (Baker 2020) Praktiken des kollaborativen Arbeitens bzw. der Kooperation im Genre des Poesiefilms und dadurch die Möglichkeit, Pluralität entstehen zu lassen, nachgezeichnet. Anhand einer multimodalen Text/Bild/Ton-Analyse werden abschließend visuelle Strategien des Poesiefilms analysiert, um dessen Beitrag zur Stärkung von lesbischer Sichtbarkeit herauszuarbeiten.

Künstlerische Zusammenarbeit und das steigende Interesse an der Arbeit von Künstler:innen- bzw. Kurator:innenkollektiven sind in den letzten Jahren verstärkt in den Fokus des zeitgenössischen Kunstdiskurses gerückt. So entspricht es diesem Zeitgeist, dass im Jahr 2022 die documenta fifteen zum ersten Mal in ihrer Geschichte von einem Künstler:innen-Kollektiv, der indonesischen Gruppe ruangrupa, kuratiert wurde. Dieses Aufbrechen der jahrzehntelangen Praxis, ein bis zwei etablierte Kurator:innen die wichtigste Ausstellung für zeitgenössische Kunst organisieren zu lassen (vgl. weiterführend hierzu Figge 2019), war ein wichtiger, wenn nicht sogar notwendiger Schritt und die konsequente Weiterführung des „Sich-Öffnens". Auch bei der Verleihung des bedeutendsten Kunstpreises in der Bildenden Kunst, dem Turner Prize, kam es 2019 zu einem Novum: Um ein

Zeichen der „Gemeinsamkeit, Vielfalt und Solidarität"[1] in einer Zeit der politischen Krise zu setzen, formulierten die vier nominierten Lawrence Abu Hamdan, Helen Cammock, Oscar Murillo und Tai Shani ihre Bitte an die Jury des Turner Prize 2019, den Preis an alle vier gemeinsam zu übergeben. 2021 wurden für den Turner Prize sogar nur noch Kollektive nominiert.

Auch wenn die Kunstwissenschaftlerin Rachel Mader betont, dass es gar nicht klar ist, ob es gegenwärtig tatsächlich zu einer Vermehrung von kollektiven Praktiken in der Kunst kommt, oder ob es nur den Anschein macht, „dass damit eher die thesenhafte Losung für einen Zeitgeist gefunden worden ist" (Mader 2020, 263), so ist doch zumindest ein gestiegenes Interesse an kollektiven Praktiken beobachtbar. „Kooperation und Kollaboration sind Schlüsselbegriffe des globalisierten Kunstfeldes" (Hausladen und Lipinsky de Orlov 2021, 6), meinen die Herausgeber:innen von *Texte zur Kunst* und fragen in ihrer Dezemberausgabe 2021 unter dem Titel *Collectivity* nach dem Verhältnis von Kunst und Aktivismus sowie nach dem Selbstverständnis von Künstler:innen, die in Kollektiven zusammenarbeiten.

Diese Betrachtungsweise ist kennzeichnend für den von der Kuratorin Maria Lind 2007 als solchen benannten *collaborative turn*, der die Tendenz zum Kollektiven und zu kollaborativen Praktiken in der zeitgenössischen Kunst beschreibt und in einen gesamtgesellschaftlichen Kontext einbettet. Lind bezieht sich hierbei unter anderem auf den von Gilles Deleuze und Félix Guattari entwickelten Begriff des Rhizom sowie auf Michael Hardts und Antonio Negris Idee des Gemeinsamen (vgl. Lind 2007, 16) und betont, dass der Wunsch nach (künstlerischer) Kollektivität keineswegs ein gänzlich neues Phänomen ist: „Dreams of collectivism have undoubtedly been a driving force in society since the advent of Modernism [...]" (Lind 2007, 18). Im Diskurs um kooperatives bzw. kollaboratives Agieren in der Kunst taucht auch ein weiterer Begriff häufig auf, namentlich die Komplizenschaft. Als Beispiel kann hier das Zentrum für Politische Schönheit (ZPS) genannt werden, das auf ihrer Homepage dazu auffordert, „Kompliz:in" zu werden, um so die Arbeit des Kollektivs zu unterstützen und sich vor allem zu solidarisieren.[2] Der ausschlaggebende Grund dafür war die im Januar 2022 vom Landeskriminalamt angeordnete Hausdurchsuchung von mehreren Objekten des ZPS in Berlin und die darauffolgende Beschlagnahmung verschiedenster Gegenstände. Um ein Zeichen gegen diesen Angriff auf ihre Kunstfreiheit zu setzen, rief das ZPS die Zivilgesellschaft dazu auf, Kompliz:in zu werden und gemeinsam auf der Anklagebank Platz zu nehmen. Hat sich der negativ konnotierte Beigeschmack des Begriffs Kollaboration auch im

---

1 Siehe https://turnercontemporary.org/news/03/12/2019/winners-turner-prize-2019/; dort auf Englisch: „commonality, multiplicity and solidarity".
2 Siehe https://politicalbeauty.de.

deutschsprachigen Raum neutralisiert, so haftet dem Begriff der Komplizenschaft implizit weiterhin etwas Listiges, am Rande der Legalität Liegendes an.

Diese Beispiele zeugen davon, dass eine Fülle an Begrifflichkeiten zur Beschreibung (künstlerischer) Zusammenarbeit besteht. In Ermangelung einer eindeutigen Definition sind es eher Versuche der Zuordnung, in denen vor allem die Begriffe Kooperation und Kollaboration oftmals fast gleichbedeutend eingesetzt werden. Der Künstler und Essayist Florian Schneider bemängelt diese synonyme Verwendung und schlägt eine Definition von Kollaboration in Abgrenzung zu Kooperation vor, die vor allem von den unterschiedlichen Realitäten der Akteur:innen ausgeht:

> In contrast to cooperation, collaboration is driven by complex and often diverse realities rather than by romantic notions of a common ground or commonality of interests. It is an ambivalent process, constituted by a set of paradoxical relationships between co-producers who affect each other. (Schneider 2010, 83)

Gleichzeitig lässt sich beobachten, dass im Gebrauch all dieser Begriffe häufig die Intention mitschwingt, „eine Alternative zu singularisierten Autorschaften zu bieten und damit zugleich ethisch-politische Ansprüche (Demokratie, Selbstermächtigung, Gerechtigkeit) einzulösen." (Barner et al. 2022, 12) Hinsichtlich der Wahrnehmung von Autor:innenschaft ist gerade das Thema der Gerechtigkeit ein zentraler Aspekt, da im Kunst- und Kulturbereich gerne die vielen Beteiligten vergessen werden, die zum Gelingen eines Kunstwerkes beitragen. Künstlerische Zusammenarbeit, sei es in Form von Kooperationen, Kollaborationen oder der Arbeit im Kollektiv, ist immer geprägt durch eine „Vielgliedrigkeit und ihre[n] relationale[n] Charakter" (Barner et al. 2022, 4). Diese kreativen Zusammenschlüsse können sowohl langfristig aufgebaut sein als auch nur sehr flüchtig: von der jahrelangen Verbundenheit in der Arbeit eines Kollektivs bis zu einer punktuellen, temporären Zusammenarbeit, die sich ohne vielen Zutuns wieder auflösen lässt.

Für das folgende Poesiefilm-Beispiel eignet sich der Begriff der Kollaboration, weil in diesem künstlerischen Genre die Abkehr von einer singulären Autor:innenschaft schon in seiner Medialität begründet liegt. Den Poesiefilm als ein Artefakt pluraler Autor:innenschaft zu sehen, entspricht auch der Definition von Ines Barner, Anja Schürmann und Kathrin Yacavone. Sie bemerken, dass der Begriff der pluralen Autor:innenschaft oftmals dann eingesetzt wird, wenn sich ein Medienwechsel zwischen zeitlich getrennten Werkphasen beobachten lässt, der mit ästhetischen Übersetzungsleistungen verbunden ist (vgl. Barner et al. 2022, 19f.). Wenn sich Filmemacher:innen einem Gedicht zuwenden – und damit auch Poet:innen –, um aus deren Gedichten eine filmische Form zu realisieren, stellen sich folgende Fragen der Herangehensweise: Inwiefern geht mit diesem Prozess der Annäherung auch eine Aneignung einher? Findet durch die Transformation des

Gedichts in einen Poesiefilm *per se* eine poetische Pluralisierung statt? Oftmals besteht wohl ein geteiltes Interesse der Kunstschaffenden, etwa eine verwandte politische Einstellung, die vielleicht am gewählten Thema des Gedichts zu erkennen ist. Oder es führt ein ähnliches Gespür für sprachliche Ästhetik dazu, dass Filmemacher:innen bei ihrer Recherche zu einem Poesiefilm auf ein bestimmtes Gedicht oder auf Gedichtfragmente verschiedener Poet:innen stoßen und sich damit beschäftigen, um dann daraus eine visuelle Form abzuleiten.

Beim Poesiefilm handelt es sich also nicht lediglich um eine Addition zweier künstlerischer Ausdrucksformen, sondern um eine gegenseitig aufeinander einwirkende, synergetische Verbindung: Das Bewegtbild fügt dem Gedicht nicht nur etwas hinzu, das Bild verwandelt vielmehr das poetische Klanggeschehen, welches seinerseits einwirkt auf das, was visuell sichtbar ist. Dabei lassen sich Poesiefilme als audiovisuelle Kunstwerke charakterisieren, die Gedichte auf unterschiedlichste Art und Weise aufgreifen. Ihre Anfänge reichen bis weit in die Filmgeschichte zurück und haben auch im deutschsprachigen Raum in den 1950er und 1960er Jahren durch experimentelle Filme von Lyriker:innen wie Friederike Mayröcker, Ernst Jandl oder Gerhard Rühm einen Höhepunkt erfahren (vgl. Orphal 2014, 96–114). Die Vielfältigkeit dieses Genres lässt sich auch an der Fülle von Begrifflichkeiten erkennen, die neben „Poesiefilm" je nach Betrachtungsweise und Schwerpunktsetzung kursieren. So spricht z. B. der kanadische Dichter und Filmemacher Tom Konyves von „Videopoesie" und betont die Wichtigkeit, diese Bezeichnung als Einheit zu begreifen:

> Für mich ist es wichtig, dass Videopoesie ein Wort ist; dass es nicht mit Bindestrich geschrieben oder getrennt wird, denn als ein Wort zeigt es an, dass eine Verschmelzung des Visuellen und des Verbalen stattgefunden hat, die zu einer neuen, anderen Form des Ausdrucks einer poetischen Erfahrung führt. (Konyves 2020)

Für Konyves beginnt die Verschmelzung der beiden Kunstgattungen also schon in der Gestalt des Begriffes. Poesiefilme lassen sich in ihrer Hybridität ferner als intermediale Kunstwerke bezeichnen. Das Potenzial, das sich dadurch ergibt, beschreibt Jürgen E. Müller folgendermaßen:

> Meines Erachtens beruht das Potential des Intermedialitätsbegriffs auf der Tatsache, dass Intermedia die Beschränkung der Untersuchung auf das Medium ‚Literatur' aufhebt; dass er eine differenzierte Analyse der Interaktionen und Interferenzen ZWISCHEN mehreren unterschiedlichen Medien erlaubt und die Forschungsausrichtung um den Aspekt der Materialität und die soziale Funktion dieser Prozesse bereichert. (Müller 2008, 38f., zit. n. Pfeiler 2010, 51)

Den zentralen Aspekt der Intermedialität betont Konyves ebenfalls: Während sich das Medium Poesiefilm im Video materialisiere, entfalte sich das Genre durch den poetischen Text (vgl. Konyves 2020). Statt sich also nur auf die literarischen oder auf die filmischen Ebenen zu konzentrieren, wird durch die Betonung der intermedialen Beschaffenheit von Poesiefilmen der Fokus auf ihr Zusammenspiel sowie auf die daraus entstehende mediale und materielle Pluralität gelenkt.

Wie sich kollaborative Prozesse gestalten können, wird im Folgenden anhand des Poesiefilms *LESBIAN* dargelegt, um die Entstehung der *poetischen Pluralität* nachzuzeichnen. lisa luxx, Lyrikerin, Performerin und politische Aktivistin, schrieb das Gedicht „Lesbian" 2019 als Reaktion auf einen homophoben und misogynen Übergriff, der sich im Mai des selben Jahres in einem Londoner Bus ereignet hat.[3] luxx performte das Gedicht auf zahlreichen Spoken Word Events und hatte Interesse daran, ihre Rezitation von „Lesbian" zu verfilmen, wie ein Social-Media-Post von ihr verrät. 2019 suchte sie über ihren Twitter-Account nach einer Zusammenarbeit mit einer Filmemacherin: „I wrote a new poem how as lesbian's [sic!] we've been made homeless in language. Our word is a taboo, a porn category, even a supposed enemy of the queer movement. I'm looking for a filmmaker to collab on making a poetry video for it." (lisaluxx_, 13. Juni 2019) Mit der Filmemacherin Tamara Al-Mashouk ist die erste filmische Umsetzung, in der luxx das Gedicht in einem reduzierten Setting performt, entstanden. Das Video wurde auf YouTube veröffentlicht und kann bis Februar 2023 über 5000 Aufrufe verzeichnen.[4] Vor dem nachfolgend analysierten Poesiefilm *LESBIAN* existierte also schon eine andere audiovisuelle Realisierung.

Im Sommer 2019 wurde Rosemary Baker, Filmemacherin aus Wales, von den Sendungsverantwortlichen von Random Acts eingeladen, an einem Pitch für einen neuen Film teilzunehmen. Dafür gab es eine Bedingung: Der Film sollte auf einem schon existierenden „piece of spoken word art"[5] basieren, das mit der eigenen Identität als Filmemacherin korrespondiere. Baker stieß auf das Gedicht „Lesbian", das sie sofort faszinierte: „I identify as a lesbian, and so I set about looking for poetic works which spoke to the experiences of lesbians." Daraufhin fragte sie luxx, ob die Lyrikerin Interesse an einer filmischen Kollaboration habe, stellte der Kommission von Channel 4 ihre Idee vor und bekam die Zusage zur Förderung. Auch wenn sich das Drehbuch und die finale Realisierung im Laufe des Entstehungsprozesses stark veränderten, war für Baker von Anfang an klar, dass luxx eine zentrale Rolle als Performerin in der Verfilmung haben solle und somit auch Teil des Prozesses sein würde. Bereits in der Konzeptionsphase zeigt

---

[3] Siehe etwa den BBC-Artikel „London Bus Attack" vom 7. Juni 2019, https://www.bbc.com/news/uk-england-london-48555889.
[4] Siehe https://www.youtube.com/watch?v=P3am7eVdhis.
[5] Alle Zitate von Rosemary Baker hier und im Weiteren stammen – wenn nicht anders nachgewiesen – aus einem Interview, das ich mit der Filmemacherin am 29. Juni und am 3. Juli 2022 geführt habe.

sich *LESBIAN* also als eine künstlerische Arbeit, in deren Produktion emanzipatorische Kräfte durch Kollaboration entfesselt werden können:

> In Abgrenzung von gängigen Formen der Arbeitsteilung, die mit Vorstellungen von Zusammenarbeit verbunden sind, sind kollaborative Beziehungen als hierarchiefreie oder doch zumindest -kritische angelegt. Ihre revolutionäre Kraft gewinnt Kollaboration aus der produktiven Beteiligung und der im laufenden Arbeitsprozess erfolgenden Optimierung soziotechnischer Medien. (Ghanbari et al. 2018, 1)

Solche produktiven Beteiligungen, die bei der künstlerischen Kollaboration entstehen, zeigten sich vor allem in der Prozesshaftigkeit und dem Dialog, der die gesamte Konzeptionsphase der audiovisuellen Realisierung von *LESBIAN* begleitete. Das im Zitat angesprochene hierarchiekritische Moment der Kollaboration kann auch über die künstlerische Zusammenarbeit hinaus gehen und als Möglichkeit gesehen werden, sowohl Präsentations-, Produktions- und Rezeptionsbedingungen von Kunstschaffenden kritisch zu hinterfragen.

Da die künstlerische Kollaboration von luxx und Baker in einem Film mündete, der auch abseits der Poesiefilmszene bei renommierten Filmfestivals wie z. B. dem European Short Film Festival einen großen Erfolg verbuchen kann, rückt die Frage nach der Autor:innenschaft wieder vermehrt ins Zentrum der Betrachtung: Wem wird das Kunstwerk urheberrechtlich zugeschrieben? Welche beteiligten Personen werden sichtbar gemacht, welche bleiben unsichtbar? Untersuchenswert erscheint hier in jedem Fall der Umgang mit der pluralisierten Autor:innenschaft in Hinblick auf den Social-Media-Auftritt beider Akteurinnen: Sowohl Baker als auch luxx haben einen professionellen Account auf der Plattform Instagram sowie bei dem Kurznachrichtendienst Twitter und sind dort sehr aktiv. Dass der Poesiefilm *LESBIAN* seit 2020 auf diversen Festivals gezeigt wird, für Preise nominiert wurde und diese z. T. auch gewonnen hat,[6] wird auf den Social-Media-Kanälen von luxx und Baker vielfach geteilt. Dabei ist zu beobachten, dass sich hinsichtlich der Zuweisung der Autor:innenschaft ein plurales „wir" bzw. „unser Film" etabliert hat. Baker und luxx berichten laufend über Screenings und Erfolge von *LESBIAN* – und das immer aus einer pluralen Perspektive. In einem der ersten Instagram-Postings von Baker über *LESBIAN* werden beide Akteurinnen als Urheberinnen des Films genannt: „First stills from mine and @luxxy_luxx's film for @c4randomacts have landed" (rosedoesdrawings, 6. September 2020). Am 5. Februar 2021 schreibt lisa luxx auf ihrem Account: „Coming very soon: our award-winning poetry film ‚Les-

---

[6] Gewinnerfilm in den folgenden Kategorien und Festivals: Best Short Form – Celtic Media Awards 2022; Welsh Film Prize – Cardiff Mini Film Festival 2021; Best LGBTQ Short – International Shorts Awards September 2020; Best First Time Director (Female) – Independent Shorts Awards September 2020.

bian' is set for release on @c4randomacts" (lisaminervaluxx, 5. Februar 2021). Diese programmatisch konsequente Schreibweise zieht sich durch sämtliche Postings und kann als gelebte kollektive Autor:innenschaft (vgl. Gamper 2001; Mader 2012) bezeichnet werden. Damit scheinen ähnliche Ziele verfolgt zu werden wie in Praktiken von Künstler:innenkollektiven, namentlich die gemeinsame Durchsetzung ästhetischer Positionen und kultur-ökonomischer Absichten oder des politischen Anliegens einer autonomieversprechenden, emanzipatorischen Praxis, die sich von gegebenen Strukturen absetzen möchte (vgl. Barner et al. 2022, 18).

Das Wir drückt den Umstand der Verbindlichkeit dieser Kollaboration aus und wird durch jedes neue Posting, jeden Retweet verstärkt. Es werden aber nicht nur die Erfolge des Films gemeinsam geteilt, sondern auch die gegenseitigen Verweise darauf, wie sehr die Zusammenarbeit in sämtliche Bereiche des eigenen Identitätsverständnisses als lesbische, queere Filmemacherin bzw. Autorin gedrungen ist und diese nachhaltig verändert haben. Beispielsweise veröffentlichte Baker am 5. Februar 2022 auf ihrem Instagram-Account folgende Nachricht:

> Happy birthday to mine & @luxxy_luxx's baby, released on All4 a year ago today. 15 festivals, 4 wins, 5 industry award nominations and a linear broadcast later, and still the story continues. It's gone further around the world than either of us imagined and completely changed me, as a person and as a filmmaker. I am, as I will always be, very grateful. She (Lisa Luxx) transformed me into a lesbian who can say the word „lesbian" and finally hear it in my own voice. (rosedoesdrawings, 5. Februar 2022)

Die Kollaboration brachte also nicht nur einen künstlerischen Mehrwert in Form der poetischen Pluralität bzw. der intermedialen Verschmelzung von Visuellem und Verbalen im Poesiefilm mit sich. Darüberhinausgehend hatte die Zusammenarbeit auch direkte und langfristige Effekte auf das Selbstbild der Künstlerinnen.

Das plurale poetische Potenzial des Poesiefilms *LESBIAN*

Am Poesiefilm *LESBIAN* lässt sich das beschriebene plurale poetische Potenzial, das durch die Kollaboration von Filmemacherin und Poetin entstehen kann, besonders gut nachzeichnen, da er sich durch den elaborierten Umgang mit lyrischer und filmischer Bildsprache sowie durch das Produktivmachen von Wechselbeziehungen zwischen visueller Kunst und Sprachkunst auszeichnet. Der Leiter der Akademie für Lyrikkritik, Asmus Trautsch, spricht Poesiefilmen das Potenzial zu, eine völlig neue Form zwischen Text und Bild zu erschaffen:

> Im schlechtesten Falle entsteht einfach eine Illustration des Gedichttextes, im besten Fall entsteht wirklich etwas Intermediales, eine neue Form, die auch eine neue poetische Erfahrung erzeugt, in der Bild, Klang und lyrischer Text oder lyrischer Klang zusammenwirken und sich gegenseitig konterkarieren, sich unterstreichen und in verschiedene Verhältnisse treten. (Trautsch 2021)

Diese neue poetische Erfahrung entsteht demnach eben nicht, wenn allein der Versuch unternommen wird, den lyrischen Text starr umzusetzen (d. h. wenn dessen Inhalte einfach bebildert werden, indem etwa beim Wort Rose das Bild einer Rose eingespielt würde). Hingegen vermögen es gerade die Poesiefilme, die über das Offensichtliche hinausgehen, in einem intermedialen Dialog neue Ausdrucksweisen, Deutungsmöglichkeiten und Atmosphären entstehen zu lassen.

Den Beginn des dialogischen Austauschs zwischen luxx und Baker stellt wie oben beschrieben die Faszination dar, die luxx' Gedicht auf Baker ausgeübt hat. Diese liegt vor allem in ähnlichen persönlichen Erfahrungen begründet und führte schließlich zur produktiven Verbindung der lyrischen Sprache der Poetin und der Bildsprache der Filmemacherin. luxx traf bei Baker einen wunden Punkt, dem sie selbst zuvor aber noch nicht nachgegangen war:

> As a lesbian woman who has never felt fully comfortable with the word „lesbian", this film is extremely personal to me. Lisa Luxx's poem nails an aspect of the queer female experience in 2020 which, to my mind, no other person or piece of work has managed to put its finger on. Uniquely, too, it's addressed as much to lesbians as it is to the rest of the world. When I first heard it, I felt called out: why did I feel uncomfortable calling myself a lesbian, and isn't it time that changed? (Baker 2021)

Diese Identifikation Bakers mit dem Gedicht von luxx sollte auch in den Film transferiert und dabei auf ein bildliches Repertoire zurückgegriffen werden, mit dem sich ihrerseits luxx identifizieren könne. Baker zählt in einem Statement drei Aspekte auf, die für ihre filmische Realisierung wichtig waren: „1) the film should centre on Lisa delivering her poem straight to camera as a direct address, 2) it needed to feature a diverse cast of real lesbians of different ethnicities and faiths, with trans lesbians explicitly included, and 3) the film should evoke a safe space made unsafe." (Baker 2021) In der Analyse des Films *LESBIAN* stellen sich die Fragen, in welchen Punkten das Bewegtbild dem gesprochenen Text etwas hinzufügen kann, diesen verändert, verstärkt oder vielleicht gar unterläuft, und wie sich wiederum der gesprochene Text auf die Wahrnehmung der visuellen Ebene auswirken kann. Für die Untersuchung von Poesiefilmen generell gilt, dass die sprachkünstlerische Performance und die unterschiedlichen akustischen Ton- bzw. Bildebenen nicht getrennt, sondern in ihren Wechselwirkungen analysiert werden sollten.

LESBIAN beginnt visuell mit fünf kurzen, statisch gehaltenen Close-ups auf jeweils ein bzw. mehrere Ausstattungsdetails, die im Laufe des Films immer wieder zu sehen sein werden. Diese Close-ups gehen in eine extrem schnell abgespielte Einzelbildmontage über, in der z. T. schon gezeigte, als auch neue Details wie z. B. ein Lippenstift oder eine kitschige Porzellanfigur (als kulturell weiblich konnotierte Requisiten) erscheinen. Es sind dies einerseits gerahmte Bilder, die Rosemary Baker, die auch als bildende Künstlerin tätig ist, selbst gefertigt hat. Die Filmemacherin hat sich dadurch nicht nur hinter der Kamera, sondern auch davor visuell in den Poesiefilm eingeschrieben. Andererseits sind es Fotografien, die in unterschiedlicher Explizität lesbische Sexualität bis hin zu pornografischen Szenen enthalten – was durchaus in Zusammenhang mit luxx' eingangs zitierter Kritik an der Assoziierung von lesbischer Liebe mit Pornografie gelesen werden kann. Die Intermedialität des Poesiefilms wird mithin durch den Einbezug der visuellen Medien Malerei und Fotografie erweitert. In der exzessiven Verwendung von Klischeebildern hinterfragen luxx und Baker kulturell vermittelte Vorstellungen, die von lesbisch/queer lebenden Menschen kursieren und durchkreuzen somit hegemoniale Normen der Darstellungen, die immer wieder reproduziert werden. Auf humorvolle Weise werden dabei auch Codes bedient, die wahrscheinlich vornehmlich in der lesbischen Community sofort decodiert werden können – als Beispiel kann Bakers Zeichnung von Justin Bieber genannt werden, die zu Beginn des Films zu sehen ist, dessen Frisur als stereotyper Look lesbischer Frauen gilt, was in der Community als eine Art Insider-Witz kursiert.

Nach der Anfangssequenz werden vier Darstellerinnen in Halbtotalen vor den Bilderwänden vermeintlicher Wohnzimmerräume, ähnlich eines *establishing shots*, vorgestellt. Eine kaum wahrnehmbare Kamerafahrt unterstützt den Fokus auf die Protagonistinnen, die durch Lichtsetzung und Maske mit dem Hintergrund verschmelzen, immer wieder unterbrochen durch eine rhythmische Abfolge von kurzen Detailaufnahmen, die als *subliminals* nur auf einer unbewussten Ebene wahrgenommen werden können. Während die vier Darstellerinnen im Wechsel zu sehen sind, setzt lisa luxx' Rezitation des Gedichts ein und bildet den Schwerpunkt, um den sich der Film aufbaut, weshalb von einem performanceorientierten Poesiefilm gesprochen werden kann. Auf auditiver Ebene beginnt *LESBIAN* mit einem pluralen Wir: „we have been made homeless in language". Das lyrische Ich bzw. Wir, dem luxx ihre Stimme verleiht, spricht nicht nur von und über sich selbst, es spricht somit *über* die ganze lesbische Community, die im Film durch die Poetin und die weiteren Protagonistinnen (audio-)visuell repräsentiert wird.

Durch die Beanspruchung eines kollektiven *We* findet eine Pluralisierung auf mehreren Ebenen statt: Das lyrische Ich scheint mit luxx, deren Biographie und Identität als lesbische Frau den Rezipient:innen durch Paratexte (Interviews, Online-Auftritte etc.) zugänglich ist, zu verschmelzen; gleichzeitig spricht es für die gesamte lesbische Community. Das Individuelle wird im *We* und der Vielzahl an Akteurinnen zu einer universalen Erfahrung gemacht, während die Grenze zwischen lyrischem Ich und Autorin durchlässig wird, weil sie selbst den Text spricht/performt. Dieser Authentizitätseffekt wird vor allem Gedichten zugeschrieben, die in der ersten Person verfasst sind und von Autor:innen selbst vorgetragen werden (vgl. Novak 2017, 158–160). Julia Novak hält in diesem Zusammenhang fest: „[...] in cases when the textual speaker articulates experiences that pertain to, or qualities that characterize, the poet-performer, the performance may then suggest ‚I have really experienced this; it is true'." (Novak 2020, 327) Bei diesem Wahrnehmungseffekt klingt also ein Lyrikverständnis an, Gedichte als eine Aussage von Autor:innen über ihre außertextliche Realität aufzufassen (vgl. Hillebrandt et al. 2017, 5), in diesem Fall über negative Zuschreibungen und Erfahrungen als lesbische Frau in der Gesellschaft.

Die Tragik der Metapher „homeless in language" zieht sich in Form eines Gefühls des Unbehagens, des Feindlichen, auch auf visueller Ebene durch den gesamten Poesiefilm. Die Lichtsetzung ist in *LESBIAN* eine wichtige Komponente und ein Vehikel um den ästhetisch-poetischen Effekt des Düsteren, Unwirtlichen zu unterstreichen. Die einzelnen Settings wurden mit *practicals* (kleinen Lampen) ausgestattet, die als zusätzliche, integrierte Lichtquellen funktionieren. In der Postproduktion wurden die meisten Einstellungen so bearbeitet, dass die Hälfte des Raumes dunkler erscheint. Dadurch wird ferner ein Gefühl der Unsicherheit transportiert, das direkt mit dem eingangs erwähnten konkreten Ereignis korrespondiert: Das Gedicht „Lesbian" wurde als Reaktion auf den homophoben und misogynen Überfall, der sich im Mai 2019 in einem Londoner Bus ereignet hat, geschrieben. Ausgangspunkt war insbesondere nicht nur der Gewaltakt selbst, sondern die Art und Weise, wie Medien darüber berichtet bzw. was sie *nicht* gesagt haben. Im Gedicht bekommt diese Sprachlosigkeit eine zentrale Bedeutung, da sich in ihr die Unsichtbarkeit zeigt, die durch das Unvermögen der öffentlichen Medien entsteht, die beiden Frauen als lesbisches Paar zu benennen:

> The Metro article about Melania and Chris
> That we all circulated
> Didn't use the word ‚lesbian'

Auch im Film *LESBIAN* ist dieser Moment der emotionale *turning point*: Es kommt zu einer Verdichtung von Rezitation, Filmsound und visueller Ebene. Die Stimme von luxx wird (ein wenig) lauter, der letzte Vers wird akzentuiert und mit kurzen, den einzelnen Wörtern Gewicht gebenden, Pausen versehen: „Didn't / use / the / word / ‚lesbian'". Die sich so aufbauende Spannung wird sowohl durch den ansteigenden Sound als auch durch die Abfolge der filmischen Bilder unterstrichen: eine rasche Schnittabfolge von einzelnen Close-ups der vier Darstellerinnen, die sich nacheinander mit der Hand den eigenen Mund zuhalten. Die Sprachlosigkeit wird so visualisiert und dadurch um die Ebene des Nicht-sprechen-Dürfens erweitert. Auditiv erfahrbar wird diese Ebene durch das stockende und abgehackte Artikulieren dieses Verses. Auch da es sich dabei im Film ebenso wie im lyrischen Text um den Höhepunkt handelt, werden, um die Spannung auf visueller Ebene zu steigern, zwischen diesen vier Close-ups wieder ein bis zwei Einzelbilder als *subliminals* eingefügt. Die Hände vor den Mündern symbolisieren in einer gewissen Art und Weise auch die durch die Medien repräsentierte Mehrheitsgesellschaft, die nicht dazu in der Lage scheint, das Wort *lesbian* auszusprechen (Abb. 16).

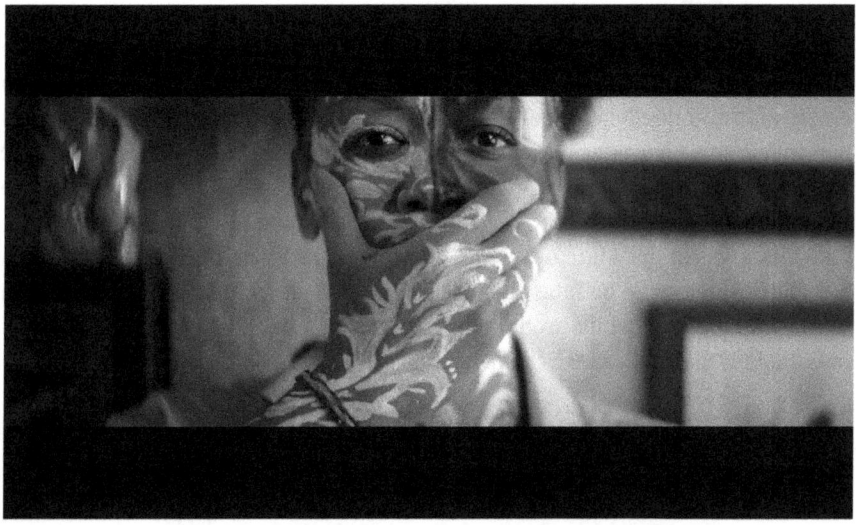

Abb. 16: Still aus *LESBIAN* (00:41). Reg. Rosemary Baker. Gedicht: lisa luxx. 2020.

Die Geste impliziert außerdem, dass die vier Protagonistinnen kollektiv den Atem anhalten. Erst als luxx noch einmal eindrücklich *L-E-S-B-I-A-N* mit einem stark betonten *s* ausspricht und darauf in die Kamera sagt: „Say it!", ändert sich die Stimmung im Film. Wurden die Schauspielerinnen bis zu diesem Zeitpunkt statisch frontal in die Kamera blickend und durch die Bodypainting-Farbe mit dem gleichen Muster der Wand als verschmelzende Körper dargestellt, ist der Imperativ „Say it!" die Aufforderung zum Handeln. Aus der Geste des Sich-den-Mund-Zuhaltens folgt eine Bewegung als Akt der Emanzipation: Langsam beginnen die vier Darstellerinnen die Farbe von Gesicht, Hals und Händen abzuwischen – sie legen ihre Camouflage ab und treten sozusagen in die Sichtbarkeit. Geht es im Gedicht „Lesbian" sehr stark darum, das Publikum bzw. die Rezipierenden in einem immer wiederkehrenden Imperativ aufzufordern, das Wort *lesbian* ohne Scham auszusprechen:

> Say it without seeing us as currency to spend
> Say it knowing we have to steal our bodies back from men
> Say it. Say it above a whisper, say it as easily as you say gay.
> Say it like it's my name,

reagieren die Bilder auf diesen sprachlich gesetzten Imperativ mit betont ruhigen, aber dezidierten Bewegungen. Was wir sehen, ist der emanzipatorische Akt, sich gesellschaftlichen Zuschreibungen, die im Film als farbige Schichten auf dem Körper repräsentiert werden, zu entledigen: Die eigene Haut wird wieder sichtbar, die eigenen Körper ebenso wie die eigene Sprache zurückgewonnen. Die Protagonistinnen treten aus dem Hintergrund in den Vordergrund des Bildes, in einem klar und deutlich ausgeführten Akt der Selbstbestimmung. Verstärkt wird der appellative Charakter dieser Szene zudem durch die Wahl einer *anamorphic lense*, die auf das Breitbandformat CinemaScope verweist. Die somit entstehende Vignettierung, das leichte Ausfransen der Schärfe an den Bildrändern, hat den Effekt, alles, was in der Mitte des Bildes zu sehen ist, stärker zu betonen. Während auf Plattformen wie YouTube oder TikTok oft auf diesen Effekt zurückgegriffen wird, um zu bewerbende Produkte bestmöglich in den Fokus zu rücken, gerät hier die Botschaft selbst ins Scheinwerferlicht.

Audiovisueller Rhythmus im Poesiefilm *LESBIAN*

Poesiefilme sehen sich vielfach mit Vorurteilen konfrontiert, einerseits damit, dass die Verfilmung eines Gedichts die visuelle Komponente zu stark in den Vordergrund rückt (vgl. Höllrigl 2016, 18), andererseits wird oft von einer Redundanz der Sprachbilder im Visuellen gesprochen. Stefanie Orphal stellt hierzu jedoch die berechtigte Frage, „inwieweit angesichts der medialen Inkommensurabilität von Wort und Bild überhaupt von einer Redundanz beider Phänomene auszugehen ist." (Orphal 2014, 242) Tatsächlich sei es viel eher so, dass „jedes Bild einen Überschuss an visuellen Informationen hinzufügt, indem es mehr zeigt, als sich mit Sprache sagen ließe, und jeder Satz bzw. Vers drückt anderes aus, als es ein Bild vermöchte. Eine vollkommene Identität von Bild und Wort ist also nie möglich." (Orphal 2014, 242) Zwischen den beiden Polen Verdoppelung und Ergänzung des Bilds liegt eine Fülle an Möglichkeiten, durch die sich Wort und Bild gegenseitig unterstützen oder konterkarieren können. Wenn beispielsweise die filmische Umsetzung des Verses „Droplets giggled down her neck" vor Augen geführt wird, sehen wir dabei luxx, die diesen Vers bildhaft unterstreicht, indem sie eine Bewegung den Hals hinunter mit ihren Fingern andeutet. Der Schnitt zeigt im Bild danach die Detailaufnahme des Halses einer anderen Darstellerin. Da luxx schon weiter rezitiert, setzt sich das Bild also in den nächsten Vers fort – „Across that plate of stone between the breasts" – und kommentiert diesen.

In diesem Zusammenhang wird im Folgenden ein besonderes Augenmerk auf den audiovisuellen Rhythmus gelegt. Die Analyse des Rhythmus ist für ein tiefergehendes Verständnis von *LESBIAN* essenziell, da sich Rhythmus als Gestaltungsform nicht nur auf der Tonspur, sondern auch stark in der visuellen Umsetzung widerspiegelt. Diese Ebenen können nicht getrennt betrachtet werden: „Vielmehr bilden sich intermodale Wahrnehmungen. Nicht nur die sichtbaren Bilder und hörbaren Töne werden kombiniert, sondern auch die ‚verkreuzten' Sinneseindrücke (crossmodal perception), also hörbare Bilder und sichtbare Töne." (Lommel 2008, 79) Da *LESBIAN* ein performanceorientierter Poesiefilm ist, sollte die gesamte wahrnehmbare Rezitation von luxx betrachtet werden, der Einsatz ihres Körpers, ihre pointiert gesetzten, das gesprochene Wort unterstreichenden Gesten.

luxx' Rezitation ihres Gedichts beruht auf einer Choreografie, die sich bereits in der ersten filmischen Bearbeitung ihres Gedichts „Lesbian" beobachten lässt. Wenn man *LESBIAN* mit der Version auf YouTube vergleicht, fällt auf, dass zwar nicht jede Bewegung synchron ist, allerdings gibt es sprachliche Realisierungen, die eine fest zugewiesene Bewegung erhalten haben. luxx unterstreicht nicht nur bestimmte Wörter mit passenden Gesten, sondern setzt ihren gesamten Körper ein. Wenn sie die Stelle: „Everyday my shoulder is a stack of sandbags / brows lifting above the parapet, check / Baby, are we safe yet?" rezitiert, bewegt sie automatisch die Hand zur Schulter und weiter zur Stirn, als ob sie die Umgebung absuchen würde. Ihre Augen bewegen sich schnell hin und her, der Kopf dreht sich und wirft einen Blick hinter die Schulter, um sicherzugehen, dass sie nicht verfolgt wird. Der Sound, der den gesamten Film in einen elegischen, sonoren Klangteppich hüllt, ist mal stärker zu hören, mal schwächer, und erzeugt sowohl eine andauernde Spannung, als auch ein leichtes Unbehagen.

Der rhythmisierende Beat ergibt sich auf auditiver Ebene überwiegend durch die sprechkünstlerische Performance von luxx' Rezitation und auf visueller Ebene durch den Filmschnitt. Noch bevor luxx mit der Rezitation des Gedichts beginnt, wird das vermeintlich Statische durch eine staccatoartige Abfolge von filmischen Bildern unterbrochen. Diese Schnitttechnik, die extrem schnell abgespielte Einzelbildmontage, bei der die Frames nur für Sekundenbruchteile zu sehen und als einzelne Einstellungen nicht fassbar sind, setzt Baker im Film insgesamt sechs Mal ein. Jedes Mal unterbricht sie damit einen Rhythmus, der gerade im Begriff war, sich aufzubauen. Begleitet wird diese Montage von einem lauten Geräusch, das an einen schnell abgespielten technischen Apparat erinnert – ein Filmapparat, der zurückgespult wird, oder eine Druckerpresse. Es wird also nicht nur die Bildebene immer wieder kurz durchbrochen, sondern auch die Tonebene.

Diese staccatoartigen Bildabfolgen stören immer wieder die Betrachtung, wirken irritierend und unterlaufen den Rhythmus. Sie werden zur Verstärkung des Unbehagens eingesetzt und führen zu einer Ent-Automatisierung der Wahrnehmung. Das heißt, die Materialität von Bild und Ton wird in den Vordergrund gerückt, mithin poetisch in Szene gesetzt, und dadurch bewusst wahrgenommen – in den Worten des russischen Formalisten Viktor Shklovsky wird hier der „Stein steinig" gemacht (vgl. Shklovsky 1990, 6; vgl. auch Benthien et al. 2019, 21; Zechner 2014, 132). Michel Chion bezeichnet solche Phänomene im Film als *scansions* (Akzentuierungen), wie Orphal erklärt (vgl. Orphal 2014, 247). Der gesprochene Text wird durch ein bestimmtes, lautes Geräusch, durch den Filmschnitt, oder durch eine Kombination aus beidem unterbrochen, punktiert oder rhythmisiert: „Es handelt sich um Effekte der Signifikantenebene (effet de signifiant), die nicht mit einer bestimmten Bedeutung verbunden sein müssen. Sie können die Worte jedoch gewichten, hervorheben und segmentieren." (Orphal 2014, 247) Diese Effekte erzeugen jene „Spürbarkeit der Zeichen" (vgl. Jakobson 1960, 365), die mit der Ent-Automatisierung der Wahrnehmung einhergeht (vgl. Benthien et al. 2019, 25).

In dem Gedicht „Lesbian" geht es um die sprachliche Rückeroberung und die Wiederaneignung des Begriffs *lesbian*, der meistens als *queer* oder *gay* subsumiert wird, aber es geht auch um die Rückeroberung eines Blicks. Der Moment, in dem luxx rezitiert: „Say it without thinking phase, without thinking male gaze", ist eine der Schlüsselszenen in Bezug auf die visuelle poetische Pluralisierung, da luxx' Gedicht in der filmischen Umsetzung um Bakers Blick erweitert und für die Zuseher:innen in diesem Moment auch ein Hinterfragen des eigenen *Gaze* vollzogen wird. Der in der feministischen Filmgeschichte von Laura Mulvey geprägte Begriff des *male gaze* (vgl. Mulvey 1999), den luxx thematisiert, wird hier auf unterschiedliche Art und Weise dekonstruiert: luxx spricht die Verse in den Spiegel, ohne diesen als Blickumleitung zu nutzen, um in die Kamera zu sehen. Die äußeren Zuschreibungen werden in diesem Moment des ‚zu sich selbst Sprechens' ausgeblendet. Es ist ein Moment der Selbstermächtigung, sich nicht durch Zuschreibungen und Blicke von außen definieren zu lassen. Erst am Ende der Textpassage, wenn sie rezitiert: „Say it like it is my name", sieht luxx wieder über den Spiegel in die Kamera (Abb. 17). So durchbricht sie den voyeuristischen Kamerablick und stellt das Blickregime (vgl. Kravagna 1997; Schade und Wenk 2011) infrage. Den Rezipient:innen soll in dieser Szene bewusst gemacht werden, wie sehr sie selbst als Schauende von Blickregimen, die bestimmte Wahrnehmungen dirigieren, geleitet sind (vgl. Froschauer 2014, 17).

Die poetische Pluralität, die sich im Film *LESBIAN* entwickelt, kann auch hinsichtlich der Wahrnehmung von Poesiefilmen im Allgemeinen festgemacht wer-

Abb. 17: Still aus *LESBIAN* (02:04). Reg. Rosemary Baker. Gedicht: lisa luxx. 2020.

den. Wenngleich sich sowohl verschiedene Lyrikformate als auch Kurzfilme in den letzten zehn bis fünfzehn Jahren einer erhöhten Beliebtheit erfreuen durften, hat es die Kombination der beiden zum Poesiefilm in punkto Sichtbarkeit um einiges schwerer. Sigrun Höllrigl, Leiterin des Art Visuals and Poetry Filmfestival in Wien, formuliert diesen Umstand sogar noch drastischer: „Der Poetry Film wird in der Filmwelt belächelt, nicht zuletzt deshalb, weil sehr wenig Geld zu holen ist." (Höllrigl 2016, 18) Poesiefilme werden meist auf eigens dafür konzipierten Festivals gezeigt.[7] Manche werden aber auch auf breiter angelegten Filmfestivals präsentiert und eröffnen dem Genre Chancen auf mehr Sichtbarkeit und Wahrnehmung. „Es geht darum, den Poetry Film im Festivalbetrieb zu verankern. Ausnahmefilme werben für das Genre, das in der Filmszene immer noch eine große Außenseiterrolle einnimmt" (Höllrigl 2016, 18). *LESBIAN* kann in jedem Fall als Ausnahmefilm bezeichnet werden, da er auf eine sehr große Resonanz gestoßen ist. Bis dato war Bakers Poesiefilm auf 15 Festivals zu sehen und hat vier Preise gewonnen. Beim Iris Prize 2021 war *LESBIAN* sowohl auf der Shortlist für den „International Prize" als auch für den „Best British Prize". Beim Celtic Media Festival, ein Filmfestival, das im Juni 2022 im französischen Quimper stattgefunden hat,

---

7 Zu erwähnen ist hier auf jeden Fall das größte Poesiefilmfestival im deutschsprachigen Raum: das ZEBRA Poetry Film Festival, das letztes Jahr vom 3. bis zum 6. November 2022 in Berlin stattgefunden hat.

gewann er den Hauptpreis in der Kategorie „short form". *LESBIAN* wird also nicht nur auf Poesiefilmfestivals, sondern auf ganz unterschiedlichen Filmfestivals in Großbritannien, aber auch darüber hinaus, gezeigt, was der Popularität von Poesiefilmen im Allgemeinen zuträglich ist.

Queering the image – Lesbianize the image!

Ein weiterer Aspekt, der nicht minder spannend ist, ist die Betrachtung des Poesiefilms *LESBIAN* aus einer queer-feministischen politischen Perspektive und damit in Hinblick auf seinen Beitrag zur Stärkung lesbischer Bildwelten. Da der Film explizit *Queering* von Bildern (vgl. Paul und Schaffer 2009, 13) aufbaut, kann der Film auch als Beitrag zu einem visuellen queer-feministischen Bildarchiv beitragen. Barbara Paul und Johanna Schaffer machen in ihrem Band *Mehr(wert) queer* darauf aufmerksam, „dass wir (ansonsten) einem Übergewicht schwul konnotierter Zeichen und Bildsprachen in Kontexten, die sich explizit um queere Visualität bemühen und vornehmlich popkulturelle Bezüge praktiziert haben, gegenüberstehen" (Paul und Schaffer 2009, 13). So kann *LESBIAN* als eine Art queer-feministisches Manifest nicht nur gegen die vorherrschenden patriarchal-sexistischen, heteronormativen Strukturen im Allgemeinen verstanden werden, sondern auch als eine Antwort auf die Dominanz dezidiert schwuler Bilder. In der Tradition queer-feministischer Theoretikerinnen wie Monique Wittig, Audre Lorde, Adrienne Rich und Gloria Anzaldúa, die ihre Theorieproduktion als politische Praxis verstehen, die ihren Ausgangspunkt in (den eigenen) unmittelbar erlebten Erfahrungen haben (vgl. Klapeer 2015, 28), kann auch luxx' Textproduktion gelesen bzw. gesehen werden. Die Identifizierung mit dem eigenen queeren/lesbischen Körper wird also nicht nur als bloßer „Rahmen" des Schreibens gefasst, sondern als (Rückkopplungs-)Effekte einer theoretischen Reflexion auf das „Selbst", einer Beschäftigung mit der eigenen Identität und dem Körper (vgl. Klapeer 2015, 28).

Die Verfilmung des Gedichts hat diese Beschäftigung noch auf eine andere Ebene gebracht. Die Auseinandersetzung mit einer filmischen Form und das Experimentieren mit unterschiedlichen Möglichkeiten der Umsetzung vor Ort führte luxx zudem zu einer neuen Sichtweise auf ihr eigenes Gedicht. Durch das Rezitieren des Textes in den Spiegel konfrontierte sich luxx auf einmal selbst mit den Imperativen, die sonst an das Publikum gerichtet waren:

> [This was improvised] and changed the whole poem for me. It was always a poem directed at the audience or listener. When we were filming we experimented with reading it into the

mirror and I looked myself in the eye and said those lines and it shook me. I felt a pain in my chest, my eyes filled with tears. I hadn't realized I was also speaking to myself.[8]

In luxx' Aussage wird deutlich, dass auch Räume und unterschiedliche Settings einen (lyrischen) Text verändern können. Es ist ein Unterschied, ob man auf einer Bühne steht oder einen Text vielleicht mithilfe von Requisiten in eine Kamera rezitiert. Ohne das unmittelbare Publikum und deren Reaktionen wird man als Künstlerin viel eher auf sich selbst zurückgeworfen, wie luxx' Erfahrungsbericht verdeutlicht.

Conclusio

Poetische Pluralität – das hat der vorliegende Beitrag gezeigt – spielt sich im Poesiefilm auf mehreren Ebenen ab: In seinem Potenzial, singuläre Autor:innenschaft zu überwinden, in seiner spezifischen Medialität, die geschriebenen Text, gesprochenes Wort und bewegte Bilder in Verbindung treten lässt, und in seiner Prozesshaftigkeit, die Kollaboration in allen Phasen des Entstehungsprozesses als synergetische Verbindung zu begreifen. Am Beispiel *LESBIAN* wurde dargelegt, dass sich die poetische Pluralität oft im Dazwischen, im Zusammenspiel und in der Ergänzung aller auf audiovisueller Ebene wahrnehmbaren Elemente, die aufeinander einwirken, entfaltet. Rosemary Baker und lisa luxx haben es in der filmischen Realisation vor allem durch die Verbindung von luxx sprachkünstlerischem Talent und Bakers Gespür für filmische Zwischentöne geschafft, die poetische Pluralität so auszuarbeiten, dass eine neue Form, eine neuartige poetische Erfahrung entstanden ist.

In der exzessiven Verwendung von Klischeebildern hinterfragen luxx und Baker kulturell vermittelte Vorstellungen, die von lesbisch/queer lebenden Menschen kursieren und durchkreuzen somit hegemoniale Normen von Darstellungen. Dabei wird die Intermedialität des Poesiefilms durch den Einbezug weiterer visueller Medien, namentlich Malerei und Fotografie, erweitert. Ebenso tragen neben der sprachlichen Performance des Gedichttexts Maske, Lichtsetzung und Rhythmus (auf auditiver Ebene und durch die Schnitttechnik) zum Spannungsaufbau des Films bei. Wird zunächst ein ästhetisch-poetischer Effekt des Düsteren, Unwirtlichen erzeugt, so kulminieren die symbolträchtigen Bilder und die nachdrückliche Rezitation in einem Akt der Emanzipation. Die anfänglich thema-

---

8 Dieses Zitat stammt aus einem E-Mail-Interview mit Luxx, das ich am 18. Oktober 2022 für diesen Beitrag geführt habe.

tisierte Unsichtbarkeit und Sprachlosigkeit wandeln sich in einen Beitrag zur Stärkung lesbischer Sichtbarkeit und in eine Rückeroberung der Sprache, insbesondere der Aussprache des Wortes *lesbian*. Dabei wird der Begriff auf sich selbst zurückgeworfen und in poetischer Weise neu und positiv verhandelt.

Am Beispiel *LESBIAN* konnte auch das Potenzial von kollaborativen Prozessen, singuläre Autor:innenschaft zu überwinden, diskutiert werden. Durch die Kollaboration von luxx und Baker ist ein künstlerisches Artefakt entstanden, das sich ohne die gemeinsame Arbeit in dieser Form nie realisiert hätte: „The motivation to collaborate is that it has to result in something that would otherwise not take place, it simply has to make possible that which is otherwise impossible." (Lind 2007, 29) Anhand der Analyse der Social-Media-Auftritte von luxx und Baker konnte gezeigt werden, dass aus dieser zeitlich begrenzten Zusammenarbeit eine Verbindlichkeit entstand, die über die Arbeit an dem Poesiefilm hinausging. Nicht zuletzt verdeutlicht *LESBIAN* auch das subversive Potential, sprachliche, patriarchale Narrative und sexistische Bildwelten aufzubrechen und den Blick auf den eigenen queeren/lesbischen Körper zurückzugewinnen.

Quellenverzeichnis

Baker, Rosemary (Reg.). *LESBIAN*. Gedicht von lisa luxx. Random Acts. 2020, https://vimeo.com/507509252 (12. Februar 2023).

Baker, Rosemary. „Director's Statement". *LGBT+ Toronto Film Festival*. 25. August 2021, https://lgbttorontofilmfestival.com/2021/08/25/director-biography-rosemary-baker-lesbian/ (12. Februar 2023).

Barner, Ines, Anja Schürmann und Kathrin Yacavone. „Kooperation, Kollaboration, Kollektivität: Geteilte Autorschaften und pluralisierte Werke aus interdisziplinärer Perspektive". *Journal of Literary Theory* 16.1 (2022): 3–28.

Benthien, Claudia, Jordis Lau und Maraike M. Marxsen. *The Literariness of Media Art*. London und New York: Routledge, 2019.

BBC. „London Bus Attack". 7. Juni 2019, https://www.bbc.com/news/uk-england-london-48555889 (12. Februar 2023).

Figge, Katrin. „Ruangruppa leitet eine neue Ära der dokumenta ein". *Goethe-Institut Magazin*. Februar 2019, https://www.goethe.de/ins/hu/de/m/kul/mag/21500627.html (12. Februar 2023).

Froschauer, Eva Maria. „Blickregime". *Z.B. Humboldt-Box. Zwanzig architekturwissenschaftliche Essays über ein Berliner Provisorium*. Hg. Sabine Ammon, Eva Maria Froschauer, Julia Gill und Constanze A. Petrow. Bielefeld: Transcript, 2014. 17–24.

Gamper, Michael. „Kollektive Autorschaft/kollektive Intelligenz 1800–2000". *Jahrbuch der deutschen Schillergesellschaft* 45 (2001): 380–403.

Ghanbari, Nacim, Isabell Otto, Samantha Schramm und Tristan Thielmann. „Einleitung". *Kollaboration. Beiträge zur Medientheorie und Kulturgeschichte der Zusammenarbeit*. Hg. Nacim

Ghanbari, Isabell Otto, Samantha Schramm und Tristan Thielmann. Paderborn: Wilhelm Fink, 2018. 1–17.

Haraway, Donna J. *Unruhig bleiben. Die Verwandtschaft der Arten im Chthuluzän*. Frankfurt a. M. und New York: Campus, 2018.

Hausladen, Katharina und Genevieve Lipinsky de Orlov. „Vorwort". *Collectivity. Texte zur Kunst* 124 (2021): 6, https://www.textezurkunst.de/de/124/katharina-hausladen-genevieve-lipinsky-de-orlov-vorwort/ (12. Februar 2023).

Hillebrandt, Claudia, Sonja Klimek, Ralph Müller, William Waters und Rüdiger Zymner. „Theories of Lyric". *Journal of Literary Theory* 11.1 (2017): 1–11.

Höllrigl, Sigrun. „Meine dreifache Faszination für den Poetry Film". *Poetryfilm Magazin. Faszination Poetryfilm?* 1 (2016): 18–19.

Jakobson, Roman. „Closing Statement: Linguistics and Poetics". *Style in Language*. Hg. Thomas A. Sebeok. Cambridge, MA: MIT Press, 1960. 350–377.

Klapeer, Christine M. „Lesbian Trouble(s): Queere Theorievergessenheit und die Bedeutung lesbisch-feministischer ‚Klassikerinnen' für andere Versionen und Visionen von Queer/ing". *Femina Politika. Zeitschrift für feministische Politikwissenschaft* 1 (2015): 25–38.

Konyves, Tom. „Was ist ein Poesiefilm". *Art Visuals & Poetry*. Juni 2020, https://www.poetryfilm-vienna.com/de/node/303 (12. Februar 2023).

Kravagna, Christian. *Privileg Blick. Kritik der visuellen Kultur*. Berlin: Ed. ID-Archiv, 1997.

Lind, Maria „The Collaborative Turn". *Taking the Matter into Common Hands. On Contemporary Art and Collaborative Practices*. Hg. Johanna Billing, Maria Lind und Lars Nilsson. London: Black Dog Publishing, 2007. 15–31.

Lommel, Michael. „Der Rhythmus als intermodale Kategorie". *Intermedialität – analog/digital. Theorien, Methoden, Analysen*. Hg. Joachim Paech. München: Fink, 2008. 79–89.

luxx, lisa. „Lesbian". *Trust Your Outrage*. London: Design Print Bind, 2020. 8.

Mader, Rachel. „Das Kollektive in der Kunst zwischen Autor*innenschaft, Arbeitsorganisation, Systemkritik und Gesellschaftsentwurf". *Journal of Literary Theory* 16.1 (2022): 174–195.

Mader, Rachel. „Neue Verbindlichkeit. Kunstkollektive im 21. Jahrhundert". *Geteilte Arbeit. Praktiken künstlerischer Kooperation*. Hg. Magdalena Bushart, Henrike Haug und Stefanie Stallschus. Köln: Böhlau, 2020. 263–279.

Mader, Rachel. „Kollektive Autorschaft in der Kunst". *Kollektive Autorschaft in der Kunst. Alternatives Handeln und Denkmodell*. Hg. Rachel Mader. Bern: Peter Lang, 2012. 7–22.

Mulvey, Laura. „Visual Pleasure and Narrative Cinema". *Film Theory and Criticism. Introductory Readings*. Hg. Leo Braudy und Marshall Cohen. New York: Oxford UP, 1999. 833–44.

Novak, Julia. „Live-Lyrik. Körperbedeutung und Performativität in Lyrik-Performances". *Phänomene des Performativen. Systematische Entwürfe und historische Fallbeispiele*. Hg. Anna Bers und Peer Trilcke. Göttingen: Wallstein, 2017. 147–162.

Novak, Julia. „Performing Black British Memory: Kat François's Spoken-Word Show Raising Lazarus as Embodied Auto/Biography". *Journal of Postcolonial Writing* 56.3 (2020): 324–334.

Orphal, Stefanie. *Poesiefilm: Lyrik im audiovisuellen Medium*. Berlin und Boston, MA: De Gruyter, 2014.

Paul, Barbara und Johanna Schaffer. „Einleitung: Queer als visuelle politische Praxis". *Mehr(wert) queer. Visuelle Kultur, Kunst und Gender-Politiken*. Hg. Barbara Paul und Johanna Schaffer. Bielefeld: Transcript, 2009. 7–20.

Pfeiler, Martina. *Poetry goes Intermedia. US-amerikanische Lyrik des 20. und 21. Jahrhunderts aus kultur- und medienwissenschaftlicher Perspektive*. Tübingen: Narr Francke Attempto, 2010.

Rajewsky, Irina O. „Das Potential der Grenze. Überlegungen zu aktuellen Fragen der Intermedialitätsforschung". *Textprofile intermedial*. Hg. Dagmar Hoff und Bernhard Spies. München: Meidenbauer, 2008. 19–47.

Rajewsky, Irina O. „Intermedialität und Remediation. Überlegungen zu einigen Problemfeldern der jüngeren Intermedialitätsforschung". *Intermedialität – analog/digital. Theorien, Methoden, Analysen*. Hg. Joachim Paech. München: Fink, 2008. 47–60.

RELAX. „Alleine denken ist kriminell". Interview der Stadt Zürich mit dem Schweizer Architekt: innenkollektiv. 2017, https://www.stadt-zuerich.ch/kultur/de/index/foerderung/bildende_kunst/kunst-newsletter/NL_2017_1_Alleine_denken_ist_kriminell.html (12. Februar 2023).

Rippl, Gabriele. „Intermedialität: Text/Bild-Verhältnisse". *Handbuch Literatur & Visuelle Kultur*. Hg. Claudia Benthien und Brigitte Weingart. Berlin und Boston, MA: De Gruyter, 2014. 139–158.

Schade, Sigrid und Silke Wenk (Hg.). *Studien zur visuellen Kultur. Einführung in ein transdisziplinäres Forschungsfeld*. Bielefeld: Transcript, 2011.

Schneider, Florian. „The Dark Site of the Multitude". *Vielleicht küsst uns ja die Muse*. Hg. Barbara Kapusta, Nathalie Koger, Simona Obholzer und Marlies Pöschl. Wien: Schlebrügge, 2010. 83–85.

Shklovsky, Viktor. „Art as Device". *Theory of Prose*. Übers. Benjamin Sher. Elmwood Park, IL: Dalkey Archive Press, 1990. 1–14.

Trautsch, Asmus. „Poesiefilm, Videopoesie, Cinépoèm: Kritik von Dichtung im bewegten Bild" [Einführung der gleichnamigen Lecture Performance]. Akademie für Lyrikkritik. November 2021, https://www.kanalfuerpoesie.org/medien/akademie-fuer-lyrikkritik-6/ (12. Februar 2023).

Turner Contemporary. „Winners Turner Prize 2019". 3. Dezember 2019, https://turnercontemporary.org/news/03/12/2019/winners-turner-prize-2019/ (12. Februar 2023).

Zechner, Anke. „Stillstand der Narration und Wahrnehmung der Dinge – Entautomatisierung im Kino". *Entautomatisierung*. Hg. Annette Brauerhoch, Norbert Otto Eke, Renate Wieser und Anke Zechner. Padernborn: Wilhelm Fink, 2014. 125–146.

Zentrum für politische Schönheit. 2009–2023, https://politicalbeauty.de (12. Februar 2023).

3 Viewpoints: Artistic Practices in Digital Poetry and Poetry Films

Chris Kerr and Daniel Holden

Optimizing Code for Performance: Reading *./code --poetry*

Introduction: code poetry's compound eye

There is something unnerving about staring at an eye, especially one that meets your gaze. In our book *./code --poetry*, "compound_eye.rb" (see Holden and Kerr 2016a) spans two facing pages, and it appears to look at the reader from each page. "compound_eye.rb" is a code poem, written in the Ruby programming language.[1] We can think of code poetry as a subset of Alan Sondheim's category "'Codework' – the computer stirring into the text, and the text stirring the computer." Sondheim also describes codework as part of a movement "concerned with the intermingling of human and machine" (Sondheim 2001, 1). A close reading, and seeing, of "compound_eye.rb" will serve as an introduction to our project *./code --poetry*, and to the visual aesthetics of code poetry in general.

On the right-hand page is a functional computer program that has been altered poetically in a way that is human-readable. The code poem is arranged on the page so that the central section looks like a hexagonal ommatidium: one of the many units that make up an insect's eye. On the left-hand side of the page are five snapshots from an animation that the code poem creates when it is run on a computer. Like the code poem, the output is made of alphanumeric characters. The output is an example of ASCII art, comprised of characters defined by the American Standard Code for Information Interchange. The text describes a patient who has undergone surgery. The patient experiences insects crawling on their body. The insects may or may not be hallucinations.

So far, we have described the print version of "compound_eye.rb," but it also exists online. The website https://code-poetry.com (see Holden and Kerr 2016b) hosts some of the code poems from our book. In the online version, we see not static flipbook frames but a moving ASCII animation, a looping GIF of the code poem's output. There is no single object to look at here: the code poem exists as input and output, in print and online (Fig. 18).

W. J. T. Mitchell writes that "the very notion of vision as a *cultural* activity necessarily entails an investigation of its non-cultural dimensions, its pervasiveness as a sensory mechanism that operates in animal organisms all the way from the flea to the elephant" (Mitchell 2002, 92). "compound_eye.rb," with its flea's

---

1 https://www.ruby-lang.org/en/.

Open Access. © 2023 the author(s), published by De Gruyter. This work is licensed under the Creative Commons Attribution-NonCommercial-NoDerivatives 4.0 International License.
https://doi.org/10.1515/9783111299334-009

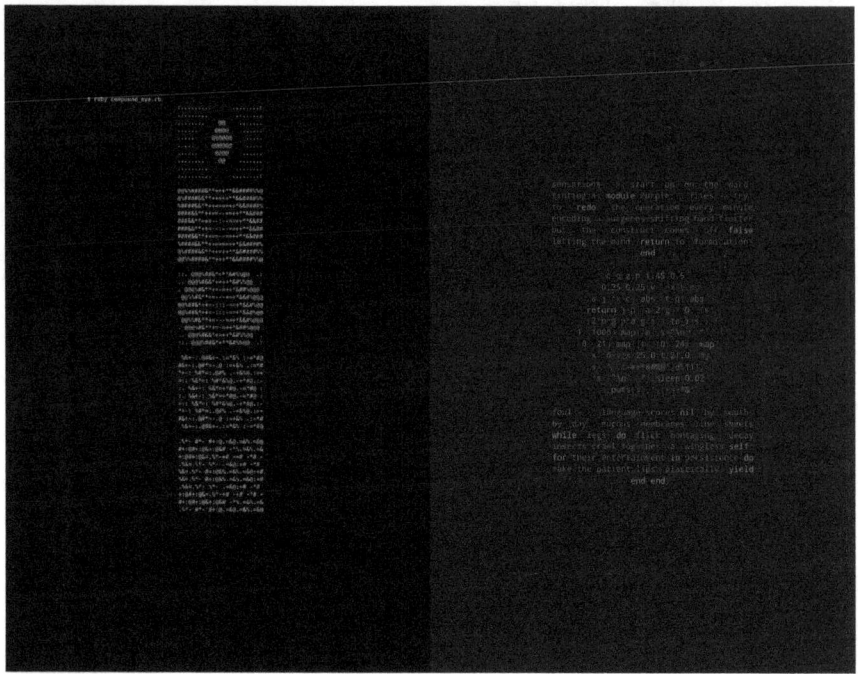

Fig. 18: Daniel Holden and Chris Kerr. "compound_eye.rb." ./code --poetry. 2016a.

eye, can be seen as an investigation of the non-cultural, or scientific dimensions of vision. Code poetry, grounded in computer science, might be an ideal medium for this scientific element of vision. However, code poetry should not be seen as a neutral escape from the cultural aspect of vision: it has a many-eyed, cultural element, too, because science is always culturally embedded.

"compound_eye.rb" is written in a monospaced font, the signature aesthetic of code poetry. Programmers use these fonts, where each character occupies the same horizontal space. It is used in *code {poems}* as well, an anthology of code poetry edited by Ishac Bertran, for example in "UNTITLED (LOVE)" by Nataliya Petkova (2018). This aspect of code poetry owes a debt to twentieth century typewriter art, for instance Peter Finch's "texture poem for the moons of stars" (1972). We argue that code poetry is a continuation of these practices with digital means and is therefore digital concrete poetry. Both the input and output of "compound_eye.rb" consist of ASCII characters. For example, the characters "= - > {" appear n the first line of the code poem, where they are a functional part of the program. In the output, these symbols are used in a purely visual way, to paint an animation. Unusual syntax is another characteristic of code poetry. In "mucous membranes line sheets while legs do flick," for instance, the word "do" is seemingly redundant, even archaic. This syntactical contortion is a sign that the text is being written for two audiences, one human, one computational. The word "do" is in fact a functional keyword in the Ruby programming language. Addressing different kinds of "readers" as well as combining alphanumeric symbols and unusual syntax are central features of code poetry in general such as Francesco Aprile's "laravel poems" (2020).

Finally, the code poem has coloured, bold, italic, underlined and emphasized text, which replicates the syntax highlighting of code text editors, which colour elements of the code according to their category in the language, and might, like this poem, have a dark background. The colouring of the syntax highlighting helps programmers to read the code more efficiently. In "compound_eye.rb," the syntax highlighting, too, sometimes serves a functional role as a readability aid: "do" is purple because it is a keyword in the programming language Ruby. At other times, the syntax highlighting has a more aesthetic function. The central hexagon of the code poem is bright red, to mimic the brilliant red of an ommatidium. This is an aesthetic choice: the colouring can be freely adapted for artistic effect. The red draws the reader's eye, as if to a cross-section of a visual organ, held on a microscope's slide by the surrounding text. In addition, this red hexagon might also remind the reader of the logo for the Ruby language: its clean angles resemble a faceted gem. For an example of syntax highlighting in another code poem, see "//Lockdown Dérive" by Brian James (2020, 11).

The aesthetics of syntax highlighting can be read in the light of visual culture studies. One of Mitchell's "eight counter-theses on visual culture" is as follows: "Visual culture entails a meditation on blindness, the invisible, the unseen, the unseeable, and the overlooked; also on deafness and the visible language of gesture; it also compels attention to the tactile, the auditory, the haptic, and the phenomenon of synesthesia" (Mitchell 2002, 90). "compound_eye.rb" asks us to look at a visual organ too small to be seen clearly by the eye, on an animal we might be too disgusted to look at. This disgust is compounded by the tactile impression conveyed by the word "formication" in the code poem: this impression becomes entangled with the texture of the ASCII characters in the output. When the viewer looks at this animation, are they looking at a single eye, or a swarm of ASCII character insects, out of which an eye emerges like a hallucination? Moreover, we can even detect Mitchell's synaesthetic component in syntax highlighting, which recalls colour-grapheme synaesthesia, where alphanumeric characters are strongly associated with specific colours (cf. Bhanoo 2011).

Code poetry, with its visual, tactile, synaesthetic language is a rich site for exploring visual culture in Mitchell's terms. Code poetry is a multisensory field, where visual art, literature, print and online words mix. But what about Mitchell's "auditory" component? In "compound_eye.rb" the "patient lips plastically [...] yield" to the insects. The lips are the patient's, yet they are also patient in another sense, waiting, silent, passive, to be entered. Can the animation be seen as a mouth, as well as an eye? This code poem, in its muteness, seems to be crying out to be voiced, or performed. If code poetry is concerned with how language looks, it is also concerned, synaesthetically, with how the visual sounds.

Human and computer performance: a code poetry typology

Performance has three aspects in the context of code poetry. First, like other types of poetry, code poetry can be performed by a human, i.e., it can be read aloud. Second, a computer can also read (that is to say, interpret, or run) a program. Thus, reading code poetry entails both human and non-human types of reading. Performance has another meaning in a computing context. The Oxford English Dictionary defines one meaning of "performance" as "the capabilities, productivity, or success of a machine, product, or person when measured against a standard" (OED Online 2022). In an environment where computer memory is scarce, the performance of a program can refer to how efficiently it uses memory. Conversely, in an environment with more abundant memory, the speed at which the program runs might be more important. Code can be optimized for performance, whether at work, to keep the client happy, or after hours, for the love and challenge of it. Finally, some code poetry can perform, or produce an output. In other words, code poems can have outputs just as "compound_eye.rb" performs its animated output. Code poetry can be optimized for performance in all three senses.

Scholars of digital literature have highlighted performance as an important, definitive dimension of code poetry. Geoff Cox writes that "[l]ike poetry, the aesthetic value of code lies in its execution, not simply its written form" (Cox et al. 2001, 30). Elsewhere, Cox, Alex McLean and Adrian Ward see "code as performative: that which both performs and is performed" (Cox et al. 2004, 161). We can use the three senses of performance that we have identified to build a tentative typology of code poetry: human-readable code poetry, machine-readable code poetry, and code poetry that produces an output. For an example of another typology of code poetry, see Alan Sondheim's three-part "tree [. . .] taxonomy" of codework (Sondheim 2001, 4). In brief, Sondheim's taxonomy is hierarchical, differentiating between work with "surface language" and work with "submerged code." This "submerged code" may or may not become "emergent content," breaking through to the surface (Sondheim 2001, 4). Sondheim's typology moves from the surface leafs to the invisible roots of a tree. By contrast, our typology is a non-hierarchical matrix, which uses types of performance rather than surface and depth as its criteria.

In the following table (Tab. 1), we propose that code poetry can be classified into eight types, according to whether it can be performed by humans, by computers and whether it, in turn, performs, or produces an output.

Tab. 1: Code poetry typology by Daniel Holden and Chris Kerr.

Type	Human performable?	Computer performable?	Performs (output)?
1	N	N	N
2	N	Y	N
3	N	Y	Y
4	N	N	Y
5	Y	N	N
6	Y	Y	N
7	Y	Y	Y
8	Y	N	Y

In the following, we will provide examples of some of these types of code poetry. Due to the page limit of the article, however, there is not enough space to discuss all the types listed in the table.

Type 5 (YNN) code poetry can be performed by humans, but not computers, and therefore does not produce any output on-screen. An example is Mez Breeze's pseudo-code language mezangelle, where "syntactical notation is taken from wildcards and regular expressions in programming languages and Unix command line interpreters forming an archetypical world" (Cramer 2005, 11). In this extract from Breeze's poem "_archi[ng]pelagos of d.sire_ (2004-02-08 17:27)" from *Human Readable Messages* square brackets are used to reveal words hidden in other words: "[eyes.of.smolder+graceless.ener[vation]gy]" (Breeze 2011, 76). When a reader reads this text aloud, they must choose whether to say "energy" or "enervation" or perhaps both in quick succession. The path that the reader chooses opens and closes off potential ways of performing the work. As McKenzie Wark writes: "Mez introduces the hypertext principle of multiplicity into the word itself. Rather than produce alternative trajectories through the text on the hypertext principle of 'choice', here they co-exist within the same textual space" (Wark 2001, 5). While it is challenging to perform, this work is nevertheless human-performable, as the title of Breeze's book *Human Readable Messages* suggests.

Type 6 (YYN) code poetry can be read aloud by humans, read by a computer, but the code itself does not perform any action. In other words, the computer recognizes the poem as valid, according to the rules of the programming language, but the program does not produce an output. An example is "Black Perl" (2003), an anonymous poem written in the Perl programming language. This poem is made of English words and a few other symbols, so it is easy for a person to read. The first line of the poem is "BEFOREHAND: close door, each window & exit; wait until time." When the Perl interpreter executes the code poem, it exits upon reaching the function "exit" in the first line.[2] The code poem terminates before it can produce an output. By contrast, a reader performing this poem aloud can read all twenty-four lines.

Type 7 (YYY) code poetry can be performed by humans and computers, and the code poems also perform an action. The code poems in our *./code --poetry* project fall into this type. This includes "compound_eye.rb," and another poem we will now turn our attention to, "chernobyl.rkt" (see Holden and Kerr 2016a). The code poem (the input) is written in the style of a report by a Communist Party official recording the fictional words of a resident of Chernobyl, or perhaps nearby Pripyat, after the disaster of 1986. The visual art that the code poem creates (the output), is a mutated version of the same report: in the animation the text scrolls faster and faster until it is replaced with non-semantic alphanumeric characters. This effect adds a glitch aesthetic to the artwork. "chernobyl.rkt" is written in the racket language,[3] and this is an aesthetic choice: each code poem in *./code --poetry* is written in a different programming language, and expresses the unique character of that language. Racket contains a lot of nested parentheses, which are used to define a hierarchical tree structure in the code.[4] "chernobyl.rkt" celebrates this feature of the language. The parentheses are markers of the meandering sub-clauses slurred by the drunken speaker of the poem. At the same time, the parentheses function to define the hierarchy of the text in the program, which determines how the text is spliced together in the output (Fig. 19).

This code poem is amenable to vocal performance for two reasons. First, the more unpronounceable symbols and keywords are hidden at the top of the poem. This encourages the human performer to focus on the body of the code poem, which contains readable English speech. Second, the parentheses help the performer, by acting like stage directions for a series of nested asides in a dramatic monologue. They suggest pauses and words to emphasize and also map the psy-

---

2 https://perldoc.perl.org/functions/exit.
3 https://racket-lang.org/.
4 https://docs.racket-lang.org/pict/Tree_Layout.html.

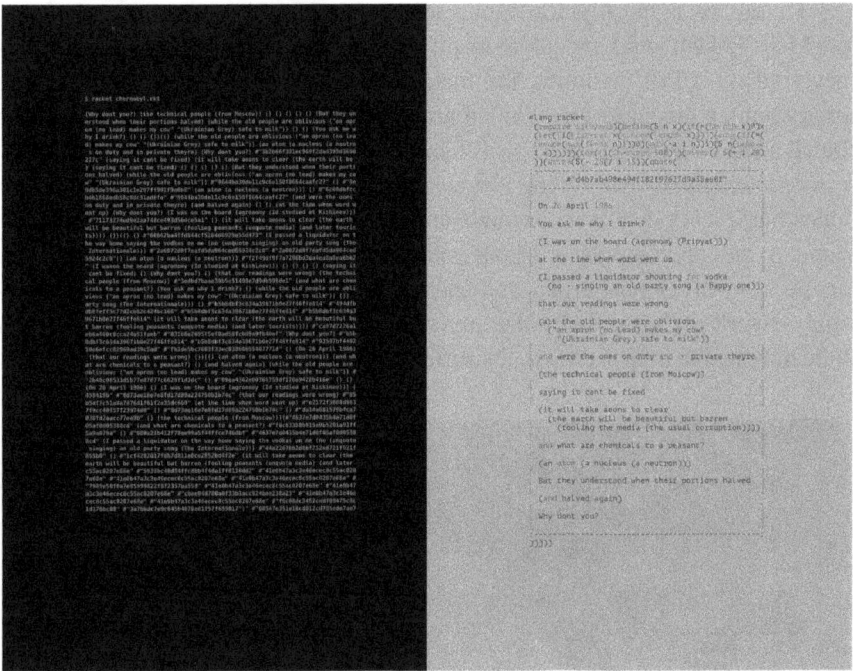

Fig. 19: Daniel Holden and Chris Kerr. "chernobyl.rkt." ./code --poetry. 2016a.

chology of the speaker's voice. One could say that the character of the programming language becomes the character of its speaker.

The next two examples in this typology incorporate images and play with the visual aspects of performing code poetry. Hannes Bajohr presents Allison Parrish's *Ahe Thd Yearidy Ti Isa* (2019), a visual-textual artwork made with multi-modal AI and points out that Parrish takes a neural network that is optimized for generating images, and feeds the neural network images of text. In Bajohr's words, Parrish's artwork "treats text *as* image, reverses the appropriate neural net architectures, and plays with the asemic effects" (Bajohr 2022, 228). Bajohr describes the images that the neural network produces as follows: "bitmaps of words are human-readable, but not machine-readable; they do not register as text" (Bajohr 2022, 228). These images are not programs: they do not do anything. Therefore, these images are examples of Type 5 (YNN) which moreover illustrate how different this work is to Breeze's of the same type. In the final step of the process, Parrish feeds the images into character recognition software (cf. Bajohr 2022, 229), making the work machine-readable after all. This demonstrates that the definitional borders around the proposed categories are blurred.

Finally, an atypical work in our *./code --poetry* project uses images. "bark.png" (see Holden and Kerr 2016a) might look like the output of a process, but it is nevertheless in fact the input. The image is a code poem written in the esoteric programming language Piet, named after Piet Mondrian, the twentieth century Dutch artist.[5] "bark.png," a framed image of a bark-like texture, consists of a series of instructions that tell the Piet compiler to output a haiku, which is in turn about bark. "bark.png" is an example of Type 3 (NYY): its input cannot be read by humans, but it is computer readable, and it produces a poetic output. Later in this article, we will see how artists and poets have invented strategies for making visual artwork performable by the human voice. Nevertheless, "bark.png" has no human-readable information on its surface (Fig. 20).

Fig. 20: Daniel Holden and Chris Kerr. "bark.png." *./code --poetry*. 2016a.

The computer programmer Daniel Shiffman demonstrates that, in a digital context, alphanumeric characters and images are not as distinct as we might think: "[a] digital image is nothing more than data – numbers indicating variations of

---

5 https://www.dangermouse.net/esoteric/piet.html.

red, green, and blue at a particular location on a grid of pixels. Most of the time, we view these pixels as miniature rectangles sandwiched together on a computer screen." (Shiffman 2015, 301) Shiffman's words suggest another way of reading "bark.png" and its haiku output: this artwork is a transformation of image into text, yes, but it is also, simultaneously, alphanumeric data translated into alphanumeric data. These last two examples show that any framework of code poetry performance must account for the visual qualities of text, and the numerical and textual properties of images. In the next section, we will describe how code poems like "compound_eye.rb" and "chernobyl.rkt" can be made, or optimized for human and computer performance.

Poetic practice

In our book, *./code --poetry*, the creation of each code poem is performed via the merging of two texts: a conventional poem, and a minimal, functional program that produces the output seen on the left-hand page. This merging process is bi-directional. In an effort to retain the functionality of the program, we must constrain, restrict, and adjust the original poem to fit into a form dictated by the programming language, and the syntax and structure it allows. Meanwhile, the original poem serves as the main inspiration for the choice of adjustments we make to the program: the poem guides the process of transforming the program from a form that is purely functional to a form that is both poetic and functional. Indeed, in the final code poem, even the functional aspects are poetic as the functional elements are an intrinsic part of the code poem. The process of combination is afforded by the technology of the programming language and us as poets. James J. Gibson defines the concept of affordances as follows:

> The *affordances* of the environment are what it *offers* the animal, what it *provides* or *furnishes*, either for good or ill. The verb *to afford* is found in the dictionary, but the noun *affordance* is not. I have made it up. I mean by it something that refers to both the environment and the animal in a way that no existing term does. It implies the complementarity of the animal and the environment. (Gibson 2015 [1979], 119)

This concept provides another framework for viewing the process, in addition to that of Oulipian constraint: the poets and the technology are in an ecological, complementary relationship. This integration process is a unique and challenging form of constrained poetry that requires programming expertise. We must capture the essence of the poem while limiting ourselves to transformations that do not change the functionality of the program. While many transformations are possible, there are various tactics that can be used to integrate a poem into a program without changing its behaviour, many of which are common across multiple programming languages. For example, arbitrary text can be inserted into programs as "comments" – additional text used to help readers of the code understand the intention of the programmer. The computer ignores these comments when it runs the program. In code poetry, "comments" can be used to directly insert segments of the original poem. While this technique is simple, it fails to account for the unique characteristics of the program, or the programming language it is written in.

Another similar technique that is common across many programming languages is to manipulate the names of "variables": named values that are used to refer to data stored in memory. The name given to variables can be changed to match words in the poem, or additional, unused variables can be declared and used in a way that does not change the program's functionality. Often, if the functional part of the program is too long or difficult to merge with the non-functional text, it can be minimized and hidden, for instance, by using single letters and symbols for variables, removing spaces and tabs, and compacting the program as much as possible. Then, the poem can be inserted into a non-functional section of the program, creating a code poem in two parts: a small functional program connected as an appendage to the larger, non-functional body. An example of this strategy can be seen in "chernobyl.rkt."

However, the goal of this merging process is to find more complex and satisfying techniques that involve some symbiosis between poem and program, preserving the signature elements of the poem, the program, and the programming language. Throughout this process, the layout of the code poem on the page can be adjusted. Because most programming languages ignore any whitespace when they functionally interpret the program, there is great freedom here. The text can be laid out on the page to create visual impressions and ASCII art, as "compound-_eye.rb" demonstrates. The whitespace, discounted by the programming language, nevertheless plays an active aesthetic role for the reader, like the role it plays in concrete poetry. Finally, the syntax highlighting can be adjusted, and colours, bold, italic, underlined formatting and highlighting can be applied to specific sections and keywords in the program in a way that foregrounds both the character of the programming language, and the poem. We can see this whole process as a form of optimization, where instead of execution speed or memory usage, a program is optimized for artistic value. In brief, this is a dual optimization with both human and computer performers in mind.

Visual scores for performance

We will now return to the human performance of code poetry. As we have noted above, "chernobyl.rkt" is relatively easy for a person to voice. But what if a reader wanted to perform the symbols and keywords from the top of "chernobyl.rkt," as well as the English words in the main body of the poem? "by_conspiracy_or_design.js" (see Holden and Kerr 2016a), another poem in ./code --poetry, presents even greater challenges for vocal performance, because the English words are mixed with large numbers of alphanumeric symbols (Fig. 21).

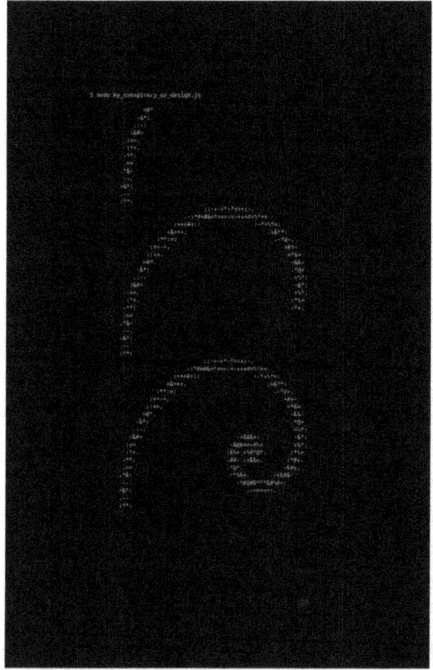

Fig. 21: Daniel Holden and Chris Kerr. "by_conspiracy_or_design.js." ./code --poetry. 2016a.

This code poem is written in JavaScript.[6] It features the voice of a ranting American conspiracy theorist who believes they have discovered the golden ratio in the vapour trails left by airplanes in the sky (or as the speaker has it "CHEMTRAILS"). The golden ratio (which is related to the golden section) is an irrational number

---

6 https://www.ecma-international.org/publications-and-standards/standards/ecma-262/.

said to have aesthetic properties.[7] The speaker appropriates feminist and Native American perspectives in a patronizing and shallow way, and mixes in pseudoscientific quantum physics concepts, all in the service of their illogical spell against supposed government conspiracy. The first part of the infinite golden ratio appears in the second line of the code poem. This number defines the shape of the visual output: a spiral that conforms to this ratio. It is made of ASCII characters, including plus, minus, equals, asterisk, ampersand signs and more. Karen Cham provides a visual culture context for the golden section:

> Any discussion of aesthetics and interactivity must first transgress the divide in modern western Art History between art and technology. Despite the fact that technical principles have always underpinned fine art production (rules of perspective, proportion and the golden section for example) photography, film, television and video are still marginalised in art-historical dialogues. (Cham 2009, 15)

To extend Cham's words from discussion to artforms, code poetry bridges the divide between literature and art on the one hand and science and technology on the other. "by_conspiracy_or_design.js" is well placed to explore the frictions at this divide: in this code poem, the golden ratio is a functional and mathematical rule as well as a spur for a kind of paranoid aesthetic thinking, where the art historian's desire to systematize and fit artwork to a scheme might have something in common with a conspiracy theorist's conviction that a pattern is everywhere they look. Nevertheless, the undeniable presence of the golden ratio in "by_conspiracy_or_design.js," might encourage the reader to consider parallels between this code poem and other visual art.

We will now turn to some examples of visual art being used as scores for sound poetry performance, to inform methods of vocally performing "by_conspiarcy_or_design.js." In this context, a score is the equivalent to printed notation of a musical or dance performance. The first example is the visual scores for sound poetry performance created by poets associated with the British Poetry Revival movement in the 1960s and 1970s. In one videoed collaborative performance with P. C. Fencott, Cobbing and Fencott use visual artworks as scores for elaborate, live performance, making animalistic sounds (see Johnson 1982). Bob Cobbing, a central figure in this movement, and Fencott talk about the relationship between the marks in the artwork and the dynamics of their performance, e.g., by equating the thickness of the mark with the volume of their voices. McCaffery and Nichol quote Sten Hanson, who asserts that Cobbing's sound poem scores have a significant visual component, cautioning that the sound element should not be privileged over the visual, or vice versa:

---

7 https://www.britannica.com/science/golden-ratio.

> The written versions of Cobbing's sound poems are not to be regarded merely as score for performance. They are poems in their own right and have important visual qualities which alone justify their existence as printed poetry. They can be appreciated without knowledge of their sound interpretations even though that knowledge would add a dimension to them. (McCaffery 1978, 102)

The second example of visual art being used as score for performance is the Fluxus art movement, also from the 1960s and 1970s. One important element of Fluxus was the production of scores for performance "events." Jackson Mac Low is an American poet associated with Fluxus who created poetic scores for performance. He described his "Asymmetries" series as "poems of which the words, punctuation, typography and spacing on the page are determined by chance operations" (Mac Low 1963). In his "BASIC METHOD" for reading Asymmetries, Mac Low defined what blank spaces, typography and punctuation indicated to the performer: "Blank spaces before, after and between words or parts of words, between lines of words, and before whole poems are rendered as silences equal in duration to the time it wd [sic!] take to read aloud the words printed anywhere above or below them" (Mac Low 1963). In this performance score, blank spaces become meaningful in the performance of the poem. This feature is analogous to some programming languages, for instance Python,[8] in which whitespace impacts how or whether programs run.

Both these examples offer possible methods for vocally performing visual art, with its marks and white spaces. Cobbing's methods in particular could be used to perform the seemingly unperformable "bark.png." Indeed, Cobbing and the poet-artist Paula Claire used patterned objects like bark as scores for performance:

> One of Cobbing's lasting contributions to text-sound activity is his revolutionising of what can constitute a 'text'. Cobbing (along with Paula Claire) has frequently abandoned the graphic imprint and received 'song signals' from natural objects: a cross-section of a cabbage, a stone, a piece of rope, the textured surface of bricks, cloth etc. (McCaffery and Nichol 1978, 14)

However, the vocal performance of visual art is perhaps necessarily idiosyncratic and unrepeatable across multiple live performances and performers, because its methods are so individual and impressionistic. That said, this art-historical context can encourage the viewer to see the works in ./code --poetry in a new light. Almost all the code poems in this project take text as input and produce text-based visual artworks as output (with the exception of "bark.png," which reverses this operation to produce text from an image). Therefore, these code poems can be seen as ekphrastic machines, which enact the translation between visual and

---

8 https://docs.python.org/3/reference/lexical_analysis.html.

textual modes in a way that is repeatable, in contrast to Cobbing and Claire's virtuosic performances.

Performing alphanumeric symbols

The context for the performance of visual art that we have outlined above will be helpful to explore methods of vocally performing alphanumeric symbols, like those that appear in "by_conspiracy_or_design.js." Our exploration of how to perform this code poem is informed by approaches to performing visual art scores as well as alphanumeric symbols. We will describe three ways of voicing the (in common usage) peculiar signs in code poetry. One strategy is to pass over the alphanumeric symbols silently as the British-Canadian artist and writer, J. R. Carpenter, did when she was invited to perform her poem "Etheric Ocean":

> I devised a print script for two voices, to be read along with a projection of the digital work being navigated from left to right. The print script soon became annotated with stage directions scribbled in pencil. As I would be reading long lists of arguments copied and pasted from JavaScript arrays, I found it useful to ['retain the JavaScript syntax in the print script', 'to guide me through otherwise grammatically impossible sentences']. (Carpenter 2021)

Carpenter uses the square brackets and single quotation marks that define JavaScript arrays to inform her performance, but she does not voice these symbols. In a second method for performing symbols, their names are read out in full. Gary Barwin's *Servants of Dust: Shakespeare Sonnets 1–20* (2021) uses a voice synthesizer to read out only the punctuation marks from Shakespeare's sonnets, like "comma" and "colon," over music. The sonnet form is surfaced indirectly, through the proxy formal container of punctuation. A third method for reading alphanumeric symbols aloud is to assign sounds to them, rather than pronouncing their names. The British performance artist Nathan Walker created an artwork using JavaScript called "Sounding.js." Walker describes this piece as follows:

> My work, "Sounding.js", is both a live sound-poem and an online interactive website that enables the user to "activate" a recording of the performance by moving their cursor over the digital score. Composed using a complete and fully functional JavaScript, the code is presented as a phonic utterance; a vocal exploration of non-phonic programming language and the spatial and temporal possibilities of embodying the digital text in performance. (Walker 2013, 63)

Another example of this third method of performing alphanumeric symbols is more functional than artistic. Tavis Rudd, a software developer, created a speech-to-text interface in the Python programming language that allowed him to code by voice, after experiencing a repetitive strain injury from typing (cf. Rudd 2013). Naming each symbol would take too long, so he defined a short vocal sound for each symbol. As well as assigning sounds to individual symbols, Rudd's system also accounts for the macroscopic structures of code. For example, for square brackets, he uses rhyming sounds to open ("lack") and close ("rack") the brackets.

Which of these three methods is appropriate for "by_conspiracy_or_design.js"? Given that the speaker of this code poem is a logically incoherent ranting conspiracy theorist, the third method (assigning sounds to symbols) seems the most appropriate, because these sounds make his speech more unintelligible. Different styles of performance suit different code poems. When the symbols are assigned to sounds in a similar way to Rudd's system, a script for the third, fourth and fifth lines of "by_conspiracy_or_design.js" might look like this:

> caps INFINITE naps eek spiral dot log par DIVINE tar slash par spiral dot PI slash 2 tar sem
> if par 0 tar brace function caps CHEMTRAILS naps par spirit tar brace return brack
> spiral dot cos par spirit tar star spiral dot exp par caps INFINITE naps star spirit tar com

Note that the capitalized words in this script were capitalized in the original code poem, inspired by the typography of conspiratorial websites. That said, capitalization does encourage the performer to shout these words. The speed of a vocal performance can be optimized by analogy to the way in which a program is optimized to perform quickly on a computer. Like a computer, a human performer can run slowly and quickly. Still, in vocal performance, there are also variables without direct computer analogues, like volume and pitch. A vocal performance could also move away from words like "naps" to other forms of human vocal articulation, like clicks.

Finally, a vocal performance of "by_conspiracy_or_design.js" could respond to the visual qualities of the code poem. The code poem is centre-aligned on the page, and the lines are of varying length. Inspired by Cobbing and adjusting his voice to the width of the marks on the page, a performer could say the shorter lines more quietly and the longer lines more loudly. A performer could also use syntax highlighting as part of their script, employing different colours as performance cues. Then, the syntax highlighting would be arranged with both vocal performance as well as visual balance in mind.

Conclusion: "optimized for performance"

In this article, we have demonstrated some ways in which code poetry can be optimized for human as well as computer performance. The techniques presented are informed by the history of the performance of visual art and alphanumeric symbols. Furthermore, code poetry can be categorized in terms of whether it can be performed by humans, computers, and whether it in turn performs, or outputs something. We assert that the struggle of human and computer voice over a single artistic and functional space presents new opportunities for dramatic ironies. The speaker of the poem can do things that the program does not register, and the program can do things that the speaker does not know about. Like plays, code poems are made of characters, in the sense of letters, numbers, and other symbols. Code poems present an opportunity for the visual personality of each of these characters to be performed on multiple levels. As J. R. Carpenter writes, a "single missing or misplaced comma, bracket, or quotation mark will cause a program not to run" (Carpenter 2021). The attention to detail required by a programmer can train the reader and viewer of code poetry to pay a similar level of attention to individual glyphs. To focus in this way on linguistic signs is to see them as visual artefacts, and not only elements of text. Such a focus is encouraged in *./code --poetry* where ASCII characters are used as the elementary units of visual artwork. Consequently, the categories of text and image blur.

The dramatic character of code poetry can be seen clearly in the esoteric programming language Shakespeare, where programs appear to be play scripts (cf. Lang 2017). In "shakespeare.spl," a currently unpublished poem in our *./code --poetry* project that is written in this language, the following words form part of a program that outputs a list of Shakespeare's sonnets: "Thou art the sum of a handsome beautiful fair flower and a plum. Thou art the sum of the square of thyself and a golden rose." Similarly, J. R. Carpenter sees JavaScript as inherently performative and dramatic: "It is no coincidence that the word 'script' appears in the name 'JavaScript' – JavaScript is a procedural language. Like a script for live performance, JavaScript must be written and read in a particular order in order to be performed by the web browser" (Carpenter 2021). *./code --poetry* also explores characters in a different sense, namely the character or personalities of programming languages themselves. There is a ghostly voice behind each code poem, which is the voice of the language it is written in, whether that is the digressive and meandering quality of Racket, with its endless asides or the chaotic energy of JavaScript, freely filling the space on the page or screen like a conspiracy theorist. In this regard, code poetry is moreover an ideal medium for dramatic irony. In "by_conspiracy_or_design.js," the syntax "/native-American/" is highlighted pink. The computer knows something about the word "native" that the deluded speaker of the poem does not: it is a reserved word in JavaScript, i.e., it cannot be used to define a variable, function or label name. The casual racism of the speaker is complicated by the functioning of the technology of the code poem. Finally, this dramatic irony has a visual component. The pink syntax highlighting acts like a stage direction here, drawing attention to the double status of the word "native," and perhaps alluding to the identity of the code poem's speaker, who a reader might read as white. In code poetry, the visual, too, is optimized for performance.

References

Anonymous. "Black Perl updated for Perl 5." 2003, https://www.perlmonks.org/?node_id=237465 (January 15, 2023).
Aprile, Francesco. "laravel poems." *Code Poems. 2010–2019*. Minneapolis, MN: Post-Asemic Press, 2020. 17–20.
Bajohr, Hannes. "Algorithmic Empathy: Toward a Critique of Aesthetic AI." *Configurations* 30 (2022): 203–231.
Barwin, Gary. *Servants of Dust. Shakespeare Sonnets 1–20*. 2021, https://www.youtube.com/watch?v=PvQiuigBm7s (January 15, 2023).
Bhanoo, Sindya N. "Getting a Handle on Why 4 Equals Green." *The New York Times*. November 21, 2011, https://www.nytimes.com/2011/11/22/science/mapping-grapheme-color-synesthesia-in-the-brain.html (January 15, 2023).
Breeze, Mez. *Human Readable Messages: [Mezangelle 2003–2011]*. Vienna: Traumawein, 2011.
Carlson, Stephan C. "golden ratio." 2023, https://www.britannica.com/science/golden-ratio (January 15, 2023).
Carpenter, J. R. "Straight Quotes, Square Brackets: Page-Based Poetics Inflected with the Syntax and Grammar of Code Languages." *Hybrid* 7 (2021): n. pag. https://journals.openedition.org/hybrid/684 (January 15, 2023).
Cham, Karen. "Aesthetics and Interactive Art." *Digital Visual Culture. Theory and Practice*. Ed. Anna Bentkowska-Kafel, Trish Cashen, and Hazel Gardiner. Bristol and Chicago, IL: Intellect Books, 2009. 15–21.
Cox, Geoff, Alex McLean, and Adrian Ward. "Coding Praxis: Reconsidering the Aesthetics of Code." *read_me: Software Art and Cultures*. Ed. Olga Goriunova and Alexei Shulgin. Aarhus: Aarhus Univ. Press, 2004. 161–174.
Cox, Geoff, Alex McLean, and Adrian Ward. "The Aesthetics of Generative Code." *Hard Code*. Ed. Eugene Thacker. Boulder, CO: ALT-X, 2001. 22–34.
Cramer, Florian. *Words Made Flesh: Code, Culture, Imagination*. Rotterdam: Piet Zwart Institute, 2005.
"ECMA-262." Ecma International. June 2022, https://www.ecma-international.org/publications-and-standards/standards/ecma-262/ (October 31, 2022).
"exit." Perldoc Browser. https://perldoc.perl.org/functions/exit (January 15, 2023).
Finch, Peter. "Texture Poem for the Moons of Stars." *Typewriter Poems*. Cardiff: Second Aeon Publications, 1972. 34.
Gibson, James J. *The Ecological Approach to Visual Perception*. New York: Psychology Press, 2015 [1979].
Holden, Daniel, and Chris Kerr. *./code --poetry*. Authors' edition: CreateSpace self-publishing service, 2016a. n. pag.
Holden, Daniel, and Chris Kerr. *./code --poetry*. 2016b, https://code-poetry.com/ (January 15, 2023).
James, Brian. "Lockdown Dérive." *code::art* 1 (2020): 11.
Johnson, Josephine (Dir.). *Performing Concrete Poetry*. 1982, https://www.ubu.com/film/cobbing_fencott.html (January 15, 2023).

Lang, Mirco. "Shakespeare Programming Language." 2017, https://www.dev-insider.de/shakespeare-programming-language-a-617430/ (October 31, 2022).

"Lexical analysis." Python. 2023, https://docs.python.org/3/reference/lexical_analysis.html (January 15, 2023).

Mac Low, Jackson. "Methods for Reading Asymmetries." *An Anthology of Chance Operations*. Ed. La Monte Young and Jackson Mac Low. New York: Authors' edition, 1963. n. pag.

McCaffery, Steve, and bpNichol. "Biographies." *Sound Poetry. A Catalogue*. Ed. Steve McCaffery and bpNichol. Toronto: Underwhich Editions, 1978. 91–111.

McCaffery, Steve. "Sound Poetry. A Survey." *Sound Poetry. A Catalogue*. Ed. Steve McCaffery and bpNichol. Toronto: Underwhich Editions, 1978. 6–18.

Mitchell, W. J. T. "Showing Seeing: A Critique of Visual Culture." *The Visual Culture Reader*. Ed. Nicholas Mirzoeff. London and New York: Routledge, 2002. 86–101.

Morgan-Mar, David. "DM's Esoteric Programming Languages – Piet." 2018, https://www.dangermouse.net/esoteric/piet.html (January 15, 2023).

"performance, n." OED Online. September 2022, www.oed.com/view/Entry/140783 (January 15, 2023).

Petkova, Nataliya. "UNTITLED (LOVE)." *code {poems}*. Ed. Ishac Bertran. Barcelona: Imprenta Badia, 2018. 21.

Racket. https://racket-lang.org/ (January 15, 2023).

Ruby Programming Language. https://www.ruby-lang.org/en/ (January 15, 2023).

Rudd, Tavis. "Using Python to Code by Voice." 2013, https://www.youtube.com/watch?v=8SkdfdXWYaI (January 15, 2023).

Shiffman, Daniel. *Learning Processing. A Beginner's Guide to Programming Images, Animation, and Interaction*. Amsterdam: Elsevier, 2015.

Sondheim, Alan. "Introduction: Codework." *American Book Review* 22.6 (2001): 1, 4.

Walker, Nathan. "Transitional Materialities and the Performance of JavaScript." *Performance Research* 18.5 (2013): 63–68.

Wark, McKenzie. "Essay: Codework." *American Book Review* 22.6 (2001): 1, 5.

María Mencía
Navigating the Poetic-Aesthetic Space of E-Poetry

> Que la crítica borre toda mi poesía, si le parece. Pero este poema, que hoy recuerdo, no podrá borrarlo nadie.
> ("The critics may erase all of my poetry. But this poem, that I today remember, nobody will be able to erase." Pablo Neruda, "Indelible poem"; own translation)

These words by Neruda were, as the Winnipeg boat was, about to part from the port of Trompeloup-Pauillac in France to Valparaiso, Chile on August 4, 1939. Neruda in his role as the Chilean Consul Immigration Officer had organised the Winnipeg boat in order to rescue and evacuate around 2,500 Spanish Civil War exiles from concentration camps in France. In his "Indelible poem," charged with the emotional atmosphere of the farewells in the port and of the passengers navigating on the Winnipeg boat into what was the unknown for most of them, expands the notion of poetry to the human experience of the event – that 'poetic moment' in time where feelings of loss, deportation, displacement, exile, and solitude are manifested.

This ability to capture a moment in time in the poetic-aesthetic space is explored through e-poetry works like my interactive piece *The Winnipeg: The Poem that Crossed the Atlantic*; that moment where feelings are represented in a multimodal way, where the visual and the semantic come together in the digital space (whether text, sound or image) to engage the reader in looking both through the text and at the text (cf. Lanham 1993, 5). I have spent my career exploring this in-between space in which the experience of the poetic is captured by shifting from the semantic linguistic meaning to the visual; from the literal, the legible, the transparent to the abstract language, creating simultaneously a poetic space of readable and visual textualities. It is in this oscillation between text and image or sound and image, and code and image, in the shifting between these ways of expression where I argue the poetic-aesthetic space can be brought to life.

The article furthermore examines the influence of experimental poetry and notions of the *in-betweenness* in and of poetic language (cf. Kristeva 1984). It explores how artistic approaches from experimental avant-garde literary and artistic traditions of the twentieth century, such as the use of typography, words which do not make sense, broken narratives, and calligrammes, can serve to highlight the impact of the intertwining of the visual and the textual. I have used these techniques to underpin my creative practice and its contextualisation in the fields of language media arts, digital art and e-poetry. I also continue to explore

Open Access. © 2023 the author(s), published by De Gruyter. This work is licensed under the Creative Commons Attribution-NonCommercial-NoDerivatives 4.0 International License.
https://doi.org/10.1515/9783111299334-010

the role of electronic literature and e-poetry in culture and society with topics on gender and identity, migration, displacement and exile, linguistic and cultural diversity, historical memory, art and healing practices.

From visual poetry to digital poetic-aesthetics: the origins

The interweaving of image, sound and text has been one of the foundations of my artistic research through the use of visual metaphors, data visualisation, phonetic sounds, animations, interactivity and multimodal, multilinguistic, generative hybrid textualities. These practices have been explored through methodologies of collaboration, co-creation, translation, transcreation, storytelling and the use of technology, software and programming languages. Through these digital and collaborative approaches, I have continued to explore the fusion of word and image or text and image to play with the visual materiality of language in my e-poetry, where language – whether visual or semantic – is the foundation of the work. In the chapter titled "Transient Self-Portrait: The Data Self" in the anthology of *#WomenTechLit*, I state how language is the key material of my creative practice to explore "the *in-between* space where the legible/illegible and intelligible/unintelligible meet in a form of symbiosis to create new landscapes of expression and new meanings" (Mencía 2017b, 190). This materialises in different ways such as through multilingual soundscapes, visual linguistic forms, and multimodal textualities.

In her book *Poesía Visual en España* (*Visual Poetry in Spain*, 2012), Blanca Millán Domínguez explains the concept of a visual poem with reference to Fernando Millán's *La Escritura en Libertad: Antologia de Poesia Experimental* (*Writing in Freedom: Anthology of Experimental Poetry*), which was published in 1975, coinciding with the death of the dictator Francisco Franco. She quotes the German poet Franz Mon: "La lengua desaparece en su medium, pero el medium, la escritura, se convierte de la misma manera en una lengua" (Millán Dominguez 2012, 100; "The language disappears in its medium, but the medium, the writing, simultaneously becomes a language"; own translation). Thus, the *visual writing* ["la escritura visual"] becomes another language, another way of expression in its materiality, maintaining the aspect of the linguistic in addition to the visual signification. This is what Millán refers to as the *writing in freedom* ["escritura en libertad"], also appropriate considering the publication was at the end of a forty-year dictatorship. This writing space set free from the constrains of the conventions of language – with its focus on its flexibility or plasticity – is where I argue, both the poetic and the aesthetic qualities fuse together. To understand this intersection of art and language in my e-poetry works, it is worth giving a short overview of certain avant-garde approaches from the beginning of the twentieth century. These aesthetic practices highly influenced my own art because of their quest for a new language interconnecting the verbal and the visual and the interchange of signs.

Historically, there have been many movements interested in the interconnection of the verbal and the visual, exploring the meaning of the visuality and aurality of language. Johanna Drucker argues that the tradition of visual poetry commenced as long ago as the beginning of writing itself (cf. Drucker 1998, 110). According to Richard Lanham in *The Electronic Word* (1993), the interaction of word and image goes back at least to the Greek poet Simias in the fourth century BC.[1] Many traditions in art and poetry have merged the verbal and the visual, artists have painted words and poets have made poems into shapes; the visual arrangement of the words and sentences add layers of meaning through the fusion of the linguistic and the visual.

In this article, I primarily focus on work from the beginning of the twentieth century, which will establish the background influences for my own creative practice and with this, my position and understanding of poetry within the fields of visual culture, electronic literature and media arts will become clear. Willard Bohn in *The Aesthetics of Visual Poetry* defines visual poetry as "poetry meant to be seen" (Bohn 1986, 2). This open definition brings up many categories of experimentation within the visual and literary genres. He further elaborates this in his publication *Reading Visual Poetry* and his fascinating chapter "The Word Made Flesh," where he underlines how this genre requires both a reader and a viewer due to words becoming elements of the visual arrangement of the poem (cf. Bohn 2011, 13). The American artist Dick Higgins, co-founder of the Fluxus international artistic movement, also discusses this aspect of the fusion of the verbal and the visual in connection to pattern poetry (cf. Higgins 1987). However, to me it is the French symbolist poet Stephane Mallarmé and his poem "Un Coup de dés jamais n'abolira le hasard" ("A Throw of the Dice," 1897) where the concrete, the materiality of the word, its visual presence and meaning versus the semantic, become manifest. In my opinion, this poem is one of the strongest examples of visual poetry in the western world.

Stephane Mallarmé is one of the pillars of my artistic research because of the way he dealt with notions of reading and viewing the text, i.e., the writing space.

---

[1] Sections of this article like the following passage on Mallarmé and Apollinaire together with the influence of Julia Kristeva's *Revolution in Poetic Language* (1984) are the foundations of my creative research practice and are adapted from my unpublished PhD dissertation *From Visual Poetry to Digital Art: Image, Sound Text and the Developments of New Media Languages* (2003). I have presented these ideas in academic and creative research events and educational settings.

His exploration of the text on the page demands that a reader employs an entirely different technique of reading: Mallarmé's poem "A Throw of the Dice" forces the reader to take a position, to be actively involved in the reading process, which in itself is more similar to how we read on screens today, scanning the poem for meaning. Mallarmé challenges the notion of coherence and rationality by destroying the linearity of thought conventionally created by syntax. The lack of punctuation in the poem allows for more fluidity, creating a sense both of insecurity and freedom. The concept of page changes to that of a space with visual signification being put into question. Alvaro Seiça writes: "*Un Coup de dés* is notorious for the displacement of words in space, creating voids and pauses in the free poetic line, and extending the reading area to the double-page spread." (Seiça 2021, 175) One of the pleasures of the poem – precisely because of this reading space – is that we are presented with a text, which permits multiple perspectives we can also find when looking at a drawing or illustration. Its richness comes from a tension between seeing and reading (cf. Benthien et al. 2019, 82).

Apollinaire's *calligrammes* (1918) are also part of the foundation of this tradition. A calligramme, at its simplest, is when a text is set out in a way to form an image, like a hat or face, and it can have a linguistic/visual plurality. This ambiguity of meaning, where the oscillation of looking and reading is significant determines in how far calligrammes are interpreted. Both the written language and the semantic possibilities of visual form come together to engage the eye as well as the mind. They abolish the hierarchy of language by being represented in a variety of patterns interconnecting the semantic and visual forms. As Foucault describes in his book *This is Not a Pipe*: "The calligramme aspires playfully to efface the oldest oppositions of our alphabetical civilization: to show and to name; to shape and to say; to reproduce and to articulate; to imitate and to signify; to look and to read." (Foucault 1983, 21) The simultaneous act of looking and reading is representative of this kind of legibility and visibility in the calligramme. Its visual and spatial elements are an important development in these written poems, which are highly influenced by painting. Apollinaire wanted to publish these poems under the title "I, too, am a painter" (Apollinaire 1980, 10). He created a new visual/linguistic sign; a *calligrammatological* sign to describe a form of poetry, which intended to employ words much as a painter would use representational forms. As with Mallarmé, poetry existed autonomously in space and the linguistic sign acquired a new signifier by being part of a visual signifier.

Further influences of avant-garde and concrete poetry

In addition to the above-mentioned literary examples, we also find other artistic avant-garde movements, which deal with similar ideas. Some are experimenting and integrating genres of poetry by breaking with linguistic meanings and by using visual language in a variety of media to question creative expression. The approaches used in the experimental literary practices mentioned above (Mallarmé, Apollinaire) and the avant-garde movements discussed in the following shape my understanding of poetry – a poetry which is readable and visible, intelligible and unintelligible, transparent and abstract, and therefore involves the viewer/reader in an interplay of intersemiotic signs. Amongst these avant-garde movements are the Italian Futurists and Dadaists, which arose as a reaction to the First World War, to nationalism and to conservative values or established rules. The Italian futurist Marinetti used a technique in his poetry called *parole in libertà* ("words in freedom") to liberate the word from the restrictions of language through typographical explorations. The Dadaist movement used a variety of strategies and aesthetic approaches from photomontages, collages to ready-mades, comprised of a mixture of languages, letters and symbols, and nonsense words, to force readers into questioning what they were reading. Suzanne Delehanty in the book *Sound by Artists* (1990) emphasises the interest shown by painters and poets after the First World War in the visuality and the aurality of letters and their value as visual images and aural signs. Poetry was filled with images and the visual arts with words. She states:

> The word alone as a pure abstraction, like a musical note, gave birth not only to Kandinsky's poetry and to the mystical incarnations of Hugo Ball but also to families of secret languages, in which the word lost its original meaning and assumed mutable interpretations in the fictive realm of artistic creation. (Delehanty 1990, 28)

In 1965, Jasia Reichardt curated the exhibition *Between Poetry and Painting* at the Institute of Contemporary Arts in London, where, as its title indicates, work blurring the boundaries between these creative fields was presented. The exhibition had a worldwide representation, with poets like Franz Mon, Ferdinand Kriwet, Bob Cobbing, and the group Noigandres. It was questioning literary content through artists making visual images out of words such as the Ragazzi/Porta collaboration. Reichardt writes: "This type of poetry serves to examine what happens to language through a certain type of visual presentation, and what becomes of an abstract image simultaneously endowed with a literary meaning." (Reichardt 1965, 9) This exhibition brought together artistic practices, where either through poetry or the visual arts, language in its visual materiality questions the literary text and its aesthetics possibilities.

The meaning of art, in its conventional sense is obliterated, opening up avenues for the creation of other meanings. The separate categories of viewer and reader are ruptured as the viewer is invited to read words and the reader to look at words. It is evident that the visual and the literary arts have been influencing each other throughout history, writers would become artists and artists would question language through their visual work. Hence, these artistic and literary approaches showcase a wide range of techniques where reading and viewing became one in the visual arts as well as in visual poetry with concrete and sound poetry. Whether in their abstraction, in secret or playful representations or interpretations, most of them originated in language itself: the syntax, structure, grammar, as well as idiosyncrasies, verisimilitudes, and puns found in language.

In the 1950s and 1960s, the experimentations of concrete poetry and sound poetry were breaking into the international arena. Concrete poetry and visual poetry have been defined in many different ways; we could say the difference is that concrete poetry is mainly formed by text, while visual poetry can include images as well as writing. Drucker in *Figuring the Word*, describes the distinction as follows: "In its most generic application, the term 'concrete poetry' is used to designate all manner of shaped, typographically complex, visually self-conscious poetic works. The term visual poetry is more general and thus more aptly used to describe a history which is as old as writing itself." (Drucker 1998, 110) This brings an understanding of concrete poetry as an internationally explored genre within the umbrella of visual poetry. In Switzerland in the 1950s, Eugen Gomringer had been producing experimental poetry, which he denominated as 'concrete,' at the same time the Brazilian group Noigandres constituted by Augusto de Campos, Haroldo de Campos and Decio Pignatari, were exploring concrete poetry as a three-dimensional, *verbi-voco-visual* object – a 3-D poetic object comprised of concrete poems fusing the verbal, vocal and visual capabilities of poetry. Poets in Germany, France, Spain and Canada were also experimenting with these visual linguistic forms.

The letters of the alphabet in concrete poetry become detached from their roles as mere signs in the system of communication and take on a visual importance of their own. They assume independent status as letters and their significance goes beyond the semantic content. Words are transformed into images, sentences are no longer readable, which is when the letter becomes concrete, visual. A poet using these techniques, and being recognised by his trademark of phonetic spelling in his concrete/sound poems, is the Canadian bill bissett. If we take his poem "yu cum" (1970) as an example, bissett plays with the typography to such a degree that he destroys the semantic aspect of language. The letters in this poem are so overtyped in some areas, that the visual rhythm of the poem becomes almost tangible. This is the space between legibility and illegibility, between transparency and abstraction. As Steve McCaffery, another Canadian poet, and writer points out:

> Overprinting (the laying of text over the text to the point of obliterating all legibility) is bissett's method of deterritorializing linguistic codes and placing language in a state of vertical excess. Overprint destroys the temporal condition of logic and causality, obliterating articulation and destroying message by its own super-abundance. (McCaffery 1986, 103)

This opposition of the legible and the illegible, where language materialises through the ink, the erasures, are what McCaffery describes as "writing is outside writing." (McCaffery 1986, 100) It is an area of unknown codes, grammar and syntax, open and free, and yet still within a structure. It is both within the linguistic and outside of it. As readers and linguistic beings, we see language and we want to find semantic meaning, but we cannot because we are 'within language but outside language.' That is, we are reading the visual which references language. bissett not only rejects all rules but urges the reader to do the same. In fact, in *what fuckan theory* he presents the following theoretical rejections:

> So yu dont need th sentence
> yu dont need correct spelling
> yu dont need correct grammar
> yu dont need th margins
> yu dont need regulation use of capital nd lower case
> yu dont need sense or skill
> yu dont need this
> what dew yu need
> (bissett 1971, 100)

The violation of these rules becomes a semantic attack, which allows language to flow freely. Inspired by bissett's approach and engagement with language and the visual – through language – I created a series of experimental generative poems. For this I used the Processing programming language, during a fellowship in the Key Centre of Design Computing and Cognition at the University of Sydney in 2007. I developed the poems further by taking Hansjorg Mayer's *alphabetenquadratbuch* (1965) poem "[alphabet in a square]" as a starting point. The linguistic is embedded in the poem, even in its title the visual is concrete in its minimalist form of multiple layers. Both, Mayer's and bissett's poems, bring up the materiality of language, the *in-betweenness*, the legible and the illegible.

In my computer-generated poetry, such as in the series "Generative Poems" (Fig. 22), the sound of the voice acts as the means to generate the poems by activating the letters. The viewers are presented with an empty screen and it is not

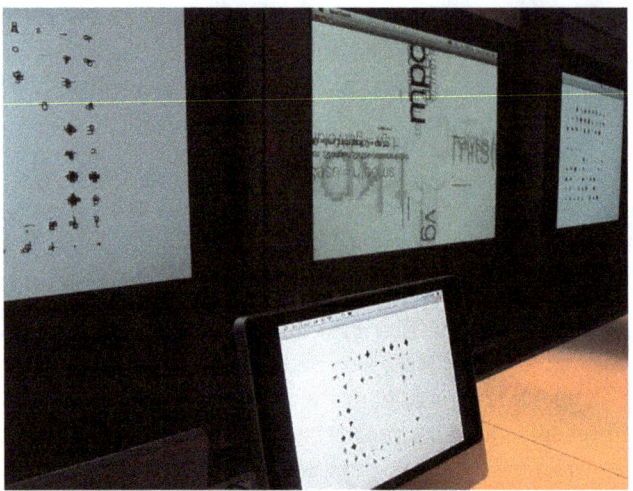

Fig. 22: María Mencía. "Generative Poems." 2010.

until sound is produced that the viewable space is filled in with letters. Sound and silence are part of the 'reading-viewing' experience of the participant. In this way, four communication systems come together: visual, writing, the underlying code, and sound. If there is no sound, there are no visuals, if the sound is loud, the letters are thicker and bigger. That is, the continuously generated writing is subjugated to the pitch of the sound.

The first two poems developed here have the shape of a square formed by the letters of the alphabet in ten rows. They are titled "Square 01" and "Square 02." In "Square 01," the letters appear lineally: line after line, the letters accumulate on top of each other in the different rows until they become a blob. This is the structure that builds up the poem. In "Square 02," the letters appear in the form of a spiral, which goes on forever producing a square.

In 2010, I revisited these poems for an exhibition at the Palazzo delle Arti in Naples, Italy, and they developed into a series of three interactive square poems titled "the alphabetic" (2010). They have as many rows as there are letters in the western alphabet (28), to follow Mayer's *alphabetenquadratbuch* structure. They also follow the conceptualisation of one of my early interactive digital artworks, "Another Kind of Language" (2001), which consists of three different layers of stills as well as moving images and phonetic sounds from Arabic, Chinese and English. The user needs to interact with the work by utilising the mouse and moving it over the screen, to activate the sounds and images. The three pieces of "the alphabetic" are also inspired by the different reading methods of these three languages: from right to left, left to right, and top to bottom. As with bissett's or Mayer's poems, I sought to create an obsessive repetition and a desire to escape from the linguistic through an obliteration of the letters. But the viewer should remain entrapped in a square (the shape of the poems). I think this condition is even more emphatic in the already described generative poems, as there is also an element of time present in them. In "Square 02" the enclosure is in the structure of the ongoing spiral. Once more, the shifting from the visual to the linguistic creates the poetic-aesthetic space of the *in-between* state of verbal-visual energy found in the in-between of the image-sound-text relation.

The in-between image-sound-text

In *Revolution in Poetic Language* Kristeva discusses the function and place of the pre-verbal semiotic and how it is revealed in language and speech. She claims that the semiotic is the period prior to the symbolic before the child separates him/herself from the mother (the semiotic and symbolic are equivalent to the pre-linguistic and linguistic; cf. Kristeva 1984, 24). The subject moves from the realm of the semiotic, the *chora*, through the *thetic* into the realm of the symbolic. Thus, the *thetic* is what allows the subject to liberate the energies from the *chora* into the symbolic and here they get trapped into language. However, there is also the area she calls the second *thetic*, where these aspects of the semiotic – impulses, energies, moods, feelings, movements, desires – are present within the symbolic and vice-versa: the *in-between*. According to Kristeva, the subject's memory of the contact with its mother's body, which is established in the semiotic, never vanishes. Instead, the speaking subject still uses it: "Because the subject is always both semiotic and symbolic, no signifying system he produces can be either 'exclusively' semiotic or 'exclusively' symbolic and is instead necessarily marked by indebtedness to both." (Kristeva 1984, 24) For her, this dialectical condition of the subject in language is represented in avant-garde literature and a desire in language is found in the struggle between the semiotic and the symbolic. I see this desire in language, in the in-between space sketched before, as that moment when the semiotic and the symbolic become one, whilst paradoxically retaining their own identities: where the semantic meaning of the word escapes and yet remains. Concrete poetry incorporates this in-between area within its visual and linguistic structures.

McCaffery also discusses this in-between area in relationship to language poetry in *North of Intention* (1986). He claims that language poetry, with its desire to break the rules of language, primarily considers the human subject in its realm of the symbolic and the biological – the latter term is similar to the pre-linguistic or in Kristeva's terms, to the semiotic, whereas the in-between of these two realms for him is the libidinal economy (cf. McCaffery 1986, 100). This is an area formed by libidinal intensities, which liberate the energy trapped by linguistic structures and, thus, could be compared to the second degree *thetic* in Kristeva's theory. There, the subject goes back from the symbolic into the semiotic in a conscious manner, so that aspects of the semiotic are used within the signifying devices of language. McCaffery finds the aspect of excess and libidinal flow in bill bissett's work (cf. McCaffery 1986, 100). It occurs by breaking all the mechanisms that restrict the flow of non-verbal impulses such as grammatical rules, reading order and orthography. He describes how these energies force passage through language: there is a desire, which operates throughout and aside from language – the 'outside' of language but 'within' language referred to earlier. bissett clearly not only rejects all rules but urges the reader to do the same in his theoretical rejections, as stated previously. When we look at bissett's work and at many other examples of concrete visual poetry, we try to find linguistic signification because we recognise it is made of language. However, we are 'outside' this linguistic signification and we are confronted with an aesthetic visual signification instead, which references language as such. Thus, this kind of poetry can be said to be an embodiment of the concept 'within language but outside' of language.

In digital environments, as with printed visual poetry, the in-between, the pre-linguistic, and the linguistic are equally found in the oscillation between text and image, sound and image or even code and image. It is in the shifting between these ways of expression, where I argue the digital poetic-aesthetic space is located and where we find the experience of what is 'outside' but also 'within' language. The process of reading and viewing, moving from the linguistic to the visual language, can furthermore be associated with Richard Lanham's notion of "looking at" and "looking through" the malleable text of transparent and abstract landscapes of visual text (Lanham 1993, 5). This also applies to my own works of linguistic soundscapes with a shift from the intelligible to the unintelligible. The reader/viewer is invited to look at the text, the surface, the materiality, and the visual meaning of the abstract visual text, while simultaneously looking through the text, the semantic, transparent meaning of language. As Apollinaire intended with his calligrammes, the reader is invited to simultaneously engage the eye and the brain to reveal the semantic and visual meaning of the text. This process is reflected in all my digital art/poems. If we look at, for example, my interactive work "Connected Memories" (2010), developed with the technical help of the creative programmer José Carlos Silvestre, we find a fluid interactive poetic generative hyper-textual narrative without a focused point, beginning or end. The work is opposed to systems founded upon ideas of centre, margin, hierarchy, and linearity. It consists of a series of interviews conducted with refugees living in London and it is activated by clicking on common keywords that link their stories. Within this digital platform to archive, interconnect, share and perform these stories, they are themselves transformed into generative visual poems (Fig. 23):

> It was my intention to blend two meanings together; one the literal part of the work; the narrative as a fundamental of human communication and the reading of legible extracts. The other, the textual narratives in the form of generative visual poems, where simultaneously the eye and the brain are functioning to reveal the semantic meaning, as well as the visual abstraction of the text. As the participant explores and experiences the work by connecting the extracts from the narratives appearing on the screen, the fortuitous position of extracts produces new relationships, and in the process, a constant current of meanings, connections and narratives; shifting from the semantic linguistic meaning to the visual, from the literal, the legible, the transparent to the abstract memory; and simultaneously creating a poetic space of readable and visual textualities, connecting memories, blending them and making them disappear in turn to make other memories appear. (Mencía 2015, 34)

I designed the work with the aim of generating the fractured realities of the refugees' stories into what looks like explosions of text, connecting their memories by clicking the common keywords in the stories (colour-activated hyperlinked words). The content of the refugees' stories served as the concept to visualise them in a poetic textual manner, inviting the reader to *look at* the poems, the surface, the materiality of the text, and to *look through* the text, the semantic meaning of language.

Fig. 23: María Mencía. "Connected Memories." 2013.

Visual poetics, conceptual and language-based media arts

Developing from the poetics and aesthetics approaches of the avant-garde at the beginning of the twentieth century, we find visual and conceptual artists during the 1960s and 1970s further engaged with breaking this barrier between the visual and the linguistic for creative expression. A well-known artist, poet and filmmaker working in many different media, with whom I felt a special connection for his conceptualisation of ideas through objects, language and projections, is Marcel Broodthaers. In contrast to concrete poetry, which challenged the notion of reading, Broodthaers challenged the notion of looking, by making language visible and object-like and by creating poems out of visual materials. As he was a writer and a filmmaker before becoming an artist, he had the ability to use the individual elements of his pieces interchangeably in the same manner words are used in different contexts, creating in this way a vocabulary of objects, words, and images. He was interested in establishing a relationship between literature and art, text and image. In 1969 he created a work in response to Mallarmé's "Un coup de dés jamais n'abolira le hazard." In the same-titled piece, Broodthaers obliterates the sentences of the original work by creating solid black lines, thereby creating a divorce from the words' linguistic meaning. Through that, the spatial and visual features of the work are highlighted, turning it into an abstract image. Thus, Broodthaers is bringing up the notion of space and image in this visual work by referring to Mallarmé's poem. The words turn into images, into little squares in Broodthaers' work, which is why he calls the poem "Image" instead of the original "Poéme" (cf. Broodthaers 1969).

There are many other conceptual artists who are both exploring language as a material for their work and who are following similar artistic and poetic interests to their early twentieth century avant-garde predecessors. In doing so, they are simultaneously establishing a ground for language-based media art and poetry in the digital age. They include, for example, Sol LeWitt, Joseph Kosuth, John Baldessari, Bruce Newman, Jenny Holzer, Gisselle Beiguelman, Eduardo Kac and Barbara Kruger. Although there is ample research on these artists, I have selected them with the aim to highlight particular concerns these artists deal with – user participation, language signification, materiality of language, use of typography – which they explore through a variety of creative practices such as paintings, billboards, installations, photography, holography. These approaches are also shared by language-based media artists and e-poets. For instance, LeWitt questions whether the idea for a work of art is art. He does this by writing instructions for the viewers to interpret and make the artwork. In this way he engages the viewers in collaborating and becoming the artists, by writing the instructions for them to create the artwork. Involving the audience in a collaborative way, is resonant with media art practices. It is also a primal feature of many pieces of electronic literature and e-poetry, where the user's interaction with the work is necessary for it to exist. The interaction can be realized through cutting and dragging words or sentences together, by clicking on hypertextual words to generate other words, by touching the screen to bring up sound compositions, by using voice to generate images and so on. These interactive gestures are all defining characteristics of my own work and they are used to engage the readers/users.

Language signification and the questioning of the signifier and signified in language is one of the underlying principles in visual poetry which Joseph Kosuth, although known as a conceptual artist, questions through his work *One and Three Chairs* (1965).[2] Here, he represents three chairs: as an object, i.e., a wooden chair; a photograph with an image of a chair, and through a text with the definition of a chair. Visual and linguistic representation and signification are put into question, in this case through the representation of a chair. Although Kosuth is categorised as a conceptual artist, he clearly engages with meaning making through the use of image and text. This is a common interest in poetry and in all the examples of literary and artistic avant-garde presented in this article. Another artist who is engaged in similar ideas and highlights the materiality of language is John Baldessari. His extensive repetition of the sentence *I Will Not Make Any More Boring Art* (1971) in a lithograph is an excellent example of writing being materialised into a visual concrete poem.[3] Following the Brazilian tradition of concrete poetry and approaches of the Noigandres group and thus the fusion of language and image to create *verbi-voco-visual* objects, is Eduardo Kac. The Brazilian artist, who is living in the States, is a contemporary poet, writer and theoretician whose current work is widely exhibited in the field of art and science. Kac is a pioneer in language-based media art and visual poetry with his holographic poems, which are fusing word and image.[4]

Also Brazilian is the artist and researcher Giselle Beiguelman, who has engaged with e-poetry since the end of the 1990s.[5] She has brought the poetry movement to the public space as Jenny Holzer has done with her well-known *Truisms* (1977–79) on notice boards and on projections in urban spaces. The page has moved not only to the screen but to billboards in the urban environment. Beiguelman's work is furthermore well-known in the field of electronic poetry and she

---

2 See https://www.moma.org/learn/moma_learning/joseph-kosuth-one-and-three-chairs-1965/.
3 See https://www.moma.org/collection/works/59546.
4 See https://ekac.org/holofrag.html.
5 See https://www.desvirtual.com/.

has extensively contributed to e-poetry conferences, exhibitions and publications; the artist is considered to be a pioneer in this field with works in different media. She also participated in the digital poetry exhibition *p0es1s. Digitale Poesie* in 2004 with her work "Poétrica" as part of the series "ad_oetries" (ads + poetry), which was specifically conceived for that particular exhibition by invitation of the curator Friedrich Block. "Poetrica" was displayed in Berlin on electronic billboards and shown in movie theatres, also in a trailer format, thereby announcing the poetry show.[6] Barbara Kruger is relevant to mention here, as well, because of her engagement with typography in immersive installations[7] – a method highly experimented with in avant-garde poetics as well as in new genres of kinetic poetry. The exploration of kinetic poetry was particularly significant in this poetry movement considering the use of the popular software Adobe Flash (formerly Macromedia), which allowed creators to inspect poetry in digital environments. Consequently, this digital and artistic practice created the Flash generation of e-poets, existing until January 2021, when Flash was deactivated and not supported by browsers anymore.

There is a huge amount of research undertaken in this particular area in the field of electronic literature and I should reference one of my early works here. "Birds Singing other Bird's Songs" (Mencía 2006) is regarded as a pioneering example of this type of kinetic poetry. As most creative media fields, the field of electronic literature is constantly evolving, digital writing is about experimentation with text, poetics and aesthetics, and narrative forms. N. Katherine Hayles defined it as a literary avant-garde in which new literary works were meant to be read only in the digital medium and not in print. She writes: "Electronic literature, generally considered to exclude print literature that has been digitized, is by contrast 'digital born,' a first-generation digital object created on a computer and (usually) meant to be read on a computer." (Hayles 2008, 3) Today we could extend this definition by adding that electronic literature is also created on and with smart and mobile devices, online platforms, and all kinds of other digital devices. It involves going beyond mainstream media platforms and stretching the possibilities of media technologies in order to question communication, the reader/writer experience, collaborative communities, remote virtual social spaces, socially engaged issues, and human and non-human interactions. My own creative practice is placed within both areas, digital art and electronic literature. It supports my academic work by using emergent technologies, the Internet, computer software, and programming languages in order to make images, sound and text coexist in the dig-

---

6 See https://desvirtual.com/poetrica/english/p0es1s.htm.
7 See https://www.moma.org/artists/3266.

ital space. Thereby, I also question the nature of language, poetry and media communication.

A fascinating, early twenty-first century digital artwork, which for me has a strong connection to visual and sound poetry, is *The Listening Post* (2001–2002). This is a collaboration between artist/technologist Ben Rubin and Mark Hanson, a strong conceptual and technical realisation. The installation consists of sounds of chanting and synthesized voices reading text fragments, which were pulled from thousands of unrestricted chat rooms and other forums on the Internet and were sampled in real time.[8] We could argue that these spaces construct the poetry machine of our times when emitting messages from chatrooms in the form of sound. With this, the digital artwork reflects Internet conversations and performs them as poetry with a rhythm, a repetition, and synthesized voices. Another Internet work using real time is Julius Popp's *bit.fall pulse* (first version 2001), which is referring to the "falling" of "bits," one of the smallest units of digital memory. The work uses an algorithm, which captures the frequency of words used in Internet news feeds and forms the most common words into a motion of "water droplet words."[9] These take on the form of animated visual poems, falling at a rhythm that lets the viewer read the words as they fall, like a pulse in a cascade of water. Metaphorically speaking, this movement represents the transient and ephemeral nature of information distributed around the world. Rather than focusing on the individual meaning and value of the words falling, *bit.fall pulse* makes us reflect about the consumption of information, mirroring today's information-overloaded society.

Both these works, *bit.fall pulse* and *The Listening Post*, move the text and the word to another level, where text is generative and the Internet is the medium. They do as they work with networked communication, algorithmic thinking, visual representation of information, ephemerality, and data. We could argue that these media and platforms write the poetry representative of our age, with poets utilising their technological advances and uncovering the visual culture of the Internet and network communications. Although the last two presented works are not associated with niche fields like that of electronic literature or e-poetry, there are clear cross overs with these artistic and literary practices in their exploration of language, data visualisation, technology, communication, networks, and programming. In the next section, I will discuss a couple of my research projects dealing with notions of data visualisation as well as current social driven issues of migration, displacement, identity and community; both with a strong visual

---

8 See http://www.digiart21.org/art/the-listening-post.
9 See https://www.youtube.com/watch?v=ygQHj1W0PPM.

presence and semantic signification in the production of poetic-aesthetic spaces in an online visual culture of interaction, documentation, archiving, and social explorations.

Visual navigations: the poetics of data

There are a couple of projects which I placed under the umbrella of "visual navigations: the poetics of data," where I, myself, have explored the use of data visualisation as a methodology for poetic-artistic expression. I have done so by using open data, archival research, life stories, and user-generated content. Both of the following projects are web-based visual digital artefacts, and both involve boats, water, rivers or oceans, thus, the use of the term "navigation" as a metaphor to explore them.

The first, *Gateway to the World* (GttW) (2014–2017), is a data visualisation piece – consisting of different iterations – originally created specifically for an exhibition in Hamburg, Germany. It highlights the city of Hamburg, as having one of the largest ports in the world. The port with its flow of vessels became a metaphor for the flow of information on the Internet, its meaning of openness and outreach in the World Wide Web, also as a gateway. The conceptualisation of the project was to explore *data visualisation poetics* by using open data from the maritime databases to visualise the routes of the vessels arriving to and from the port as well as having the vessels' names mapped and connected to Wikipedia. The vessels function as writing tools to reveal a string of text, thereby creating *calligrammatic* strings of readable information gathered from the Wikipedia entries about the names of all vessels entering and leaving the port (Fig. 24). These create a textual remix – in relation to the name of each boat – that combines information about the vessels (on containers, cargo ships, tankers and carriers) with the names of characters in literary works, plays, and mythological stories. One example is the vessel named Fortuna, the name of which is centred in the etymology and history of Greek mythology, thus offering information on the gods and myths of ancient Greece. In other cases, such as with a ship called Rita, it connects the multiple uses of that name, whether it is of a person, the title of an opera or a martial art school. Other included vessels' names are Summer Flower, City of Hamburg, City of Beirut, Nagoya, and several personal names such as Peter, Jamie, Viktoria, Gerda, Jana and Suzana.

In *Gateway to the World* data is acting as the software tool to animate the vessels and these function as writing tools. Initially, the writing of generative animated text placed in the river Elbe is readable until the text mixes with many

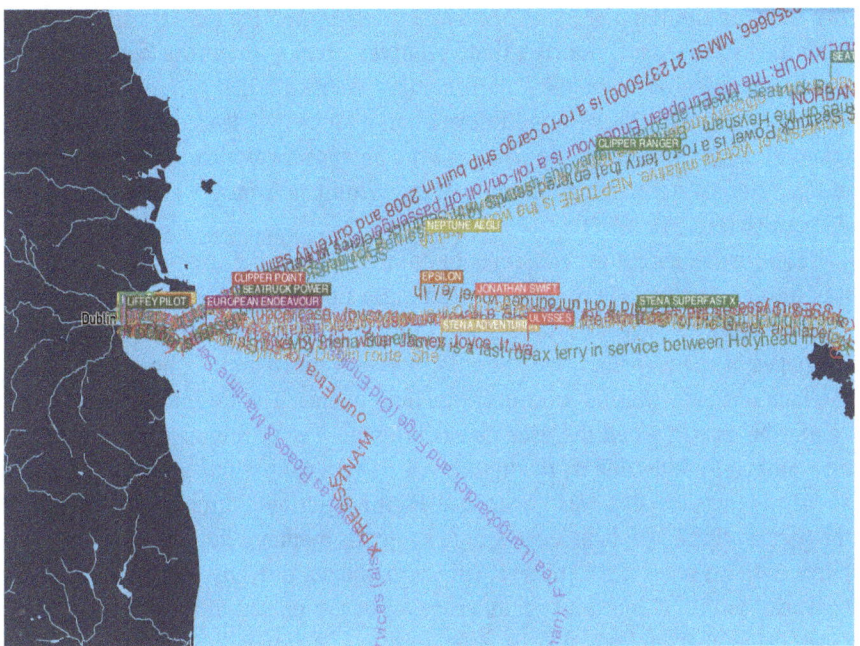

Fig. 24: María Mencía. Screenshot from *Gateway to the World*. 2014–2017.

other strings of texts from different vessels, especially with regard to moving elements. This then creates a *data visualisation poetics* of unreadable colourful letter flows, shadows, layers, and ripple effects. The work connects animation, visual semiotics, textual and visual poetics with interaction. The user can interact with this maritime landscape through an iPad or a similar device. They can zoom in and out with the gesture of pinching and stretching the image with their fingers to see the close-ups of ripple effects formed by the text – which simulate the movement of water – and they can read the colourful strings of text linked to the vessels (cf. Mencía 2017a).

The second of my works discussed here is called *The Winnipeg: The Poem that Crossed the Atlantic* (2018). This project builds on Pablo Neruda's Winnipeg boat and reflects pertinent critical issues of migration, displacement and the search for survival so apparent in current worldwide events. As mentioned at the beginning of this article, it is inspired by my own personal story rooted in historical events of the Spanish Civil War and the evacuation and rescue of Spanish civil war exiles. Amongst them were my grandfather and his brother, who were saved by Neruda from the internment camps in France and brought to Valparaiso, Chile on August 4, 1939. My aim was to create an interactive, online poetic narrative,

The Poem or *The Winnipeg: The Poem that Crossed the Atlantic* – consisting of the Winnipeg's passengers' stories, their relatives, stories about the boat, Neruda's poems – and an accompanying documentary website called "The Winnipeg. The Boat of Hope" with background information about the research. The index page (opening page) introduces the names of the passengers, which appear as a string of text, thereby delineating the route of the Winnipeg from the Paulliac region to Valparaiso (Fig. 25).

The further pages provide links to an area, where the users can submit stories, and an archive where they can find these stories, the interactive, generative "Poem," and the page with background information about this event. In one of the pages of the website titled "Neruda," we find the Winnipeg boat parting and the face of Pablo Neruda with his "Indelible poem." The interactive digital text cannot be erased when the user moves the mouse over the text, thus, it is literally/materially indelible in its digitality. It is said that when the Winnipeg was about to leave, Neruda was so touched by the emotional atmosphere created at the port with the people leaving, that to keep this memory, he said: "Que la crítica borre toda mi poesía, si le parece. Pero este poema, que hoy recuerdo, no podrá borrarlo nadie." ("The critics may erase all of my poetry. But this poem, that I today remember, nobody will be able to erase it.") This is the reason I titled the work *The Poem that Crossed the Atlantic*. I was interested in the idea of the boat, the story of the poem expanding the notion of poetry to the human experience of the event; that poetic moment in time where feelings of loss, deportation, displacement, exile and solitude are manifested. The interactive "Poem" is a multi-linguistic sea of networked poetic interactive narratives, fed by the stories from posts uploaded to the website. These stories have been translated into French and English. The interlacing of the stories continuously increases with the number of posts, resulting in an on-going community-based poem at the heart of the work. The Spanish and Chilean historical memory comes together in this poetic research of life stories, writings by Neruda, and social and political issues (cf. Mencía 2019).

The design and conceptualisation of this work – with its sea of linear stories evolving over time into visual generative poetry of words, letters, and typographical characters and creating simultaneous forms of expression, similar to the visual arts – draws from the poetic and artistic history discussed in this article, thus visual, concrete poetry and language-based media art. Kristeva's pre-verbal semiotic and symbolic and the in-between of text and image, the legible and illegible is explored through the use of programming to create that space where poetics and aesthetics come together in language. It results in new ways of expression and also brings up socially engaged issues.

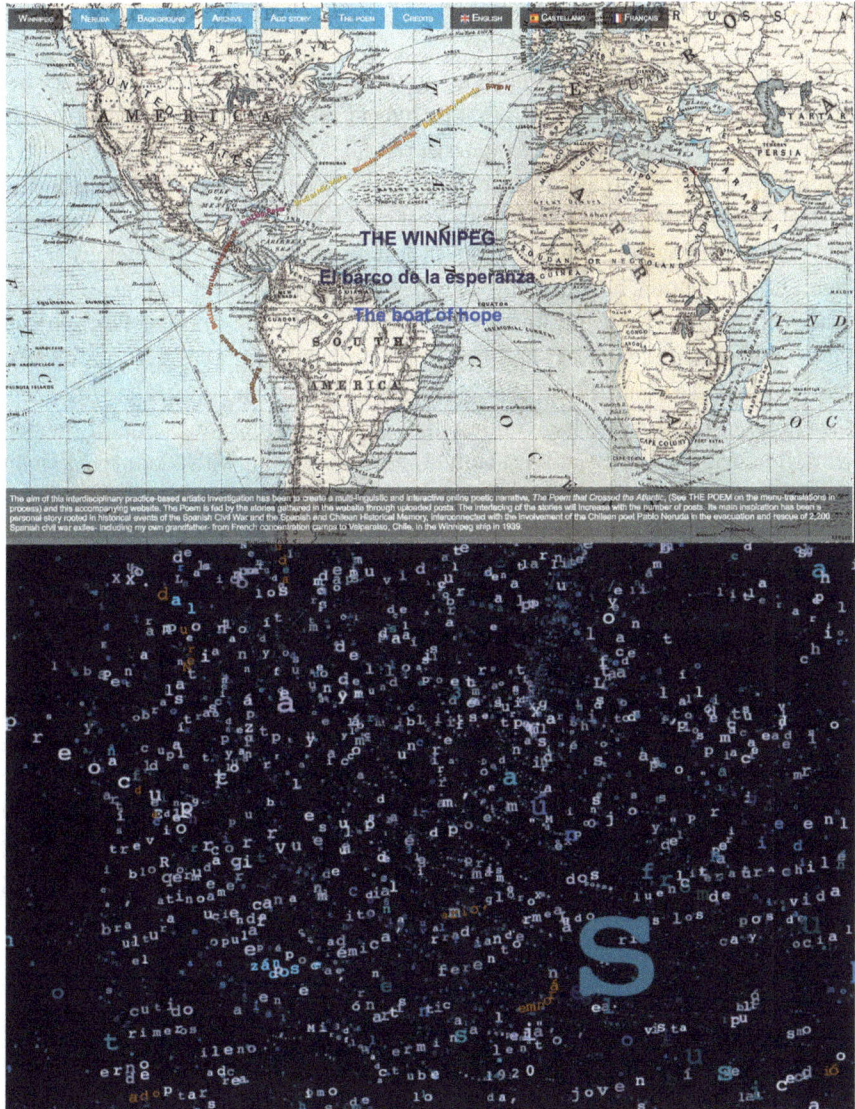

Fig. 25: María Mencía. Screenshots of "The Winnipeg. The Boat of Hope" and of *The Poem that Crossed the Atlantic*. 2018.

Conclusion

The study of the production of meaning in multimodal textualities – the space between image, sound, and text – and in hybrid digital multilingual poetics has been one of the focal points of my research (cf. Mencía 2020). I explored these aspects through my creative practice since the beginning of my interest in the field of e-poetry in the year 2000, with works such as "Another Kind of Language" and "Birds Singing Other Birds' Songs." These projects brought up themes of foreignness, translation, and multilingualism, which evolved towards more poignant issues of displacement and human relocation like in the previously discussed piece "Connected Memories" and in further projects such as "Cityscapes: Social Poetics/Public Textualities" (2005), developed in Melbourne, Australia. *The Poem that Crossed the Atlantic* is a continuation of these explorations and of the artwork *Gateway to the World*. With both of these works and with "Connected Memories," the text shifts from linear narratives, which evolve in time, to a multi-dimensional poetic and artistic expression of visual poetry that is blending two meanings together: one being the literal part of the work, the narrative as a fundamental element of human communication and the reading of legible texts; and another the poetic-aesthetic space in the form of the *calligrammatic*, such as texts and generative visual texts, respectively.

Again, Lanham's notion of "looking at" and "looking through" (Lanham 1993, 5), that is, the process of reading and viewing by shifting from the linguistic to the visual language is also part of the experience of an exploration of these pieces. The readers/viewers are invited to look at the text, the surface, the materiality, and the visual meaning of the abstract visual text, while they are simultaneously looking through the text, the semantic, transparent meaning of language. In this shifting from text to image the poetic-aesthetic space appears and exists.

References

Apollinaire, Guillaume. *Calligrammes. Poems of Peace and War (1913–1916)*. Transl. Anne Hyde Greet. Berkeley, CA: Univ. of California Press. 1980.
Bann, Stephen. *Concrete Poetry*. London: Magazine Editions, 1967.
Bayard, Caroline. *The New Poetics in Canada and Quebec. From Concretism to Post-Modernism*. Toronto, Buffalo, NY, and London: Univ. of Toronto Press, 1989.
Benthien, Claudia, Jordis Lau, and Maraike M. Marxsen. *The Literariness of Media Art*. New York: Routledge, 2019.
bissett, bill. *RUSH: what fuckan theory. A study uv language*. Toronto: Gronk Press, 1971.
Bohn, Willard. *The Aesthetics of Visual Poetry 1914–1928*. Cambridge: Cambridge Univ. Press, 1986.

Bohn, Willard. *Reading Visual Poetry*. Vancouver: Fairleigh Dickinson Univ. Press, 2011.
Broodthaers, Marcel. "A Throw of the Dice Will Never Abolish Chance." MoMA/The Museum of Modern Art New York. 1969, https://www.moma.org/collection/works/146983 (February 19, 2023).
Delehanty, Suzanne. "Soundings." *Sound by Artists*. Ed. Dan Lander and Micah Lexier. Toronto: Charivari Press, 1990. 21–38.
Drucker, Johanna. *Figuring the Word. Essays on Books, Writing and Visual Poetics*. New York: Granary Books, 1998.
Freeman, Judi. *The Dada and Surrealist Word-Image*. London: MIT Press, 1989.
Foucault, Michel. *This is Not a Pipe*. Berkeley, CA and London: Univ. of California Press, 1983.
Hayles, N. Katherine. *Electronic Literature. New Horizons for the Literary*. Notre Dame, ID: Univ. of Notre Dame Press, 2008.
Higgins, Dick. *Pattern Poetry. Guide to an Unknown Literature*. Albany, NY: State Univ. of New York Press, 1987.
Kac, Eduardo. *Holopoetry. Essays, Manifestoes, Critical and Theoretical Writings*. Lexington, KY: New Media Editions, 1995.
Kristeva, Julia. *Revolution in Poetic Language*. New York: Columbia Univ. Press, 1984.
Lanham, Richard. A. *The Electronic Word*. London: The Univ. of Chicago Press, 1993.
McCaffery, Steve. *North of Intention. Critical Writings, 1973–86*. New York and Toronto: Roof Books, 1986.
McCaffery, Steve, and bpNichol (Ed.). *Sound Poetry. A Catalogue for the Eleventh International Sound Poetry Festival*. Toronto: Underwhich Editions, 1978.
Mencía, María. "Multimodal Textualities: Poetic Aesthetic Digital Space." *Romance Notes* 60.1 (2020): 179–186.
Mencía, María. "The Winnipeg: The Poem that Crossed the Atlantic." *Hyperrhiz: New Media Cultures* 20 (2019): http://hyperrhiz.io/hyperrhiz20/moving-texts/2-mencia-the-winnipeg.html (February 13, 2023).
Mencía, María. *The Winnipeg: The Poem that Crossed the Atlantic*. 2018, http://winnipeg.mariamencia.com/?lang=en/ (January 7, 2023).
Mencía, María. *Gateway to the World*. 2014–2017, http://www.mariamencia.com/pages/gatewaytotheworld.html (January 7, 2023).
Mencía, María. "Gateway to the World: Data Visualisation Poetics." *GRAMMA. Journal of Theory and Criticism Digital Literary Production and the Humanities* 23 (2017a): 173–186.
Mencía, María. "Transient Self-Portrait: The Data Self." *#WomenTechLit*. Ed. María Mencía. Morgantown: West Virginia Univ. Press, 2017b. 189–209.
Mencía, María. "Connected Memories." *Creative Manual for Repurposing in Electronic Literature*. ENTER+ 16 (2015): 33–36.
Mencía, María. "Connected Memories." 2010, https://mariamencia.com/pages/connected_memories.html (February 19, 2023).
Mencía, María. "Generative Poems." 2007–2010, http://www.mariamencia.com/pages/generative_poems.html (February 19, 2023).
Mencía, María. "Birds Singing other Bird's Songs." *Electronic Literature Collection* 1 (2006): https://the-next.eliterature.org/works/626/0/0/ (February 19, 2023).
Mencía, María. *From Visual Poetry to Digital Art: Image-Sound-Text, Convergent Media, and the Development of New Media Languages*. London: Univ. of the Arts London, 2003.
Mencía, María. "Another Kind of Language." 2001, http://www.mariamencia.com/pages/anotherkindof.html (19 February 2023).

Millán Domínguez, Blanca. *Poesía Visual en España*. Colmenar Viejo: Información y producciones S.L., 2012.
Reichardt, Jasia. *Between Poetry and Painting*. Exhibition Catalogue. London: Institute of Contemporary Arts, 1965.
Seiça, Alvaro. "Kinetic Poetry." *Electronic Literature as Digital Humanities. Contexts, Forms, and Practices*. Ed. O'Sullivan James and Grigar Dene. London: ELO Bloomsbury, 2021. 173–202.

Lucy English
Finding a New Approach: The Use of Visual Images in Spoken Word Poetry Film

An Experience-Based Artist's Report with Reference to the Poetry Film Collection *The Book of Hours* and the Poetry Film *I Want to Breathe Sweet Air*

Introduction

Spoken word poetry is often perceived to be the public delivery of noisy crowd-pleasing material, which is certainly the case with poetry slams, but, for many, the lasting appeal of spoken word is its ability to create an emotional connection with an audience. Spoken word can be intimate and deeply personal. How can this intimacy and connection be translated into the medium of poetry film? This essay explores artistic approaches for using or adapting these to contain spoken word poetry. For many filmmakers the most obvious choice is to present the poet speaking or performing the poem. Organisations such as the UK based Apples and Snakes and current spoken word poets such as Hollie McNish use this method when creating their spoken word poetry films. However, there are a variety of other approaches.

Canadian theorist Tom Konyves identifies five major categories of what he describes as "video poems": Kinetic text, where the text on the screen is animated; sound text, where the poetry is spoken, either by the poet or through a voice-over; visual text, where the text is featured on the film like a subtitle; performance, which includes the human body; and cine(e) poetry, which uses recognisable film sequences as well as animation (cf. Konyves 2012, 7). He claims a video poem must contain the following elements: text, either on screen or voiced; a narration to propel the viewer; poetic juxtaposition, which he defines as the placement of words and images which create different "meanings" or interpretations; and a "poetic experience," which he further defines as "fragmented expressions of the artist's imagination, suggestive of meaning, yet denying clarification of the purported meaning." A video poem, he claims, should produce in the viewer "unprecedented and unlimited associations between image, text and sound" (Konyves 2012, 5). It must also include rhythm, illustration, collaboration and have a duration of "not longer than 300 seconds." He claims that a true poetry film must express a blended nature: "In the measured blending of these three elements (visual, text and sound) it produces in the viewer the realisation of a 'poetic experi-

Open Access. © 2023 the author(s), published by De Gruyter. This work is licensed under the Creative Commons Attribution-NonCommercial-NoDerivatives 4.0 International License.
https://doi.org/10.1515/9783111299334-011

ence'" (Konyves 2012, 5). These parameters, although debateable, are a good starting point when creating a poetry film.

Sarah Tremlett in her comprehensive *Poetics of Poetry Film* (2021) acknowledges Konyves' categories and also adds video haikus, dance, documentary, and ecopoetry. How useful are these definitions when creating a spoken word poetry film? I will argue that a variety of methods, as well as performance, can enhance the placement of a spoken word poem in a poetry film and that the physical presence of the poet, or even their voice, is not necessarily needed. I will refer to my own project *The Book of Hours* (English 2017) and to my recent spoken word project with US filmmakers Pamela Falkenberg and Jack Cochran, *I Want to Breathe Sweet Air* (Cochran and Falkenberg 2020). Furthermore, I will discuss how spoken word poetry is translated into imagery in a spoken word poetry film.

A brief definition of poetry film and the origins of *The Book of Hours*

Firstly, what are poetry films? One thing they are not (although they can be) is films of people reading or reciting poetry. Even the name of the genre is disputed. Poetry films appear under different guises as "poetryfilms," "filmpoems," "video poems," "multimedia poetry," "e-poetry," and "screen poetry." Broadly speaking, they are a combining of poetry/words, displayed as text or spoken, with accompanying images and viewed on a screen. They can be created by the poet but they are usually a collaboration between poet and filmmaker. This is not a new subject; some of the earliest films, created by the Dadaists, were what we would now call poetry films and Susan McCabe has examined the use of film by the early Modernist poets, including Gertrude Stein, Hilda Doolittle or H.D, and Marianne Moore. "Rather than perceiving film as extraneous to their poetic styles [. . .] the poets engaged the modern crisis of embodiment with an awareness of the medium's tangible synchronicity, multiplicity and evanescence." (McCabe 2005, 17) In more recent years, with easier access to new media technology, more poetry films are being created and shown to audiences in festivals such as the Zebra Poetry Film Festival in Berlin, which is dedicated to this art form. Unlike the narrative led films of Hollywood, poetry films are tiny, exquisite and mesmerising and, if a filmmaker is involved, the relationship of the filmmaker to poet can be seen as a "creative editor" (MacDonald 2007, 22) who presents the text to new audiences.

For my own project, *The Book of Hours*,[1] I wanted to explore how spoken word poetry can be used in poetry film. Rather than present the films as a series of readings or performances I wanted to translate the immediacy and vibrancy of spoken word into the poetry film form and create a project which is experimental in its use of spoken word in poetry film, and also innovative in its approach to creating a themed collection of poetry films. This project, which contains 48 poetry films, was begun in 2014, made available online from 2015 during the process of construction and finally completed in 2018. *The Book of Hours* contains layers of experience for the reader, through sound, visual image, and text with the poetry delivered as spoken word. These poetry films present a constantly changing commentary on the passage of time. This is a loose replication of the original Books of Hours, highly decorative medieval illustrated manuscripts, which provided readers with religious texts in sections connected to the times of the day and religious festivals. The reader of the original books could choose which texts to read and when. In *The Book of Hours*, the first film displayed represents the current month and the time of day the viewer has accessed the website, such as "May, afternoon," or "November, night," but the viewer can also browse through the complete collection. *The Book of Hours* is therefore a calendar of poetry films which represent four times of day for each month of the year. Films from this project have been screened at over 40 international film festivals, won several awards, and the entire project was shortlisted for the New Media Writing Prize in 2019. *The Book of Hours* is now kept in the British Library archive as an example of a digital project. My role in this project was to write the poetry, record the poems in my voice, and act as artistic director (cf. English 2017).

As with all forms of art, there are factions, and allegiances. For my exploration of *The Book of Hours* I will use the term "poetry film," with no hyphen, throughout. Tremlett mentions that the inclusion or not of a hyphen for the term "poetry film" is still a source of debate (cf. Tremlett 2021, 25). However, my decision not to use a hyphen emphasises that for this project I have understood a poetry film to be a blended entity, as described by Konyves, of both poetry and film, and in my case, these elements have been created separately but in collaboration between a poet and a filmmaker.

As mentioned earlier, the poetry in *The Book of Hours* is in the form of spoken word. I write poetry to be performed or heard. I want the sound of the language and the emotional response of the audience to be an important part of the experience. Claudia Benthien, Jordis Lau, and Maraike M. Marxsen explore how even in a recording of a poem the recorded voice "can have the power to create a

---

[1] www.thebookofhours.org.

strong intimacy with listeners." (Benthien et al. 2019, 50) My poetry can also be described as lyrical. "Lyric (or lyrical poetry) is subjective in its approach, expressing the feelings, thoughts and visions of the poet directly and often very personally" (Stillman 1966, xii). The lyrical nature of the poetry, I hoped, could be translated to the poetry films. Benthien, Lau, and Marxsen propose that when "works of media use poetic structures, they predominantly refer to lyric poetry" (Benthien et al. 2019, 114). Although I experimented with several forms in *The Book of Hours*, those which I were most drawn to were the ones where the lyrical poetry could be best appreciated: 'sound text,' as it uses the human voice and 'visual text,' which "displays the text on screen, superimposed over images captured or found" (Konyves 2012, 5). A few of the poetry films for *The Book of Hours* are also cine(e) poetry in that they have been created by a filmmaker using storyboards, actors, soundtracks and all the elements used in cinema films (cf. Konyves 2012, 5).

The development of *The Book of Hours*

One of the early filmmakers involved in the project was Helen Dewbery, a photographer, poetry filmmaker and organiser of the Poetry Film Live Online Magazine (see Dewbery 2019). In 2014 she was in the early stages of her poetry film making career and wanted plenty of discussion about the project and the films we could create. We discussed the concept of *The Book of Hours*, and its intention to create reflective experience in the viewer. Reflective moments in contemporary life were at the centre of our discussions, and strangely we both came up with the same location, a motorway service station. The result of this conversation was the realisation of artistic possibility in the anonymous quality of a service station and its existence as a place 'out of time'; a place where time can get lost. Dewbery sent me a selection of short filmic sequences and images taken at the Gordano Service Station near Bristol. The aim was to find a new way of creating a poetry film other than me 'giving' her a poem to interpret. The visual images were a starting point that would drive the viewer's interest in the poetry film as much as the poem itself. Dewbery would indeed be what McDonald calls "a creative editor" in that she would be adding to the audience's interpretation of the poem by the use of visual language. P. Adams Sitney calls this "[t]he poetics of filmmaking" and his analysis of the work of Andrei Tarkovsky shows how "[t]he elements of dream and memory interpenetrate one another in a tight network of associations" (Sitney 2015, 87). These were certainly our aspirations for this poetry film.

One of Dewbery's filmed sequences was a car journey at night. Mundane images that could be interpreted in a variety of ways. The following questions were at the centre of a contemplation of these images and the motif of journeys: Where were all those cars going? What was the purpose of those journeys? How many journeys do we take in our lives? Dying is also referred to as 'the last journey' in our culture. To further explicate this, I want to include a specifically artistic and personal point of view in the production of the poem "Drive Through the Night" here. Death was very much on my mind at this time as my brother was in the final stages of cancer.

Based on this experience I wrote the poem and sent it to Helen Dewbery to work with. Her final film uses the repeating sequence of cars driving in the night. Against the placement of the words, this seemingly mundane image becomes ominous, even foreboding. She also included a fleeting image of a wolf, which was an important and discussed figure throughout the process of writing the poetry film. In our conversations during the production of this poetry film we decided to keep the image of the wolf as the animal seems to represent both the uneasiness about facing death but also a sort of spirit guide to the after-world. In the Native American pantheon of spirit guides, the wolf is connection to intuition and spiritual path finding. Collaboration is a shared space but it is also a space where individual talent can thrive and be celebrated. In a filmmaker's hands, the poetry film becomes more than the poem; the images and sound used, expand the interpretation of the poem rather than merely 'illustrate' it; the poetry film explores those unconscious elements of dream and memory. "Drive Through the Night" reveals Helen Dewbery's skill as a creative editor in placing images with the words, which give the poem a deeper meaning (Fig. 26). The images leave space for the audience's interpretation (cf. MacDonald 2007, 22).

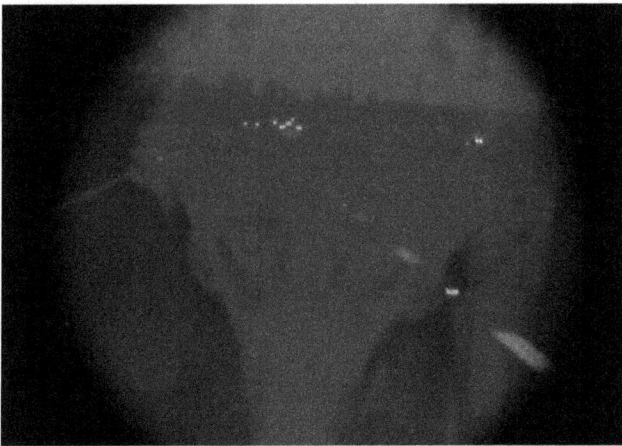

Fig. 26: Still from "Drive Through the Night." Dir. Helen Dewbery. Poem: Lucy English. 2014.

A challenge in the writing of the poetry for *The Book of Hours* was to find a contemplative form of spoken word that could be translated to poetry film. My own personal experience is that in writing poetry the tasks are to choose a narrative structure, to develop a story within the poem/s, and to use lyrical language to enhance meaning. However, any narrative structure had to be more condensed in a poetry film, or even abandoned. Detailed descriptions, explanations and dialogue, the bedrock of much of previous spoken word poetry, proved to be too long and complicated. Claudia Kappenberg discusses this effect in her analysis of the work of Maya Deren, a filmmaker who wanted to move away from the "shorthand of narrative" in mainstream films, and to explore "[t]he real potential of cinema, which resides in the realm of the visual experience" (Kappenberg 2017, 108). A poetry film does not need so many words since the images, and indeed the sound, also carry meaning; much of the text has to be sacrificed to the image. A current approach, when combining spoken word poetry with film, is to create a film of the poet reading or performing the poem. Apples and Snakes, the leading UK promoter of spoken word poetry, for its Blackbox project, has filmed a series of spoken word poets which can be viewed online. These are quality films and were recorded in partnership with ESA Productions, the in-house production company of Elstree Screen Arts Academy (see Apples and Snakes 2022). These recreate the atmosphere of a live performance with a stage, background lighting, and in a venue, which looks like a theatre. These films and many other spoken word films, like music videos, tend to rely on the physical presence of the performer. For my project I felt that such an approach was limiting. *The Book of Hours* is not about 'me'; it is designed to convey mood, or a reflection on place.

As a poet I am passionately concerned that *The Book of Hours* contains writing of a high literary standard, which can be critiqued as poetry. My spoken word poetry tends to be narrative, often improvised, and although it contains lyrical writing, the story predominates. The poetry I wrote for *The Book of Hours* conveys a mood, thought or emotion. Stories began to appear, as it seems that I cannot leave story behind, but they were more within the overarching narrative of the work rather than the individual poems. My 'chatty' spoken word voice still needed to be pared down even more to create more space for the visual experience. What I learned in these early collaborations was that I needed to take the poem to a place 'outside' of itself where it could blend more effectively with the sound and the images. I took these discoveries into the subsequent collaborations with the other filmmakers.

One of the filmmakers who developed the impact of the image in *The Book of Hours* was Eduardo Yagüe. He is Spanish and currently lives in Stockholm. Like many poetry filmmakers he had a complex route into filmmaking. He studied drama and has had a career as an actor, a teacher of drama, and a writer. He started making poetry films in 2012. *The Book of Hours* was conceptualized to be a transnational project so I was keen to find filmmakers whose first language was not English. His approach to poetry film creation is very different to that of Helen Dewbery. Yagüe storyboards the films, creates narratives and uses actors and locations, much like a traditional concept of 'film' and what Konyves calls cine(e) poetry (cf. Konyves 2012, 5). In 2015 he described his working methods to me via email: "I am interested in exploring the limits of poetic and cinematographic languages. I love working with the actors in my videos, leaving them exposed and giving pure emotions, I love suggested stories with an open reading, all with the base of touching and intense poems." I was familiar with his work through moving-poems.com and sent him "High Summer." I was not sure what he would make of this poem written during a hot day in August and which conveys a particularly British summer:

> Full bosomed and bellied, heavy and slow.
> A bus shelter covered in ivy
> by a crossroads where the road dips
> to a brown sludge of stream.
> The sticky smell of meadowsweet.
> Honeysuckle hair and eyes like brown moths.
> (English 2018, 44)

He said he would "deeply study it" before he responded with ideas. He decided to have it translated into Spanish so he could fully understand it. The idea he suggested to me was this: "I would like to make a contrast between the light of the words of the poem that go from the field to the tough city where we will find a woman (or a man, I am not already sure), who is imagining the poem." He also suggested that he would approach it like a haiku and try to translate the structure of a haiku into a visual form. A month later he had made the film. The words were placed on the screen rather than spoken and it was intended to add a voice-over later, either in Spanish or in English. In "High Summer" Yagüe has used a story of a woman writing a poem about a British summer in a winter urban Spanish environment. He has, as Sitney suggested that the Italian filmmaker Pasolini does in his films, "[i]nvested his images with his subjectivity" (Sitney 2015, 22). There is tension between the placement of the words and the images. We read "honeysuckle hair" and we look at an image of dead plants in a drain pipe. We have to re-evaluate our attitude towards the urban environment, wet and dreary and filmed in black and white, whilst we read words about heat, meadows and ditches. There is a mystery about the film: Why is it a poem about summer in the middle of winter? When we first see the woman, we are not sure who she is and why she is so deep in thought. We only realise that she is the writer towards the end of the film when we see her in her kitchen, looking for inspiration and finding it in the figure of a cow fridge magnet. It is a tender evocation of the act of creation and the power of imagination. This is why we decided collaboratively that this film did not need a voiceover.

For our second collaboration it seemed fitting to try a Spanish language film. A more narrative poem was chosen to accompany as Yagüe's films are excellent visual storytelling. The poem "What is Love" was selected because of its recognisable storyline; a snapshot of a relationship between a man and woman who meet in romantic circumstances but, as their lives progress, they have to navigate more ordinary challenges:

> What is love? I think it is a new house.
> Piling up fast with stuff in every room.
> How can she have so many dresses, shoes, cooking pots?
> How can he have so many retro computer games?
> (English 2018, 38)

By the time they are old "with icing sugar hair" they no longer remember the circumstances of when they first met but they are still together. It is a gentle poem and so there was plenty in the poem for Eduardo to storyboard. The poetry film Yagüe then created, "Qué es el Amor? (What is Love)" has become one of the most widely screened films in *The Book of Hours*. It was awarded video poem of the week on the online poetry film journal *Versogramas* (Montero 2016), second prize in the *Atticus Review* videopoem contest (2018) and has been screened at many other festivals. What Yagüe has done is to find a story within the story of the poem. Instead of focusing on the simple "boy meets girl" narrative he places his film in the future. As Belen Montero points out on the *Versogramas* webpage:

> The contrast between the poem and the video is absolutely devastating, thus effective. A parallel history emerges in our minds: one of the protagonists of the poem, now an old man, alone in a big empty house, tries to spend time while remembering, in absolute solitude and sadness, when "they never felt alone." (Montero 2016)

Filmed in black in white and with a Spanish voiceover it has the power of a full-length drama and seems much longer than three and half minutes thanks to its emotional impact. It conveys all the emptiness and longing of grief. In the film an old man sits by a window, wanders through an empty apartment and picks up the gloves of his dead wife and inhales the scent. While none of this is mentioned in the poem, a visual 'story' with these images was created in the poetry film, which lends added depth and poignancy to the words. Dave Bonta comments further on movingpoems.com:

The geographic/linguistic distance and change in the expected sex of the narrator [most of the other poetry films are narrated by me, a woman. This is narrated by a man.] create additional resonances. And actor Steffan Carlson's silence is so eloquent as to supply almost a third voice to the mix. *Qué es el amor?* is a brilliant demonstration of how to use the narrative style of filmmaking to comment upon and transform a lyric poem. (Bonta 2016)

Marie Craven as the judge of the *Atticus Review* videopoem contest mentions why it was awarded a prize. "Masterfully directed and profoundly moving, the film is a meditation on a near-universal experience as we approach end of life." (*Atticus Review* 2019) Through a visualisation of the poem in the poetry film this specific example has become more than the poem through the adept use of images that has truly enhanced and expanded the words.

The next film I am going to discuss is "The Sundial" created with filmmaker and visual artist Lucia Sellars (2017). Previously working with Sellars for *The Book of Hours* the resulting discovery was that parts of the entire poem can suffice for a poetry film. In our previous collaboration Sellars edited my poem and even cut out several lines. I am a poet and like many artists I want artistic control but I had to learn not to feel precious about my words; I was willing to let the words go for the success of the collaboration. I realised that a poetry film did indeed not need all of the details in the text, even if they are spoken, because the visuals were 'carrying' this information. In "The Sundial" Sellars altered the sequence of the words and the phrase "Do not talk to me today" is repeated like a phrase of bird song. A wistful mood of a summer's day is suggested by using pastel colours and the effect of the sun through clouds, but the images in the poetry film also reveal the uneasiness about being a human in the natural world. A hummingbird flits restlessly across the screen and the outstretched hand could be interpreted as a lost attempt to connect.

These collaborations showed me how much time and effort all collaborators were putting into the poetry films, which in most cases, are not more than three minutes long. A poetry film is not merely a set of images to accompany words, it is a crafted visual and sound journey with the audiences' experience very much in mind; this specifically refers to what Tom Konyves called "a measured blending" (Konyves 2012, 2). In the film created with Sarah Tremlett, "Solstice Sol Invictus," the collaborative nature was explored further in the actual creation of the poem as well as in the construction of the film. In *The Book of Hours,* the two Solstice poetry films represent the sun at its lightest and darkest points of the year. Because of the status of these films in the series it was important for me to choose a filmmaker who could understand the significance; Sarah Tremlett prepared to take on this challenge.

Tremlett is the UK's foremost theorist on poetry film and her *The Poetics of Poetry Film* is a comprehensive overview of the theory and practice of poetry film creation and an important attempt to define the genre. In her preface she states that "poetry films and videopoems are *not* vehicles for poets solely reciting to camera, [. . .]. Ultimately, all forms hinge on creating the *perception* of a relationship [. . .] between the elements, and it is this dialectic that creates such an imaginative leap [. . .]" (Tremlett 2021, xxi). She also states that poetry itself creates *"meaningful relations* between words and sounds" (Tremlett 2021, 49) and poetry films are furthering this poetic experience. Tremlett is an artist and writer and her poetry films combine her multifaceted skills. Her direct involvement in the writing of this poem took on a deeper significance as the 2016 Refugee Crisis unfolded across Europe. We wrote a verse each and recorded our voices: Sarah's evokes the emergence of the light at Solstice, and my verse asks us to consider "even in the dark days there is hope." The verse written by Tremlett is spoken by Helmi Stil, and she also co-speaks some of the words herself. Towards the end of the poetry film the three voices combine in a choral crescendo; a sonorous experience. The three female voices could represent the Celtic triple goddess and the rising soundtrack emphasises the gravitas of the message. The images are of a rising sun and the background colours move from darker tones towards the bright green and yellows of spring. It seems particularly relevant today when the 'dark days' appear even more extreme.

Before deciding to speak the poems in my own voice, I experimented with other methods, such as text on screen, and the use of other narrators. This decision was more complex than any concerns about the quality of delivery of the poems by other readers. My readers have added a multiplicity of voices with a range of ages, gender, and nationalities but I wanted to establish that I am a spoken word poet and my craft is in the writing and speaking of my work. I feel strongly that spoken word is not confined to the young, urban, and apparently artless. I am sixty-four years old and have over twenty years' experience as a poet. I craft my work with care. I argue accordingly that the strengths of spoken word in poetry film are the choice of words and the way they are spoken. Unlike a live performance I did not have the use of my body to convey meaning and emotion. Julia Novak calls this "body communication" and has discussed in length the use of bodily actions and facial expressions in my and other spoken word poets' live poetry (cf. Novak 2011, 151–153). For *The Book of Hours* my bodily actions were not part of the film, so I could only use my voice. Norrie Neumark examines how even a recorded voice still has the impact of a live voice and we respond to it as though it were physically present even though it is in the digital realm: "The performative voice is quintessentially paradoxical [. . .] it carried a trace of its 'home,' the body of the speaker, but leaves that home to perform speaking" (Neumark 2010, 97). John Durham Peters also explores the power of the spoken voice in modern media which "leaves the voice in curious limbo between body and machine, text and performance, animal and angel," (Peters 2004, 9) because we can keep returning to it to find further meaning.

For a poetry film the physical presence of the poet is unnecessary; spoken word poets do not always realise how good they are at the verbal delivery of their work. The purpose should be to connect to their audiences with their poet's voice. Novak examines how spoken word poets "enact the irregular rhythms of ordinary speech" (Novak 2011, 95) to create this emotional bond. From an audience's point of view the poet's voice seems so natural their skill in doing this can be overlooked. It is this entire aspect of spoken word poetry that is often neglected. I am aware that my viewer will experience the poetry in *The Book of Hours* through images and sound rather than through gestures or body movements. I have been told that I am a good reader of my work. Pauses and emphasis of certain words are used in my delivery to bring out the meaning and emotions. For example, the sadness of the mother whose grown-up daughter has not stayed long enough in "River Girl" is an integral part of the poem. When I read the poem, my voice is almost a whisper and it sounds like I am on the verge of tears.

> When she's gone I wash the plates. Do the laundry.
> Her dress is on the floor. Crumpled in a corner.
> A thrush on the steps breaks open a snail
> (English 2018, 33)

I wonder if filmmakers of spoken word poetry have felt too much the need to show the face of the poet, as if trying to replicate the live performance, rather than focusing on the quality of the delivery of the words and the quality of the images. For example, the 2018 ZEBRA Poetry Film Festival contained a separate screening of spoken word poetry films, "Fokus Spoken Word." The programme notes describe a clear relationship between these films and music videos: "In the music industry video clips have been an established medium for the transfer onto the screen for more than 30 years. Spoken Word artists use this format as well in order to performatively present eloquent texts." (Zandegiacomo Del Bel 2018, 50) In Germany there is a growing audience for these spoken word clips, and the ones I viewed at this screening did indeed have the energy and impact of a live performance, but most of the impact was through the sound of the words. There are many opportunities for exploring spoken word in poetry film and my hope is that festivals such as ZEBRA will keep creating separate spoken word screenings so that this sub-genre will develop further. For this purpose, I would propose a collaborative process where both filmmaker and poet are prepared to actively put aside their usual ways of working and find alternative ways of representing spoken word on screen. If a poet has to be placed in front of a camera, it should at least be made visually engaging, such as Salena Godden's anarchic *RED*

(2016) where she gets red paint chucked at her as she performs a poem about menstruation or Kae Tempest's recent *Salt Coast* (2022) which has the moody quality of film noir.

Further explorations since the completion of *The Book of Hours*

All the *The Book of Hours* films were completed by 2018 and are available to view on the website. Since then my poetic work has been centred on creating poetry films with an environmental message in the form of ecopoetry films as mentioned by Sarah Tremlett (cf. Tremlett 2021, 310). Ecopoetry can be described as poetry which focuses on climate change and its effects on our daily lives such as soaring temperatures, flooding, and melting of polar ice. These poetry films draw attention to the destruction and changes in the natural world. With this aim I approached the US filmmakers Pamela Falkenberg and Jack Cochran who run Outlier Moving Pictures[2] and were collaborators for two poetry films for *The Book of Hours*, "The Shadow" and "The Names of Trees." The reason behind this choice was their use of experimental techniques in filming, and their compelling images of the American landscape. Between 2018 and 2019 they had been filming in the Permian Basin in Texas (the largest oil basin in the US) and around Dallas and Austin, documenting freeway construction and new suburban development. They had also filmed the prairie restorations and wetlands nature preserves near Rockford, Illinois in the US, the nuclear power plant and the wind turbine installations. In an email to me Falkenberg explained their methodological approach to filmmaking:

> On a shooting road trip, we are usually searching for arresting images and beautiful light. On this trip, we scan the landscape, like advance scouts on expedition, but instead of water holes or the best trail, we are looking for visible signs of man's destructive impact on the environment (Falkenberg 2020).

The poetry film *I Want to Breathe Sweet Air* was created during the global Covid-19 Pandemic and I wrote the poem during lockdown in the UK. Whilst in lockdown many people discovered or rediscovered their connection with the natural world and this poetry film starts with the desire to reconnect with nature. "Take me far away from here / to a grass meadow in The Basin." (Cochran and Falkenberg 2020) In our previous collaborations for *The Book of Hours*, we explored in-

---

2 https://www.outliermovingpictures.com/.

dividual emotional responses to landscapes: In "The Shadow" a woman cannot feel the wonder and beauty of the Oregon mountains until she understands that she is merely a "shadow" on the landscape; in "The Names of Trees" she realises that she does not know what the trees are called in her lover's country, and feels that she does not belong there (cf. English 2017). *I Want to Breathe Sweet Air* takes this uneasiness further. How do we feel when we see a meadow of prairie flowers growing outside a nuclear power plant? Are the flowers a compensation for the destruction of the natural world? I felt that such an enormous topic as climate change had to start with a personal narrative, which viewers could relate to. "The same flowers grow in the buffer zone / near the nuclear power plant / as the flowers in my great-grandmother's farm. Gallardias and Gauras." (Cochran and Falkenberg 2020) The words of the poem combined with the images create in the film a mystery and also awe, similar to what McCabe calls "an awareness of the medium's tangible, synchronicity, multiplicity and evanescence" (McCabe 2005, 17). We are stunned by the beauty of the Permian Basin but also the vastness of the industrial activities (Fig. 27).

Fig. 27: Still from *I Want to Breathe Sweet Air*. Dir. Jack Cochran and Pamela Falkenberg. Poem: Lucy English. 2020.

In *I Want to Breathe Sweet Air* the camera scans the landscape but instead of prairie meadows one sees the visible signs of man's destructive impact. What appears to be a natural hillside is, in fact, a mound of landfill. The film reveals the buffer areas around nuclear power plants, and strip mines, where wild flowers bloom, birds sing, and insects buzz. Shots framed to exclude the excavations and installations look like nature reserves. Viewers' assumptions about what constitutes beauty in landscape are unsettled. The poem appears as text on the screen and reveals a desire to escape "this concrete land" and find a place to "breathe cool sweet air." But the journey along the freeways in Texas only lead back to the city where the unhoused are living in tent villages. Human lives as well as landscapes are being disrupted by global industrialisation.

The film was originally created as a single reel but was later changed into a Triptych of images where the viewer watches three reels at once in order to have more impact. These three reels loop through the sequences of freeways, prairies and industrial landscape combined with a soundtrack of industrial noise, cars, and bird song. The effect is deliberately unsettling and disturbing. The poem ends with a determination to return to the river, the source of life, and a renewed sense of connection to nature and a desire to adopt a more robust stance to prevent further destruction. The aim was for our viewers to feel uncomfortable, learn more, and support/take action.

> Take me far away from here.
> I want to breathe cool sweet air
> and listen to the black throated blue warbler's song
> and smell the dry wind from the rocky hill,
> and walk through prairie flowers to the lake
> and sink my fingers in the mud
> and wipe the mud across my face
> (Cochran and Falkenberg 2020)

I did not use my voice in *I Want to Breathe Sweet Air* and the poem appears in the film as text on screen. Although the poem is spoken word, in that it is written to sound like a person speaking, I did not feel that my own voice was suitable due to my very British accent. The placement of the words replicates the "irregular rhythms" of natural speech which Novak (2011, 95) mentioned that we respond to emotionally. The placement of the text on the screen lends a certain gravitas to the words.

My experiments with spoken word in poetry film have led me to explore further approaches other than placing me in front of a camera. I have found that the 'narrative' of images can give deeper meaning to the poem, whether by placement of words with images, as in "Drive Through the Night," images that further enhance the interpretation of the poem, as in "Solstice Sol Invictus," and the condensation of the words can enhance the experience of the poems, as in "The Sundial." The filmmaker can create a separate 'story' which runs alongside the poem, as in "Qué es el Amor? (What is Love)." Experiments in the way in which the poetry film is viewed, by creating a three-reel film where the viewer experiences a sound and visual overload as in *I Want to Breathe Sweet Air*, reveal that there is much that can still be explored in the creation of the viewing experience (Fig. 28).

Fig. 28: Still from *I Want to Breathe Sweet Air*. Dir. Jack Cochran and Pamela Falkenberg. Poem: Lucy English. 2020.

My belief is that spoken poets must remember that their art is about craft, not appearance. They are not music stars, they do not need to sell their work by how they look on screen. The big players in spoken word, Shane Koyczen, Buddy Wakefield, and Kae Tempest, are not cute or manufactured. Their power is in their ability to connect with people through their words and voices. I would therefore suggest the development of a new definition, the *lyrical spoken word poetry film*. In a lyrical spoken word poetry film, the poet's other skills, such as the use of language, and delivery of the words, can be enhanced and the placement of the images by the filmmaker can be fully explored. For the placement of spoken word in poetry film I would propose the following: a lyrical spoken word poetry film need not contain the same poetry as a live performance since the type of poetry needs to be leaner, and more concise to give necessary space for the visual material; a lyrical spoken word poetry film can explore language as well as narrative content, but the quality of the language should be a high consideration; a lyrical spoken word poetry film can convey emotion as much as a live performance does but it may be conveyed in a more subtle way via the accompanying images; a lyrical spoken word poetry film should give opportunities for the viewer to revisit it to find further detail and nuance. There is much scope for spoken word poets to have more detailed and engaged conversations with collaborators on how to create spoken word poetry films which best combine aspects of poetry, sound, and moving image.

References

Apples and Snakes. 2022, www.applesandsnakes.org (February 10, 2023).
Atticus Review Videopoem Contest. January 11, 2019, https://atticusreview.org/winning-entries-of-the-2018-atticus-review-videopoem-contest/ (February 10, 2023).
Benthien, Claudia, Jordis Lau, and Maraike M. Marxsen. *The Literariness of Media Art*. London: Routledge, 2019.
Bonta, Dave. *Moving Poems. The Best Video Poems on the Web*. June 2, 2016, http://movingpoems.com/filmmaker/eduardo-yague/page/2/ (February 10, 2023).
Cochran, Jack, and Pamela Falkenberg. *I Want to Breathe Sweet Air*. [poetry film] 2020, https://www.outliermovingpictures.com/i-want-to-breathe-sweet-air (February 10, 2023).
Dewbery, Helen. *Poetry Film Live*. 2019, https://poetryfilmlive.com/ (February 10, 2023).
English, Lucy. *The Book of Hours*. Portishead: Burning Eye Books, 2018.
English, Lucy. *The Book of Hours*. [poetry film collection] 2017, www.thebookofhours.org (February 10, 2023).
Godden, Salena. *RED*. [poetry film] 2016, https://www.youtube.com/watch?v=My85dDqMkDw (February 10, 2023).
Kappenberg, Claudia. "Film as Poetry." *The International Journal of Screendance* (2017): 101–119.
Konyves, Tom. "Videopoetry a Manifesto." *Critical Inquiry* (2012): 1–7. https://critinq.wordpress.com/2012/10/13/videopoetry-a-manifesto-by-tom-konyves/ (February 10, 2023).
MacDonald, Scott. "Poetry and Avant Garde Film: Three Recent Contributions." *Poetics Today* 28.1 (2007): 1–41.
McCabe, Susan. *Cinematic Modernism. Modernist Poetry and Film*. Cambridge: Cambridge Univ. Press, 2005.
Montero, Belen. "Videopoem of the Week." *Versogramas*. 2016, https://www.versogramas.com/love-eduardo-yague/ (February 10, 2023).
Neumark, Norie. "Introduction: The Paradox of Voice." *Voice. Vocal Aesthics in Digital Arts and Media*. Ed. Norie Neumark, Ross Gibson, and Theo van Leeuwen. Cambridge, MA: MIT Press, 2010. xv–xxxiii.
Novak, Julia. *Live Poetry. An Integrated Approach to Poetry in Performance*. New York: Rodopi, 2011.
Peters, John Durham. "The Voice and Modern Media." *Kunst-Stimmen*. Ed. Doris Kolesch and Jenny Schroedl. Berlin: Theater der Zeit, 2004. 85–100.
Sitney, P. Adams. *The Cinema of Poetry*. Oxford and New York: Oxford Univ. Press, 2015.
Stillman, Frances. *The Poet's Manual and Rhyming Dictionary*. London: Thames and Hudson, 1966.
Tempest, Kae. Homepage. 2022, www.kaetempest.co.uk (February 10, 2023).
Tremlett, Sarah. *The Poetics of Poetry Film. Film Poetry, Videopoetry, Lyric Voice, Reflection*. Bristol: Intellect Books, 2021.
Yagüe, Eduardo. "Videopoetry." 2017, http://eduardoyague.wixsite.com/videopoetry (February 10, 2023).
Zandegiacomo Del Bel, Thomas. *ZEBRA Poetry Film Festival Programme*. Berlin and Münster: Filmwerkstatt Münster, 2018.

4 **Poetic Images: (Audio)Visuality in Contemporary Book Poetry**

Esther Kilchmann
Vexierbild Gedicht: Schriftbildlichkeit, intermediale und interlinguale Translation in der Lyrik Heike Fiedlers und Jörg Piringers

Mit Heike Fiedler und Jörg Piringer untersucht dieser Aufsatz zwei bislang von der Forschung vergleichsweise wenig beachtete Gegenwartslyriker:innen, die die Materialität von Sprache und Schrift in vielfältiger Weise poetisch inszenieren. Wie zu argumentieren sein wird, spielt dabei die visuelle Gestaltung von Schrift unter den medialen Bedingungen der Digitalisierung ebenso wie die von Translationsprozessen eine besondere Rolle. Anteil an zeitgenössischer visueller Kultur haben Fiedler und Piringer insofern sie in teils digital gestützter Weiterentwicklung lyrischer Untergattungen wie Figuren-, Plakatgedicht und konkreter Poesie die grafisch-bildliche Seite der Schrift hervortreten lassen. Gelockert von der Einbindung in semantische Zusammenhänge werden Zeichen und Wörter so für die Leser:innen optisch erfahrbar oder, um es in der Terminologie Roman Jakobsons zu formulieren, „spürbar" (Jakobson 1979b, 93). Indem die Arbeiten Fiedlers und Piringers einzelne Zeichen und Wörter aus ihrer semantischen, syntaktischen und linearen Anordnung herauslösen und anschließend nach visuellen Parametern wie grafischen Formen oder Ähnlichkeiten zwischen Buchstabenformen neu gruppieren, schließen sie an avantgardistische Verfahren zur Unterlaufung standardisierter Sprach- und Zeichenordnungen an (vgl. Schaffner 2006, 2011). Den Leser:innen wird so zum einen die „fundamentale Dichotomie der Zeichen und Objekte" (Jakobson 1979b, 93) plastisch vorgeführt und zum anderen die allem Geschriebenen inhärente Dimension der Schriftbildlichkeit, die nach Sibylle Krämer dadurch definiert ist, dass Schrift gleich Bildern „auch ‚zu den Augen' [spricht], ihr Metier ist nicht nur das Sagen, sondern auch das Zeigen." (Krämer 2012, 14) Mithin reflektiert Fiedlers und Piringers Lyrik grundlegende Einsichten sowohl in die Beschaffenheit des sprachlichen Zeichens als auch in die der Schrift als Mischung von Bild und Sprache.

In ihren computergestützten Animationen insbesondere von Buchstaben, veranschaulichen sie darüber hinaus die These, dass gerade die poetische Schriftgestaltung den Fokus auf die Beschaffenheit von Schrift überhaupt im digitalen Medium lenken kann, die generell gegenüber dem Druck durch Beweglichkeit, Formbarkeit und Flüchtigkeit gekennzeichnet ist (vgl. Strehovec 2010, 213). Die Gedichte können dabei mit Vexierbildern verglichen werden, in denen gleichzeitig unterschiedliche Figuren präsent sind, zwischen denen das Auge ‚springen' kann.

Ebenso visualisieren sie, wie im Folgenden darzulegen sein wird, intermediale und interlinguale Übergänge zwischen Schrift und Bild, zwischen natürlichen wie zwischen menschlichen und computergenerierten Sprachen. Der Schrift als Ort visueller ebenso wie poetischer Gestaltung von Sprache kommt dabei eine zentrale Stellung zu. Fiedler und Piringer partizipieren von Seiten der Lyrik an jenem neuen Nachdenken über Schriftlichkeit, das Martin Bartelmus und Alexander Nebrig in ihrem aktuellen Band *Schriftlichkeit. Aktivität, Agentialität und Aktanten der Schrift* (2022) angesichts des digitalen Umbruchs fordern. Ausgangspunkt ist, dass Schrift heute weitgehend maschinell bedingt ist und dadurch entschiedener als je zuvor die Auffassung zu verabschieden ist, es handle sich dabei in erster Linie um eine Notation natürlicher mündlicher Sprache. Piringer und Fiedler zeigen stattdessen Schriftbilder, an denen nicht-menschliche Aktanten in der medialen wie interlingualen Transformation beteiligt sind. In ihrer Zentrierung auf Materialität und Medialität der Schrift erinnern sie zudem daran, dass diese immer schon Ergebnis bestimmter Medialisierungen ist und intermediale wie interlinguale Übersetzungen so gesehen eine genealogische Weiterentwicklung zeichenfokussierter Verarbeitungsverfahren von Wirklichkeit darstellen, zu denen nicht zuletzt auch die Poesie gehört.

Insgesamt geht es Fiedler und Piringer aber nicht allein um einen experimentell und poetologisch motivierten Zugriff auf das Sprachmaterial. Vielmehr verhandeln beide Lyriker:innen in ihren Texten explizit auch aktuelle gesellschaftliche Fragen. Bei Fiedler sind es insbesondere soziopolitische Themen wie Migration und Ökokritik, Piringer befragt die Macht von Algorithmen und Sprachtechnologie. Beide Autor:innen begreifen das Gedicht mithin als einen Ort intensiver Spracharbeit, an dem ganz im Sinne Jakobsons zusammen mit konventionellen Zeichenordnungen auch die Wahrnehmung der Wirklichkeit kritisch befragt und verändert werden soll (vgl. Jakobsons 1979a, 79). Bezüglich der genutzten medialen Formate unterscheiden sich Fiedler und Piringer dabei durchaus. Piringer schreibt *digital poetry* im engeren Sinne, die nach Funkhouser kennzeichnet, dass sich darin „crafted language with new media technology and techniques enabled by such equipment" (Funkhouser 2007, 319) verbinden und die digitale Technik so in ästhetischer Weise eingesetzt wird. Hierzu gehört, dass das Produkt mithilfe von Computerprogrammen auf Bildschirmen präsentiert wird: „A poem is a digital poem if computer programming or processes (software, etc.) are distinctively used in the composition, generation, or presentation of the text (or combinations of texts)." (Funkhouser 2007, 319) Piringers Arbeiten entsprechen dieser Definition, insofern darin sowohl Generierung als auch Präsentation der Texte digital gestützt erfolgt. Die Text- und Buchstabeninstallationen sind auf seiner Homepage publiziert, teilweise auch auf der Social-Media-Plattform Instagram. Zusätzlich hat Piringer eine App erstellt, mit der interaktiv Buchstaben- und Lautfolgen erstellt werden können. Schließlich bringt er seine Arbeiten in intermedialen audiovisuellen Performances auf die Bühne. Dass Piringer auch die Programmierung seiner Wortkunstwerke selbst vornimmt, macht ihn zu einem „poet-programmer" im Sinne Funkhousers (2007, 330).

Fiedlers Werk, das in Gestalt mehrerer Gedichtbände sowie poetologischer Essays und einem Roman in Buchform vorliegt, wirkt dagegen auf den ersten Blick ‚weniger' digital. Gleichwohl präsentiert auch Fiedler ihre Gedichte in computergestützten audiovisuellen Performances, wofür sie eine *looping*-Software nutzt. Diese Aufführungen unterscheiden sich von herkömmlichen Lesungen vor allem dadurch, dass sich die Gedichte durch die eingesetzte Technik verändern und so während der Performances neue Texte entstehen, die sich aufgrund ihrer Flüchtigkeit und Intermedialität von der gedruckten ‚Vorlage' unterscheiden und sich nicht unmittelbar in das Printmedium zurückübersetzen lassen. Die Performance erscheint damit als eigener Teil des Werkes und rückt dieses durch die darin in Szene gesetzten Wechselwirkungen zwischen gedrucktem Gedicht und seiner medialen Transformierbarkeit durchaus in die Nähe digital erzeugter Literatur. Fiedlers Arbeiten betonen so in der Verflechtung von Druck und computergestützter Performance die Kondition des „postprint", die N. Katherine Hayles (2021) zufolge für die gegenwärtige Textproduktion prägend ist. Dabei macht sie auf die enge Verbindung aufmerksam, die heute zwischen Büchern und Computern besteht und fordert, dass die technische Produktion jedes Textes mitreflektiert werden sollte, auch wenn dieser am Ende in Gestalt eines konventionellen Buches gedruckt erscheint. Denn letztlich verändert diese Verbindung Hayles zufolge grundlegend, wie Texte produziert und rezipiert werden können und lässt überdies die gedruckte Version lediglich als eine mögliche Repräsentation eines Textes unter anderen erscheinen (vgl. Hayles 2021, 1–39).

Aufgrund der unterschiedlichen Nutzung computergestützter Tools in Generierung und Präsentation der Gedichte können anhand der Arbeiten Fiedlers und Piringers verschiedene Aspekte von Schriftbildlichkeit, intermedialer Transformation und Translation im Lyrikschaffen im digitalen Zeitalter beleuchtet werden. Im Folgenden ist nun an exemplarischen Texten zu untersuchen, wie darin Schrift visuell inszeniert und zugleich künstlerische Forschung am Sprachmaterial mitsamt seiner Transformationsmöglichkeiten betrieben wird. Ein besonderes Augenmerk liegt darauf, wie in den Arbeiten herkömmlicherweise unsichtbare Translationsprozesse visualisiert und dabei *en passant* Korrespondenzen zwischen intermedialen und interlingualen Übersetzungsvorgängen sichtbar gemacht werden. Ferner soll gezeigt werden, wie Fiedler und Piringer mit ihrer Lyrik einen Beitrag zur Reflexion des Stellenwertes von Schrift im digitalen Zeitalter leisten und zugleich die spezifische Rolle, die Translationsprozessen in diesem Kontext zukommt, in den Fokus rücken.

Poetische Visualisierungen von Schriftbildlichkeit

Indem Fiedler und Piringer in ihren Arbeiten „Visuales und Skripturales in dynamischen Konstellationen [verweben]" (Benthien und Weingart 2014, 10), sind sie Teil des aktuellen Feldes von Literatur und Visualität. In der Spannung von *linguistic turn* und *visual turn* wird dabei die bildliche Seite von Schrift betont. Gleichzeitig verschwindet darin aber die textuelle Beschaffenheit des poetischen Materials nicht, vielmehr ist es weiterhin das sprachliche Zeichen, das als vorherrschend erscheint und im Mittelpunkt des gestalterischen ebenso wie des forschenden Interesses an medialer Transformation steht. Mit Ludwig Jäger gesprochen, wird das Sprachzeichen dabei als eine Art „primäres Medium" (Jäger 2000, 12) in den Fokus gerückt. Weitere Medialisierungen erscheinen daher als eine Fortentwicklung poetischer – im Sinne von zeichenfokussierter – Verarbeitungsverfahren von Wirklichkeit und mithin ihrerseits als eine Form von Schrift. So im Zyklus „Visuelle Poesie" aus Fiedlers Band *sie will mehr* (2013), der aus zweiundzwanzig Gedichten besteht, in denen alphanumerische Zeichen, deutsche und französische Wörter mit grafischen Formen kombiniert werden. Dabei werden die für konventionelle Schriftsysteme wesentlichen Abgrenzungen zwischen Text und Bild, zwischen Buchstaben und Zahl wie zwischen einzelnen Sprachen überschritten und alternative Formen der Bedeutungsgenerierung erkundet.

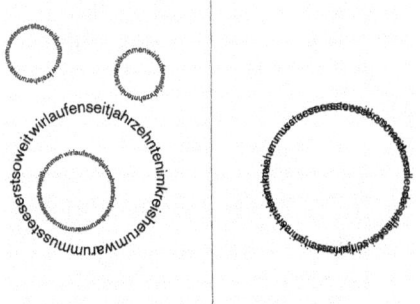

Abb. 29: Heike Fiedler. „wirlaufenseitjahrzehnten". *sie will mehr*. 2013. 82–83.

Im doppelseitig gedruckten Gedicht „wirlaufenseitjahrzehnten" wird der Satz „Wir laufen seit Jahrzehnten im Kreis herum warum musste es erst soweit kommen" ohne Wortabstand in mehreren Kreisformen angeordnet (Abb. 29). Nach Vorbild des Figurengedichtes wird dabei das Beschriebene zugleich plastisch gezeigt. Durch die Reproduktion der Kreise lassen sich zusätzlich Ausdrücke wie Gedankenkreise oder Leerlauf assoziieren, die gleichsam verkörpert werden. Die visuelle Dimension lenkt aber auch vom Textinhalt ab. Auf der gegenüberliegenden Seite wird die Schrift übereinander gedruckt, sodass der Inhalt unlesbar wird und nur die grafische Kreisform erkennbar bleibt. In der Gegenüberstellung der beiden Seiten wird Krämers These unterstrichen, der zufolge Schrift immer „ein Doppelleben im Spannungsverhältnis von Materialität und Interpretierbarkeit" (Krämer 2012, 24) führt. So erscheint das Gedicht als vexierbildartiger Ort, an dem es jenseits konventioneller Repräsentationsordnungen gelingt, die mediale Spezifik der Schriftbildlichkeit als „Kippfigur" (Assmann 2012, 235) zwischen Text und Bild zur Darstellung zu bringen.

Mehrere andere Gedichte des Zyklus sind ähnlich komponiert. In „hier" und „übergang" (Fiedler 2013, 92–93) werden die Worte in Gestalt eines Pfeiles bzw. einer Brücke arrangiert, wobei ansatzweise mit der linearen Schriftordnung auch die Buchstabenfolge in den Worten gelöst wird. Fortgesetzt wird dies in „REINRAUS" (Fiedler 2013, 91). Hier werden die beiden titelgebenden Worte im ersten Vers übereinander gedruckt und dann versweise um Buchstabenlänge auseinandergeschoben, bis in der Mitte des Gedichtes „REIN RAUS" lesbar wird. Anschließend werden sie in umgekehrter Richtung verrückt, wobei zusätzlich Buchstaben verschoben werden, sodass im letzten Vers „RAUS RIEN" entsteht. Die Lockerung der linearen Textanordnung zugunsten des Fokus auf das Schriftbild zieht dabei die Lockerung der Buchstabenfolge im Wortgefüge ebenso nach sich wie die zwischen den Sprachen. Mit der Verdrehung von „E" und „I" in „REIN" verschiebt sich das Wort zu „RIEN" und damit ins Französische (frz. „rien", dt.: „nichts"). Ebenso wie im Gedicht „temps" (Fiedler 2013, 90) wird so die mediale Transformation von Text in Bild mit einer interlingualen Übersetzung kombiniert. Der gemeinsame Fluchtpunkt scheint die Aushebelung konventioneller Sprachordnungen zu sein, zu der neben Linearität auch Einsprachigkeit gehört. Wird hingegen der Fokus auf das Visuelle gelegt, lässt sich Schrift nicht nur auf der Fläche anders anordnen, auch die Buchstaben lassen sich neu kombinieren und die textorientierten Repräsentationsnormen treten insgesamt zurück. Poetologisch reflektiert wird dieses Vorgehen im selbstreferentiellen Gedicht „p-o-e" (Abb. 30).

Unter Auflösung des Wortzusammenhangs und der linearen Schriftanordnung wird aus der Buchstabenfolge p-o-e-s-i-e ein Schriftbild generiert, in dem sich die einzelnen Buchstaben als eine Art Gestöber über die Seite ausbreiten und Poesie selbstreferentiell als ästhetisch-visuelle Kombination von an sich bedeutungslosen Buchstabenformen erscheint.

Piringer spitzt dieses poetologische Prinzip in seinen digitalen Buchstabeninszenierungen zu. In den digitalen Poemen „abcdefghijklmnopqrstuvwxyz" sowie denen der „insta visuel poetry" werden einzelne Buchstaben in unterschiedlichen Laufrichtungen über den Bildschirm bewegt. Die Zeichen werden so, wie Simanowski es formuliert hat, vom Sinnträger zum „visuellen Objekt" (Simanowski 2012, 5). Ihr Lauf folgt dabei simulierten physikalischen Gesetzen, zufälligen An-

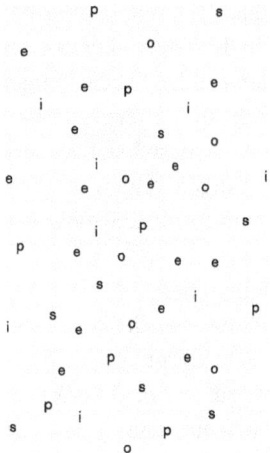

Abb. 30: Heike Fiedler. „p-o-e". *sie will mehr.* 2013. 85.

ordnungen oder auch bestimmten Figuren. Andere Arbeiten Piringers gruppieren Zeichen und Buchstaben aufgrund von Formähnlichkeiten. So werden in „unicode infinite" Glyphen des Unicode-Standards in einen automatisierten Ablauf gebracht, der diese nach Formähnlichkeit ordnet und damit aus ihrer Zugehörigkeit zu unterschiedlichen Schriftsystemen löst (vgl. Portela 2017, 107).

Gegenüber den gedruckten Gedichten Fiedlers reflektiert Piringers *digital poetry* zusätzlich zur Schriftbildlichkeit die Frage nach deren Erscheinungsweise, bzw. der Erscheinung von Schrift überhaupt in der Transformation ins Digitale und damit den Einfluss des Mediums auf die Repräsentation wie Wahrnehmung von Schrift. Dabei richten die Arbeiten Piringers den Fokus darauf, dass die auf traditionellen Trägermaterialen wie Papier, Stein etc. mit Attributen wie „fest" und „unverrückbar" verbundene Schrift in der Transformation ins Digitale andere Qualitäten bekommt. In erster Linie gehören nun Beweglichkeit und Flüchtigkeit zu ihrem Erscheinungsbild. Die Medientheoretiker:innen Hayles und Strehovec sprechen von „flickering signifiers" (Hayles 1999, 27) bzw. davon, dass das Wort im digitalen Medium seine „authority and solidity" verliere und „as a raw material for numerous transformations" (Strehovec 2010, 213) erscheine.

Die Buchstabengedichte Piringers – und ebenso die digitalen Gedicht-Performances Fiedlers – gewinnen einen guten Teil ihrer ästhetischen Faszination dadurch, dass sie diese Veränderung der Schrift durch die digitale Transformation visuell erfahrbar werden lassen. Fiedlers Gedichtbände zeigen ihrerseits, dass Schrift auch im Druck bereits als beweglich inszeniert werden kann und gestalten entsprechend, ganz im Sinne Hayles, eine Zone des Übergangs von Print und Postprint (vgl. Hayles 2021). Wie im Folgenden darzulegen ist, lenken beide Lyriker:innen überdies den Blick darauf, dass mit dieser Medialisierung, mit den jeweiligen medialen Transformationen von Schrift, die in den Gedichten sichtbar gemacht wird, immer auch Prozesse der Übersetzung verbunden sind.

Poetische Visualisierungen von Translation

In literatur- und kulturtheoretischen Auseinandersetzungen mit Schrift und Digitalisierung erfährt der Komplex der Translation bislang wenig Aufmerksamkeit. Eher beiläufig wird konstatiert, dass Digitalisierung Übersetzungsvorgänge erfordert. So hält Krämer fest, dass Digitalisierung im Kern darauf beruhe, „Medienformate ineinander übersetzen zu können" (Krämer 2012, 22). Julia Nantke präzisiert dies in ihren Ausführungen zu den komplexen Übersetzungsprozessen, die insbesondere die Digitalisierung von avantgardistischen Schrift-Bild-Artefakten erfordern. Ihr zufolge besteht die zentrale Leistung des Computers darin, „Zeichenformate ineinander übersetzen zu können." (Nantke 2022, 43) Zugleich werde dies von Prozessen der Normalisierung begleitet, durch die Übersetzbarkeit erst hergestellt werden kann. Anschließend daran lässt sich argumentieren, dass der Computer verstärkt nicht nur als „Schriftmaschine" (Krämer 2012, 22) sondern auch als Übersetzungsmaschine begriffen werden müsste. Und dies nicht allein im metaphorischen oder im weiteren Sinne einer ‚medialen Transformation', sondern durchaus im Sinne von Jakobsons „translation proper", die als „interpretation of verbal signs by means of some other language" (Jakobson 1959, 233) definiert ist. Eine solche Übertragung von Sinn von einem standardisierten System in ein anderes durch die Verknüpfung jeweils bedeutungsäquivalenter Zeichen, stellt nicht nur die Translation zwischen natürlichen Sprachen, sondern auch die nach eben diesem Muster ablaufende Translation zwischen natürlichen menschlichen Sprachen und Programmiersprachen und Codes dar.

Der computergestützten Sprach- und Schriftverarbeitung liegt mithin eine „translation proper" zugrunde. Wie Beat Suter und René Bauer es formuliert haben, wird dabei, „jedem Zeichen eines Zeichenvorrats eindeutig ein Zeichen oder eine Zeichenfolge aus einem möglicherweise anderen Zeichenvorrat" (Suter und Bauer 2016, 73) zugeordnet. Wie bei der Translation zwischen natürlichen Sprachen auch, wird dabei unter der Vorgabe der eindeutigen Zuordnung von Zeichen eine Auswahl getroffen. Insgesamt aber bleiben maschinell prozessierte Übersetzungsprozesse ebenso wie traditionell die Arbeit der Übersetzer:innen dem Auge der Leser:innen bzw. User:innen vermeintlich entzogen. Auf der Nutzer:innenoberfläche des Bildschirmes erscheinen sie nur, wenn Störungen auftreten, wie Nantke (vgl. 2022, 43) konstatiert. Auch darin ist die Ähnlichkeit computerbasierter Sprachverarbeitung mit herkömmlicher interlingualer Translation unübersehbar, die, wie es im berühmten Aperçu Norman Shapiros heißt, einer Glasscheibe (zit. in Venuti 1995, 14) gleichen sollte, die nur sichtbar wird, wenn sie zerkratzt ist.

Digitale Sprach- und Schriftverarbeitung ist mithin von jener „Unsichtbarkeit der Übersetzung" begleitet, die Lawrence Venuti in seinem translationswissenschaftlichen Klassiker *The Translator's Invisibility* grundlegend kritisiert. In dieser Perspektive folgt der Übertragungsprozess zwischen natürlicher menschlicher Ausgangssprache und ihrer computerbasierten Verarbeitung sowie der anschließenden Lesbarkeit für menschliche Nutzer:innen auf dem Bildschirm dem Modell der domestizierenden Übertragung. Sie ist dadurch gekennzeichnet, dass der Text aus der Ausgangssprache so in die Zielsprache übertragen wird, dass er sich hier standardisierten Sprachstrukturen und Ausdrucksweisen reibungslos anpasst. Venuti hat demgegenüber dafür plädiert, den Übertragungsvorgang sowohl in der Translationsarbeit selbst als auch in der philologischen Beschäftigung damit sichtbar zu machen. Übersetzung sollte so als eigenständige Konstitution von Bedeutung in den Blick rücken und damit die Bedeutungsgenerierung mitsamt der ihnen zugrunde liegenden Interpretationen, Hierarchisierungen und Machtverhältnisse (vgl. Venuti 1995).

Anschließend daran forderte jüngst auch Birgit Neumann, die mit Übersetzungsprozessen verbundenen „wechselseitigen Verstrickungen, Veränderungen und Neuformationen" (Neumann 2021, 11) besser zu erkennen und sie als spezifische Form von Lektüreprozessen zu verstehen. Übersetzungen sollten folglich als Möglichkeit begriffen werden, sich mit Mehrdeutigkeiten auseinanderzusetzen und damit auf sprachphilosophische Betrachtungen hin geöffnet zu werden, wie dies Walter Benjamin in seinem Aufsatz „Die Aufgabe des Übersetzers" fordert. Ihm zufolge ist „alle Übersetzung nur eine irgendwie vorläufige Art [...], sich mit der Fremdheit der Sprachen auseinanderzusetzen." (Benjamin 1991, 14) Sie sollte diese nicht unsichtbar machen, sondern im Gegenteil spürbar werden lassen. Folgerichtig ist für Benjamin die gelungenste Übersetzung deshalb eine poetische; er nennt in diesem Zusammenhang jene Hölderlins von Sophokles, in der die Sprache hervortritt und der Sinn sich zu verlieren droht.

Wie im Folgenden zu zeigen sein wird, sind Fiedlers und Piringers poetische Gestaltungen von Übersetzungsszenarien vor diesem Hintergrund einer Visualisierung von sprachlicher Materialität und Schriftbildlichkeit zu lesen. Die materiellen Aspekte von Sprache und Schrift, die „Spürbarkeit der Zeichen" (Jakobson 1979b, 93) wird so neben den bereits ausgeführten poetischen Verfahren über Verfahren der Übersetzung hervorgehoben. Dabei werden sowohl Translationsszenarien zwischen natürlichen Sprachen wie zwischen natürlichen und maschinellen Sprachen gezeigt.

In Fiedlers Werk sticht zunächst dessen translinguale Anlage hervor. Die Autorin publiziert auf Deutsch und Französisch und in ihren Gedichten spielen neben diesen beiden hauptsächlich verwandten Sprachen polyglotte Versatzstücke aus dem Englischen, Russischen, Italienischen und Spanischen eine Rolle. Während sich die Mischung von Deutsch und Französisch mit Fiedlers biografischem Lebensmittelpunkt in der französischsprachigen Schweiz verknüpfen lässt, lenkt der Einbezug weiterer Sprachen, der nahtlos auch ins Lautmalerische und die bereits erläuterte Darstellung asemantischer Zeichen übergeht, von der biografischen Begründung ab. Anders als in der Forschung zur translingualen Lyrik, die diese immer noch biografisch und thematisch begründet sieht (vgl. etwa Zemanek 2016; Gunkel 2020), erscheint Vielsprachigkeit hier auch als Konsequenz poetischer Überschreitungen konventioneller Sprach- und Schriftordnung. Ihre poetologische Bemerkung, sie habe „eine Art Mischpult im Kopf, das ununterbrochen Wörter in Laute zerlege und auf ihre Bedeutungsvielfalt in anderen Sprachen untersuche" (Fiedler 2010, 156), lässt das translinguale Spiel ihrer Lyrik ebenso sehr wie aus dem biografischen Erfahrungsraum aus ihrem medial vermittelten Zugriff auf Sprache und aus der Aufmerksamkeit für deren audiovisuelle Materialität entstehen. Entsprechend erscheint, wo sie in ihren Gedichten auftaucht, die interlinguale Übersetzung als ein Strang in Fiedlers experimenteller Arbeit am in intermedialen Transformationsprozessen befindlichen Sprachmaterial. Ihrem ersten Gedichtband *langues de meehr* (Fiedler 2010, 9) ist entsprechend folgendes Poem als Motto vorangestellt:

> lau   tt   teil
> ,entre sons et fragments, le sens se crée
> dans l'inattendu, dans les interstices de
>   nos attentes.

Der erste Vers besteht aus dem Neologismus „lautteil". Durch die optische Anordnung wird die Aufmerksamkeit auf den verdoppelten Mittellaut „tt" gelenkt, der zugleich als jener semantisch unbestimmte Teil eines Lautes gelesen werden kann, den der Neologismus bezeichnen soll. Der Vers richtet mithin autoreferentiell die Aufmerksamkeit auf das Zusammenspiel bzw. das Auseinanderdriften von materiellem Laut und Bedeutung. Die folgenden Verse präsentieren eine Übersetzung des lyrischen Spiels in eine poetologische Reflexion, durch das Französische sind sie zusätzlich von der Sprachform des ersten Verses unterschieden, in den wiederkehrenden und verdoppelten t's bleiben sie ihm aber auf semiotischer Ebene auch verbunden. Die poetologische Aussage des Gedichtes, zu Deutsch: „Zwischen Tönen und Fragmenten entsteht der Sinn im Unerwarteten, in den Lücken unserer Erwartungen", betont ihrerseits Vorgänge des Übergangs und der Übertragung. Auf diese Weise fordert das Gedicht von den Leser:innen eine mehrfache Übersetzungsleistung: französischer und deutscher Teil, poetisches Spiel und poetologische Sentenz sollen – vermittelt durch die visuelle Anordnung – aufeinander bezogen werden. Als Motto des gesamten Bandes stellen die Verse zudem eine Leseanleitung dar, in der darauf hingewiesen wird, dass in den Zwischenräumen zwischen Lauten und Fragmenten wie Schriftzeichen, über die lesend buchstäblich ‚übergesetzt' werden muss, unerwartet Sinn entstehen kann. Sowohl in der zweisprachigen Anordnung des Gedichtes als auch in der Kombination von optischer Poesie und poetologischer Reflexion bringt Fiedler so das Gedicht selbst als Ort der Übersetzung zur Darstellung.

Diese Auffassung findet sich wieder im Titel des jüngsten Gedichtbandes *Tu es! hier* (Fiedler 2022). Der Titel lässt sich sowohl Deutsch („Tu es hier") als auch Französisch („Tu es hier", dt.: „Du bist gestern") lesen. Auf diese Weise erscheint er als Vexierbild, in dem je nachdem die eine oder andere Lesart bzw. Übersetzung hervortritt. Das eingeschobene Ausrufezeichen verweist überdies darauf, dass hier nicht allein Sprachen, sondern der alphanumerische Code poetisch in Bewegung gebracht wird und gleichzeitig eben dadurch auch sprachliche Zugehörigkeiten entstehen, bzw. zerfallen. Insgesamt erscheinen die natürlichen Sprachen Deutsch und Französisch nicht als kategorial voneinander geschieden, sondern lediglich als mögliche Realisierungen des gleichen Schriftbildes. Mit Claudia Benthien lässt sich diese in *Tu es! hier* aufscheinende besondere Spielart translingualer Schreibweise auch als „visuelle Polyphonie" (Benthien 2017, 135) bezeichnen, bei der die ‚Mehrstimmigkeit' gerade nicht hörbar ist, sondern nur auf visueller Ebene erzeugt wird. Der Titel reflektiert so eine „Bimodalität der Sprache: zwischen (tendenziell mehrdeutiger) Schriftsprache und (eher eindeutiger) mündlicher Sprache, die zwangsläufig immer eine ‚Realisation' im Wortsinn ist." (Benthien 2017, 136) Gleichzeitig wird im Sinne Jacques Derridas Kritik am Phonozentrismus die Ebene der Schrift, der *écriture*, als Ort der Bedeutungsgenerierung und -transformation hervorgehoben. Fiedler bringt darüber hinaus die Schrift als Ort translatorischer Bewegung zwischen Bild und Text wie zwischen den Sprachen zur Darstellung. Explizit kombiniert wird Schriftbildlichkeit und interlinguale Translation in dem Poem „a line" (Abb. 31):

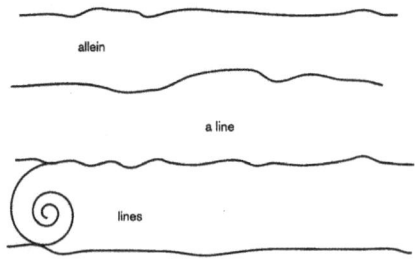

Abb. 31: Heike Fiedler. „a line". *sie will mehr.* 2013. 97.

In diesem Gedicht werden semantische Übersetzung und homophone Übertragung kombiniert. Zwischen dem ausgangssprachlichen „allein" und dessen Übersetzung „alone" in der Zielsprache stehen die Oberflächenübersetzungen „a line" und „lines", die zusätzlich ins Figürliche, in Linien und Spirale übertragen werden. Auch hier wird mithin eine Vielfalt möglicher Übersetzungsbewegungen sichtbar gemacht, die in einer vereindeutigenden Translation (*allein – alone*) unterdrückt werden müssen, die aber gerade für das poetische Interesse an Übersetzung als Ort der Wortvermehrung und entsprechender Mehrdeutigkeit zentral ist.

Als letztes sei auf Fiedlers Gedicht mit dem programmatischen Titel „Von einer Sprache" (Fiedler 2022, 54) aus *Tu es! hier* eingegangen. Der Titel ruft zunächst die Erwartung auf, dass von *einer* Sprache gehandelt werde, die gleich zu Beginn des Gedichtes dadurch gebrochen wird, das „Von einer Sprache" nur den Ausgangspunkt einer Bewegung benennt, die „in die andere" führt. Beweglichkeit und Flüchtigkeit werden so als wesentliche Merkmale von Sprache hervorgehoben: „Von einer Sprache / in die andere / g/leiten". Die französische Übersetzung wird spiegelbildlich dazu angeordnet: „g/lisser / d'une langue / à l'autre". Dabei erlaubt es gerade die unterschiedliche syntaktische Wortstellung von Deutsch und Französisch, die Sprachen über das Verb, das im Deutschen am Ende des Satzes steht, im Französischen am Anfang, zu verbinden. Mit „gleiten" und „glisser" ist zudem ein Wortpaar gefunden, das nicht nur die Bedeutung teilt, sondern auch auf Ebene des Schriftbildes starke Ähnlichkeiten aufweist und so auch eine Oberflächenübersetzung erlaubt. Das Gedicht betont dies noch in der Separierung des Anfangsbuchstabens ‚g', der die verschiedensprachigen Wörter verbindet und zugleich in der Mitte des Gedichtes eine Stelle interlingualen Umschlags markiert.

Zusammenfassend lässt sich sagen, dass Fiedler in ihren Gedichten ein im Sinne Jakobsons poetisches Interesse an der Übersetzung zur Darstellung bringt, das daran ansetzt, dass ein Wort in ein – oder mehrere – andere übertragen wird. Am Übergang zwischen den Sprachen eröffnen sich dabei Uneindeutigkeiten und Bedeutungsspielräume, kurz, es werden Differenzen sichtbar, die sich wiederum im Gedicht ausstellen lassen. Dabei scheint mir gerade im visuellen Raum, den das Gedicht durch seine spezifische Anordnung zu gestalten vermag, die Möglichkeit gegeben, Übersetzungsprozesse sichtbar zu machen, die sonst durch ihre lineare Normierung in Gestalt der Überführung eines linearen Ausgangs- in einen ebensolchen Zieltext unsichtbar gemacht werden. Damit einhergeht, dass die Übertragung des Sinns als oberstes Ziel der konventionellen Übersetzung zugunsten einer mehrdeutigen Oberflächengestaltung zurückgenommen wird.

Abschließend soll anhand von Texten Jörg Piringers diskutiert werden, wie auch Übersetzungsvorgänge zwischen Text und unsichtbarer digitaler Sprachverarbeitung poetisch visualisiert werden können. Als digitaler Lyriker entwirft Piringer nicht nur die bereits diskutierten Schriftinstallationen, es ist ihm zudem ein Anliegen, computerbasierte Sprachtechnologie und ihr Funktionieren mit den Mitteln künstlerischer Forschung zu erkunden und ihre Auswirkungen für seine Leser:innen in experimentellen poetischen Anordnungen darzustellen. Wie jene anderer digitaler Lyriker:innen zielt seine Arbeit „auf das Sichtbarmachen der Arbeitsweisen von Quellcodes und Algorithmen, die der auf dem Interface lesbaren Schrift zugrunde liegen." (Vorrath 2022, 55) Dies geschieht aus einer kulturkritischen Haltung heraus: „in zukunft", so Piringer in der Vorrede zu seiner Publikation *datenpoesie*, wird es „die digitale sprachtechnologie der konzerne sein, die die bedingungen von poesie und sprache verändert." (Piringer 2018, 6) Aufgrund dieser tiefgreifenden Veränderungen, die gegenwärtig nicht zuletzt durch die Entwicklung von ChatGPTs rasant fortschreiten, stellt er folgende Fragen: „wie funktioniert die maschine? welchen beschränkungen ist das programm unterworfen? [...] kann ich die verborgenen strukturen und neigungen der ursprünglichen programmierer zu tage fördern?" Piringers Datenpoesie will „diese strukturen und algorithmen, die unsere kommunikation und weltwahrnehmung zunehmend beeinflussen" reflektieren und „deren materialität an die oberfläche" (Piringer 2018, 7) bringen. Dazu müssen insbesondere die verborgenen Übersetzungsprozesse zwischen menschlicher Sprache und deren maschineller Verarbeitung fokussiert werden.

Exemplarisch geschieht dies in der Arbeit „allgemein erklar menschenrecht" (Piringer 2018, 152). Darin wird die 1948 von der Generalversammlung der Vereinten Nationen in Paris verkündete „Allgemeine Erklärung der Menschenrechte" in ihrer deutschen Fassung dem gleichen automatischen Prozess unterzogen, mittels dessen Suchmaschinen relevante Informationen aus Texten herausfiltern. Dies geschieht Piringer zufolge in erster Linie durch das Entfernen als unwichtig erachteter Wörter (sogenannter Stopp-Wörter wie Artikel, Pronomen u. a.) sowie durch die Reduzierung auf den Wortstamm (vgl. Piringer 2018, 280). Übersetzt in die maschinelle Lesbarkeit lautet der Beginn der Erklärung entsprechend: „da anerkenn angebor wurd gleich unverausser recht mitglied gemeinschaft mensch grundlag freiheit gerechtig fried welt bildet nichtanerkenn veracht menschenrecht akt barbarei" (Piringer 2018, 152). Sichtbar wird so eine deutliche Reduktion als Resultat der Translation zwischen natürlicher und maschinell verarbeitbarer Sprache, wie Vorrath in ihrer Interpretation des Textes bereits dargelegt hat (vgl. Vorrath 2022, 66). Mit Blick auf die Textvorlage, die die Transformation eines emphatischen humanistischen Dokuments zu einer „verstümmelten sprache" (Piringer 2018, 280) zeigt, wird gefragt, inwiefern eine solche Translation auch eine bestimmte Bedeutung, bzw. Lesart des Dokumentes befördert. Piringer stellt zudem die These einer kulturellen Verzerrung auf, die daraus resultiere, dass die Sprachalgorithmen möglicherweise „auf die morphologisch ärmere englische sprache optimiert wurden." (Piringer 2018, 281) Entsprechend spiegelten sich in der computergestützten Sprachverarbeitung gesellschaftliche und kulturelle Machtverhältnisse und würden gegebenenfalls weiter befestigt. Mit Blick auf die Geschlechterordnung macht Piringer dies in der Arbeit „tätigkeiten" (Piringer 2018, 62–63) sichtbar:

> sie ist ärztin.
> *O bir doktor.*
> er ist ein arzt.
>
> er arbeitet als krankenpfleger.
> *O bir hemşire olarak çalışıyor.*
> sie arbeitet als krankenschwester.
>
> [...]

Hier wurde mittels eines nicht weiter identifizierten Übersetzungsprogramms vom Deutschen ins Türkische und zurück übersetzt. Da Piringers Angaben zufolge türkische Personalpronomina geschlechtsneutral sind, wählt der Übersetzungsalgorithmus bei der Rückübersetzung ins Deutsche ein Geschlecht und orientiert sich dabei an dominanten kulturellen Zuschreibungen. Ähnlich wie Venuti kritisiert Piringer mit diesen Arbeiten, dass im Grunde weitreichende Eingriffe in die Sprache, wie die Zuschreibungen von Geschlechterspezifik, durch den Übersetzungsprozess strukturell unsichtbar bleiben. Die poetischen Eingriffe zielen demgegenüber darauf ab, dies sichtbar zu machen.

Dass das Resultat dabei auch weniger kulturkritisch als in den eben besprochenen Arbeiten ausfallen kann und die Sichtbarmachung von Übersetzung stattdessen ihrerseits einen mehrdeutigen poetischen Text hervorbringen kann, zeigt Piringer in „übersetzungen" (2018, 50–57). Hierfür wurde die erste Strophe aus Matthias Claudius' Gedicht „Der Mond ist aufgegangen" mittels automatischer Übersetzung in eine Zielsprache und weiter in eine nächste übertragen. Nach 82 solcher Translationen folgt die Rückübersetzung ins Deutsche. Aus „der mond ist aufgegangen / die goldenen sternlein prangen / am himmel hell und klar" entstand so: „ein monat / papua / abstimmung". Offen bleibt dabei, inwiefern es die maschinelle Übersetzung ist, die die Generierung von Mehrdeutigkeit und Poetizität befördert, oder ob es die Poetizität des Ausgangstextes ist, die die maschinelle Übersetzungsarbeit stört und so Widerstand gegen ihre computerbasierte Verarbeitung leistet. Beides ließe sich im Sinne Piringers auslegen, demzufolge es die poetische Spracharbeit ist, die dazu in der Lage ist, unsichtbare Sprachverarbeitungsprozesse in ihrer Materialität sichtbar werden zu lassen.

Fazit

Heike Fiedler und Jörg Piringer beschäftigen sich in ihrem lyrischen Werk mit vielgesichtigen Transformationsprozessen und gestalten in ihren visuellen Schriftanordnungen Momente des Umschlages zwischen Text und Bild, zwischen menschlicher Sprache und ihrer computerbasierten Verarbeitung sowie zwischen unterschiedlichen natürlichen Sprachen. Der Aufsatz untersuchte ihr Werk vor dem Hintergrund aktueller medientheoretischer und literaturwissenschaftlicher Fragestellungen zur Veränderung von Schrift und Sprache unter den Bedingungen der Digitalisierung, zu neuen Formen intermedialer Schriftbildlichkeit sowie der künstlerischen Reflexion der Materialität und Medialität sprachlicher Zeichen. Ferner wurde hervorgehoben, dass die lyrische Gestaltung der Übergänge zwischen natürlichen und computergenerierten Sprachen stärker als bislang berücksichtigt als Übersetzungen nach dem Vorbild interlingualer Translationen lesbar ist. Das Gedicht als Ort intensiver Spracharbeit, wo im Sinne Jakobsons die poetische Funktion hervorgehoben wird, ist dabei gleichzeitig der Ort, an dem seine mehrfache Lesbarkeit ausgestellt wird: Dies nicht nur bezogen auf die semantische Ebene, sondern ebenso auf die intermediale, in der die Deutung als Schrift oder Bild möglich ist, sowie auf die interlinguale, indem einzelne Wortzusammenstellungen in unterschiedlichen Sprachen, beispielsweise Deutsch und Französisch, gelesen werden können. Auf diese Weise entstehen Gedichte, die insofern Vexierbildern ähneln, als in ihnen unterschiedliche Figuren – oder präziser: Aktualisierungen von Schrift – *gleichzeitig* dargestellt werden, die sich aber nur *nacheinander* lesen, bzw. aktualisieren lassen. Auf diese Weise können die Leser:innen in der Lyrik Fiedlers und Piringers intermediale wie interlinguale Translationsvorgänge, die konventioneller Weise unsichtbar bleiben, visuell erkunden.

In Fiedlers Gedichten liegt der Schwerpunkt dabei in Anlehnung an Verfahren konkreter Poesie auf der Gestaltung von Schriftbildlichkeit, wobei in diesem Kontext programmatisch auch interlinguale Übersetzungsszenarien gestaltet werden, wie u. a. an dem Gedicht „a line" gezeigt wurde, das die grafische Umsetzung der benannten Linie mit homophonen und semantischen Translationen in „allein" und „alone" kombiniert. Intermediale und interlinguale Translationen erscheinen dabei als zwei verwandte Verfahren, die ihren gemeinsamen Ausgangspunkt in der mehrfachen Ausdeutbarkeit von Schrift bzw. Buchstabenanordnungen haben. Piringer bezieht demgegenüber stärker digitale Verfahren ebenso wie deren Reflexion mit ein. Seine computerbasierten bewegten Buchstabenpoeme wie „abcdefghijklmnopqrstuvwxyz" inszenieren intermediale Transformationen von Schrift sowohl auf technischer wie ästhetischer Ebene. In der Auseinandersetzung mit Sprachtechnologie wie automatisierten Übersetzungsprogrammen macht er ferner die mit der Translation verbundenen Umwandlungen sichtbar und fragt nach ihren möglichen gesellschaftlichen

Auswirkungen. Gemeinsam ist beiden Autor:innen, dass sie lyrische Verfahren als Ort der künstlerischen Erkundung der Materialität der Schrift selbst verstehen, mit der wiederum (einzel-)sprachliche wie mediale und kulturelle Mehrdeutigkeiten verknüpft sind, die in Translationsprozessen nicht unsichtbar gemacht, sondern vielmehr entfaltet werden sollten.

Quellenverzeichnis

Assmann, Aleida. „Lesen als Kippfigur. Buchstaben zwischen Transparenz und Bildlichkeit".
 Schriftbildlichkeit. Wahrnehmbarkeit, Materialität und Operativität von Notationen. Hg. Sybille Krämer, Eva Cancik-Kirschbaum und Rainer Totzke. Berlin: Akademie Verlag, 2012. 235–244.
Bartelmus, Martin und Alexander Nebrig. „Schriftlichkeit und die Agentilität der Schrift".
 Schriftlichkeit. Aktivität, Agentialität und Aktanden der Schrift. Hg. Martin Bartelmus und Alexander Nebrig. Bielefeld: Transcript, 2022. 7–38.
Benjamin, Walter. „Die Aufgabe des Übersetzers". *Gesammelte Schriften*. Bd. IV/1. Hg. Rolf Tiedemann und Herrmann Schweppenhäuser. Frankfurt a. M.: Suhrkamp, 1991. 9–21.
Benthien, Claudia. „Visuelle Polyphonie. Cia Rinnes archives zaroum als mediale Reflexion konkreter Poesie". *Übersetzen und Rahmen. Praktiken medialer Transformationen*. Hg. Claudia Benthien und Gabriele Klein. Paderborn: Fink, 2017. 123–140.
Benthien, Claudia und Brigitte Weingart. „Einleitung". *Handbuch Literatur & Visuelle Kultur*. Hg. Claudia Benthien und Brigitte Weingart. Berlin: De Gruyter, 2014. 1–30.
Fiedler, Heike. *langues de meehr*. Luzern: Der gesunde Menschenversand, 2010.
Fiedler, Heike. *sie will mehr*. Luzern: Der gesunde Menschenversand, 2013.
Fiedler, Heike. *Tu es! hier*. Luzern: Der gesunde Menschenversand, 2022.
Funkhouser, Christopher. „Digital Poetry: A Look at Generative, Visual, and Interconnected Possibilities in its First Four Decades". *A Companion to Digital Literary Studies*. Hg. Ray Siemens und Susan Schreibman. Malden, MA: Blackwell, 2007. 318–335.
Gunkel, Katrin. *Poesie und Poetik translingualer Vielfalt. Zum Englischen in der deutschen Gegenwartslyrik*. Wien: Praesens, 2020.
Hayles, N. Katherine. *How We Became Posthuman. Virtual Bodies in Cybernetics, Literature, and Informatics*. Chicago: Univ. of Chicago Press, 1999.
Hayles, N. Katherine. *Postprint. Books and Becoming Computational*. New York: Columbia Univ. Press, 2021.
Jäger, Ludwig. „Die Sprachvergessenheit der Medientheorie. Ein Plädoyer für das Medium Sprache".
 Sprache und neue Medien. Hg. Werner Kallmeyer. Berlin: De Gruyter, 2000. 9–30.
Jakobson, Roman. „On Linguistic Aspects of Translation". *On Translation*. Hg. Reuben Arthur Browner. Cambridge, MA: Harvard Univ. Press, 1959. 232–239.
Jakobson, Roman. „Was ist Poesie". *Poetik*. Hg. und Übers. Elmar Holenstein und Tarcisius Schelbert. Frankfurt a. M.: Suhrkamp, 1979a. 67–82.
Jakobson, Roman. „Linguistik und Poetik". *Poetik*. Hg. und Übers. Elmar Holenstein und Tarcisius Schelbert. Frankfurt a. M.: Suhrkamp, 1979b. 83–121.
Krämer, Sybille, Eva Cancik-Kirschbaum und Rainer Totzke. „Einleitung. Was bedeutet Schriftbildlichkeit?". *Schriftbildlichkeit. Wahrnehmbarkeit, Materialität und Operativität von*

Notationen. Hg. Sybille Krämer, Eva Cancik-Kirschbaum und Rainer Totzke. Berlin: Akademie Verlag, 2012. 13–38.

Nantke, Julia. „Normalisierung als Bedingung von Schriftlichkeit am Beispiel digitaler Repräsentationen von Schrift". *Schriftlichkeit. Aktivität, Agentialität und Aktanden der Schrift*. Hg. Martin Bartelmus und Alexander Nebrig. Bielefeld: Transcript, 2022. 39–54.

Neumann, Birgit. *Die Sichtbarkeit der Übersetzung. Zielsprache Deutsch*. Tübingen: narr, 2021.

Piringer, Jörg. *datenpoesie*. Klagenfurt: Ritter, 2018.

Portela, Manuel. „Signs in the Machine. The Poem as Data Flow". *Media Theories and Cultural Technologies*. Hg. Maria Teresa Cruz. Cambridge: Cambridge Scholars Publishing, 2017. 99–115.

Schaffner, Anna Katharina. „Assaulting the Order of Signs". *Dada Culture. Critical Texts on the Avant-Garde*. Hg. Dafydd Jones. Amsterdam: Rodopoi, 2006. 117–133.

Schaffner, Anna Katharina. „Dissecting the Order of Signs. On the Textual Politics of Dada Poetics". *Dada and Beyond*. Bd. 1: *Dada Discourses*. Hg. Elza Adamovicz und Eric Robertson. Amsterdam: Rodopoi, 2011. 37–50.

Simanowski, Roberto. *Textmaschinen – Kinetische Poesie – Interaktive Installation. Zum Verstehen von Kunst in digitalen Medien*. Bielefeld: Transcript, 2012.

Strehovec, Janez. „Alphabet on the Move. Digital Poetry and the Realm of Language". *Reading Moving Letters*. Hg. Roberto Simanowski, Jörgen Schäfer und Peter Gendolla. Bielefeld: Transcript, 2010. 207–230.

Suter, Beat und René Bauer. „Code und Wirkung". *Code und Konzept. Literatur und das Digitale*. Hg. Hannes Bajohr. Berlin: Frohmann, 2016. 71–87.

Venuti, Lawrence. *The Translator's Invisibility. A History of Translation*. London: Routledge, 1995.

Vorrath, Wiebke. „Unter der Oberfläche? Programmierte Schriftlichkeit in digitaler Lyrik". *Schriftlichkeit. Aktivität, Agentialität und Aktanden der Schrift*. Hg. Martin Bartelmus und Alexander Nebrig. Bielefeld: Transcript, 2022. 55–69.

Zemanek, Evi. „Exophone, transkulturelle, polyglotte Lyrik". *Handbuch Lyrik*. Hg. Dieter Lamping. Stuttgart: Metzler, 2016. 478–479.

Hiroshi Yamamoto
„Schneiden, Spleißen und punktgenaue Mutation!" Zu Text-Bild-Korrespondenzen im digitalen Zeitalter in Gerhard Falkners und Yves Netzhammers *Ignatien*

2016 hat der Literaturwissenschaftler Michael Braun den Band *Die zweite Schöpfung. Poesie und Bildende Kunst* herausgegeben, in dem er mit Klaus Merz, Nico Bleutge, Gerhard Falkner, Marcus Roloff und Silke Scheuermann Gespräche über deren Bildgedichte führt. Es ist bemerkenswert, dass einzig Gerhard Falkner, der zweitälteste unter den fünf interviewten Dichter:innen, auf digitale Kunst Bezug nimmt. Dies ist zunächst verblüffend, denn seine skeptische Haltung gegenüber den neuen Medien und dem „‚Vampirismus' in der gegenwärtigen Kultur" (Braun und Falkner 2016, 42) ist bekannt: Falkner äußerte in diesem Interview weiter, „dass die Kommunikation über die sozialen Medien und über die neuen technischen Möglichkeiten Massenbetäubungsmittel darstellt" (Braun und Falkner 2016, 43). Allerdings ist er kein konservativer Dichter, der sich bloß von der Wirklichkeit im digitalen Zeitalter abwenden und sich mit dem Vokabular aus der konventionellen Naturlyrik begnügen würde. So liest man in einem seiner Gedichte:

> Den Mond und die Wiesen sind wir
> endgültig los, den Hain und die Linde.
> Wir sind allein aufs Sein gestellt, wir Schließlichen.
> Wir leben zwischen ökologischem Algorithmus
> und metrosexuellem Download
> als individueller Strahlungswiderstand.
> (Falkner 2014, 60)[1]

Im digitalen Zeitalter wird selbst die Natur nach dem mathematischen Algorithmus kalkuliert und nahezu vollständig kontrolliert, während man in der Metropole in körperlosen Cybersex verfällt. Statt zu bestätigen, appelliert das Gedicht eher an „uns", „Sand, nicht Öl im Getriebe der Welt" (Eich 1991, 384) zu werden.

Als er 2014 in Zusammenarbeit mit dem Medienkünstler Yves Netzhammer den bebilderten Gedichtband *Ignatien. Elegien am Rande des Nervenzusammen-*

---

[1] Nachfolgend werden die Nachweise der Gedichtzitate aus *Ignatien* (Falkner und Netzhammer 2014) der besseren Lesbarkeit wegen jeweils nur mit (Falkner 2014) angegeben, während die Bilder aus demselben Band mit (Netzhammer 2014) nachgewiesen werden.

Open Access. © 2023 bei den Autorinnen und Autoren, publiziert von De Gruyter. [CC BY-NC-ND] Dieses Werk ist lizensiert unter der Creative Commons Namensnennung - Nicht-kommerziell - Keine Bearbeitungen 4.0 International Lizenz.
https://doi.org/10.1515/9783111299334-013

bruchs publizierte, erfolgte die Auswahl des künstlerischen Partners zwar nicht aus freien Stücken, sondern im Auftrag des Verlegers, jedoch hat Falkner die vielen „überraschende[n] Korrespondenzen" (Braun und Falkner 2016, 44) zwischen sich und Netzhammer umgehend festgestellt. Offensichtlich gefällt Falkner, dass Netzhammer ebenso wie er selbst „mit dieser Verbindung von exaktem, technischem und formalem Kalkül mit der surrealistischen Bildmetapher" (Braun und Falkner 2016, 44) arbeitet. Der Künstler, für den der digitale Raum mit „dem Raum der Imagination eng verwandt" ist, versucht, mit Computertechniken traumähnliche Szenarien zu kreieren (vgl. Keller 2018). Auch dem Dichter scheint es daran gelegen, angesichts der „Sprechnot" „in einer totalitär durchrationalisierten, verwalteten, digitalisierten Welt" (Geist 2007, 642) die Möglichkeiten und die Grenzen der Poesie auszuloten. Das Ergebnis der dichterisch-künstlerischen Zusammenarbeit als Bildgedicht im konventionellen Sinne zu bezeichnen, wäre jedoch irreführend. Wie die englische Übersetzung der Dichterin Ann Cotten, mit der der Band versehen ist, nicht immer wortgetreu umgesetzt ist, sondern an einigen Stellen *transmuted* wird, so fällt es schwer, zwischen den 20 Gedichten Falkners und den 30 Bildern Netzhammers einen direkten Bezug auszumachen: Es bleibt letztlich unklar, ob die Bilder den Gedichten als Vorlage dienen oder umgekehrt, bzw. ob überhaupt von einer Entsprechung zwischen den lyrischen und künstlerischen Arbeiten die Rede sein kann. Fest steht nur, dass Falkner die Ansätze weiterführt, die er bei Netzhammer vorfindet, und umgekehrt.

Falkner verschließt sich auch nicht der aktuellen Populärkultur, wenn er etwa den deutschen Untertitel für den oben genannten Band aus dem auch in Deutschland bekannten spanischen Spielfilm *Frauen am Rande des Nervenzusammenbruchs* entleiht. Wenn er das einzelne Gedicht als „Ignatia" bezeichnet und deren Sammlung mit *Ignatien* betitelt, mag dies den Verdacht nahelegen, dass er damit auf einen ironisch-komischen Effekt abzielt, handelt es sich in der Homöopathie bei der „Ignatia" oder bei der „Ignazbohne" doch um ein höchst fragwürdiges Hausmittel gegen die „bipolare[] Störung, also d[ie] manisch-depressive[] Erkrankung" (Braun und Falkner 2016, 40). Insofern erscheinen die Gedichte als manisches Sprechen und homöopathisches Mittel zugleich, die als eine Art Reaktion auf die oben zitierte „Sprechnot in der durchrationalisierten digitalen Welt" interpretiert werden könnten. In *Ignatien* geht es Falkner allerdings tatsächlich darum, nicht einfach manisches Sprechen in der Dichtung zu präsentieren, wie es in der Antike bei „der ekstatischen Prophetie und de[m] göttlich inspirierten Orakel[]" (Braun und Falkner 2016, 40 f.), oder auch in der Moderne, beispielsweise in den *Dionysos-Dithyramben* von Nietzsche, zu finden ist, sondern es „durch wissenschaftliche Sprache gegenzukaschieren" (Braun und Falkner 2016, 41). Wie dieser Fachausdruck aus der Buchbinderei nahelegt, der so viel wie die Rückseite eines Bildes zu stabilisieren bedeutet, wird hier dazu aufgefordert, das ‚manische

Sprechen' mit der wissenschaftlichen Sprache gleichzeitig zu unterstützen und zu bezähmen, damit sie nicht gänzlich ins Irrationale abdriftet.

Wenn Falkner Manie nicht nur als furchterregend und angsteinflößend, sondern auch als heilig bezeichnet (vgl. Braun und Falkner 2016), dann ruft er wohl in Erinnerung, was Sokrates in Phaidros über die „herrliche[n] Wirkungen des von den Göttern kommenden Rausches" (Platon 1979, 41) äußert, den Ausdruck „Mania" (Platon 1979, 40) also in einem gänzlich positiven Sinne verwendet. In jedem heiligen Rausch spielen wie im Tanz, in der ekstatischen Prophetie und in der Liebesraserei die unkontrollierbaren Körper eine wichtige Rolle. Sie können einerseits als Störfaktor den reibungslosen technologischen Abläufen Widerstand leisten. Die vereinfachten und mutierten Körper und Körperteile der Menschen und der Tiere, die in den Bildern Netzhammers und in den Gedichten Falkners auffallen, zeigen andererseits wohl, wie sehr sich das moderne Konzept des einheitlichen Körpers im digitalen Zeitalter verwandelt hat. Im Folgenden soll unter besonderer Berücksichtigung des Körpers im technisch-imaginären Raum untersucht werden, welche Korrespondenzen zwischen Kunst und Dichtung in *Ignatien* entstehen.

Yves Netzhammers digitale Bildästhetik

In der Forschung zu den computergenerierten Zeichnungen und Animationen Netzhammers wird immer wieder dessen „durch Sterilität und Glätte gekennzeichneter ,Bildkosmos'" (Burkhard 2018, 6) hervorgehoben: In einem leeren Raum, meistens in einem fensterlosen dunklen Innenraum, bewegen sich nackte geschlechtsneutrale Marionetten mit „[m]akellose[n], plastikähnliche[n] und glänzende[n] Oberflächen", die „in ihren illustrierenden Vereinfachungen an Gebrauchsgrafik und Comics" (Kaufhold 2001, 17) erinnern. Diese Figuren kommen auf eine intime, aber auch gewaltige Weise in Berührung mit anderen Puppen oder mit Pflanzen und mit Tieren wie Affen und Vögeln, um sich in verschiedene Mischwesen zu verwandeln wie zu einem Baummenschen, aus dessen Körper Äste und Blätter wie aus einem Baumstamm sprießen. Mal werden den Lebewesen auch leblose Dinge implantiert, zum Beispiel Spiegel, mal wird eine abgetrennte Hand mit einem Vogel verwachsen dargestellt, indem das zerrissene Handgelenk zu einem Flügel und zwei der Finger zu Hühnerbeinen transformiert werden. Was Netzhammers Werk faszinierend macht, liegt gerade darin, dass er immer wieder einen solchen Prozess der Metamorphosen in Gang setzt.

Yves Netzhammer wird, ebenso wie Gerhard Mantz, Gero Gries, Martin Dörbaum und Yoichiro Kawaguchi, als repräsentativer Produzent der „kameralose[n]

Digitalbilder" (Kaufhold 2001, 8) bezeichnet. In Abgrenzung zur vorherrschenden Computerästhetik, die aus der kameratechnisch abgebildeten Wirklichkeit hervorgeht, beginnt ihre Arbeit am leeren Bildschirm. Ohne jeden Bezug auf Vorbilder in der Wirklichkeit, schöpfen sie die Bilder aus der eigenen Fantasie und brechen auf diese Weise mit dem mimetischen Prinzip – dem hartnäckigen Vorurteil zum Trotz, dass digitale Techniken den Künstler:innen für die schöpferische Verwendung keinen Spielraum ließen. Sie hinterlassen in den computergenerierten Bildern gleichsam ihre eigenen handwerklichen Spuren. An der Art und Weise, wie Netzhammer einerseits die Bild- und Formsprache bewusst reduziert und andererseits die Mutationen wie Kettenreaktionen abwickelt, kann man so auch „unterschiedliche Emotionswerte und individuelle Gefühle" (Kaufhold 2001, 23) erkennen. Netzhammer selbst versteht sich als „Zeichner mit ganz klassischer Ausbildung" (Netzhammer und Jocks 2007, 194). Seine Digitalästhetik wird von der Kritik als „fortschrittlich-

Abb. 32: Yves Netzhammer. Ohne Titel. *Ignatien*. 2014. 30.

archaisch[]" (Röller 2008, 174) bezeichnet: Bei der Nutzung der digitalen Ausdrucksformen verzichtet er auf zeitgemäße effektvolle *Raytracing*-Programme. Stattdessen bringt er von Anfang an eine heutzutage veraltete, zeitaufwendige CAD-Software zum Einsatz, „die ursprünglich für architektonische Entwürfe entwickelt wurde" (Kania 2016, 69).

Der Künstler selbst betont immer wieder, „dass man auch in eine ganz einfache Computerzeichnung viel Subjektivität stecken kann" (Netzhammer und Gasser 2011, 98). Wenn die Computerästhetik gemeinhin „mit Kühlheit und Distanz" gleichgesetzt wird, so fasse man sie zu eng. Die digitale Kunst kann und soll Netzhammer zufolge „eine eigenständige Sprache [...] generieren" (Netzhammer und Gasser 2011, 104). Die Möglichkeit für seine eigene Handschrift, sieht er allerdings weniger in einer medienspezifischen „Geschwindigkeit" und in einer genauen, detailtreuen Wiedergabe der Wirklichkeit als vielmehr in einer Inszenierung der Künstlichkeit und einer „eigenwillige[n], bewusst reduzierte[n] Bild- und Formensprache" (Netzhammer und Gasser 2011, 96). Die Oberflächentextur der Figuren und der Dinge ist glatt, selbst die Menschen und die Tiere haben „ihre schrundige unregelmäßige Haut gegen eine künstliche, blanke eingetauscht" (Stegmann 1999). Sowohl in der Farbgebung als auch in der Darstellung der Bewegung verhält sich der Künstler dezent. Während die Gangart der Figuren „tastend[]" (Schmidt 2003, 29) und „schablonenhaft" (Ermacora 2003, 11) ist, verwendet Netzhammer nur sehr wenige Farben, die abgesehen von Grau und Rosa für die Puppenkörper fast ausschließlich aus den drei Grundfarben Gelb, Rot und Blau sowie aus Schwarz und Weiß besteht.

Die Pointe seiner künstlerischen Ausdrucksform liegt jedoch darin, dass seine „reduzierte[] und abstrahierte[] Stilistik" (Netzhammer und Gasser 2011, 99) mit zahlreichen Leerstellen, die einen Bruch mit naturalistischen Darstellungsweisen markieren, gerade die Phantasie der Zuschauer:innen stärker anregen. In seiner Ästhetik stellt die künstliche Szenerie eine „eigengesetzliche Gegenwelt" dar, denn die Arbeit am Computer zwingt Netzhammer, sich „aus verbalen, gesellschaftlich etablierten Kommunikationsformen" herauszunehmen (Netzhammer und Jocks 2007, 198). Allerdings will sich der Künstler keineswegs selbstgenügsam in einer solipsistischen Festung verschanzen. Durch den ständigen Prozess der Mutation mit dem Disparaten, in den sich alle Lebewesen und Dinge in seiner Bilderwelt verwickeln, sprengt er immer wieder „die Vorstellung des einen geschlossenen Körperpanzers" (Volkart 2015, 94). Insofern kann der räumliche Gegenentwurf zur Realität keinen stabilen Fluchtort darstellen, sondern er ist auch zu jeder Zeit den Möglichkeiten der Transformationen ausgesetzt.

Wenn Netzhammer früher in den statischen Digitalzeichnungen eher auf ein „Netzwerk an Bildern" setzte, so versucht er seit Beginn des 21. Jahrhunderts auch in Form von Animationsfilmen oder Installationen kompliziertere Geschichten zu erzählen. Sie sind allerdings nicht etwa „auf narrative Stringenz" (Netzhammer und Stegmann 2014) ausgerichtet, wie beispielsweise auf eine konsequente Handlung oder einen individuell geprägten Charakter. Vor allem „mit ihren permanenten Brüchen, Kehrtwendungen und parallelen Ebene[n]" (Netzhammer und Stegmann 2014) werden sie bewusst gestört. Um „[m]it scheinbar einfachsten ‚Formulierung[en]'" Begriffsverwirrung zu stiften (Kaufhold 2001, 18), kommen zwei Effekte zum Einsatz, durch die sich das kameralose Digitalbild auszeichnet: „die gleichmäßige Konturschärfe in allen Ebenen" und „die Variationsmöglichkeiten der Perspektive" (Kaufhold 2001, 22). Das virtuelle Licht wird auch in weitumfassenden Brechungen und Spiegelungen eingesetzt. So entziehen sich seine Digitalbilder dem photographischen Realismus. In vielerlei Hinsicht steht die eigenständige Bildsprache Netzhammers, wie im Folgenden näher erläutert wird, in engem Zusammenhang mit der lyrischen Sprache Falkners, insbesondere mit Reduktion, Künstlichkeit und Sinnverwirrung.

Die Engel vor den Portalen von Facebook

Ein Hauptmerkmal der Text-Bild-Korrespondenzen in *Ignatien* besteht nicht bloß im Verzicht der Gedichte, die Bilder des Künstlers einfach zu beschreiben, sondern vielmehr darin, die Überlegungen über die Genese und die Ästhetik der digitalen Kunst und die Auswirkungen der neuen Medien auf das Leben und den Körper der Menschen in der genuin lyrischen Sprache anzustellen – wodurch ein inhaltlicher Bezug zu Netzhammers Bildern gegeben ist. In den Gedichten führt Falkner neben verschiedenen griechischen und germanischen Gött:innen Philosophen wie Hegel, Derrida und de Saussure sowie Naturwissenschaftler wie die DNA-Entdecker James Watson und Francis Crick namentlich und teilweise sprachspielerisch an: „Derrida! die Blumen sind da!" (Falkner 2014, 31). Auch zahlreiche Fachbegriffe aus diversen Wissensbereichen kommen zum Vorschein, deren Tragweite von der Soziologie („emergente Ordnung") über die Biologie („Homöobox") bis zur Informatik („Webarchitekt", „Notebook" und „Gigabyte") reicht. Dabei liegt der Akzent eindeutig auf Begriffen des digitalen Zeitalters, etwa die heutige Informationstechnologie und die sozialen Netzwerke betreffend.

Die Bezugnahme Falkners auf das Internet erschöpft sich allerdings nicht bloß in der Nennung einzelner Begriffe, sondern sie durchdringt sowohl die thematische als auch die stilistische Ebene der Gedichtsammlung. Nachdem im Gedicht „Ignatia 9" der Gründer des sozialen Netzwerks Facebook, Mark Zuckerberg, erwähnt wurde, treten die Schlüsselverse in Erscheinung, in denen die Subjekte und die Räume im digitalen Zeitalter gedacht werden, und die insbesondere für das Verständnis des dichterischen Konzepts von *Ignatien* relevant sind: „Die Engel liegen als Punks mit gepiercten Augen / vor den Portalen von Facebook." (Falkner 2014, 51) Diese Verse, die an Kafkas Parabel *Vor dem Gesetz* erinnern, stellen den Cyberspace vor als einen verschlossenen Raum mit zahlreichen Toren. Angenommen, dass die Engel hier für Menschen im digitalen Zeitalter stehen, so sinken sie vor der gigantischen Macht des Plattformbetreibenden in Ohnmacht und haben aus Verzweiflung ihrem eigenen Körper Wunden zugefügt. Es ist allerdings nicht zu übersehen, dass sie sich nicht wie der tragische Held Ödipus selbst geblendet haben, sondern weiterhin sehen können. Die Engel stellen bloß, aus einem anderen Gesichtspunkt betrachtet, mit ihren Piercings bewusst eine Körpermodifikation zur Schau. Diesen Engeln, die in sich die Tragik und die Maskierungs- und Inszenierungslust miteinander verbinden, kommt ein janusköpfiger Charakter zu, der auch der hier erörterten Gedichtsammlung zugrunde liegt.

Wenn in den Computerzeichnungen und Animationen Netzhammers die beständige Metamorphose auf die Realität im digitalen Zeitalter Bezug nimmt, in der das moderne Konzept vom einheitlichen autonomen Individuum außer Kraft gesetzt wurde, so wird der Mensch auch in den *Ignatien*-Gedichten einfach als „Auslaufmodell Mensch" (Falkner 2014, 25) oder als „das schwer mit Prothesen bewaffnete / völlig entgeisterte Ungetüm Mensch" (Falkner 2014, 60) bezeichnet. An seine Stelle treten einmal Mischwesen, wie sie auch bei Netzhammer immer wieder anzutreffen sind, und ein anderes Mal eben Engel. Allerdings stehen diese nicht bloß für Menschen, sondern sie sind auch in einem literatur- und kunsthistorischen Kontext zu sehen. Falkner hat angemerkt, dass das Buch mit dem Untertitel *Elegien* „als ein fernes Echo auf die Duineser Elegien" (Braun und Falkner 2016, 39) von Rilke konzipiert wurde. Abgesehen davon, dass in Allen Ginsbergs Langgedicht „Howl (Das Geheul)", das Falkner im Gespräch neben Nietzsches *Dionysos-Dithyramben* als Paradebeispiel des manischen Sprechens in der Poesie erwähnt, viele Engel vorkommen, wird ferner ein Engel aus der Kunstgeschichte zweimal im Gedichtband in Erinnerung gerufen: Der Engel Michael aus dem Gemälde *Verkündigung an Maria*, das aus der Feder des italienischen Renaissancemalers Lorenzo Lotto stammt (vgl. Falkner 2014, 20; 55). Darin bricht der Künstler insofern mit den Konventionen des *Annuntiatio*-Stoffs, als er die bekannte biblische Geschichte auf eine bewusst einfache und direkte Weise erzählt, um sie dem alltäglichen Realismus anzunähern. In den Vordergrund tritt so der Engel mit den kräftigen Gliedern, der eher wie ein Einbrecher als ein heiliger Gottesbote wirkt, und vor dem Maria überbestürzt flüchtet. Indem Falkner im Gedicht diesen Engel als „Inbegriff von Wollust und Eile" (Falkner 2014, 55) bezeichnet, treibt er nicht nur den Bruch mit der Tradition auf die Spitze, sondern er bewirkt nach der Manier Netzhammers eine kleine Verschiebung:

> Der Engel Lorenzo Lottos erscheint
> und übernimmt die Verkündigung:
> Wenn die Sprache spricht, geschieht, was sie sagt!
> sagt er. [...]
>
> (Falkner 2014, 20)

Durch das Ersetzen des „Gottes" durch „die Sprache" in der biblischen Wendung „Wenn er spricht, so geschieht's" (Psalm 33, 9) wird das Augenmerk von dem Urheber auf das Medium bzw. den Boten gelenkt. Wie in der performativen Sprechakttheorie Austins wird hier die Sprache zum Schöpfer. In diesem Kontext lohnt es sich, die Überlegungen Michel Serres in seinen Schriften *Die Legende der Engel* und *Der Parasit* in Betracht zu ziehen. In der heutigen Informationswelt, in der „flüssige[n], fließende[n] und manchmal sogar fluktuierende[n] Welt" (Serres 1995, 44), nehmen die Engel als Austauschende und Übersetzende an den Knotenpunkten im Netz der milliardenfach in sich verschlungenen Beziehungen Platz, um sie untereinander zu verbinden und miteinander kommunizierbar zu machen. Allerdings halten diese Vermittler:innen nicht immer systemkonform den Verkehr unter Kontrolle, sondern verursachen auch oft wie Parasiten im Netzwerk Verwirrung. Durch die parasitären Eingriffe, die „Unterbrechungen und Störungen" im Kommunikationsfluss, wird die

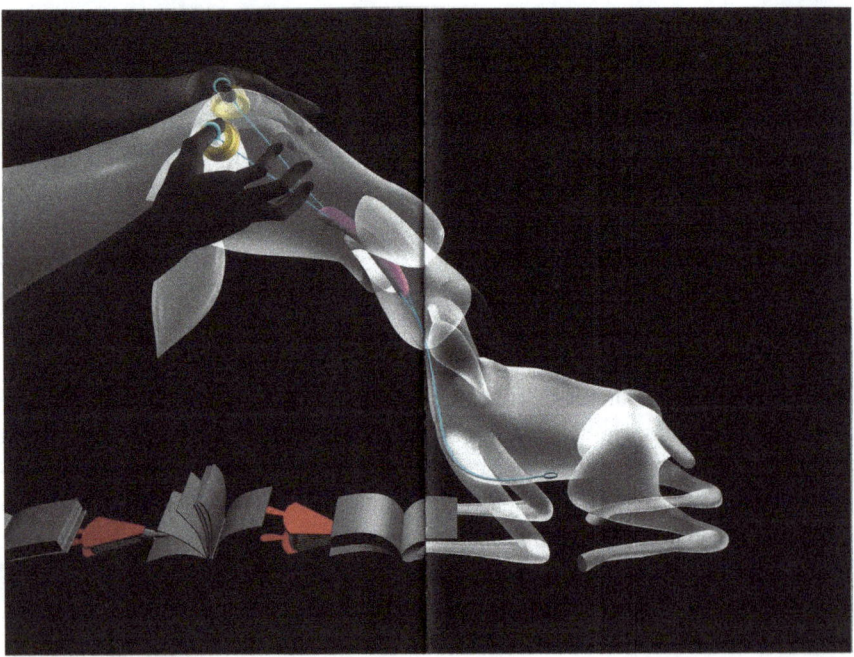

Abb. 33: Yves Netzhammer. Ohne Titel. *Ignatien*. 2014. 64–65.

Botschaft nicht einfach gestört, sondern sie kann sich, so Serres in *Der Parasit*, teilweise „durch Mutation, Abwesenheit, Substitution oder Verschiebung von Elementen" (Serres 1987, 282) verändern. Die geschlechtslosen Engel bzw. Cherubim in der Gestalt des geflügelten Stiers gewährleisten „die Möglichkeit der Übergänge und die Plastizität des Kommunikationssystems" (Serres 1995, 166). Während Geschlecht Trennung bedeutet, vereinen die hermaphroditischen Engel. Die „amphibische[n] Wesen" „leben in beständigem Koitus" (Serres 1995, 166), um jede Grenze porös zu machen, was, wie gezeigt wurde, in den Bildern Netzhammers, der übrigens selbst auch seine geistige Nähe zum französischen Denker betont (vgl. Netzhammer und Jocks 2007, 200), vielfach Entsprechung findet.

Auch Falkner hebt in der Wendung „[k]ein Netz ohne Knoten" (Falkner 2014, 20) die entscheidende Rolle eines Boten im digitalen Zeitalter hervor und bringt seinen Engel ebenfalls mit Sexualität in Beziehung. Dabei lenkt er die Aufmerksamkeit insbesondere auf dessen Fluidität, die sich nur schwer sprachlich fassen lassen: Die Engel werden als „[e]ntsetzlich zart" bezeichnet, so zart „wie die Gelüste einer Frau" oder „[w]ie ein junger Mann, gestaltet wie ein Seufzer / der einen Strand entlangweht, dessen Weite ihn auslöscht" oder „[w]ie der Fühler des Zitronenfalters" (Falkner 2014, 51). Eine ähnliche Begeisterung für das Ephemere und Flüchtige lässt sich in einem weiteren Gedicht, „Ignatia 4", ausmachen:

> Hörst du es nicht?
> Dies schläfrige Anschlagen der Brandung.
> Wind
> Wimperntusche und Lipgloss.
> [...]
> Hat das Zyklopenauge der Webcams
> den Gang all dieser Dinge festgehalten
> die immer kürzere Zeit brauchen
> um im Sand zu verlaufen?
> Spurlos übergreifend ins Nebensächliche.
> So klein inzwischen
> wie der Abstand zwischen Nepal und Neapel.
> Legathenisch winzig. Wie
> die Lücke zwischen dem Jetzt und der Bahnsteigkante.
> (Falkner 2014, 25)

Es handelt sich bei „all diese[n] Dingen" um Naturerscheinungen wie „Brandung" und „Wind", die sich wie in Ewigkeit wiederholen, so dass der Gang der einzelnen Welle oder des einzelnen Luftzuges schwer feststellbar ist, oder um die Toilettenartikel, die keine Stabilität zeigen, sondern von einem Augenblick zum anderen verfließen und sich verflüchtigen wie Flügel eines Schmetterlings. Wenn „die Dinge", wie in einem anderen Gedicht bemerkt wird, „jeder Beschreibung" „spotten" (Falkner 2014, 86), so wird hier kritisch gezeigt, dass selbst das scharfsichtigste Auge der nagelneuen Digitalkamera außerstande ist, alles zu registrieren, was sich in der Welt gar nicht behaupten will, sondern schon im gleichen Augenblick, in dem es geboren wird, so unauffällig wie möglich wieder verschwindet, ohne jede Spur zu hinterlassen. Auch wenn der Apparat „den Gang" oder besser das Zittern „all dieser Dinge" optiktechnisch aufnehmen möge, so wird er jedoch im sensationssüchtigen digitalen Zeitalter wohl als langweilig gebrandmarkt und sofort aus dem allgemeinen Interesse entfernt. Außerdem wissen diese flüchtigen Dinge von einer linearen Teleologie gar nichts, sondern verfolgen „verwegen / die Richtungsarmut [ihrer] Ziele" (Falkner 2014, 89), wiederholen unendlich wie ein „Reigen" (Falkner 2014, 74) und wie „Karusselle" (Falkner 2014, 36) einen Kreislauf.

Im System kleine „Lücke[n]" oder gerade Verschiebungen wie einen Druckfehler ausfindig zu machen, darin sieht Falkner die Aufgabe seiner Dichtung. Es ist in einer gebrochenen Weise, in der er, wie oben bereits erwähnt, die *Duineser Elegien* zitiert. In der ersten „Ignatia" nimmt er auf deren berühmten Eröffnungsvers „WER, wenn ich schriee, hörte mich denn aus der Engel Ordnungen?" (Rilke 1982, 441) Bezug und formuliert diesen um in: „Wer, wenn nicht ich, hörte mich denn / aus der Enge der Ordnungen" (Falkner 2014, 11). An diesem Beispiel wird eines der poetischen Verfahren Falkners erkennbar, um die Lücke sichtbar zu machen, nämlich das der Permutation, durch das jedes Sprachgebilde seine feste Kontur verliert und in den beständigen Prozess der Transformation gerät. Darin lässt sich eine weitere Korrespondenz zwischen Lyrik und Kunst in *Ignatien* beobachten: Der Dichter versucht in den Gedichten mit den Sprachkörpern das umzusetzen, was der Künstler in den Bildern am Figurenkörper „mit kleinen morphologischen Verschiebungen" (Netzhammer und Gasser 2011, 97) geschehen lässt.

Eingefrorene Räume

Auch auf die sterilen „kühlfarbigen Szenerien" (Keller 2018), in denen die Figuren Netzhammers fast immer gefangen sind, nimmt Falkner in seiner lyrischen Topografie Bezug, wie auf deren „Öffnungen", die mal als „Schnittstellen zwischen Außen und Innen" (Lukowicz und Wagner 2016, 28), mal als „grenzüberschreitende kommunikative Kontakte" (Laukötter 2005, 12) bezeichnet werden. In den Gedichten fehlt es zwar meistens an Ortsangaben, jedoch ist nicht nur vom Tor, das auf ein geschlossenes Terrain hinweist, sondern auch immer wieder vom zu lüftenden Zimmer oder vom aufzumachenden Fenster die Rede (vgl. Falkner 2014, 60 und 71). Selbst die Landschaft draußen wird oft als totenstille Einöde dargestellt, aus der es keinen Ausweg gibt, wie eine hohe Gebirgslandschaft mit „der graslosen Nordwand" (Falkner 2014, 11) und wie eine nördliche Winterlandschaft mit dem „ewige[n] Eis" (Falkner 2014, 15). Die Erde ist nicht unendlich weit, sondern stellt wie ein Treibhaus nichts als „globale[] Abrundung" (Falkner 2014, 25) dar. Wenn der Dichter auf die räumliche Geschlossenheit und Enge fokussiert, so nimmt er nicht bloß auf die ästhetisch dargestellten Bildszenerien Netzhammers Bezug, sondern auch auf deren Rahmen, nämlich auf den computergenerierten digitalen Raum: Dieser ist, wie gezeigt wurde, von der Wirklichkeit völlig abgekoppelt. Selbst „die köstlichen alten Landschaften", die draußen nur scheinbar „prangen" (Falkner 2014, 20), sind unzugänglich, denn sie existieren ebenso lediglich auf dem digital hergestellten virtuellen Bild.

Der geschlossene Raum in den Gedichten kann ferner auch darauf bezogen werden, was in der Medienwissenschaft als Echokammer-Effekt kritisch diskutiert wird. Durch die Anwendung von Algorithmen versuchen Webseitenbetreiber:innen, den Benutzer:innen nur Informationen anzuzeigen, die ihre eigenen Ansichten unterstützen, bis diese schließlich in der „Echokammer" (Sunstein 2017, 5) oder in einer „Filterblase" (Pariser 2011, 9) völlig isoliert sind, was über den selektiven Nachrichtenkonsum zu einer Fragmentierung und Polarisierung der Gesellschaft führt (vgl. Gleich 2019).[2] Die euphorische Erwartung der frühen Tage des Internets, wonach dieses ein *Global Village* schaffe, das jede Distanz überwindet und in dem die Vision einer vollständigen Demokratie umgesetzt wird (vgl. McLuhan 1992, 13), wurde bisher nicht erfüllt. Stattdessen sind wir im Internet einer ständigen und umfassenden Kontrolle ausgesetzt, selbst unsere geheimen Wünsche und Begierden sind den Internetkonzernen bekannt und auf diese Weise manipulierbar geworden. Gerade mit diesen Problemen beschäftigen sich Falkners Gedichte, um einen Ausgang aus diesem Dilemma zu finden. Falkner weist auch auf die sogenannten „Dark Screens" (Falkner 2014, 66) bzw. den Black Screen hin, also auf einen Systemfehler. In dieser Computerwelt, in der die Wenigsten wissen, „worauf / die Erdgeschosse [des Systems] gründen, wann / das Unterirdische beginnt" (Falkner 2014, 25), in der es keine „Gewähr" (Falkner 2014, 71) gibt, kann ein kleiner *bug* zum *shutdown* des ganzen Betriebssystems führen, wie „die Division durch die Null" (Falkner 2014, 71), die insofern ein unausführbares Kommando darstellt, als sie keine einzige gültige, sondern unendlich viele Lösungen ergibt. Gerade in diesen Systemstörungen sieht Falkner, wie im Folgenden näher erläutert werden soll, die subversive Produktivität der Kunst.

Im Kontext des manischen Sprechens ist aber zunächst die Tatsache wichtig, dass die digitale Bilderwelt mit der Sprachwelt vergleichbar ist. Falkner geht von der poststrukturalistischen Prämisse aus, wonach „[d]as Bedeutende [...] seine Bedeutung" und „das Zeichen [...] das Bezeichnete [verfehlt]" (Falkner 2014, 14). Es geht ihm

---

2 Ob Echokammern tatsächlich derartige gesellschaftliche Auswirkungen haben, ist mittlerweile allerdings recht umstritten (vgl. Guess et. al. 2018).

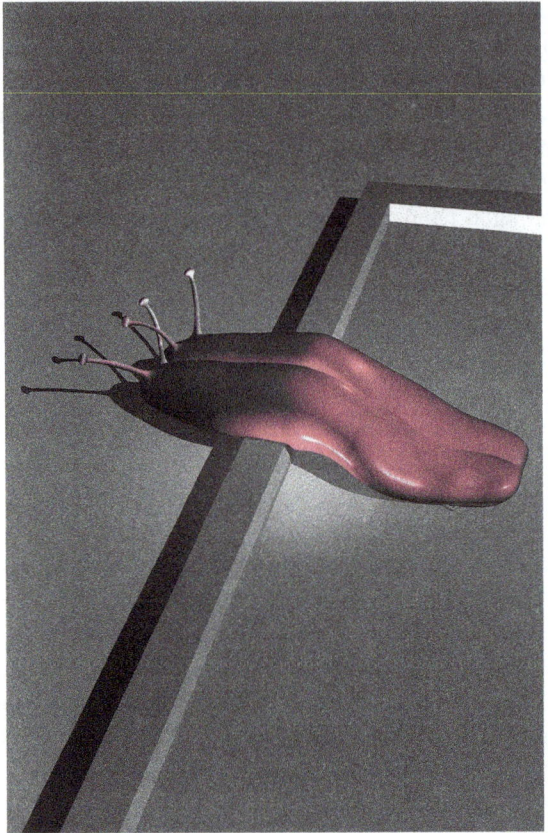

Abb. 34: Yves Netzhammer. Ohne Titel. *Ignatien*. 2014. 43.

darum, nach einem Ausweg aus dem logisch-grammatisch geregelten sprachlichen Gefängnis zu suchen. In den Gedichten wird auf verschiedenen Ebenen die Möglichkeit berücksichtigt, aus der aussichtslosen Enge, „aus der Unhintergehbarkeit / von Sprache / ins endlich Offene –" (Falkner 2014, 11) auszubrechen. Mit größter Aufmerksamkeit nimmt Falkner die kleinsten Anzeichen für den Durchbruch der geschlossenen Räume wahr und zeichnet auf, wie sich „[m]it einem leisen Kreischen" (Falkner 2014, 26) die Klettverschlüsse öffnen, wie „die Verschlusslaute p, t, k", die aus der „Magengrube" durch plötzliche Öffnung des Artikulationskanals erzeugt werden, „auf den Lippen platzen / PTK, PTK!" (Falkner 2014, 95). Es ist gerade die manische Raserei im platonischen Sinn, die in die glatte Oberfläche der geschlossenen Räume eine Ritze oder gar ein Loch reißen kann. Sie „bricht" wie „die Sonne den knarrenden Fels aus dem Eise" und lässt wie „Pulse [...] / mit gepolsterten Hämmern / Kontinentalplatten erklingen" (Falkner 2014, 86). Selbst die Haut des Menschen, die nach der Auffassung der Moderne einen „individuierten, monadischen bürgerlichen Körper" (Benthien 2001, 49) umhüllt, ist „zu Tausenden, zu Tausenden verwundet worden" (Falkner 2014, 86), so sehr, dass sie wieder „zum porösen, offenen und zugleich grotesk mit der Welt verwobenen Leib" wird (Benthien 2001, 49). Die Abgeschlossenheit in Falkners Versen bleibt somit nicht nur auf Räume bezogen, sondern auch auf Körper, wobei sie sich im manischen Sprechen öffnen und neu verbinden lassen.

Im Gedichtband tritt von den vier göttlichen Rasereien nach Platon neben der poetischen, insbesondere auch die mystische bacchantische „Turbulenz" (Falkner 2014, 61), in der geschwelgt, pokuliert und mit der Trommelmusik getanzt wird, sowie der Liebeswahn in den Vordergrund. Die liebkosende „Spitze eines Lächelns" statt einer Lanze, ist in der Lage, „die Eisflächen zu ritzen" (Falkner 2014, 86). Denn die Liebe kann aus der allmächtigen Kontrolle des „gültige[n] Algorithmus" geraten, der „bei der gleichen Voraussetzung / zum selben Ergebnis führt" (Falkner 2014, 61). In der 19. „Ignatia" bricht das lyrische Ich, als es vor sich „plötzlich ein Du, eine Referenz, ein Objekt / eine Geliebte" (Falkner 2014, 95) sieht, endlich aus dem verschlossenen Sprachgefängnis aus, um die „glitzernden prähistorischen Ebenen" zu erreichen und auf der „schriftlosen Weite die Hufe der Büffel / klappern" (Falkner 2014, 95) zu hören. Im euphorischen Augenblick, in dem im Riss des Sprachgefängnisses eine reale „Referenz" in Erscheinung tritt, verwandelt sich die logisch-grammatisch geregelte Welt in eine schriftlose, worin auch die Grenze der Wahrnehmungskategorie außer Geltung gerät. Denn das Klappern der „Hufe der Büffel" erreicht nicht nur akustisch das Ohr des lyrischen Ich, sondern die „wie bewegliche Lettern" (Falkner 2014, 95) materialisierten Geräusche, die bis ans Ohr dringen, sind zugleich lesbar und physisch verletzbar.

Allerdings bedeutet dieser überglückliche Augenblick der synästhetischen Wahrnehmung im Gedichtband keine Klimax. Im letzten Gedicht, „Ignatia 20", kehrt eine melancholische Resignation zurück. Durch den Perspektivenwechsel wird darin das Liebespaar des vorletzten Gedichts angesprochen: „Ihr, die ihr geliebt habt / die ihr den Traum des Unwahrscheinlichen geträumt habt / den die Grausamkeit Hoffnung nennt" (Falkner 2014, 101). Darauf folgt ein doppelter Imperativ, sich zu „entarte[n]" und „die Sprache / [...] ins Unenthüllte" zu „entrück[en]" (Falkner 2014, 101). Zum einen wird erwartet, in der überhellen Welt der Informationen ein mutierter Störfaktor zu werden, jener „individuelle[] Strahlungswiderstand" (Falkner 2014, 60), der bereits besprochen wurde. Zum anderen wird gefordert, die Sprache aus den Händen der reibungslosen Informationsmitteilung zu befreien und wieder für das Enigmatische der Dichtung zurückzugewinnen.

Mutation

Um den Algorithmus des Cyberspace zu unterlaufen und die glatte Oberfläche der Informationssprache ‚zu ritzen', spielt das imperativisch eingebrachte, somatische und poetische Verfahren „Schneiden, Spleißen und punktgenaue Mutation!" (Falkner 2014, 45) eine entscheidende Rolle. Dabei muss man zwei Ebenen unterscheiden. Einerseits erfahren die Figuren auf der inhaltlichen Ebene eine Metamorphose, andererseits transformiert die Sprache selbst auf der formalen Ebene ihren eigenen Körper. Es geht dabei, wie weiter unten verdeutlicht wird, um die Transformation von einzelnen Wörtern und eine dadurch erzeugte Mehrdeutigkeit. Falkner entnimmt einen bekannten Metamorphose-Stoff aus der griechischen Mythologie, um ihn parodistisch zu transformieren:

> Im Garten bei Helga spielt Gott
> den verliebten Mandanten
> er geht als goldener Regen auf sie
> nieder, durchwühlt ihr Haar
> kleckert das Manna ins köstliche Nest
> ihrer Hochsteckfrisur.
> (Falkner 2014, 90)

Hier mischt er den griechischen Mythos (Zeus als goldener Regen) – was für seine Poetik der „Kollision" (Braun 2018, 10) typisch ist – nicht nur mit dem biblischen (Manna), sondern auch mit der alltäglichen Banalität (Helga statt Danae). Diese synkretistische Transformation, die sich in Gestalt des „entlaubten Meere[s]" im nächsten Vers weiterentwickelt, wird nicht frei und willkürlich phantasiert, sondern Falkner will sie, wie schon im zitierten Interview mit Braun angedeutet, in der wissenschaftlichen Sprache bestätigt sehen. Die Metamorphose wird dem mikrobiologischen und genetischen Modell nachgebildet:

> Der Unterschied
> zwischen Curt Goetz und Rainald Goetz
> zwischen Ann Cotten und Jerry Cotton
> ist, genetisch gesehen, irrelevant.
> Alles die gleiche Homöobox
> das gleiche, trügerische Schillern von Aminosäuren
> genetische Strickleitern, codierte Erblasten.
> (Falkner 2014, 31)

Nachdem unter genetischem Gesichtspunkt der kulturell relevante Unterschied zwischen dem Komödienautor vor Jahrzehnten und dem provokativen Netzautor in der Gegenwart, zwischen der sprachbewussten Dichterin und der Figur aus einer kommerziell erfolgreichen Kriminalroman-Serie negiert wird, wird auf die Problematik verwiesen, dass „das Ich" als „konsistente, gar authentische Entität" in der Moderne insbesondere „unter hochtechnisch-kybernetischen Bedingungen" (Grimm 1993, 459) abhandengekommen sei. Allerdings macht Falkner auch auf die Möglichkeit aufmerksam, dass ein „winzig[er] Sprung / in den einfachen Chromosomensätzen / [...] uns ankündigt" (Falkner 2014, 39), d. h. den fatalen Determinismus („Alles die gleiche Homöobox") außer Kraft setzt und eine Individualität gewinnen lässt. Wie in den Gedichten Falkners die biologische Mutation mit dem manischen Sprechen der Dichtung überschnitten wird, so kann dieser Sprung als „[l]egasthenisch winzig[er]" (Falkner 2014, 25) Eingriff, als Permutation verstanden werden. Dieses poetische Verfahren hat Falkner schon im Gedichtband *wemut* (1989) erfolgreich erprobt, dessen Titelwort durch die Tilgung des Buchstaben ‚h' mehrere Bedeutungen auffaltet: Wermut, Wehmut, *we mute* (wir, die Stummen) und Wermund (Familienname, insbesondere eines mythologischen Königs von Dänemark) (vgl. Geist 2007, 642). In ähnlicher Weise wird der Name des Sprachwissenschaftlers Ferdinand de Saussure im vorliegenden Gedichtband transformiert: „alles so saussure!" (Falkner 2014, 31). Der Nachname wird sprachspielerisch in Kleinschreibung präsentiert, als wäre er aus ‚so' (eine lautliche Übertragung der französischen Silbe ‚sau', im Nachklang des vorlaufenden „so") oder ‚sau' wie in ‚saukalt' (eine Übertragung auf der

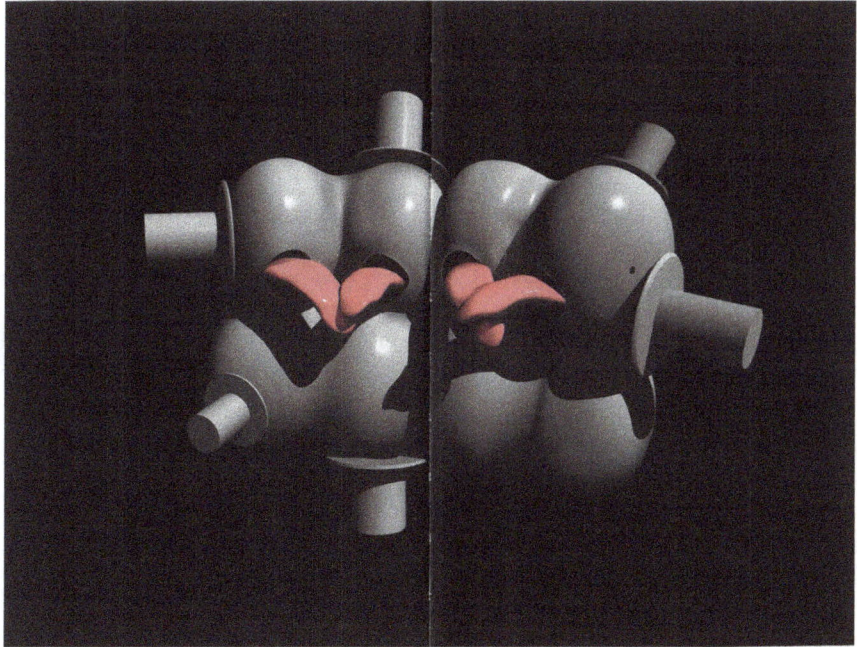

Abb. 35: Yves Netzhammer. Ohne Titel. *Ignatien*. 2014. 82–83.

visuellen Ebene) und ‚ssure' oder besser ‚sûr' (‚sicher' im Französischen) kontaminiert und wird auf diese Weise „mit einem Bedeutungsüberschuss" (Eickmeyer 2018, 226) aufgeladen. In beiden Fällen lässt sich eine polyglotte Erweiterung beobachten.

Wie die im Gedicht variierte Redewendung „das Zünglein an der Waage sich ausschlaggebend / im Gesichtspunkt niederschlägt" (Falkner 2014, 66) zeigt, kann ein kleiner Zungenschlag bei der Rede einen solchen Ausschlag geben, dass er den festgelegten Gesichtspunkt beeinträchtigt und verrückt. Ein winziger Versprecher oder ein Zungenbrecher verursacht unerwartete Sinnverwirrungen. Es gehört, wie in der Forschung gezeigt wird, zu den zentralen poetischen Techniken Falkners, „kleine bedeutungsdifferenzierende Worteelemente für ambigue sinntragende Klangfiguren" zu nutzen wie den „Metaplasmus" oder die „Paronomasie" (Grimm 2006, 2). Meistens ist es das Austauschen oder Auslassen eines einzigen Buchstabens, das eine bekannte Wendung transformiert: Dann wird aus Amor und Psyche „Amok und Psyche" (Falkner 2014, 25), sodass die Akzent- und Bedeutungsverschiebung von der einzigartigen Liebe in der Mythologie, wie sie etwa in Apuleius' *Metamorphosen* erzählt wird, zum Amokläufer mit psychischer Erkrankung, wie häufig in den Sensationsmedien dargestellt, stattfindet. In der „Ignatia 10" gelingt Falkner, mit dem mutierten Neologismus „Knallhalla" sein Zungenreden, das manische Sprechen, in Richtung auf die Kunst- und Zeithistorie hin zu erweitern.

> Hall of fame!
> Halle der Säuferinnen, Knallhalla!
> Die lallende Freya der Weltenburg
> und die torkelnde Fulla
> am Tresen der Befreiungshalle.
> Unter die rastlose Wallfahrt der Donau
> nach Wien. […]
> (Falkner 2014, 54)

Vor dem Hintergrund einer wie in akustischen Halluzinationen hartnäckig wiederholten Silbe ‚all' erfährt das Walhall, in der nordischen Mythologie der Ruheort der gefallenen Krieger, eine vielfältige Transformation. Auf der mythologischen Ebene verwandeln sich die Göttinnen auf synkretistische Weise in eine dionysische Mänade. Damit wird der heilige Ort in die „Halle der Säuferinnen" umbenannt, um so entweiht und zugleich in Beziehung mit dem heiligen Wahn Platons gesetzt zu werden. Wenn die Göttinnen in der zweiten Strophe „[w]eltweit trinkend / bacchantisch" (Falkner 2014, 55) die Wolkenweberei treiben, so fällt es im Übrigen schwer, vor dem Hintergrund der das ganze Buch durchdringenden Thematik des Internets, diese Hausarbeit nicht mit Begriffen wie Cloud und World Wide Web in Verbindung zu bringen.

„Walhalla" meint aber auch die gleichnamige nationalistische Gedenkstätte in Bayern, die im Jahr 1842 errichtet wurde, im selben Jahr wie die Befreiungshalle im nahen Ort Kehlheim im Andenken an den Sieg gegen Napoleon: Falkner stellt einige Verse später deren „Büstenhalle", in der die im 19. Jahrhundert als vorbildlich erachteten Herrscher, Feldherren, Wissenschaftler und Künstler mit Marmorbüsten geehrt wurden, mit dem Neologismus „Kehlheime" (Falkner 2014, 54) nebeneinander. So erreicht das manische Sprechen des Gedichts wieder eine Sinnverwirrung, wie Ann Cottens bewusst wörtliche Übersetzung nahelegt: „Bust halls, Throathomes" (Falkner 2014, 56). Die Wortkontamination „Knallhalla" ist auch im zeitgeschichtlichen Kontext kritisch einzuordnen, da Hitler 1937 im Walhalla die Büste seines Lieblingskomponisten Bruckner enthüllte (vgl. Kellermann). Wenn man das erste Glied ‚Knall', das mit einem Gewaltakt wie ‚schießen' und ‚schlagen' assoziiert werden kann, mit dem Vers in der zweiten Strophe („Alle Köpfe aller Meerschaumpfeifen / der Welt eröffnen das Feuer der Rede!" Falkner 2014, 54) in Verbindung setzt, so können die Formulierungen „(Knall)köpfe" und „Meerschaumpfeifen" als eine sarkastische Bemerkung verstanden werden, die durch Verdoppelung die Leerheit und Dummheit der NS-Reden hervorheben soll.

An diesen Beispielen zeigt sich, wie die manische Sprache Falkners im Wesentlichen aus „Schneiden, Spleißen und [der] punktgenaue[n] Mutation" besteht und zugleich von der wissenschaftlichen Nüchternheit ‚gegenkaschiert' wird. In diesem Sinne ist die Schlusszeile des letzten Gedichts zu verstehen: „Es schenkte uns Hypnos / den Schlaf mit offenen Augen / um ohne zu erblinden auf die Displays / einer allmächtigen Leere zu starren" (Falkner 2014, 102). Ähnlich dem Musilschen Begriff der „taghellen Mystik" (Musil 1978, 1089) markiert „der Schlaf mit offenen Augen" den Balanceakt, den Falkner, wie in der Einleitung dieses Beitrages erwähnt, zwischen dem manischen Sprechen und der wissenschaftlichen Sprache ausführt. Allerdings macht Falkner selbst diese Coda des Bandes, wie fast alle seine Aussagen, durchstreich- und ironisierbar. Denn in der Mythologie sollen die Augen des schönen Jungen Endymion nicht deswegen im Schlaf geöffnet bleiben, damit er immer sehen und Einsicht gewinnen, sondern bloß, damit sie der verliebte Gott Hypnos jederzeit sehen, d. h. sich an ihnen erfreuen kann (vgl. Scheer 2014, 1027). Insofern nimmt die Wendung „Schlaf mit den offenen Augen" eher auf eine Stumpfsinnigkeit Bezug, wie sie Falkner in seinen Gedichten der Netzwelt zuzuschreiben scheint.

Schluss

Trotz des nahezu identischen thematisch-methodischen Bezugsrahmens geben sowohl der Dichter als auch der Künstler einander keine illustrierenden Erklärungen, die zu ihrer dekonstruktiven Intention im Widerspruch stehen würden. Pflanzenartig mutierte Körper bzw. Körperteile wie die Zunge, der Finger und die Hand, Requisiten wie der Rasierapparat, die Schere und der Revolver, labyrinthartige Räume – alles das in den Bildern Befindliche macht sich zwar selbständig und entwickelt sich nach ihrer eigenen Logik. Jedoch werden die Ansätze weitergeführt, die in den Gedichten enthalten sind. Es ist z. B. nicht zu übersehen, dass die eher düsteren, sterilen Digitalbilder zweifellos in einem engen Verhältnis mit der negativen Sichtweise auf die Digitalisierung stehen, die aus den Gedichten hervorgeht. So hilft die sprachlich-bildliche Korrespondenz dem Verständnis der verschiedenen Aspekte ihrer Werke.

Zum Beispiel wird die Aufmerksamkeit zuerst auf das „Zünglein" (Falkner 2014, 66) gelenkt, da der Künstler der Zunge vier von 30 Computer-Zeichnungen widmet, wenn auch jedes Mal ein anderer Gesichtspunkt beleuchtet wird, wie der Zungenkuss einer gesichtslosen Puppe mit einem hühnerartigen Puppenspielerkopf (vgl. Abb. 32), die von der Hand eines Marionettenspielers mit Fäden kontrollierte Zunge eines durchsichtigen Hundes oder Huftieres (vgl. Abb. 33) und eine in ein Schneckenpaar verwandelte kriechende Zunge (vgl. Abb. 34). In Abb. 35 treibt Netzhammer sein reduktionistisches Verfahren auf die Spitze, um sich eine posthumane Perspektive anzueignen. Es geht nicht mehr um Lebewesen, weder um menschenähnliche Puppen noch um modellierte Tiere, sondern um zwei zusammengekoppelte Kugeln, die einen Teil oder ein Bruchstück aus einem undefinierbaren industriellen Produkt darzustellen scheinen. Vier Kugeln, die inmitten der absoluten Finsternis schweben und wie zusammengeschweißt nebeneinandergestellt sind, wirken einerseits aufgrund der hell- und dunkelbeigen Farbe und der atmosphärischen Sterilität unorganisch und dinghaft. Andererseits werden diese leblosen Figuren durch weiche, runde Formen zusammengewachsener Körperteile, durch hutförmige Handgriffe, und vor allem durch die rosa Zunge, die aus jeder Öffnung weit hinausgestreckt wird, und jene der Nachbar:innen so beschwingt berührt, dass aus der ganzen Szene ein befremdender, aber komischer Effekt hervorgeht.

Nach Peter Geist forciert Falkner neuerdings mehr „den Dialog mit anderen Künsten" und „Mehrsprachigkeit", während „Verfahren der Dekonstruktion und Palimpsestierung" „stark zurückgenommen erscheinen" (Geist 2018, 130). Wie im vorliegenden Aufsatz gezeigt, kommen sie allerdings an wichtiger Stelle effizient zum Einsatz. Im künstlerischen Gespräch mit Netzhammer konnte Falkner seinerseits in Hinblick auf den Posthumanismus seine eigene Thematik und Methodik erweitern und vertiefen. Die Mischwesen, die überall in den Gedichten nisten, sind ohne Zweifel ein Symptom für die Situation des Menschen im posthumanen Zeitalter. Vor dem Hintergrund der Digitalzeichnungen, die „die Vorstellung des einen geschlossenen Körperpanzers" (Volkart 2015, 94) auf vielfältige Weise in Frage stellen, greift der Dichter auf die „Illusion ‚Ich'" (Grimm 1995, 293) zurück, die lediglich als „eine Schnittstelle irgendwo zwischen Körper und elektronischem Netzwerk" (Grimm 1995, 288) dargestellt wird. Auf der ästhetischen Ebene kommt allerdings seine subjektive Kreativität gerade in vielerlei Arten von Mischungen zum Ausdruck, wie im Mischen von Bibelbezügen, Motiven aus der Mythologie und Begriffen aus der digitalen Sphäre oder im Austausch einzelner Buchstaben oder Silben in einem einzigen Wort. Im Gegensatz zur reibungslosen Abgeschlossenheit der gängigen Digitalästhetik und der vorherrschenden Informationssprache entwirft er jedoch auch Alternativen und setzt auf die poetischen Verfahren „Schneiden, Spleißen und punktgenaue Mutation" bzw. Permutation und Kontamination. Durch die Analyse des Zusammenwirkens wird deutlich, wie die beiden Künstler versuchen, Fehler ins System hineinschlüpfen zu lassen, damit sie wie Viren oder Krebszellen das Programm umschreiben und für ständige mikrobiologische und genetische Wandlungen, Entgrenzungen und Hybridisierungen sorgen.

Quellenverzeichnis

Benthien, Claudia. *Haut. Literaturgeschichte – Körperbilder – Grenzdiskurse*. Reinbek bei Hamburg: Rowohlt, 2001.

Braun, Michael und Gerhard Falkner. „Poesie am Rande des Nervenzusammenbruchs. Michael Braun im Gespräch mit Gerhard Falkner über seinen neuen Gedichtband Ignatien". *Die zweite Schöpfung. Poesie und Bildende Kunst*. Hg. Michael Braun. Heidelberg: Wunderhorn, 2016. 39–50.

Braun, Michael. „Lob der Unschärfe. Gerhard Falkners poetische Navigationen zwischen 1986 und 1992." *Materie: Poesie. Zum Werk Gerhard Falkners*. Hg. Constantin Lieb, Hermann Korte und Peter Geist. Heidelberg: Universitätsverlag Winter, 2018. 9–17.

Burkard, Jennifer. „Von der Bedeutung des Raums. Einführung". *Yves Netzhammer Installationen 2008–2018*. Hg. Jennifer Burkard. Berlin: Hatje Cantz, 2018. 6–7.

Eich, Günter. „Träume". *Günter Eich. Gesammelte Werke*. Bd. II: *Die Hörspiele* 1. Hg. Karl Karst. Frankfurt a. M.: Suhrkamp, 1991. 349–384.

Eickmeyer, Jost. „Bipolaroids of Yestern Times … Antike und Antikes in Gerhard Falkners Lyrik". *Materie: Poesie. Zum Werk Gerhard Falkners*. Hg. Constantin Lieb, Hermann Korte und Peter Geist. Heidelberg: Universitätsverlag Winter, 2018. 195–230.

Ermacora, Beate. „Schnittstellen". *Yves Netzhammer. Das Gefühl präziser Haltlosigkeit beim Festhalten der Dinge*. Hg. Sabine Maria Schmidt. Bielefeld: Kerber, 2003. 9–17.

Falkner, Gerhard und Yves Netzhammer. *Ignatien. Elegien am Rande des Nervenzusammenbruchs. Elegies at the Edge of Nervous Breakdown*. Translated and, but rarely, transmuted, by Ann Cotten. Fürth: starfruit, 2014.

Geist, Peter. „Gerhard Falkner". *Deutschsprachige Lyriker des 20. Jahrhunderts*. Hg. Peter Geist und Ursula Heukenkamp. Berlin: Erich Schmidt, 2007. 639–649.

Geist, Peter. „‚Im Marmor herrscht Alarm.' Beobachtungen an den neuen Gedichtbänden Gerhard Falkners". *Materie: Poesie. Zum Werk Gerhard Falkners*. Hg. Constantin Lieb, Hermann Korte und Peter Geist. Heidelberg: Universitätsverlag Winter, 2018. 129–137.

Gleich, Uli. „Auswirkungen von Echokammern auf den Prozess der Meinungsbildung". *Media Perspektiven* 2 (2019): 82–85.

Grimm, Erk. „Zwischen Sprachkörper und Körpersprache. Gerhard Falkners ‚wemut'". *Sprache im technischen Zeitalter* 128 (1993): 456–468.

Grimm, Erk. „Das Gedicht nach dem Gedicht: Über die Lesbarkeit der jüngsten Lyrik". *Deutschsprachige Gegenwartsliteratur. Wider Ihre Verächter*. Hg. Christian Döring. Frankfurt a. M.: Suhrkamp, 1995. 287–311.

Grimm, Erk. „Gerhard Falkner". *KLG – Kritisches Lexikon zur deutschsprachigen Gegenwartsliteratur*. 1. Juni 2006, http://www.munzinger.de/document/16000000137 (21. Januar 2023).

Guess, Andrew, Benjamin Lyons, Brendan Nyhan und Jason Reifler. *Avoiding the Echo Chamber About Echo Chambers. Why Selective Exposure to Like-Minded Political News is Less Prevalent than You Think*. 2018, https://www.researchgate.net/publication/330144926 (7. März 2023).

Kania, Elke. „Per Animat zur Sichtbarmachung. Zur filmischen Sprache in den zeitbasierten Arbeiten von Yves Netzhammer". *Selbstgespräche nähern sich wie scheue Rehe. Yves Netzhammer*. Hg. Hermann Arnhold. Münster: LWL-Museum für Kunst und Kultur, 2016. 69–73.

Kaufhold, Enno. „Kameralose Digitalbilder". *Natürlich künstlich. Das virtuelle Bild*. Berlin: Jovis, 2001. 6–26.

Keller, Deborah. „Yves Netzhammer". *SIKART Lexikon zur Kunst in der Schweiz*. 2018, http://www.sikart.ch/KuenstlerInnen.aspx?id=9733635&lng=de (21. September 2022).

Kellermann, Bernd. „Vor 80 Jahren nutzte Adolf Hitler die Walhalla für einen Propaganda-Auftritt". *Wochenblatt*. 11. Juli 2017, https://www.wochenblatt.de/archiv/vor-80-jahren-nutzte-adolf-hitler-die-walhalla-fuer-einen-propaganda-auftritt-12486695 (21. September 2022).

Laukötter, Frank. „Probehandeln in Bildern". *Yves Netzhammer. Die Anordnungsweise zweier Gegenteile bei der Erzeugung ihres Berührungsmaximums*. Ausst.-Kat. Kunsthalle Bremen. Hg. Frank Laukötter und Wulf Herzogenrath. Nürnberg: Verlag Moderne Kunst, 2005. 5–16.

Lukowicz, Marijke und Marianne Wagner. „Im Freigehege. Yves Netzhammers Entwürfe von Lebewesen, Welt und Dingen". *Selbstgespräche nähern sich wie scheue Rehe. Yves Netzhammer*. Hg. Hermann Arnhold. Münster: LWL-Museum für Kunst und Kultur, 2016. 25–29.

Musil, Robert. *Der Mann ohne Eigenschaften*. Reinbek bei Hamburg: Rowohlt, 1978.

McLuhan, Marschall. *Die magischen Kanäle. Understanding Media*. Düsseldorf, Wien, New York und Moskau: Econ, 1992.

Netzhammer, Yves und Heinz-Norbert Jocks. „Die Subjektivierung der Wiederholung. Ein Gespräch". *Kunstforum* 188 (2007): 194–201.

Netzhammer, Yves und Christian Gasser. „Gespräch". *Animation.ch. Vielfalt und Visionen im Schweizer Animationsfilm*. Hg. Christian Gasser und Hochschule Luzern. Bern: Benteli, 2011. 96–121.

Netzhammer, Yves und Markus Stegmann. „Erzählen als intuitiver Erkenntnisprozess". *Kunst Bulletin* 10 (2014), https://www.artlog.net/de/kunstbulletin-10-2014/yves-netzhammer-erzaehlen-als-intuitiver-erkenntnisprozess (21. September 2022).

Pariser, Eli. *The Filter Bubble. What the Internet is Hiding From You*. New York: Penguin Press 2011.

Platon. *Phaidros*. Stuttgart: Reclam, 1979.
Rilke, Rainer Maria. „Duineser Elegien". *Rainer Maria Rilke. Werke*. Bd. I.2: *Gedicht-Zyklen*. Frankfurt a. M.: Insel, 1982. 439–482.
Röller, Nils. „Figur und Instrument". *Yves Netzhammer*. Ostfildern: Hatje Cantz, 2008. 174–178.
Schmidt, Sabine Maria. „Die Formen zukünftiger Gefühle. Die Utopie der Möglichkeitswelt im Werk von Yves Netzhammer". *Yves Netzhammer. Das Gefühl präziser Haltlosigkeit beim Festhalten der Dinge*. Hg. Sabine Maria Schmidt. Bielefeld: Kerber, 2003. 18–32.
Scheer, Tanya. „Endymion". *Der neue Pauly. Enzyklopädie der Antike*. Bd. 3. Hg. Hubert Cancik und Helmuth Schneider. Stuttgart: J.B. Metzler, 2014. 1027.
Serres, Michel. *Der Parasit*. Frankfurt a. M.: Suhrkamp, 1987.
Serres, Michel. *Die Legende der Engel*. Frankfurt a. M.: Insel, 1995.
Stegmann, Markus: „Erschrecke die Schnecke nicht". *Yves Netzhammer. Wenn man etwas gegen seine Eigenschaften benützt, muss man dafür einen anderen Namen finden*. Ausst.-Kat., Kunstverein Schaffhausen. Hg. Markus Stegmann. Nürnberg: Museum zu Allerheiligen, 1999. o. S.
Sunstein, Cass R. *#Republic. Divided Democracy in the Age of Social Media*. Princeton, NJ: Princeton Univ. Press, 2017.
Volkart, Yvonne. *Fluide Subjekte. Anpassung und Widerspenstigkeit in der Medienkunst*. Bielefeld: Transcript, 2015.

Tijana Koprivica
Film Techniques and Poetic Procedures in Vladan Krečković's Poetry Collection *Pariz, Teksas*

Vladan Krečković's poetry collection *Pariz, Teksas* ("Paris, Texas") (2020) is one of the more recent books released by PPM Enklava, a fairly young, but renowned Serbian publisher focused mostly on poetry. Similar to other Serbian contemporary literary works, for instance Nikola Đurica's poetry collection *Noćne životinje* ("Nocturnal Animals") (2020) from the same publisher, Krečković's book features prominent references to films. Already the titles of these two collections of poetry, which explicitly point to Wim Wenders' and Tom Ford's cinematic achievements – *Paris, Texas* (1984) and *Nocturnal Animals* (2016) – demonstrate that visual culture and, especially film, occupy a privileged place and represents a point of departure for these two Serbian poets. If poetry in the past was thought to be one of the sources of cinematic creativity (cf. Kramer and Röhnert 2020, 5), the case of Krečković's and Đurica's works shows a shift: Here cinematic achievements become a source of poetic creativity. The approaches of these two poets to the subject, however, differ significantly, indicating that there are multiple ways in which contemporary Serbian poets treat film as a source.

On the one hand, Đurica does not explicitly refer to *Nocturnal Animals* as cinematographic work nor to the plot or scenes from Ford's film, except in the title of his work. The title of the film serves as a starting point for the development of the book's leading idea about the changeability, fickleness, and the most deeply hidden sides of human nature. Just as nocturnal animals hide from the sunlight and are only active after dark, one's genuine traits and intentions, as Đurica's book suggests, can be discerned only when one embraces one's own solitude and darkness. Krečković, on the other hand, relies on Wenders' film more openly and more often. The evocation of the plot, themes, and motifs represented in the film but also the poetical reshaping of the entire scenes, enriching them with additional observations and meditations, reveal an intermedial quality in the form of media transposition (cf. Rajewsky 2005, 51) in this book.

Furthermore, Wenders' film as the most prominent reference in the poetry collection becomes a lyrical persona's tool for introspection. Yet, the question of how the intricate relationship between poetry and film is established in Krečković's poetry collection does not only concern explicit references to the latter (as in the titles of the mentioned poetry works) or the transformation of the material from one medium into another. It also concerns the question of the film's impact

∂ Open Access. © 2023 the author(s), published by De Gruyter. [CC BY-NC-ND] This work is licensed under the Creative Commons Attribution-NonCommercial-NoDerivatives 4.0 International License.
https://doi.org/10.1515/9783111299334-014

in terms of the techniques and procedures deployed in literary work. By borrowing and imitating film techniques, as well as by referring to the film as a medium, Krečković's book develops a distinctly broad system of "intermedial references," which are deployed as "meaning constitutional strategies" (Rajewsky 2005, 52) and affect the book's signification. In other words, in Krečković's poetry collection, film as a medium serves as a structural device of the text. Finally, the references to Wenders' film as well as the references to the medium of film serve as a means of constructing and expressing subjectivity throughout the book, as will be demonstrated in this article.

This treatment will also show that *Pariz, Teksas* is a meticulously conceptualized book whose structure and meaning are reinforced by the mechanisms of film, contributing to the diversity of Krečković's lyrical expression. To date, there have still been no deeper and more detailed investigations of the relations of this poetry collection with film, of structural analogies, techniques, or procedures employed in this book. Therefore, the main focus of this article lies on *Pariz, Teksas*, and on shedding light on its relationship with Wenders' film, that is, on different modes in which film as an individual artwork and a medium appears in this poetry collection, aiming to close an outlined research gap.

From screen to poetic text

Pariz, Teksas is Krečković's first collection of poetry. Soon after its publication, it achieved great success; the poet was awarded the prestigious international literary prize Bridges of Struga established by The Struga Poetry Evenings Festival (SPE) and UNESCO. Translations into Macedonian and English followed and increased the visibility of the book, making it accessible to both regional (Balkan / South-East European) and further European audiences.[1] The title of Krečković's poetry collection alone, as well as the blurb on the back cover that indicates some of the cinematic influences and leading topics, propose a key for reading it, which has directed literary critique to focus more closely on the book's relations with film (Fig. 36). This interest resulted mostly in the detection of films that Krečković explicitly or implicitly evokes in his poetry. Other films besides Wenders' *Paris,*

---

[1] Jovica Ivanovski translated the book into Macedonian, Kruna Petrić into English; these translations first appeared together in 2021, in the trilingual edition of *Pariz, Teksas* that followed the Bridges of Struga award. Afterwards, PPM Enklava published a separate e-publication of the poetry collection's English translation. All English translations of Krečković's poems in this article will be quoted according to Kruna Petrić's translation from the trilingual edition of the book.

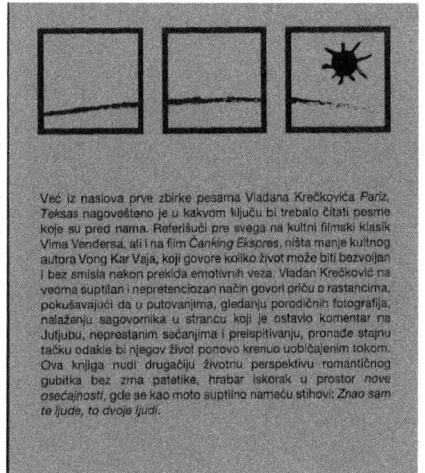

Fig. 36: Back cover of *Pariz, Teksas*. Design by Hajdana Kostić and Stefan Bulatović. 2020.

Texas (1984) that literary critiques listed as influential for Krečković's collection of poetry are *Chungking Express* (1994), *My Winnipeg* (2007), *Eternal Sunshine of the Spotless Mind* (2004), as well as David Lynch's cinematography, especially the TV series *Twin Peaks* (1990–2017). So far, the research has focused mainly on the specific cinematic atmosphere that emerges as a result of these evocations (cf. Marinkov 2020, 294–295; Đurković 2020).

Right at the outset of the collection, Krečković introduces Wenders' *Paris, Texas* by quoting a part from Sam Shepard's script of the film, referring to one of the most prominent monologues in cinematography: "He ran until the sun came up and he couldn't run any further. And when the sun went down, he ran again. For five days he ran like this until every sign of man had disappeared" (Shepard and Wenders 1983, 180; cf. Krečković 2020, 5 and 2021, 97). The quotation, which represents Travis Henderson's, the film protagonist's, monologue (played by Harry Dean Stanton; 02:08:52–02:09:24) in the film's finale, sets the thematic horizon and the atmosphere of Krečković's poems. It also serves as an indicator of the nature and sensibility of the lyrical persona and consequently of Krečković's poetry. Hence, the story of loss, loneliness, wandering, searching for the right direction, as well as deconstructing and reconstructing family and love relationships is conveyed as poetically shaped introspective insights based on the lyrical persona's experience. This is followed by the lyrical persona's double positioning, which is based on their recognition of the similarities they share with the film's characters (cf. Branigan 1984, 10). On the one hand, the lyrical persona identifies with the boy Hunter (played by Hunter Carson), Travis Henderson's son, through the feeling of being abandoned and torn apart between parents, which is for both of them based on the childhood experience of family and home disintegration (for example in the poem "The Time When Fernando Torres Was the Best Striker in the World" ["Vreme kada je Fernando Tores bio najbolji napadač na svetu"]). On the other hand, the experience of loss of love in adulthood both re-evokes and re-contextualizes feelings of loneliness, abandonment, and resignation (as in the poem "August, Once Again" ["Avgust, još jednom"]). For this reason, the lyrical persona also identifies with Travis Henderson himself and empathizes with his suffering after broken relationships.

This aspect of the lyrical persona's identification is most evident in the poem titled "Paris, Texas" (Krečković 2021, 121; cf. 2020, 38–39) which is central to Krečković's poetry collection (Fig. 37).

Fig. 37: Vladan Krečković. "Pariz, Teksas." *Pariz, Teksas*. 2020. 38–39.

This poem can be regarded as a lyrical recreation or "adaptation" (cf. Hutcheon 2006, 6) of Wenders' film. To the same degree as the quotation from the beginning of the book, this poem too points to the film's finale and thus to the explanation and unfolding of the events preceding the final meeting of Travis and Jane (played by Nastassja Kinski; 01:58:44–02:19:28) in the peep show booth. Since the process of adaptation is always a process of (re-)interpretation and (re-)creation (cf. Hutcheon 2006, 8), the film scenes serve as a source for the poetic images just as Travis' monologue's verbal content does. Prominent scenes from the film, such as the wandering through the desert, the memory loss, and the search for the missing wife and son are evoked and poetically transformed. The motifs of the camp trailer and the cowbell tied to the woman's ankle only verbally evoked in the film become an integral part of the poem, too (cf. Krečković 2021, 121). However, since an adaptation allows only for a gradual approximation of one medium to another (cf. Hutcheon 2006, 16; Benthien et al. 2019, 212–213), the dissonance between the film and the newly created poetic images emerging in the process of adaptation introduces and adds new aspects to the film scenes in question. For instance, the verbalization of the poem in first-person singular does not only reinforce the effect of the lyrical persona's identification with Travis. It also allows for the articulation of thoughts from Travis' perspective. Since the thoughts evoked in the poem are never explicitly mediated in the film, they are the product of the lyrical persona's taking over the protagonist's position. However, their verbal reconstruction as poetic images through the lyrical persona's voice compensates for the limiting possibilities of the film in representing inner states. It furthermore serves as a counterpart to the film's finale, where the results of the introspective process are visually represented as gazing (cf. Branigan 1984, 80) through the peep show window.

The investigation of the influence of Wenders' film on Krečković's poetry invites for consideration of a film genre as well: *Paris, Texas* is commonly characterized as a road movie (cf. Bromley 1997; Hark 1997, 210–214), a genre that emerged under the direct influence of on-the-road literature (cf. Kohan and Hark 1997; Kuhn and Westwell 2020), and Krečković imports specific themes inherent to this film genre into his book. These elements concern leaving home for a road trip, and thus imply various forms of mobility and means of transportation (cf. Kramer and Röhnert 2020, 7), the naming of numerous temporary destinations, as well as motifs of alienation, tension, self-discovery, and the self-reflection of the protagonist as well as the reflexivity of the genre itself (cf. Morris 2003, 24–48; see Krečković 2021, 101, 105–106, 118–120, 124–125, 131, 134, 137–139). In this sense, mobility serves as a "trigger for poetry" in Krečković's book, while poetry "makes us perceive the devices of mobility as a means to travel not only in the external world but on unforeseen roads of the mind" (Kramer and Röhnert 2020, 11). Moreover, it disguises the paths of transposition of different artistic practices and procedures into different media – in this particular case from literature to film and then back to literature.

The specific poetic quality of Wenders' film is rooted in the structuring of the film itself. Namely, this translates to the fact that the horizontal structure of the film – which concerns the narrative or the development of the plot (cf. Deren 2000, 173–174; Benthien et al. 2019, 118) – is rather simple: it is a quest for a missing wife and child. This pushes forward the film's vertical structure, which regards "what it feels like or what it [the situation] means" (Deren 2000, 173–174). This means that, in Wenders' film, Travis' experiences and feelings are in a privileged position. The audience, together with the characters in the film, learn about the events and their causality from Travis' telling. This, however, happens only when Travis is able and ready to tell his story, for at the beginning of the film he is mute and has no memory of the events that preceded and led to his initial position in the film. This constant delay of the unfolding of the events is what provokes suspense, emphasizing the change of Travis' emotional and mental states (from jealousy, fear, and anger, to disappointment and unconsciousness, to regained consciousness, understanding, and accepting responsibility) as a causative agent of the events visually represented and verbally evoked in the film. In this sense, the protagonist in *Paris, Texas* and the lyrical persona in *Pariz, Teksas* both travel on a shared 'reflexive road.'

Poetic procedures of capturing mobility

A particularly interesting aspect of the relations between film and poetry in Krečković's book is the question of how mobility affects the creation or development of a scenery. In terms of filmmaking, the scenery is first established within the screenplay; it is a more or less detailed technical description of the space where the film scenes take place (cf. Kuhn and Westwell 2020). However, only when the film scenes are shot, the scenery expresses its full potential as an element in the processes of signification and interpretation of the film. Thus, the scenery contributes to the general atmosphere of the sequence, sets the tone, reflects the characters' attitudes, feelings, and personalities, underlines the leading ideas, etc. When it comes to Krečković's poetry, the lyrical persona's mobility is the key element that distinguishes two types of scenery – the static and the dynamic one – and therefore two different poetic strategies employed in their verbal representation.

In the cases when the lyrical persona is at rest, that is, when their movement is minimized, the scenery is a static one. Often, there is no physical presence of other people in these "scenes," which creates a feeling of isolation, but also a sort of calmness. This kind of scenery is usually presented at the very beginning of the poem, or it is gradually constructed around the lyrical persona, emerging as a background for the lyrical persona's poetic introspection. Therefore, its main function can be explained as setting the atmosphere before the main ideas or feelings are articulated, which usually happens by the end of the poem, accompanied by some sort of conclusion or point. For example, in the poem "Before Midnight in Room 25 (Memories of 11 Schlösselgasse)" ["Pre ponoći u sobi 25 (sećanje na Šloselgase 11)"], the title indicates the exact position (the address) and type of a place (a hotel/hostel/motel room). The shifting of the lyrical persona's perspective from wide to a narrower one (which will be explained later on in more detail) generates the effect of going closer *into* the space. A more accurate representation of the scenery intertwined with the lyrical persona's impressions is given in the first seven lines: "I find it easier to endure / the passing of time in a rented room. /

The ceilings are high / and there's enough room for doubt / in the building where the ghosts / of previous tourists whimper, / crammed inside the floor cracks" (Krečković 2021, 126). Emphasizing the fact that the room is rented, as well as putting the architecture and purpose of the building to the fore, this poem points to the ambiguity of the space and the ambiguity of the lyrical persona's feelings about it. A hotel room is not an intimate, personal space, but a temporary residence; still, just for this reason, it alleviates the lyrical persona's existential questioning and the feeling of transience, turning the scenery not into a mere background of the poem, but into an important element of an allegorical representation of the transience of human life.

Since the mobility of Krečković's lyrical persona, similar to the protagonist in Wenders' film, has many forms (walking, running, riding) and therefore demands various means of transportation (bicycle, car, train, plane, boat), it does not surprise that this book entails a significantly larger number of poems in which the lyrical persona is on the move. The dynamic scenery, as the second type, is the dominant one in Krečković's poetry. Being mobile impacts the more or less rapid change of scenery surrounding the lyrical persona, depending on the velocity of the motion. A case in point can be found in the poem "The Return" ["Povratak"]. In contrast to Wenders' film, where Travis manages to rediscover and regain his identity through travel and movement, here a downhill ride on a bicycle for the lyrical persona exemplifies the moment of finally being nothing (cf. Krečković 2021, 134). While neutralizing all of the characteristics of the lyrical persona, the speed and movement also shift the focus to the surroundings, as seen from an unusual perspective: the poetic images of houses, courtyards, laundry, children playing, gas stations, the street and the city are quickly changing in front of the lyrical persona's eyes. This rapid change of space increases the kinesthesia (cf. Levi 2017, 75–76) of the poem.

The lyrical persona's awareness of the multiple effects of mobility on the impression of dynamism can be detected in the text. In this regard, it should be noted that the poetic images in Krečković's poems are usually introduced by the lyrical persona's explicit statement that they see, observe, look, watch, etc. (e.g. "*Gazing* at the dark water crust / in silence" (Krečković 2021, 119; own emphasis)). Moreover, there are examples where poetic images emerge from situations that imply the practices of the lyrical persona's seeing, observing, looking (e.g. "*From your bedroom window* / the slow stream of the Danube *looked like* / an exodus of oil*"* (Krečković 2021, 116; own emphasis)). Therefore, vision and the mentioned practices connected to it function as an initial "aestheticizing procedure" and the "founding gesture of spatial framing/fragmentation" (cf. Levi 2017, 62) in Krečković's poetry. In other words, isolating and putting to the fore a detail from the scene in the lyrical persona's sight by the notion of practices connected to vision, awards the text with cinematic quality.

For instance, in the poem "Delta," the lyrical persona, during a boat ride, firstly points out the preconditions for the observational practice that leads to a (desired) impression of dynamism: "We need to keep still in the boat / to let the countryside *flow past us*" (Krečković 2021, 101, own emphasis). The mobility of the surroundings is attained by the succession of the poetic images represented as seen from the boat, but top-down: roofs, cable lines, villages, and a dog on the river bank that reappears among the bulrush. Mobility is additionally emphasized by detecting other elements in space that affect the observational practice itself: "Fences, walls, windows, / religious icons – / *everything framing the scenery*, / is a collage of waste." (Krečković 2021, 101; own emphasis) Therefore, it can be said that structuring the poem according to the visual experience contributes not only to its cinematic quality but, in a form of meta-reflection, also becomes an acknowledgment of vision and visuality as a dominant mode in Krečković's poetry.

Concerning the translation of dynamism into poetic language, it should also be noted that the impression of movement depends on a formal aspect of the poem: the faster the movement, the less time the lyrical persona spends in a particular setting, and the shorter the verbal expression reflecting the individual parts of the scenery or objects/subjects in the space, and vice versa.[2] For instance, in the poem "Trains and Again Trains" ["Vozovi i opet vozovi"], the lyrical persona rides on a train and observes the landscapes passing by: "Across a dreamy space / after the Budapest suburbs / I saw meadows, chessboard pieces, / still cows and powerlines / gliding away" (Krečković 2021, 125). Sequences of the space observed and elements in it are represented either in one line (as the Budapest suburbs) or by a syntagma or a noun that is part of the line (as still cows and powerlines), rendering the poetic language very demonstrative. Moreover, the semantic field of movement adds a certain amount of dynamism to the space itself and reinforces the verbal recreation of the impression of mobility within a space (e.g. the meadows that are "gliding away" like the countryside which was previously flowing past the lyrical persona).

In contrast to these sequences, in the poem "Anima, the Movement of the Concrete" ["Anima, kretanje betona"], the mobility of the lyrical persona is based

---

[2] This can be compared with the ideas present in Miroslav Bata Petrović's short text *Šetaj i gledaj* ("Walk and Look"), where he offers a course on looking at reality. Among other things, he suggests the following: Once in a moving vehicle, one should look through the window and notice how everything is in motion – people outside, cars, trees, the vehicle itself and the observing person in it. By the movement of the head, one could affect the composition of frames, as well as change the object of observation, etc. (cf. Levi 2017, 75–77).

on walking. Here, the third, fourth, and fifth stanzas are dedicated to the representation of a cityscape. Streets and street signs, concrete walls and reinforcing steel bars, as markers of a city space, are tightly intertwined with the lyrical persona's emotional experience of this space (Krečković 2021, 99). The poetic language is thus more associative and abundant with epithets, metaphors, and comparisons. From this it becomes clear that the dynamics of movement also impact the detailedness of spatial representation, causing a constant change of focus. As the examples analyzed in this section show, one aspect of the pervasiveness of the medium of film in Krečković's poetry collection can be linked to the idea that visual representations of movement and acts of mobility in films are self-referential in terms of the illusion that films as *moving* pictures produce (cf. Kramer and Röhnert 2020, 7). Besides evoking the genre of road movies, the movements and acts of mobility represented verbally create an effect of moving pictures within the text. The poetry collection thus acquires a cinematic quality and brings the experience of reading closer to the experience of observing.

Introducing film techniques into poetry

The lyrical persona's mobility in the scenery and its verbal representation are not the sole aspect of intermedial quality in *Pariz, Teksas*. Other influences of film as a medium are also present in the book as poetic procedures used to recreate effects of various film techniques such as tracking and panning shots, point of view, and close-up shots. For example, a poetic image is sometimes comparable to the image produced by a steady camera capturing only what is within the range of the objective. In other cases, poetic images are represented as if they were captured by a camera in a fixed position, but only rotating horizontally or vertically, as in panning and tilting shots. Or the poetic image possesses dynamics as if it was captured by a completely mobile camera following the subjects and objects of interest, as the following examples indicate.

In the poem "We Finally Measured Our Love in Miles" ["Konačno smo ljubav merili u miljama"] poetic images substitute one another as a result of a car ride, which is the central theme of the poem: "The hypnosis of a monotonous panorama, / the scars on the birch trees and streets / sagging under the weight of too much industry. / A highway. / In the sky above Denver / the stars looked like piercings. / It was hard to look at / the Methodist churches by the road, / the homeless whose lives / could fit in a supermarket trolley" (Krečković 2021, 137). Movement is pointed out by naming the toponyms from the map (Denver, but further in the poem also Huron, Illinois, Sierra Azul), and referring to the topoi of the highway, that is, the motel room, gas stations, and the desert (cf. Krečković 2021, 137–139). However, the birch trees and industrial settlements evoked at the beginning of the poem are the motifs that most strongly transmit the effect of the film technique. Namely, as they are metaphorically represented as scar-like because they occasionally and suddenly appear on the horizon during the car ride and thus interrupt the monotony of the surroundings, the birch trees and industrial settlements become indicators of a movement of the lyrical persona, who is in the driving car. Therefore, the birches and settlements appear as glitches on the film frame or film screen: they interrupt the continuity of the visual (re)presentation of the panorama framed by the windshield or the window of the moving car. In this way, the aforementioned motifs both enhance the effect of the moving pictures in the poem and introduce the materiality of the medium of film into a medium of poetry. This, together with the double meaning of the lyrical persona's statement that "[i]t was hard to look at" – both physically (for the lyrical persona is on the move and thus their field of vision constantly changes) and emotionally (for the scenes leave a strong impression on the lyrical persona, even though observed for a short period of time) – contribute to the creation of the effects of a tracking shot, a shot where the camera follows the character or shows the surroundings (cf. Kuhn and Westwell 2020).

The poem "The Message I Didn't Send" ["Poruka koju nisam poslao"] brings into consideration another type of film shot. Namely, a description of a room in the middle of the night that pays close attention to items, light sources, and sounds (cf. Krečković 2021, 123) gives the impression that the lyrical persona is completely static. The lyrical persona is also only reporting on the things that are within the horizontal axis of its sight, like in a panning shot (cf. Kuhn and Westwell 2020). Visual practices, as previously stated, impose the main aestheticization procedure, which is in the poems reflected in the semantic field of sight. For that reason, as well as for the fact that it is written in the first person singular, very often in an intimate tone and with a predominantly introspective tendency, it can be argued that *Pariz, Teksas* is conceptualized as a point-of-view shot. For example, in the poem "Approaching the Sanatorium" ["Nadomak sanatorijuma"], the lyrical persona finds themselves disappointed and defeated by the loss of a beloved one. This loss is, however, only metaphorical, for the eyes of the beloved one do not reflect the person they once were (cf. Krečković 2021, 103). In the last stanza, the lyrical persona locates themselves at a bus stop and the direction of their gaze is asserted in the following lines: "At times, I'd stare / at the stave of the cables / on the telephone poles, / think about the voices / travelling across the wasteland. / Still in the distance / they will reach someone" (Krečković 2021, 103). The gaze, which is fixed on the objects (telephone poles), becomes intertwined with reflections on the objects' purpose (communication), bringing to the fore the lyrical persona's solitude and feeling of isolation as a result of the lack or absence of communication with the beloved person. As in the point-of-view shot (cf. Branigan 1984, 6), *what* the lyrical persona sees, is just as much represented as the way *how* the lyrical persona sees it.

Another example of recreating the effects of film techniques in poetry can be found in the above-mentioned poem "Anima, the Movement of the Concrete." The poem commences with an image of a woman holding a gun against her head, while special attention is paid to the hair that touches the gun barrel: "Time and again / a spectre of a woman / whose hair is touching / a 9mm gun barrel / keeps haunting me" (Krečković 2021, 99). The poetic image is built on tensity at the point of contact between hair and gun. Its sudden appearance at the very beginning of the poem without any kind of context is what immediately directs readers' attention toward the most important detail of the poem. In an analogous manner to the technique of the zoom, where the camera focuses and isolates one specific detail from the bigger picture to show it more closely, the very distinctive language and grammatical structure in this example present the audience with a very powerful poetic close-up shot.

The poem "My Dad's Photos from the West Coast" ["Fotografije moga oca sa Zapadne obale"] deploys yet another visual medium: The first five stanzas of the poem concern five different photographs of the lyrical persona's father. Although the content of the photographs is verbally articulated in the present tense as if the photographed scenes take place at the exact time of the lyrical persona's observations, they testify to the father's life in the past. This can be deduced from the opposed time adverbs "now," "[t]oday," "back then," and "then" (Krečković 2021, 112–113; cf. 2020, 29) in the second line of the fifth stanza and the first lines of the sixth and seventh stanzas. This temporal binary opposition is what indicates distancing (cf. Backman Rogers 2015, 14) between the objects (the photographs) and the viewer (the lyrical persona). While observing the photographs to learn about the father's past, the lyrical persona contextualizes each of them by remarking on what can be seen. However, indications of the time of the day, weather forecasts, occasions, and other people's presence, which the lyrical persona notices, do not suffice for the comprehension of the father's past. This leaves the lyrical persona, and the readers as well, with many assumptions and uncertainties. Therefore, to recreate "the prior condition of the existence of a photograph" (Deren 1978, 64), that is, the specific reality in which the father's photographs emerge, the lyrical persona focuses their gaze on details of the individual photographs (Fig. 38).

The fourth stanza of this poem serves as a good example: "Who were you with that night in Reno? / It's dark in front of the gambling-club, / you are holding a fan of dollars. / I won't ask you about the woman / whose locks are fluttering in

Fig. 38: Vladan Krečković. "Fotografije moga oca sa Zapadne oblae." *Pariz, Teksas*. 2020. 28–29.

the reflection / on a red Ford windshield" (Krečković 2021, 112). Here, the interchange of the wide plan and the specific details within that plan, that is, utilizing zoom as a film technique, is achieved through the rhetorical structure of the stanza. The notion of the casino in wide plan in the second line is subtly substituted with a change of focus to the representation of the father's hand and a wad of cash in the third line. Additionally, a detail that is supposed to remain outside of the photograph's focus, the "punctum" (Barthes 1982, 27), which is the reflection of the unknown woman's hair, is also brought to attention. It adds an effect of mystery and suspense to the poem as well as to the father's life.

This hidden detail becomes a justification for the posed questions: the explicit and direct one at the outset of the stanza about who the father was with in Reno; and the silent but implied one in the last three lines about the identity of the unknown woman. An explanation of the context that only pertains to what was intended to be represented in the picture – the father's hand full of dollars as a symbol of success and luck – is provided after the first question. By directing attention to the detail of the woman's hair, the lyrical persona makes her presence noticeable, potentially confirming another aspect of the father's success – his success as a lover. However, by suppressing curiosity about the unknown woman, the lyrical persona accepts the fact that they are not present in the reality of the photograph and thus can never fully comprehend its significance. The photographs verbally represented in the poem are then juxtaposed with the image of the father from the present, which in the poem emerges from the lyrical persona's direct, unmediated observation of the father (cf. Krečković 2021, 113).

Having in mind the ontological and structural relationship between photography and film (cf. Cavell 1979, 23–25; Kramer and Röhnert 2020, 9) and the fact that the film image is created of photographic still images projected at twenty-four frames per second, appearing as continuous movement (cf. Mulvey 2006, 7), it can be asserted that the succession of photographs in the recreation and reinvention of the father's past alludes to the mechanisms of the moving pictures. In other words, compensating for the lack of knowledge about the father, the lyrical persona picks up the pieces, that is, photographs, trying to give them meaning. For the photographs are evoked successively – each in an individual stanza, the blank space between these stanzas can be comprehended as the spaces between the photographs in the photo album, whereby each stanza is a verbal representation of one photograph. Furthermore, the blanks can be interpreted both as graphic equivalents clear cuts between the scenes in the hypothetical movie chronicling the father's past, but also metaphorically, as blanks in the knowledge of the lyrical persona about their father. In that sense, the poetic images of the photographs in succession constitute a procedure similar to film montage. Once the photographs are juxtaposed with the father's image in the present, an expressive value of the procedure (cf. Antoine-Dunne 2004, 5) comes to the fore, effectively conditioning the meaning of the poem. The impossibility of the lyrical persona to fully grasp the past and present identity of the father from the juxtaposed images, creates the atmosphere of wistful longing in the poem, while the unspoken issues denote the dynamics of the father-son relationship.

The connecting point of the father's images from the past and the present can be found in the details of the last photograph evoked. The father's hands, greased by the oil from a car repair (cf. Krečković 2021, 112–113) belong to both temporal dimensions: the one in which the lyrical persona is not present, which exists only in photographs, and the one in which the lyrical persona recognizes and remembers their father's touches activating multiple senses – vision, olfaction, and the tactile sense. This zoomed-in detail of the photograph, therefore, triggers associations in the lyrical persona, but it is also an invitation for readers to liberate themselves from passive, automatized perception (cf. Benthien et al. 2019, 112, 117) by activating their senses and thus engaging in the process of signification.

Rethinking the process of poetry creation

The influence of the film in Krečković's poetry is notable in its metapoetic and self-reflexive moments as well. The most evident instance of these facets of the book can be found in the poem "The Ability of an Owl" ["Sposobnost sove"]: "Tonight I need neither / assonance nor alliteration, // but like in horror films / to turn my head / through one hundred and eighty degrees / and see the sneaking of nothingness. // In the morning, when the poem is ready, / under the pine tree in the yard / I'll find mice bones" (Krečković 2021, 117; cf. 2020, 33). By rejecting assonance and alliteration as poetic means in the first three lines of the poem, the lyrical persona for the first time fully exposes themselves as a poet. Along the same lines, a preference for cinematographic, rather than poetic strategies, is clearly stated. More precisely, the metapoetic remarks in these lines explicitly connect the creation process of a poem to a specific film genre. Interestingly, the poem refers to horror films and their peculiarities rather than to the road movie as an influential film genre (Fig. 39).

Sposobnost sove

Večeras mi ne treba
ni asonanca ni aliteracija,

već kao u horor filmovima
da okrenem glavu
za sto osamdeset stepeni
i vidim prikradanje ništavila.

Ujutru, kad pesma bude spremna,
pronaći ću ispod bora u dvorištu
kosti miševa.

32
33

Fig. 39: Vladan Krečković. "Sposobnost sove." *Pariz, Teksas*. 2020. 33.

The creation of a poem is thus compared with the experience of watching scenes that provoke feelings of fear, anxiety, and terror, on the one hand. On the other hand, these very feelings become the effect of the poem while reading it: The lyrical persona identifies themselves with an owl, placing themselves within the horror film. This implies several meanings. First off, because of its nocturnal nature and general ambiguity, the owl features prominently in horror films as a bad omen. Consequently, besides alluding to Lynch's *Twin Peaks* and evoking the dark and gloomy atmosphere of the TV series, the owl in this poem reveals the lyrical persona's deep-seated negative self-understanding. The lyrical persona, who is a poet, adopts all of the ominous traits of an owl. Next, just as the owl's ability to turn its head around its axis is unique and uncanny, so too is the lyrical persona's capacity to create poems conveyed as an uncanny activity. Additionally, if the owl's ability to rotate its head is compared to the panning shot film technique, the lyrical persona's field of vision expands to match an owl's field of view and perspective. Furthermore, by taking the owl's place and appropriating its characteristics, this mystification of the lyrical persona underscores the idea of poetic creation as an act of transgressing the given possibilities of vision. This newly acquired special type of vision enables *looking into nothingness* behind one's back, which is represented as the source of poetic creation. Moreover, it points directly to the filmic representations of introspection in the form of *gazing* or *staring* (into nothingness), which suggests that the object of a gaze is inward (cf. Braning 1984, 80). The creation of the poem is thus not initially connected with writing but with vision itself and with its various practices. In Krečković's poetry, writing happens only afterward, serving as "the camera operator's proto-apparatus" (Levi 2017, 73) *to record* the visual experience.

Some other poems use a similar method to subtly emphasize the value of vision in the poetry creation process. The lyrical persona's acceptance of the impossibility of language to express experience is stated throughout the book, for example in the poem "All That Ramirez Said" ["Sve što je rekao Ramirez"]: "Feel the magnetic needle between your eyebrows. / Language is of no use anymore. / You have to follow the syntax of the pupil, / Step inside yourself through a full stop" (Krečković 2021, 102). Here, the syntax of vision dominates and overpowers the syntax of language. As a result, vision becomes crucial not only for creation but also for introspection, the results of which are most frequently Krečković's poetry's subject. Consequently, visual images and their verbal representations become critical for the articulation of thought processes and emotions.

Another aspect of the metapoetic quality of Krečković's poetry is to be found in poems about dreams and dreaming, as well as in poems about memory and remembering. Here, the metapoetic quality reveals itself through the presence of meta-images. If the concept of the meta-image is understood as any kind of (visual, verbal, mental) image present within another image (cf. Mitchell 1994, 56–57), then the poetic images in Krečković's poetry that verbally represent dream and memory sequences as mental images can also be considered meta-images. For instance, in the poem "Omens" ["Predskazanja"], the lyrical persona states the following: "Last night I dreamt about / my father all in sepia, he spoke quietly and backwards. / The title was in Russian" (Krečković 2021, 115). The father's unusual manner of speaking – quietly, backwards, and in a foreign language – builds up tension in the poem. This further leads to the almost diabolical representation of the father in the lyrical persona's dream and consequently in the poetic image conveying the dream.

Additionally, this dream sequence once again puts the importance of film as a medium to the fore, rendering the meta-aspect of Krečković's book even more complex. The common idea that the structure of film most closely resembles the structure of dreams, for they both dissolve time and space boundaries and their images express a latent message of desires and fears (cf. Morin 1967, 77–78), is introduced in this poem: The notion of subtitles underlines the cinematic character of the lyrical persona's dream sequence, adding another layer to the meta-image of the father. The dream as a mental image, which is perceived and represented as film-like, is verbally shaped into a poetic image. Furthermore, the mother's repeated question about the deathly omens' presence in the dream – that of either the father's or the lyrical persona's teeth falling out (cf. Krečković 2021, 115) – not only intensifies the already existing tension in the poem, but it also places the lyrical persona into the role of an (unintentional) filmmaker. The mother's urge to interpret the dream and comprehend its latent message cannot be satisfied without the knowledge of the omens' presence. By providing her with this information, the lyrical persona takes responsibility for setting the semantic range of the dream.

When it comes to the question of memory and remembering in Krečković's poetry, as was shown in the case of the poem "My Dad's Photos from the West Coast," it is usually connected to the observation of photographs. A similar strategy occurs in the poem "Cracks in the Ceiling" ["Pukotine na plafonu"], in which, at the request of the dying grandfather, photo albums are displayed back to front: "We faded away / in his arms, / the house shrank / floor by floor, the blurry faces / of my parents' wedding guests, / my father in a suit, / for the first and only time. / A veil on my mother's face / like a mist" (Krečković 2021, 108). Memories as mental images are embedded in photographs, that is, visual images, which are then represented as poetic images in the poem. When being displayed or represented in the opposite order to their emergence, the poetic images of the evoked photographs and thus memories achieve the filmic effect of reverse motion, conveying the impression of the undoing of time (cf. Deren 1978, 68). By achieving the uncanny effect of turning stillness into movement and the past into the present (Backman Rogers 2015, 13), the photographs are transporting the dying grandfather to the beginning. A somewhat analogous interpretation can be connected to the following lines as well: "If they look for me, / the trail leads to the pines and other / power lines, / where the flame, paper / and my memories / rewind to the beginning" (Krečković 2021, 109). Here, the lyrical persona explicitly associates their memories with a film tape and turns it into the foundation of their existence. The hypothetical disappearance of the lyric persona (that is, their hypothetical end) suggested by the conditional clause, however, rests in the return to the beginnings of their memory. Thus, memory is simultaneously perceived as fundamental and destructive to the lyrical persona's identity exploration.

Watching and producing films in *Pariz, Teksas*

In this last section, the privileged position of film in Krečković's poetry collection will be reviewed concerning the aspect of film reception in general. More accurately, in addition to the question of which films the lyrical persona in this book watches – to which Wenders' filmography is one of the answers – it will be examined what kinds of films they are and how these films are being watched. If one closely follows the lyrical persona's explicit statements about the practice of watching films, such as "I would like to tell you / how many nights I've stayed awake / rewatching / Paris, Texas" (Krečković 2021, 113), it is clear that this activity belongs to an intimate setting, like a lyrical persona's home or bedroom. This has various implications. Firstly, the lines cited demonstrate the need for a different kind of privacy and intimacy than was considered to exist in the context of movie theaters (cf. Levi 2017, 34). Being regarded as an experience that guaranteed a high degree of privacy for the audience (cf. Barthes 1995, 418–421), going to the cinema is in Krečković's poetry replaced with home screenings of films. By excluding or at least limiting the presence of others while watching films, the private screening thus becomes an intimate experience in the narrower sense; one could even say an isolating experience. In other words, although displaced from the cinema, film screening in Krečković's poetry retains some of the elements of "the absolute isolation of absorbed viewing" (Mulvey 2006, 27) – the darkness and the absence of intrusions.

Secondly, private screenings exemplify how widely accessible diverse ranges of content, including film, are in the contemporary era. This means that, aside from selecting content and the circumstances under which it is consumed, one has a nearly unlimited possibility of repeating these actions. As implied in the lines above, repeated watching of films allows for the multiplication of their meanings and influences potential interpretations, while also emphasizing the films' aesthetics and visuality. Moreover, since in this poem the lyrical persona most presumably alludes to the screening of a film's digital copy, the question of the film's materiality is again brought to attention. Diverse modes of watching a film in a private setting (such as pausing, skipping, repeating, enlarging, etc.), on the one side point towards "interactive spectatorship" (Mulvey 2006, 190), and, on the other, to the cinema's rootedness in the still image (cf. Backman Rogers 2015, 12; Mulvey 2006, 27–28). Digital technology "enables a spectator to still a film" (Mulvey 2006, 22) and therefore to recreate the presence of a single celluloid film frame. The ability to pause a film image reinforces the importance of consumption and interpretation of films for the lyrical persona's introspection, as well as for the conceptualization of Krečković's book.

In this regard, the genre of home movies, which finds its place in Krečković's poetry as well, should also be mentioned. When evoked, similarly to photographs, home movies are usually brought into connection with the past and memories. They are frequently referred to by the metonymy "VHS tapes," and serve as testimonies of earlier film production and reception. On the one hand, creating home movies shows the integration of cinematic technology into everyday life (cf. Mulvey 2006, 36), meaning that the filmmaking process is not reserved for artists or professionals but is an activity that anyone can practice. On the other hand, the fact that they were supposed to be shown in a private context, stresses their emotional and sentimental rather than their artistic and expressive functions. Therefore, accessibility concerns not only the reception of the film but its production as well.

Still, in the case of Krečković's poetry, making a home movie does not always bring about only a sentimental tone. This can be detected in the poem "My Mother's Portrait in High Resolution" ["Portret moje majke u visokoj rezoluciji"]. Here, the lyrical persona observes a photograph of their mother in her youth, attempting to reconstruct her childhood and recognize the similarities between the photographed and present woman while also remembering their own childhood (cf. Krečković 2021, 110–111). When failing in these attempts, the lyrical persona creates a new portrait in the form of a digital film. This portrait is meant to last forever as an alternative way of remembering the mother: "only the digital god remembers forever" (Krečković 2021, 110). By filming her while she expresses her message as a testimony for the future, the lyrical persona breaks the material connection between the object and its image through the conversion of the recorded information into a numeric system (cf. Mulvey 2006, 19), thereby ensures their mother's eternal existence. Hence, in contrast to the photographs, which are, as the lyrical persona notices, "prone to dementia" (Krečković 2021, 110), digital film is regarded as 'timeless' and invulnerable. Moreover, by allowing the lyrical persona to discard photographs as the keepers of memory, and thus their cinematic potential when flicked through (as in the poems "My Dad's Photos from the West Coast" and "Cracks in the Ceiling"), and then to turn to digital technology, Krečković presents a history of cinematography in a nutshell.

Conclusion: Poetic procedures, film, and photography in *Pariz, Teksas*

This is the exact moment in which the confrontation of non-digital and digital spheres most strikingly appears in Krečković's book of poetry. For the lyrical persona, the non-digital world – the past – is one of unavoidable loneliness, distance, and isolation. The digital world provides some sort of comfort and consolation, whether by watching films in the intimacy of one's own room, which helps the lyrical persona untangle the enigma of interpersonal relationships and break away from loneliness, or by experiencing understanding from a stranger in a random comment under a YouTube video, as is the case in the poem "After-Midnight Reading of YouTube Comments" ["Posleponono čitanje komentara na Jutjubu"]. The possibilities of the digital age allow the lyrical persona to find a point of anchor: to review and comprehend everything that belongs to the non-digital sphere of life and finally express its emotions towards the past through poetic images.

As has been shown in this article, film as a major part of contemporary visual culture has an immense impact on Krečković's poetry and appears within the book in diverse modes. *Pariz, Teksas* exhibits multiple intermedial relationships between poetry and film. The explicit notions of individual cinematic achievements, of which Wim Wenders' *Paris, Texas* is the most striking influence, introduce the intermedial character of this poetry collection. Poetical reinterpretations of the film's themes, motives, and scenes appear as a means of self-identification and introspection for the lyrical persona. The peculiarities of film genres – road movies and horror films – are reflected within the structures and metapoetic layers of the poems. By evoking the genre of road movies, Krečković's poetry verbally re-enacts movement and acts of mobility, provoking the effect of moving pictures within the text. Moreover, structuring verbal expressions according to the visual experience (either during movement or during rest) also contributes to the cinematic quality of the book. References to horror films provide a strong self-reflexive spot in Krečković's poetry, revealing aspects of vision and of visuality, as well as the overstepping of their boundaries, as dominant modes for the poetry creation process and introspection.

The variety of film techniques used and evoked in the poetry creation process, such as tracking and panning shots, point-of-view shots, close-up shots, cut and montage, expand, deepen, and reinforce the intermedial referencing system of the book. Specifically, the point-of-view shot can be recognized as a primary film technique transformed into a poetic procedure in the conceptualization of *Pariz, Teksas*. The lyrical persona's use of verbs indicates practices connected to vision, inscribing in the poetical images not only into what the lyrical persona sees but how they see as well. The implementation of cinematographic strategies as poetic ones also invites reflection on the ontology and history of film. On this note, photographs embedded with memories appear to be of tremendous importance because, when observed in succession, they both point to the origins of film and enable the conversion of the past into the present in a film-like form. Additionally, poetically shaped dream sequences refer to the dream-like character of film, once again displaying meta-aspects and intermedial qualities of Krečković's poetry collection.

References

Antoine-Dunne, Jean. "Introducing Eisenstein's Theory." *The Montage Principle. Eisenstein in New Cultural and Critical Context*. Ed. Jean Antoine-Dunne and Paula Quigley. Amsterdam and New York: Rodopi, 2004. 1–14.

Backman Rogers, Anna. "Imaging Grief and Loss: Laura Mulvey's Death 24 x a Second as Film-Philosophy." *De Arte* 92 (2015): 11–18.

Barthes, Roland. *Camera Lucida. Reflections on Photography*. New York: Hill and Wang, 1982.

Barthes, Roland. "Leaving the Movie Theater." *The Art of the Personal Essay*. Ed. Phillip Lopate. New York: Anchor Books, 1995. 418–421.

Benthien, Claudia, Jordis Lau, and Maraike M. Marxsen. *The Literariness of Media Art*. London and New York: Routledge, 2019.

Branigan, Edward. *Point of View in the Cinema*. Berlin and Boston, MA: De Gruyter, 1984.

Bromley, Roger. "Traversing Identity: Home Movies and Road Movies in *Paris, Texas*." *Angelaki. Journal of the Theoretical Humanities* 2.1 (1997): 101–118.

Cavell, Stanely. *The World Viewed. Reflections on the Ontology of Film*. Cambridge, MA and London: Harvard Univ. Press, 1979 [1971].

Deren, Maya, Arthur Miller, Dylan Thomas, and Parker Tyler. "Poetry and the Film: A Symposium with Maya Deren, Arthur Miller, Dylan Thomas, Parker Tyler." *Film Culture Reader*. Ed. P. Adams Sitney. New York: Cooper Square Press, 2000 [1970]. 171–186.

Deren, Maya. "Cinematography: The Creative Use of Reality." *The Avant-Garde Film. A Reader of Theory and Criticism*. Ed. P. Adams Sitney. New York: Anthology Film Archives, 1978. 60–73.

Đurković, Uroš. "Pariz, Teksas i sve između – poetski prvenac Vladana Krečkovića (Paris, Texas and everything in between – Vladan Krečković's Poetic Debut)." *Eckermann. Web časopis za književnost* 30 (2020): https://eckermann.org.rs/article/o-vladanu-kreckovicu/ (September 14, 2022).

Hark, Ina Rae. "Fear of Flying: Yuppie Critique and the Buddy-Road Movie in the 1980s." *The Road Movie Book*. Ed. Steven Kohan and Ina Rae Hark. London and New York: Routledge, 1997. 204–229.

Hutcheon, Linda. *A Theory of Adaptation*. New York: Routledge, 2006.

Kramer, Andreas, and Jan Röhnert. "Poetry and Film in Abbas Kiarostami's and Jim Jarmusch's Cinema of Mobility." *Poetry and Film*. Ed. Andreas Kramer and Jan Röhnert. Frankfurt a. M.: Edition Faust, 2020. 5–14.

Krečković, Vladan. *Pariz, Teksas / Париз, Тексас / Paris, Texas*. Struga: Струшки вечери на поезијата (Struga Poetry Evenings), 2021.

Krečković, Vladan. *Pariz, Teksas*. Beograd: PPM Enklava, 2020.

Kuhn, Annette, and Guy Westwell. *A Dictionary of Film Studies*. Oxford: Oxford Univ. Press, 2020.

Levi, Pavle. *Jolted Images (Unbound Analytic)*. Amsterdam: Amsterdam Univ. Press, 2017.

Marinkov, Jelena. "Dalekovodi u pustinji [Powerlines in the Desert]." *Gradina* 92–93 (2020): 294–300.

Mitchell, W. J. T. *Picture Theory. Essays on Verbal and Visual Representation*. Chicago, IL: Univ. of Chicago Press, 1994.

Morin, Edgar. *The Cinema, or The Imaginary Man*. Minneapolis, MN and London: Minnesota Univ. Press, 2005.

Morris, Christopher. "The Reflexivity of the Road Film." *Film Criticism* 28 (2003): 24–52.

Mulvey, Laura. *Death 24 x a Second: Stillness and the Moving Image*. London: Reaktion Books, 2006.

Rajewsky, Irina O. "Intermediality, Intertextuality, and Remediation: A Literary Perspective on Intermediality." *Intermédialités / Intermediality* 6 (2005): 43–64.

Shepard, Sam, and Wim Wenders. *Paris, Texas*. [Screenplay] 1983, https://cinephiliabeyond.org/wp-content/uploads/2014/10/paris-texas-cont.compressed.pdf (January 18, 2023).

Wenders, Wim (Dir.). *Paris, Texas*. Road Movies Filmproduktion GmbH and Argos Films S.A. 20th Century Fox, 1984.

List of Figures

Fig. 1	Still from "Night and Refuge" [edited film version] by Caroline Bergvall. May 21, 2020, https://cementfields.org/journal/caroline-bergvall-night-and-refuge/ (March 3, 2023) © Caroline Bergvall —— **36**	
Fig. 2	Photo from "Drift" [performance] by Caroline Bergvall. 2014, https://carolinebergvall.com/work/drift-performance/ (March 3, 2023) © Caroline Bergvall —— **40**	
Fig. 3	Tom Martin. *Passenger*. 2014, http://martinandmartin.eu/#/drift/ (March 3, 2023) © Tom Martin —— **41**	
Fig. 4	e.e. cummings. "r-p-o-p-h-e-s-s-a-g-r." *Complete Poems, 1904–1962*. New York: Liveright. 2013, 396 —— **52**	
Fig. 5	Luis Camnitzer. *This Is a Mirror. You Are a Written Sentence*. 1966–1968. Daros Latinamerica Collection, Zürich. Foto: Peter Schächli —— **54**	
Fig. 6	Olga Bragina. "Excerpts from 'Kyiv Diary'." Transl. Olga Livshin. 2022, https://lcb.de/diplomatique/excerpts-from-kyiv-diary/ (January 20, 2023) —— **66**	
Fig. 7	Snapshots from "YATOO" by Zeitgenossen (Ursula Hentschläger and Zelko Wiener). 2001, http://www.zeitgenossen.info/e/zw/yatoo1.html (March 7, 2023) —— **77**	
Fig. 8	Snapshot from "Untitled" by Squid Soup. 2001, https://d-nb.info/1253929505/34 (March 8, 2023) —— **80**	
Fig. 9	Screenshots from "Enigma n" and "Enigma n^{2022}" by Jim Andrews. 2022 [1998], https://enigman.vispo.com/ and https://vispo.com/animisms/enigman/enigman.htm (March 8, 2023) —— **81**	
Fig. 10	Anna Li Bryant. "▬Anthem (a blackout poem of the National Anthem)." *Protest Through Poetry*. 2020. 36–37, https://protestthroughpoetry.com (February 27, 2023) —— **112**	
Fig. 11	westtrestle. "Black Lives Matter." Instagram. April 20, 2022 (accessed on May 11, 2022; in the meantime, the post has been deleted) —— **115**	
Fig. 12	jo.backhouse.96. "It is NOT enough to be non-racist." June 9, 2020, https://www.instagram.com/jo.backhouse.96/ (February 13, 2023) —— **116**	
Fig. 13	kursives_ich. Unnamed poem. April 15, 2021, https://www.instagram.com/p/CNsa-QuhZJl/ (November 20, 2022) © Carina Eckl —— **127**	
Fig. 14	rudkazydel. "Babskie wiersze." October 26, 2020, https://www.instagram.com/p/CG0cQtjnYUT/ (November 20, 2022) © Rudka Zydel —— **129**	
Fig. 15	holliepoetry. "pre-baby body." July 21, 2021, https://www.instagram.com/p/CRmIC8dhpr0/ (November 20, 2022) © Hollie McNish —— **135**	
Abb. 16	Still aus *LESBIAN* (00:41). Reg. Rosemary Baker. Gedicht: lisa luxx. Random Acts, 2020 © Rosemary Baker —— **155**	
Abb. 17	Still aus *LESBIAN* (02:04). Reg. Rosemary Baker. Gedicht: lisa luxx. Random Acts, 2020 © Rosemary Baker —— **159**	
Fig. 18	Daniel Holden, and Chris Kerr. "compound_eye.rb." *./code --poetry*. Authors' edition: CreateSpace self-publishing service, 2016. n. pag. © Daniel Holden and Chris Kerr —— **168**	

Fig. 19	Daniel Holden, and Chris Kerr. "chernobyl.rkt." *./code --poetry*. Authors' edition: CreateSpace self-publishing service, 2016. n. pag. © Daniel Holden and Chris Kerr —— **173**
Fig. 20	Daniel Holden, and Chris Kerr. "bark.png." *./code --poetry*. Authors' edition: CreateSpace self-publishing service, 2016. n. pag. © Daniel Holden and Chris Kerr —— **174**
Fig. 21	Daniel Holden, and Chris Kerr. "by_conspiracy_or_design.js." *./code --poetry*. Authors' edition: CreateSpace self-publishing service, 2016. n. pag. © Daniel Holden and Chris Kerr —— **177**
Fig. 22	María Mencía. "Generative Poems." Exhibition *no one can hear you scream*. Inspace Edinburgh, 2010 © María Mencía —— **192**
Fig. 23	María Mencía. "Connected Memories." Exhibition *Repurposing in Electronic Literature*. DIG Gallery Košice, 2013 © María Mencía —— **195**
Fig. 24	Screenshot from *Gateway to the World* by María Mencía. 2014–2017, http://www.mariamencia.com/pages/gatewaytotheworld.html (January 7, 2023) © María Mencía —— **201**
Fig. 25	Screenshots of "The Winnipeg. The Boat of Hope" [index page] and of *The Poem that Crossed the Atlantic* by María Mencía. 2018, http://winnipeg.mariamencia.com/?lang=en/ (January 7, 2023) © María Mencía —— **203**
Fig. 26	Still from "Drive Through the Night." Dir. Helen Dewbery. Poem: Lucy English. *The Book of Hours*, 2014 © Helen Dewbery and Lucy English —— **211**
Fig. 27	Still from *I Want to Breathe Sweet Air*. Dir. Jack Cochran and Pamela Falkenberg. Poem: Lucy English. Outlier Moving Pictures, 2020 © Jack Cochran, Pamela Falkenberg, and Lucy English —— **219**
Fig. 28	Still from *I Want to Breathe Sweet Air*. Dir. Jack Cochran and Pamela Falkenberg. Poem: Lucy English. Outlier Moving Pictures, 2020 © Jack Cochran, Pamela Falkenberg, and Lucy English —— **221**
Abb. 29	Heike Fiedler. „wirlaufenseitjahrzehnten". *sie will mehr*. Luzern: Der gesunde Menschenversand, 2013. 82–83. —— **228**
Abb. 30	Heike Fiedler. „p-o-e". *sie will mehr*. Luzern: Der gesunde Menschenversand, 2013. 85 —— **230**
Abb. 31	Heike Fiedler. „a line". *sie will mehr*. Luzern: Der gesunde Menschenversand, 2013. 97 —— **234**
Abb. 32	Yves Netzhammer. Ohne Titel. *Ignatien. Elegien am Rande des Nervenzusammenbruchs. Elegies at the Edge of Nervous Breakdown*. Fürth: starfruit, 2014. 30 © starfruit publications —— **244**
Abb. 33	Yves Netzhammer. Ohne Titel. *Ignatien. Elegien am Rande des Nervenzusammenbruchs. Elegies at the Edge of Nervous Breakdown*. Fürth: starfruit, 2014. 64–65 © starfruit publications —— **248**
Abb. 34	Yves Netzhammer. Ohne Titel. *Ignatien. Elegien am Rande des Nervenzusammenbruchs. Elegies at the Edge of Nervous Breakdown*. Fürth: starfruit, 2014. 43 © starfruit publications —— **252**
Abb. 35	Yves Netzhammer. Ohne Titel. *Ignatien. Elegien am Rande des Nervenzusammenbruchs. Elegies at the Edge of Nervous Breakdown*. Fürth: starfruit, 2014. 82–83 © starfruit publications —— **255**
Fig. 36	Back cover of Vladan Krečković's *Pariz, Teksas*. Design by Hajdana Kostić and Stefan Bulatović. Beograd: PPM Enklava, 2020 —— **265**

Fig. 37 Vladan Krečković. "Pariz, Teksas." *Pariz, Texas*. Beograd: PPM Enklava, 2020. 38–39 —— **266**
Fig. 38 Vladan Krečković. "Fotografije moga oca sa Zapadne obIae." *Pariz, Teksas*. Beograd: PPM Enklava, 2020. 28–29 —— **274**
Fig. 39 Vladan Krečković. "Sposobnost sove." *Pariz, Teksas*. Beograd: PPM Enklava, 2020. 33 —— **276**

Authors

Prof. Dr. Astrid Böger is professor of North American Literature and Culture at Universität Hamburg where she co-directs the Research Center for Graphic Literature. She conducts research on U.S. American literature from the nineteenth century to the present with a focus on visual media and popular culture.

Prof. Dr. Heinz Drügh ist Professor für Neuere deutsche Literatur und Ästhetik an der Goethe-Universität Frankfurt am Main. Er forscht unter anderem zu Literatur und Populärkultur, Warenästhetik und Postmoderne sowie zur Literaturgeschichte des 18. und 19. Jahrhunderts.

Dr Lucy English is a poet and professor of Creative Enterprise and the Spoken Word at Bath Spa University, GB. Her recent poetry film project *The Book of Hours* was shortlisted for the New Media Writing prize in 2019 and is now held on the British Library database of digital work.

Sophie Ertel, MMag.a ist Filmemacherin und Erwachsenentrainerin in Wien, AT. Sie hat Bildende Kunst an der Akademie der bildenden Künste in Wien sowie Slawistik an der Universität Wien studiert und an Universitäten in Serbien (Belgrad 2017/18) und China (Peking 2016) unterrichtet.

Dr. habil. Vladimir Feshchenko is senior research fellow at the Institute of Linguistics of the Russian Academy of Sciences, Moscow, RUS. His research focuses on theoretical linguistics, poetics, semiotics, and avant-garde poetry, and he translates Anglo-American prose and poetry into Russian.

Daniel Holden is a programmer and writer working in R&D in the games industry in Montréal, CA. He studies how machine learning can be applied to create more realistic character animation systems in games. His poetry, visual artwork, and short fiction have appeared in *Tentacular*, *Battalion*, and *Montréal Writes*.

Chris Kerr is a poet based in London, UK. He creates analogue and digital visual poetry as well as code poetry. Together with Daniel Holden, he co-authored the collection *./code --poetry* (2016) and its expanded edition (2023). Among his book publications are *Nam Gal Sips Clark* (2021) and *Extra Long Matches* (2022).

PD Dr. Esther Kilchmann ist Literatur- und Kulturwissenschafterin. Zu ihren Forschungsschwerpunkten gehören unter anderem literarische Mehrsprachigkeit, sprachexperimentelle Literatur und Narrative transkultureller Erinnerungen. Sie wurde 2022 an der Universität Hamburg habilitiert.

Tijana Koprivica, M.A. is a PhD candidate in Slavic studies at the University of Vienna, AT and editor at the Web Literary Magazine Eckermann. She studied Serbian Literature and Language with Comparative Literature at the University of Belgrade and Slavic studies at the University of Cologne.

Magdalena Elisabeth Korecka, M.A. is a PhD candidate and research associate in the ERC project *Poetry in the Digital Age* at the Universität Hamburg. In her dissertation project, she investigates the interrelation of visual aesthetics and sociopolitical messaging in platformized social media poetry.

Dr María Mencía is a media artist and associate professor in Media Arts and Digital Poetics at Kingston School of Art, London, UK. Her research areas include the intersection of language, art, and digital technology, as well as virtual aesthetic spaces in-between the visual, the aural, and the semantic.

Prof. Karin Nykvist, PhD is associate professor and senior lecturer of Comparative Literature at Lund University, SE. Her main research field is contemporary and multimodal Nordic poetry. Another area of her research is the construction of 'the child' in Swedish literature since the period of Romanticism.

Prof. Dr. Roberto Simanowski is a literary and media scholar and founder of the online journal *Dichtung-Digital*. His research focuses on literature and art in digital media. He published numerous books and articles in the field, most recently on aesthetic and cultural aspects of algorithms and AI.

Dr. habil. Olga Sokolova is senior research fellow at the Institute of Linguistics of the Russian Academy of Sciences, Moscow, RUS. Her research specializes in the theory of discourse, linguistic pragmatics and poetics, and the language of avant-garde. She translates Italian and Anglo-American prose and poetry into Russian.

Dr. Wiebke Vorrath is a literary scholar and research associate in the ERC project *Poetry in the Digital Age* at the Universität Hamburg. She examines visual digital poetry with a special focus on aesthetics of kinetic typography as well as on functions and effects of algorithms and AI.

Prof. Hiroshi Yamamoto ist Professor für Neuere deutsche Literatur am Institut für Germanistik der Waseda Universität in Tokyo, JP. Er forscht unter anderem zu Gulag-Literatur aus zweiter Hand, Autofiktion sowie Translation Studies und übersetzt deutschsprachige Literatur ins Japanische.

www.ingramcontent.com/pod-product-compliance
Lightning Source LLC
Chambersburg PA
CBHW050517170426
43201CB00013B/1987